Asian American
Basketball

Asian American Basketball

A Century of Sport, Community and Culture

Joel S. Franks

McFarland & Company, Inc., Publishers

Jefferson, North Carolina

Library of Congress Cataloguing-in-Publication Data

Names: Franks, Joel S.
Title: Asian American basketball : a century of sport, community and culture / Joel S. Franks.
Description: Jefferson, North Carolina : McFarland & Company, Inc., Publishers, 2016 | Includes bibliographical references and index.
Identifiers: LCCN 2016008798 | ISBN 9780786497188 (softcover : acid free paper) ∞
Subjects: LCSH: Basketball—United States—History. | Basketball players—United States—History. | Asian Americans—Sports—History. | Pacific Islander Americans—Sports—History.
Classification: LCC GV885.7 .F73 2016 | DDC 796.3230973—dc23
LC record available at http://lccn.loc.gov/2016008798

British Library cataloguing data are available

ISBN (print) 978-0-7864-9718-8
ISBN (ebook) 978-1-4766-2049-7

On the cover: basketball team (© 2016 XiXinXing/Thinstock); Manzanar Relocation Center, Manzanar, California, 1943 (National Archives); girl with ball (© 2016 Blend Images/Thinkstock)

Printed in the United States of America

McFarland & Company, Inc., Publishers
 Box 611, Jefferson, North Carolina 28640
  www.mcfarlandpub.com

To my wife, Cheryl,
and my children, Kaitlin and Spencer—
with all my love

Acknowledgments

Inspiration for this book derives from many sources. To be sure, it came from watching and coaching my children, Kait and Spencer, as they sometimes struggled and sometimes triumphed in mastering the difficult game of basketball. Likewise, their teammates, opponents, coaches, and even referees inspired me. In particular, I want to remember one of my son's earliest coaches, the late Art Wong, who earnestly and patiently taught fundamentals to sometimes impatient seven-year-olds for Palo Alto Youth Services.

I have been helped along the way by conversations via telephone and e-mail with Mary Lai, Florence Chinn, Mel Orphilla, Peter Jamero, Colleen Matsuhara, and Chris Pung. In addition, my research has been aided by the Interlibrary Loan Department at San Jose State University; Santa Clara University's Department of Archives and Special Collections; Special Collections at California State University, Sacramento; Special Collections and University Archives, San Jose State; the University of San Francisco Archives; Schlesinger Library, Radcliffe Institute, Harvard University; University Archives for the University of Portland; David Silverman and the Harvard Athletics Department; Associated Students of UCLA; Oregon Nikkei Endowment; Fullerton Community College Library; Whitman University Special Collections; University of California, Irvine, Media Relations; University of Southern California Special Collections; University of Missouri Athletic Department; Long Island University Athletic Department; and the Japanese American National Museum.

Table of Contents

Preface

I have to confess that this book was inspired by "Linsanity." As I write these words, there have already been numerous articles, books, and at least one documentary on the market examining Jeremy Lin's young life, struggles, and faith in the wake of the Taiwanese American's emergence as a surprising, excessively hyped, albeit perhaps temporary, National Basketball Association (NBA) star in the winter and early spring of 2012. And as I write these words, it is hard to predict where Lin's professional basketball career will go. He left the New York Knicks, for whom he excelled for several weeks in 2012 before a knee injury put him on a shelf. Instead of plying his trade in New York City, he headed to Texas on the winds of free agency and was most recently in Houston, performing for the Rockets. Thus far, he seems to have disappointed his most rabid detractors and fans. That is, he has evidenced the talent, courage, and basketball know-how to become a productive NBA player for many years, but probably not a superstar or even a star. Regardless, even if he stopped playing basketball at the end of the 2013–2014 season, we should still consider Lin a source of pride to his family and those communities, spiritual and secular, which matter the most to him. But more than that, his deft moves at driving the lane compelled many Americans to consider, if but for a moment, the complex experiences of Asian Americans and that maybe the stereotypes that have comforted many of us were dissolving.

Thus, while motivated in part by the Bay Area–raised and Harvard-graduated Lin, this book is more concerned with one of the things that Jeremy Lin seemed to represent to people in the late winter of 2012—the legacy of Asian American basketball, which has nourished not only Jeremy Lin but countless children and adults of Asian ancestry who have played, coached, and watched basketball in the United States for decades. And perhaps just as important, if not more so, people found in Jeremy Lin a way to interpret the experiences of Asian Americans in general.

As someone who has taught Asian American studies, researched and written books about Asian American athletic and nonathletic experiences, and coached in an Asian American youth league in the Bay Area, I found much of the reaction to Jeremy Lin's success as a New York Knick in 2012 somewhat curious. Like many, I, too, was surprised that a Harvard grad could hold his own against the finest basketball players in the world. Like many, I, too, was surprised that a basketball player cut by not one but two NBA teams, including my favorite NBA contingent, the Golden State Warriors, could not just find a place on the Knicks' bench but at the time substantially shape the Knicks into one of the most exciting teams in the NBA. Unlike many, however, I was not surprised that a person of Asian ancestry could develop into a decent NBA or, for that matter, Women's National Basketball Association (WNBA) performer. But I remained at least somewhat surprised and disappointed that it had taken so long for it to happen.

Perhaps cultural, economic, and demographic factors have stymied the fostering of a visible cohort of Asian American elite basketball players. Moreover, we need always consider the haunting presence of racism. Indeed, despite the fact that horrors such as the Chinese Exclusion Act and Japanese American internment camps in World War II might seem well behind the United States in the second decade of the twenty-first century, "racism's traveling eye," to borrow a phrase from scholar Elaine Kim, trails Asian Americans, if not as closely as other nonwhite Americans, closely enough. Still, wherever Americans of Asian ancestry have put down roots, they have played basketball with passion and frequently skill. And that is why I remain a bit astonished that so many are astonished that somebody of Jeremy Lin's racial identity should be able to find at least a modicum of success in the NBA.[1]

Accordingly, it seems to me that Asian American basketball's most consequential stories transcend Jeremy Lin. One of these stories concerns the Asian American community teams and leagues that have historically linked generations, social classes, and males and females from Boston to Honolulu. Perhaps just as significant, another notable story concerns the relatively anonymous Asian Americans who have crossed often treacherous cultural borderlands to play on predominantly non–Asian American high school, junior college, and college teams. In other words, if Jeremy Lin had never gotten off the NBA bench, Asian American experiences with basketball in general would still be worth chronicling as a way to talk about both the limitations and possibilities of sport in America, and America itself.

Focus

The focus of this book will be on the basketball experiences of Americans, either citizens or immigrant residents, primarily possessing ancestral links to such present day nations as China, Japan, Korea, the Philippines, and India. Some of the people I will discuss will be biracial or multiracial. In Hawai'i and among Japanese Americans in general, these people are called *hapas*. Some may question the legitimacy of this, but unless we are to parse what makes a person an enthusiastic and, frequently, talented basketball player— the European, African, or Asian ancestry—then it would seem appropriate to consider biracial or multiracial hoopsters as long as they can claim Asian descent.

I have chosen to stress the story of Asian American basketball up to 1965, the year of a far-reaching immigration reform law that dramatically transformed Asian America. Admittedly, as a historian, I am more interested in early and middle twentieth-century experiences. This time period offers fascinating glimpses of Asian Americans struggling against institutionalized racism and nativism while forging community and intercultural ties through sports such as basketball. This does not mean that the post–1965 period does not deserve attention. It is significant that while Asian Americans comprised less than 1 percent of the U.S. population in 1965, over 6 percent of Americans possessed Asian ancestry in 2010. Moreover, in 1965 most Asian Americans were native born and descendants of immigrants from Japan, China, and the Philippines; since 1965, 9.5 million people migrated to the United States from China and the Philippines, but also India, Pakistan, Korea, Taiwan, Vietnam, Cambodia, Laos, Thailand, and Burma (now Myanmar). This resulted from not only the Hart-Cellar Act, which eliminated Asian immigration quotas, but also thousands of Southeast Asian refugees making their way to America in the wake of war and political turmoil in their lands. Originally, I had hoped to buck my preferences as a historian and thoroughly extend my analysis up to the twenty-first century, but doing so made the manuscript larger and more unwieldy than I had previously imagined. Yet I have not slighted post–1965 Asian American basketball entirely. I do devote a chapter and the epilogue about Jeremy Lin's arrival on the NBA scene to the ambiguous experiences of hoopsters from various Asian backgrounds in the last 50 years.[2]

Sources

Although they have their limitations, mainstream and ethnic newspapers have been vital to my research. Of course, newspapers can misspell and misrepresent names. A "Chew" in a high school box score could be Asian American, but not necessarily. Newspapers can also get names wrong—especially Asian names. Moreover, I probably underrepresent Filipino hoopsters because their surnames often resemble those of Latinos. The latter problem, too, can surface in my use of high school yearbooks.

Other issues should also be raised. Many *hapas*, of course, have had non-Asian surnames. Someone who saw a Franks in a Cupertino High School basketball box score in recent years would probably not know that my daughter and son possess Japanese ancestry. Complicating matters is the case of Wilmeth Sadat-Singh, who, in the 1930s, was a prominent college football and basketball player. His name would suggest he possessed Asian Indian descent and he was, indeed, often described in the press as such. Nevertheless, Sadat-Singh was an African American whose mother married an Indian after Sadat-Singh's birth father died. Consequently, he took the last name of his stepfather. In other words, by claiming that a Singh played center for a Southern California high school, I might not be referring to an actual Asian American, but most likely I am. Finally, an Asian surname in a high school basketball box score might actually have belonged to a national of some Asian country who was temporarily attending school in the United States. My daughter, for example, had a basketball teammate at Silicon Valley's Cupertino High who was a Japanese national. If she returned to Japan after graduating, I would not consider her experience an Asian American experience. If she remained in the United States to attend college, work, and live, then I would view her as an Asian American regardless of her citizenship status.

Mainstream newspapers are also frustrating in that they have only sporadically reported on ethnic games and tournaments. And when they have paid attention to such events they have, unsurprisingly, stressed male over female participation. For example, I have yet to discover a mainstream newspaper account of the Busy Bees, a very talented Japanese American female team based in Stockton, California, in the 1930s. To be fair, the mainstream press did not always miss out on Asian American hoops. After World War II, for example, the *San Francisco Examiner* devoted some ink to Helen Wong. A magnificent athlete out of San Francisco's Chinatown, Wong shined in both basketball and tennis. In general, ethnic newspapers offered more space to female basketball but still emphasized male hoopsters.

The mainstream press has been useful, moreover, as a barometer of racial attitudes toward Asian Americans. We will discuss anti–Asian politics and the racial nativism that justified American animus toward people of Asian ancestry historically and still sadly twists its way through the avenues of American society. For now, however, we should note that Asian American basketball often became the occasion for the mainstream press to dig up the cache of Orientalist language invented to exoticize people of Asian ancestry. To be sure, the mainstream press was not always intent on insulting Asian Americans. It could even seem generous, sometimes surprisingly so, in its appraisals of Asian American basketball.

Yet though the mainstream press was not necessarily bent on degrading Asian American hoopsters, the takeaway from much of its reportage is troubling. As historian David Welky points out regarding mainstream press coverage of Japanese athletes at the 1932 summer Olympiad in Los Angeles, even seemingly gracious journalistic accounts could, perhaps unintentionally, serve to degrade and exoticize Japanese athletic accomplishments. For example, the widespread press references to the Japanese athletes' lack of physical size were not only perhaps innocent in motivation but even aimed at praising the Japanese athletes for overcoming physical deficiencies. To readers, however, the constant use of words such as "diminutive" might have worked to diminish the Japanese athletes, portraying them as exotics at best and freaks at worst, at a time when the United States was feeling more than uneasy about Japan's military and economic advances in the Pacific Rim.[3]

The same could be said of mainstream press accounts of Asian American basketball players. Many of the high school and college Asian American hoopsters illuminating the pages of this book were called not only "diminutive" but also "tiny," "wee," and other terms to convey that the athletes under scrutiny were short. Readers of this book may not blanch at this because, after all, many of these hoopsters probably stood less than six feet tall. Moreover, five-foot-six white and black basketball players provoke similar journalistic conversations. But making an issue of height, while perhaps unavoidable to some extent in basketball and frequently done with no malice, can dehumanize no matter who is being described. Constant references to short Asians may seem even more troubling given the historical efforts of mainstream American popular culture to reinforce cultural boundaries, as well as diminish and marginalize people of Asian ancestry.

To get a sense of Asian American participation in high school and even college hoops, I have consulted various yearbooks. One of the good things about pre–1960s yearbooks is that they often display sections on girls' and women's athletics, which was typically intramural at the time. These sections will show photographs and at least surnames of those engaged in basketball, as well as other sports, such as volleyball and tennis. These yearbooks also do the same for male "lightweight" or nonvarsity basketball competitors who did not always get publicized in either the mainstream or the ethnic press. Conversely, yearbooks were not consistently well organized and the names of participants could be easily botched or not provided.

I have also used U.S. census manuscripts and, occasionally, other archival sources to trace the social and economic backgrounds of some of the people explored in this book. As a source, U.S. census manuscripts are useful but can reflect the biases and mistakes of the various census takers involved. I can also unintentionally misuse them. That is, I can mistakenly claim that I have found a certain individual in the census data and, as it turns out, it could be the wrong person. Arthur Kim was a Hawaiian of Korean descent who played basketball and coached on the islands, as well as doing stints as a professional basketball franchise owner on the mainland in the 1960s. Since Arthur Kim is not a remarkable name, how I can be sure if the one that pops up in the census manuscripts is the right Arthur Kim?

Organization

I have organized this work topically and chronologically. The introduction explores the book's major themes. It provides something of a conceptual framework assembled from scholarship associated with ethnic and Asian American studies. But more important, it explains my pursuit of a populist sport history. That is, in the case of basketball history, I am not insisting that we ignore the NBA or Dean Smith's legacy at the University of North Carolina. However, basketball history should look beyond the supremely talented players and coaches who have gotten a great deal of attention and often a great deal of money.

For many in the early months of 2012, Asian American basketball did not become a reality until Jeremy Lin started knocking down baskets for the NBA's New York Knicks. But, as I assert in future pages, Asian Americans have been playing basketball long before Jeremy Lin was a glint in his mother's eye, indeed, long before his mother was a glint in her mother's eye. And although faced with immigration restriction, institutionalized racism, class exploitation, and World War II internment, working-class Asian Americans found in basketball a sense of community, purpose, and joy. Their stories should be told.

The first two chapters cover Asian American community basketball. As explained in the introduction, community basketball provided the foundation of Asian American experiences with the sport. All major Asian American ethnic groups have used basketball to forge community ties. The love of basketball has linked Asian Americans across generational, gender, and socioeconomic distinctions. Moreover, community basketball has helped prepare some Asian Americans for excellent careers in high school and college hoops.

Chapter 1 examines Asian American community basketball up to the end of World War II. It concentrates on Chinese American and Japanese American community basketball on Hawai'i and the U.S. mainland, allowing readers glimpses at formidable Chinese American female teams in San Francisco, Portland, and Boston, in addition to Japanese American males and females swishing baskets behind the barbed wire fences of World War II internment camps.

The post–World War II period of 1945 to 1965 is the focus of the second chapter. It, too, attends mostly to Chinese American and Japanese American hoopsters, but it also looks at the vibrant world of Filipino American community basketball. While other regions entertained Asian American basketball, chapter 2 spends a great deal of time on the San Francisco Bay Area, which offered a home for highly competitive male and female teams sponsored by the St. Mary's Church in San Francisco's Chinatown. Also in San Francisco, the Filipino American Mangoes and Mangoettes played exciting hoops. And in the South Bay, the San Jose Zebras established a lively legacy of Japanese American hoops in the region.

Chapters 3 and 4 cover Asian American cultural border crossings via basketball. That is, Asian American hoopsters were not hermetically sealed off from non–Asian American ethnic groups. They traversed cultural borders separating them from non–Asian Americans when they ran on to high school basketball courts. In Hawai'i, class distinctions often shaped the social hierarchy as much, if not more, than race and ethnicity. Accordingly, multiethnic basketball thrived on the islands, at least compared to the mainland, where Jim Crow and racial nativism too often prevailed. Yet even on the mainland, Asian Americans played with and against non–Asian Americans on school teams and other fives. Chapter 3 explores Asian Americans and intercultural hoops to the end of World War II. In the process, it shows Asian Americans in the first half of the twentieth century not just making the high school five, but starring. The fourth chapter covers the same topic from 1945 to 1965. One of the highlights of this chapter, however, is the revelation of at least a few Asian American females thriving in intercultural hoops.

The fifth chapter examines Asian American college and professional hoopsters up to the mid–1960s. Admittedly, Asian American All-Americans and professional stars were nonexistent. But given the relatively small numbers of Asian Americans in the United States at this time, their experiences with college and professional hoops merit respect. We will find Asian American benchwarmers, but we also will find major and minor college basketball programs dependent on Asian Americans who may never get into the Basketball Hall of Fame but who sparked teams at the University of Washington, Oregon State, University of California, Berkeley (Cal), and, of course, the University of Hawai'i. As for professional hoops, the Asian American impact may have been slim but nevertheless interesting.

Chapter 6 takes up Asian American hoops since 1965. First, it scrutinizes the continued importance of community basketball for the United States' increasingly diverse population of Asian Americans. While attending to intercultural encounters on various courts in the United States, chapter 6 notes that thanks to the growing influence of feminism and, in particular, the 1972 passage of Title IX in the U.S. Congress, more young Asian American women have competed and excelled in interscholastic hoops. Likewise, somewhat older Asian American women have made their way on to college and even professional teams. A few have dribbled, shot, and defended to stardom. Accordingly, chapter 6 devotes attention to intercollegiate and professional hoops in the late twentieth and early twenty-first centuries. It will not just look at female elite hoopsters, of course, but their male counterparts, who have starred at UCLA, Washington State, Kansas, Missouri, and Harvard, and have played professional basketball in the NBA and around the world. Chapter 6 takes a closer look at Jeremy Lin's still youthful basketball career and elite Asian American coaches, such as Colleen Matsuhara and Erik Spoelstra.

The epilogue revisits Jeremy Lin, but more as a cultural phenomenon than a sometimes brilliant NBA performer. Yet it does more by connecting Asian American basketball to issues brought up in the introduction. That is, developing a more democratic perspective on sports history will allow us to recognize how ordinary people, in social, economic, and political terms, can embrace a sport such as basketball without expectations of fame and fortune. In these pages, we will find restaurant workers and children of laundry operators playing basketball because it helped give their lives meaning; because it allowed them to represent their neighborhoods, churches, and ethnic groups; and because it was fun.

An Apology

I have tried to show the depth and quality of Asian American basketball experiences. Some will find that I have no doubt ignored or underrepresented some of these experiences. Others may find that I overrepresented some of those experiences. To those of you who feel that I should have paid attention or at least more attention to an individual Asian American hoopster or an Asian American team, I especially apologize. Hopefully, these mistakes will encourage more research and writing on Asian American basketball. As for those of you who think I overrepresented Asian American basketball experiences, you are just wrong.

Introduction

Basketball is not an easy game to master. To do so requires, of course, excellent hand and eye coordination, with which not everyone is born. But an often overlooked aspect of the game is the interaction of foot and hand work. It is so easy for the novice to get frustrated by failing to employ his or her feet properly on offense and defense. Good footwork means you do not travel with the ball. Good footwork means you can stay in front of the person you are guarding. But good hands go with good footwork. To be more precise, good fingers go with good footwork, because you largely shoot and pass with a flick of your fingers, you dribble with your fingers, and you should try to catch passes and rebounds as much as possible with your fingers, so you are in a better position to then dribble, pass, or shoot.

The game moves so fast. It is much too possible for players to find themselves intimidated by the speed of it all and lose out to uncertainty. But it is just as possible to get caught up in the speed and move too quickly. As the inimitable John Wooden put it, "Be quick but don't hurry"—easy to say but harder to do. It takes practice, as all the best basketball players and coaches will tell you. Constant repetition in drill after drill, scrimmage after scrimmage, will build muscle memory and court vision—to know when to shoot and to pass and how to see who is on the court and where each player is positioned.

Not everyone who wants to get it, gets it. I wanted to be a good basketball player, but my ambition was doomed by lack of size. Yet no matter how short I am, if I had mastered the intricacies of the game, I might have taken my hoops career further. And even if I had been a foot taller, that career would have been stunted if I had failed to take seriously how very hard basketball can be.

Accordingly, I admire anyone who has played basketball well. To be sure, good basketball players have often been treated generously by nature. But they also have demonstrated splendid dedication, especially when well short of six feet and plagued by racial and gender stereotypes, rendering it difficult for them to earn the respect that their deadeye shooting, pinpoint passing, or tenacious defense merit. Accordingly, as well, I admire many of the Asian American hoopsters who have dribbled, screened, and rebounded through the pages of this book.

The examination of the history of Asian American basketball has provoked me to consider four interesting questions. First, what has been the interplay between Asian American basketball and the nourishment of a democratic culture in the United States? Second, has Asian American community basketball demonstrated the worthiness of the concept of cultural citizenship as a better way to understand racial and ethnic dynamics in the United States than the crusty notion of assimilation? Third, has Asian American ventures across cultural borderlands to play with and against predominantly non–Asian Americans suggest that a sport such as basketball can, under the right conditions, serve as what sociologist Elijah Anderson has called a "cosmopolitan canopy," encouraging a certain amount of respectful dealings between people of diverse racial and ethnic backgrounds? Finally, is Ronald Takaki's exploration of Asian Americans as "strangers from a different shore" applicable to Asian American basketball experiences?

Democratic Culture

Asian American experiences with basketball tell an intriguing story about the struggle for a democratic culture and, in particular, a democratic sports culture, in the United States and its empire. This is not the place to debate how democratic the United States has been or is at this moment. However, it is fair to say that even if American democracy is flawed, American society has long embraced democracy rhetorically even as too many Americans denied it to their fellow citizens.

Since most Americans seem to value democracy, they were willing to perhaps cast their suspicions aside for a while when President George W. Bush claimed that the U.S. invasion of Iraq was spurred by a desire to spread democratic rule to a seemingly benighted land. More to the point, few American sports fans dissent when they are told by those who govern professional and elite amateur athletics in the United States that democratic principles staunchly inform the way Americans do baseball, basketball, football, and other sports.

It may seem odd to extend talk of democracy to the world of jump shots and pick and rolls. Many Americans strive to confine democracy to the world of electoral politics, and often we do so in a fairly superficial manner, according to political scientists like Benjamin Barber and the late Robert Dahl. We are content that we live in a democracy because we are allowed to cast votes every so often for either Republicans or Democrats. While I do not wish to weigh this book down with political theory (and even if I did entertain such an ambition, I would rather leave the matter to those more qualified), democracy would seem to demand more than just periodic elections, but significant levels of economic and social equality among those doing the electing. If I can amass more political power than you because of my racial identity and you can amass more political power than me because of your wealth, then democracy has taken a major beating.[1]

Accordingly, if we truly honor democracy, we cannot restrict it to electoral politics and cast it adrift to fend for itself while we put together a social structure and develop our economic system in a hierarchical manner. Likewise, we would find it difficult to maintain democracy in electoral politics, unless it permeates our everyday lives. In no small measure, this means culture—how we express ourselves and the meanings we attach to how others express themselves.

A democratic culture, therefore, would foster a modicum of egalitarian respect for the myriad and varied ways we express ourselves in myriad and varied venues. It does not necessarily concede that a garage band is the equal of Springsteen's E Street Band or that a painting of a sad clown is the equal of Georgia O'Keefe's work. However, it does discourage us and others from accepting the adjective of "just" to describe how we express ourselves. A democratic culture, moreover, enables each of us as equally as possible to perform culture without denying that some cultural performances possess more beauty, skill, wit, and truth than others.

If playing a sport expresses something meaningful about us, a democratic culture might well distinguish an adult recreational basketball team from the NBA's San Antonio Spurs. It would not disrespect the team of perhaps physically over the hill men and women but respect it as one of many ways people enjoy and express themselves. A culture which delegitimizes the efforts of ordinary people to sing, dance, paint, and shoot hoops because of their class, gender, sexual orientation, race, age, religion, or physical and intellectual capacities is not a democratic culture nor a culture that a democratic society can count upon for sustenance.

I have stressed the production or performance aspect of culture because this book largely focuses on participation rather than consumption. However, if Amartya Sen is correct in saying that democracy is a conversation between equal members of a society, a democratic society should focus on not just what we say but on how others hear, understand, and interact with us. A democratic culture inspires a substantially egalitarian access to cultural performances. That is, it would not impose an onerous economic burden on middle- or working-class families if they wish to attend a museum or a ball game once in a while. A democratic culture would find a way to make certain that it is not always the wealthy who have courtside seats and not always working people located in the nose-bleed sections.[2]

Sadly, too many of us associate the fate of a sport with the fate of its most elite, most hyped practitioners, financial backers, and fans. A number of years ago, when Major League Baseball was mired in a serious and much too extensive strike, media experts wondered if baseball was doomed. To be sure, if Major League Baseball disappeared, a sad gap would have surfaced in American culture, but would people stop playing baseball and, its cousin, softball, at various parks, high school fields, and college stadiums around the nation?

Referring to America's national pastime, historian Larry Gerlach once declared, "Much of what passes for baseball history concerns only major league baseball and is presented without qualifications as though 'baseball' and 'major league' were synonymous." A great deal of the same could be said about the popular, historical, and contemporary representations of basketball.[3]

If we move beyond the assumption that American basketball is little more than the NBA and Division I National Collegiate Athletic Association (NCAA) hoops, we might discover that the sport has been perhaps surprisingly democratic in the past. Early twentieth-century basketball reveals young women playing the game interscholastically in high school and even intercollegiately with as much joy and intensity as their male counterparts. For a great deal of the twentieth century, municipalities sponsored adult and youth recreational leagues in which ordinary people of varied skill levels and racial and ethnic identities played against and with one another. Meanwhile, ethnic communities forged teams and leagues which promoted a great deal of pride and gave participants, even if standing well below six feet, and supporters a great deal of joy.

Cultural Citizenship and Community

Among other important tasks, a democratic culture would need to find a way to negotiate the difficult terrain constructed out of years of hierarchical racial and ethnic relations. Cultural distinctions have emerged based on race and ethnicity in the United States. Yet a democratic culture should transcend calls for cultural homogeneity, an unhealthy breeding ground for democracy, which requires dialogue between varied perspectives to thrive. It should also transcend cultural fragmentation, an equally unhealthy breeding ground for democracy, which requires a sense of shared purpose and respect for rules of civic participation. In other words, a democracy does not need assimilation of various racial and ethnic groups, nor does it need the kind of multiculturalism critiqued by scholar Henry Louis Gates in the early 1990s—a multiculturalism in which "each culture is fixed in place and separated by grout."[4]

The concept of cultural citizenship might offer a democratic culture an opportunity to avoid the pitfalls of assimilation and fragmentation. Cultural citizenship is a concept developed in the 1990s by Latino scholars Renato Rosaldo, William Flores, and Rina Benmayor. Flores and Benmayor define cultural citizenship as "the right to be different (in terms of race, ethnicity, or native languages) with respect to the norms of the dominant national community, without compromising one's right to belong, in the sense of participating in the nation-state's democratic processes." Cultural citizenship seems a prerequisite in a culturally diverse nation striving for democracy.[5]

To stress the role of democracy in American sports, much of this book will focus on the grass roots of American athletic experiences—ethnic community basketball teams and leagues that take pride in distinctiveness but can also reach out to other communities. As the well-cited political scientist Benedict Anderson told us, communities are imagined and invented. In his classic *Imagined Communities*, the eminent scholar wrote about the creation of nations—the effort to unite people otherwise divided by mountains and rivers, dialects and languages, time periods, and social distinctions such as race, ethnicity, gender, class, and religion.[6]

Using Anderson's work as my cue, I will employ a comparatively inclusive definition of community. While as a concept, community has typically been tied to a relatively small geographic area—a neighborhood, a cluster of adjacent neighborhoods, a village or small town—it has also been applied to larger geographic areas. Not only has Benedict Anderson called a nation a community, but we often hear people talk about something called the international community as represented by the United Nations or the World Health Organization.

Community has also been connected to identity. In other words, people who believe they have a great deal of meaningful things in common are often described as members of a community. For example, we hear about ethnic communities and gay and lesbian communities that transcend geographic borders. In recent years, the term *diasporic community* has been invented to help us understand the experiences of people who share a common geographic ancestry but live scattered throughout the world. And, at the time of this writing, there are those who consider themselves members of a community contrived through social networking.

While many analysts consider community a conceptually slippery devil, most of us, as theorist Raymond Williams asserted years ago, retain a warm and fuzzy feeling for community. We perceive community as something that brings people together, often during trying times and circumstances. Yet Williams reminded us that while we all cheer the inclusiveness of community, there seems something insidious working in the background of community building and maintenance.[7]

That is, our need to create communities often stems from the belief that there are people, substantially and ominously different from us, who have done or would do us harm. At the very least, these people are indifferent to our welfare. Accordingly, to protect ourselves we organize into an effectively unified social group. Exogenous forces, such as institutional racism and nativism, have often moved people to create and sustain ethnic community organizations. At the same time, a community, while it might possess a considerable amount of inclusiveness, has an exclusive side. A community suggests that that there are those who either choose not to be members or who are excluded from membership. In other words, not all communities are necessarily "beloved."

For many of us, however, communities reflect less a need for group insularity than the need to gather together people who share something important in common—at least, important to them. So, aside from the uncritical affection we have for community, another problem derives from its widespread use as a category to describe any group of people entranced by the same pastime or lifestyle. Over 25 years ago, a group of University of California, Berkeley, sociologists headed by Robert Bellah dismissed as "lifestyle enclaves" many groupings then widely represented, and representing themselves, as communities. Since Bellah et al. published the important *Habits of the Heart* in the mid-1980s, we have blithely ignored the authors' complaints.[8]

To be fair, we have the right to classify groupings with which we identify any way we wish. At the same time, doing so means lumping fans of a television show with oppressed early Christians facing down lions before blood-lusting ancient Romans and civil rights activists facing down shot guns, snarling police dogs, and fire hoses in the segregated south in the 1950s and 1960s. Therefore, while I might stray from strict geographically based definitions of community, I do think that Bellah et al. were on the right track when they wrote,

> A community is a group of people who are socially interdependent, who participate together in discussion and decision making, and who share certain practices... that both define the community and are nurtured by it. Such a community is not quickly formed. It almost always has a history and so is also a community of memory, defined in part by its past and its memory of its past.[9]

A community then might strike us as a neighborhood or an aggregation of neighborhoods with a collective memory. San Francisco's Chinatown comes to mind. Yet it might also appear as a racial or ethnic group residing within a nation or a transnational diasporic group with members dispersed throughout the globe. Furthermore, communities have been and are forged when people share common grievances against those who possess power based on class, race, colonialism, gender, sexual orientation, and religion.

Athletic organizations and individual athletes can help constitute and sustain a sense of community. They can represent communities to other communities. And they can build cultural bridges to other communities as well. But the relationship between sports and community has often been ambiguous. Some have understandably argued that sports offer a diversion that aggrieved or economically strapped communities cannot afford. Despite sports' sometimes sincere embrace of meritocracy, it has also helped justify exclusion and marginalization of people because of their racial identity, gender, sexual orientation, age, size, or, more trivially, because some of us would rather spend Super Bowl Sunday at a museum than glued to a television set for hours.

This book, therefore, is not aimed at romanticizing the association between a sport such as basketball and community. It does acknowledge that since at least the onset of the twentieth century, Americans of Asian ancestry have employed basketball to enhance their sense of community with others they perceive as similar to them in meaningful ways, primarily in terms of common ancestry. Second, it asserts that through basketball Americans of Asian ancestry could represent their communities in a beneficial light to those willing to shed at least some of their racial nativism. Third, it recognizes that through basketball Americans of Asian ancestry could, albeit often too briefly, bond with other communities.

Cosmopolitan Canopies

In order to link communities and foster a civic conversation so necessary to its existence, a democratic society should encourage the development of social spaces in which diverse people can move from their ethnic communities and engage one another with a significant amount of civility. Sociologist Elijah Anderson called such social spaces *cosmopolitan canopies*. In an influential study of them in Philadelphia, Anderson wrote that "cosmopolitan canopies [are] settings that offer a respite from the lingering tensions of urban life and an opportunity for diverse peoples to come together."[10]

Community teams have laid the foundation of Asian American basketball. As such, they have also launched innumerable male and female "ballers" across

In places like Silicon Valley, high school teams suiting up Asian Americans have become fairly widespread. This is my son's 2009–2010 Cupertino High School basketball team. Of the 13 players on the roster, nine possessed Asian ancestry. The handsome young man first on the left in the middle row is my son, Spencer. By the way, the team did well, making it into the postseason tournament.

cultural borderlands. Where I live, in California's Silicon Valley, it is hard to find a high school basketball team without players of Asian ancestry. During his senior year in 2010 at Cupertino High School, my son's basketball team's starting lineup included two *hapas* who possessed Japanese and European ancestry (one of whom was my son), a Chinese American, and an Indo-American. The fifth starter was a Middle Eastern American who alternated with a young man of Vietnamese and Japanese ancestry. The teams they played often possessed rosters harboring young men of similar racial and ethnic backgrounds.

But my son's high school team represented something that was not entirely new. Americans of Asian ancestry have been playing basketball with and against people of diverse racial and ethnic backgrounds for years. The practice was customary in twentieth century Hawai'i, where class distinguished people more clearly than on the U.S. mainland and to some extent eclipsed race and ethnicity as hierarchical markers. But even on the U.S. mainland, one could find elementary school, middle school, high school, junior college, and college teams suiting up Americans of Asian ancestry since the early twentieth century. Furthermore, relatively diverse youth, commercial, and church leagues have long furnished homes for the passion and skills of young and adult Asian Americans.

Perhaps, we can look upon the basketball court as a cosmopolitan canopy, "middle ground," "contact zone," "social field," or any number of spatial metaphors used to make sense of the complex relations that develop when people of diverse social backgrounds, frequently unequal in power, encounter one another. To assume that people cast their prejudices and their power aside once the ball hits the floor remains naive. Nevertheless, it is interesting that while sports such as basketball have sadly reflected hierarchical social relations, they have also facilitated cross-cultural interactions possessing at least a semblance of civility and even democratic promise.[11]

Strangers from a Different Shore

Several years ago, historian Ronald Takaki wrote a seminal history of Asian Americans. He called his book *Strangers from a Different Shore* in part because Asians in America could trace their ancestry from a significantly different part of the world than those of us who can claim our ancestors came from Europe. Moreover, while Europeans landed on the shores of the East Coast, often eyeing the Statue of Liberty in the process, Asian immigrants reached the United States by way of Honolulu, Seattle, and San Francisco. As such, Asians brought with them different cultural practices and institutions than, for examples, immigrants like my maternal grandparents, who migrated to the United States from Eastern Europe.[12]

However, Takaki was not just interested in geographical and cultural disparities. He borrowed the concept of *stranger* from classical German social theorist Georg Simmel, who argued that European Jews, no matter how much they tried to assimilate into the dominant cultures of the nations in which they resided, were and would remain permanently estranged from those cultures. For Takaki, Asian Americans have been seemingly permanent strangers, marked by America's fitful adherence to racist ideology and practices. American white supremacy, Takaki's book maintains, not only enslaved millions of Africans and their descendants and murdered and ruthlessly relocated American Indians, but also ran roughshod over the hopes of countless Asian immigrants to the United States in the nineteenth and early twentieth centuries. Asian immigrants were denied citizenship by virtue of the way white law and society identified them racially. Asian immigration was largely eliminated by World War

II. In states such as California, Asian immigrants could not own farmland for decades. In many municipalities, Asian immigrants were residentially segregated, humiliated, and threatened well into the twentieth century and beyond. And sometimes threats turned to actual violence.

Like many other Asian American scholars, many of whom were inspired by his work, Takaki understood that class and gender also imposed burdens on Asian immigrants and their offspring in the United States. Often performing "cheap labor" on Hawaiian plantations and docks and California's farms, Asian Americans could also be found working hard for little wages as industrial and domestic laborers. At times, those doing the exploiting of their labor were white; at times they may have come from similar ethnic backgrounds. Asian American females, meanwhile, were especially burdened. They might, for example, be expected to work for meager wages as domestic laborers and then perform the bulk of the household and child-rearing chores at home.

For the offspring of Asian immigrants, discrimination and isolation shadowed their experiences at least until World War II. Immigration restriction had minimized second-generation Asian Americans, but they still could be found attending public schools in Los Angeles and San Jose, hearing in classrooms that in the United States there was hope—there was "liberty and justice for all." But hope foundered as they learned about job and housing discrimination and, in the case of Japanese Americans, a nation willing to imprison them because of their race and ethnicity.

Growing up in Hawai'i, Takaki argues that Asian American experiences were different there than on the mainland. He points out that according to the 1920 U.S. census, over 60 percent of Hawai'i's population claimed some kind of Asian ancestry. In California, only 3 percent claimed Asian ancestry, and throughout the Lower 48, less than 1 percent of the population possessed Asian ancestry. Thus, intuitively one would imagine that growing up Chinese, Japanese, Korean, or Filipino in Hawai'i or California made a difference.

The quest for labor by Hawaiian sugar and then pineapple plantations inspired the large Asian presence on the islands. Significantly removed from the United States and even more removed from Europe, the Hawaiian Islands were an unlikely destination for whites seeking jobs and other economic opportunities. To fill their labor needs, large-scale employers in Hawai'i recruited principally from Asia, as well as among indigenous Hawaiians, who were diminished by intermarriage and more tragically by diseases conveyed to the islands by whites—diseases rendered more deadly by Hawaiian poverty.

Takaki hardly presents an image of Hawai'i as a land of social harmony. Racialized class lines divided the island population. That is, disproportionately the white minority held political and economic power and disproportionately Hawai'i's nonwhite people were the wage workers and small-scale shop keepers and farmers. On the plantations, there was resentment and occasionally bitter strikes. Yet aside from a major and surprisingly effective strike of Japanese and Filipino workers in 1920, few eruptions of labor militancy crossed ethnic lines, in part because the plantation management effectively manipulated ethnic tensions. At the same time, the almost entirely *haole*, or white, Hawaiian elite was playing with fire by permitting families to migrate and allowing interracial marriages. On the mainland, it was hard for an extensive second generation of American-born citizens and prospective voters to incubate among Asian ethnic groups. In Hawai'i, it was not so hard.

Moreover, inside and outside the plantations, the ethnic divisions among lower-class Hawaiians were cracking almost as soon as they appeared. Takaki asserts that Pidgin English was an important source of this breakdown. Also called by academics Creole Hawaiian, Hawaiian Pidgin English was a mishmash of English, Hawaiian, and a variety of Asian languages. Through Hawaiian Pidgin English, lower-class Hawaiians could foster a language as legitimate as any other—with a logic, a complicated structure and vocabulary. They therefore could communicate across ethnic lines about their labor grievances, organize athletic teams, socialize, and court one another. Hawaiian Pidgin English helped create the conditions for the fostering of Hawaiian local culture analogized by essayist and humorist Sara Vowell to the Hawaiian "plate lunch," where "a glop of macaroni salad" sits next to "Japanese chicken." This local culture did not and could not erase the hard history of race and ethnicity in Hawai'i, but it could complicate that history. More concretely, it could make it easier after World War II for Hawaiians of Asian and Pacific Islander ancestry to effectively and democratically assert their agency against a colonial elite.[13]

In Honolulu and larger Hawaiian municipalities, furthermore, a diversified, urban economy emerged. Given the overwhelming preponderance of Asian Hawaiians, it proved difficult for racist nativists to maintain the kind of residential and occupation separatism that existed on the mainland. Whereas jobs such as bank tellers, elementary school teachers, police officers, department store sales clerks, and hotel managers were generally closed to Asian Americans on the mainland, employers were often hard pressed to hire anyone else but Asian Americans in Hawai'i. Corresponding with the relative lack of occupational segregation was the relative lack of housing segregation, at least by race and ethnicity.

The ethnic enclaves—the Chinatowns and Little Tokyos—that one could note on the mainland were less prevalent in Hawai'i. In Hawai'i, class determined neighborhood as much as race and ethnicity, if not more so. Thus, one could grow up, go to school, and play and work with people of different ethnic backgrounds more easily than on the mainland, although as historians Allyson Varzally and Shelly Sang-Hee Lee assert, mainland racial and ethnic boundaries were frequently more fluid than many of us think, especially in places like mid-twentieth-century Los Angeles and Seattle.[14]

World War II witnessed powerful changes for Asian Americans. West Coast Japanese Americans were, of course, interned by the thousands. However, the economic tail wind produced by the war's Keynesian economics on steroids pushed many Asian Americans out of their ethnic enclaves and migratory worker circuits and into more mainstream white and blue collar jobs. Moreover, powerful policy makers believed that if the war was going to be won against fascism, the United States would have to rid itself of some of the more embarrassing legacies of institutionalized racism. If, for example, a World War II alliance with China was going to work, then it would perhaps be useful to deep six the Chinese Exclusion Act.

The Cold War and the "red scare" it inspired in the United States might have stifled the most strident demands for racial equality, but it also inspired more inclusive immigration laws. If, for example, the United States wanted to firm up an alliance with Japan in the wake of the Chinese Revolution, would it not make sense to open the doors to Japanese immigration? Thus, the McCarran-Walter Act was passed by the U.S. Congress in 1952. If the United States wished to combat Soviet influence in Asia, in general, would it not make sense to eliminate restrictive quotas from Asia and other third world nations? Thus, the relatively liberal Immigration Act of 1965 was passed.[15]

Even so, Asian immigrants and their offspring continued to confront racism and nativism, Takaki and other analysts of Asian American experiences remind us. Scholars such as Michael Omi and Howard Winant point out that the way Americans do race has not always been consistent. While accused of an incapacity to assimilate but a strong capacity for taking away the jobs of native born whites, people of Asian ancestry have been hailed in the United States as representatives of a "model minority." While its flowering took place after 1965, the model minority thesis, according to Takaki, reinforced the estrangement of Asian Americans. The model minority thesis, as applied to Asian Americans, stemmed from the joint efforts of honest social scientists and ideologically driven political leaders and media spokespersons. As such, it has been questioned vigorously by a number of Asian American scholars and activists.[16]

Introduced as a concept by sociologist William Peterson in the mid–1960s, the model minority theses was used originally to explain the relative success of Japanese Americans, despite the deep-seated racism they historically encountered. Since the mid–1960s witnessed growing militancy on the part of nonwhite activists persuaded that there was something fundamentally amiss with American institutions, the notion of Japanese, Chinese, Korean, and other Asian Americans comprising a model minority found a receptive audience among those who believed that institutional racism was but an unfortunate aberration of an otherwise generous American experience. Advocates of the model minority thesis often supported the needed passage of the Civil Rights and Voting Rights Acts of the mid–1960s; consequently, they argued that these laws eliminated substantial racial bars to upward advancement for people of color. Thus, if minority groups continued to lag behind other groups and complain about it, they needed instead to blame themselves for their inability to climb up the social ladder rather than the generally benevolent U.S. political and economic institutions.

The model minority thesis purported, therefore, that Asian Americans had achieved so much social and economic success that they were outperforming European Americans in the job market and the classroom. Despite the personal and institutional racism they had once endured, Asian Americans had succeeded by believing in the American dream—by believing that hard work, discipline, abstinence, and a heterosexually headed nuclear family paved the way for Harvard admissions and six-figure jobs. In the process, Asian Americans had eschewed welfare and political protest. Therefore, other nonwhite minority groups should pay respectful heed to Asian Americans. Otherwise, they would be culpable for their own failure to achieve the American dream.

While many Asian Americans bought into the notion that they were members of a model minority, Takaki and other Asian American critics of the model minority thesis have condemned its empirical foundations and its employment as an ideological weapon against those less taken with the veracity of American dream. Moreover, critics understandably lambasted the thesis as a stereotype, which, like other stereotypes, rob people of their complexity—of their humanity. It paints a picture of African American youth playing basketball out on the playground, while Asian American youth studiously hunker down in a library. More important, it ignores the insults and even violence visited upon Asian Americans of all ethnic backgrounds, as well as their struggle for a more democratic America.

A more recent, well-publicized version of the model minority thesis can be found in the book *Battle Hymn of the Tiger Mother* by Amy Chua. Highly controversial, this often entertaining and unsettling book has provoked condemnations from within and without Asian American communities. It argues that the key to the academic achievements of young Chinese Americans is a mother who will not accept anything less than high GPAs and SAT scores. While non–Chinese Americans are shuffling their children off to play dates and soccer practices, the "tiger mother" is making sure their children are doing their homework.[17]

Orientalism and Exoticism

Much of how Asians have been perceived historically has been filtered through the cultural construction of Orientalism. While generally negative in the sense that this construction has stereotyped and thus dehumanized millions of people, Orientalism and its use has not always been malicious in intent. That is, Orientalism has helped fashion people into strangers, exotics who are perhaps very nice but seem incapable of being like Westerners—that is, Europeans and European Americans.

According to the late scholar Edward Said, Orientalism emerged in the eighteenth and nineteenth centuries out of increasing encounters between people from the West and people residing east of Europe. Many of these encounters were determined by European imperialism and thus led to scholarly and nonscholarly efforts to represent the people of the Middle East and Asia as not just different from Westerners, but inferior to them, especially when it came to self-government. At the same time, nineteenth-century Orientalism could lead intellectuals, such as the American transcendentalists, to perhaps simplified but interesting and not necessarily offensive interpretations of Asian cultural traditions and practices. Yet as Said put it, "It is enough for 'us' to set up those boundaries in our own minds; 'they' become 'they' accordingly, and both their territory and their mentality are designated as different from 'ours.'"[18]

Orientalism, therefore, traveled different paths. It could represent "Orientals" as superstitious, violent, deceitful, and drug addicted. Yet it could represent them as gracious, artistic, wise, courageous, and darn good cooks. The point, as Rudyard Kipling underscored, was that "East is East and West is West, and never the twain shall meet." The Orient became "inscrutable" and "mysterious." To be sure, such representations could elicit Western fear but they also could elicit Western curiosity, along with Western money paid for books and movies revolving around Asian fictional villains and heroes such as Fu Manchu, on the one hand, and Charlie Chan, on the other. Sadly, Asian women were not forgotten by Orientalism. They were often branded as "dragon ladies"—corrupt and seductive, luring innocent young white men. However, they were often also branded as "China dolls"—innocent and submissive.[19]

While always overgeneralizing Asian experiences, Orientalism has cut in different directions. This nineteenth-century dime novel cover displays a vile form of Orientalism, portraying Chinese immigrants as corruptors of American innocence. Courtesy Library of Congress Prints and Photographs Division, LC-USZC4–4944.

Orientalism's effort to exoticize Asians helped fashion them into strangers to American adherents. It made it easier to dehumanize Asian Americans. And it made it easier to marginalize their efforts to represent themselves as people both distinctive and similar to other Americans.

CHAPTER 1

Pre–1945 Ethnic
Community Basketball

On the mainland and the territory of Hawai'i, Asian Americans gathered in urban and rural neighborhoods. On the mainland, they could be found substantially but not totally in the West and to a lesser extent, the Northeast. To some extent, these residential communities were a matter of choice—of familiarity based on kinship, friendship, language, and traditions. However, these residential communities were significantly fostered by racist practices bent on limiting the population of Asian Americans, while not only isolating Asian Americans from non–Asian Americans, but making their neighborhoods as uninhabitable as possible. To sustain themselves in these geographically constricted areas, Asian Americans established durable community institutions and practices, including basketball teams and leagues.

Basketball fit well the needs of those forging and maintaining a sense of community. Exogenous and endogenous forces combined to fashion basketball into an often fervently supported community sport. As designed by Springfield College's James Naismith in the early 1890s, basketball would not require much in the way of equipment or uniforms. A game would necessitate a ball, two baskets (which were really fruit baskets originally), and a referee to keep things from getting too unruly.[1]

One of the primary objectives of institutions such as Springfield College was to train physical educators for employment in various schools around the burgeoning U.S. empire, wherever American military and economic interests were apparent, as well as in religiously based youth organizations, such as the Young Men's Christian Association (YMCA) or the Young Women's Hebrew Association (YWHA). By the end of the 1890s, basketball surfaced throughout the U.S. mainland and the new U.S. territory of Hawai'i. It found enthusiastic participants in females as well as males. One of the first intercollegiate basketball games, if not the first, was played in the 1890s by young women from the University of California, Berkeley (Cal), against neighboring young women from the relatively new Stanford University. A few years later, the first professional league was formed for males on the East Coast.

Within the United States and its colonial possessions, the sport took root in the early decades of the twentieth century among culturally diverse urban, working-class, and lower- to middle-class people from Boston to Honolulu. In his pathbreaking book on Jewish American sporting experiences, historian Peter Levine argued, "Not surprisingly, in urban, ethnic, working-class neighborhoods, a game open to improvisation and requiring little space or equipment proved attractive to children." Accordingly, "smallish, white Jewish men," living in largely East Coast metropolitan Jewish neighborhoods transformed Naismith's creation into "the sport of Jews."[2]

Why a stereotypically nonathletic people would gravitate to basketball occasioned journalistic commentary during the first half of the twentieth century. Levine quoted famed writer Paul Gallico, who maintained, "Curiously ... above all others the game appeal[s] to the temperament of Jews ... a good Jewish football player is a rarity.... Jews flock to basketball by the thousands

Young women played basketball enthusiastically in the early twentieth century. This is a photograph of a group of Vassar basketball players in action around 1913. Courtesy Library of Congress Prints and Photographs Division, LC-USZ62–22263.

[because] it placed a premium on an alert, scheming, mind ... flashy trickiness, artful dodging and general smart aleckness." For Gallico, "the Hebrew" possessed these traits because of "his Oriental background."[3]

Stanley Frank echoed Gallico's efforts to racialize Jews through basketball. Racialization refers to the attribution of inherent qualities to a group of people, and Frank clearly racialized Jews when he claimed that skill at basketball required "the characteristics inherent in the Jew ... mental agility, perception ... imagination and subtlety." If given an opportunity to create a sport, Jews could not have had "a happier inspiration than basketball."[4]

To be sure, urban-based Jewish Americans played basketball passionately and skillfully. Among the more talented early twentieth-century basketball players were the Jews Barney Sedon, Dave Banks, and Nat Holman. Organized by a Philadelphia Jewish American, Eddie Gottlieb, a quintet representing the South Philadelphia Hebrew Association (the Sphas) became one of the more famous early professional teams and a forebear of the NBA's Philadelphia (now Golden State) Warriors. Yet other urban ethnic groups enthusiastically and adroitly took up basketball. For example, perhaps the greatest all-around basketball player during the first half of the twentieth century was the son of Italian immigrants living in San Francisco's North Beach: Angelo "Hank" Luisetti. Indeed, San Francisco's predominantly Italian American North Beach was widely considered a center of basketball in the city, rivaled significantly by adjacent Chinatown.

The religiously based youth organizations referenced earlier comprised part of a larger reform movement active in industrializing, urbanizing America. During the late nineteenth and early twentieth century, religious, secular, and local government organizations combined in a playground movement, seeking to divert urban, working-class youths from the real and presumed evils of crime, ethnic isolation, substance abuse, labor militancy, and political radicalism. Reformers believed that organized athletic competition played a role in all this, because they expected that a youth with a baseball bat or a basketball was less likely to join street gangs or militant labor organizations and more likely to become a dutiful, patriotic American consumer and worker.

The metropolitan settlement house supplied an appropriate site for linking basketball to social reform. Jewish American Nat Holman, who became a renowned basketball player and coach, remembered, "There is no question in my mind that the settlement houses were instrumental in popularizing the game of basketball as well as developing some of the more outstanding players in the history of the game.... Basketball was THE GAME on the Lower East Side and every youngster tried to excel at it."[5]

Transcending the urban setting, the social reformers of the playground movement insisted that a healthy body and healthy mind went hand-in-hand; they used basketball's versatility as both an indoor and outdoor sport to channel young people of varied cultural backgrounds toward what they perceived as wholesome recreational endeavors. Thus, playgrounds throughout the United States were equipped with not only sandboxes, swings, and see saws, but also basketballs, courts, backboards, and nets. At the same time, the targets of the playground movement were not just manipulated on to basketball courts. They frequently embraced basketball with passion and skill, pushing it perhaps in directions that Progressive Era reformers did not foresee.

Significantly, reform-minded physical educators often saw no harm and, indeed, substantial advantage in teaching young women basketball. They tended to view the sport as far more reputable than baseball, shadowed by often unwholesome participants and rowdy fans, and far less violent than American football, which by the early twentieth century was littering playing fields with the broken heads and bodies of many young men. Thus, college and school administrators and educators either sanctioned or ignored female students intent upon organizing basketball teams and games.

Yet the relative tolerance of female basketball in the 1890s started to give way to doubt by the early twentieth century. In 1900, the *San Francisco Examiner* reported that in a game against Cal women, a University of Nevada player sustained a skull fracture after plunging headfirst into the goal post holding the basket. The *Examiner* expressed the fear that like football, basketball was too dangerous for women. In 1905, the *Oakland Tribune* reported on a competitive high school game between females from Hayward and Alameda High Schools. The daily happily reported that no one was hurt. In 1917, Morris Dailey, who presided over San Jose Normal School, announced that women's basketball would cease on campus because it was too strenuous and injurious to the competitors.[6]

Meanwhile, the democratic potential of basketball was demonstrated by a group of American Indian women. Kansas's Fort Shaw women's team gained national fame in the early 1900s not just because the squad was entirely American Indian but because the youthful hoopsters were very good at the sport. After sweeping aside local competition, they appeared at the St. Louis World's Fair in 1904. In St. Louis, they continued their winning ways, much to the surprise of onlookers who doubted that indigenous women had the discipline to master a sport such as basketball.[7]

Negative pronouncements on female basketball did not keep women and girls off the court entirely, but it led to greater, more systematic efforts to make the sport safer and less competitive for females. This was part of a larger campaign to reign in female athletics and, for good and bad reasons, discourage women from replicating the male model of sports competition. In the 1890s, Senda Berenson, a Jewish American physical educator at Smith College, took Naismith's sport, invented but a few years earlier, and tried to transform it into something meaningful for middle- and upper-class young women. Inspired by basketball rules designed by Berenson, the female game included six players on a side, rather than the male game's five. Moreover, females were confined to certain areas of the court—guards to defend the goal, forwards to put themselves in shooting position, and centers to hang about in the middle of the court. The idea was to cut down on the physical demands on young women, hopefully rendering the sport less brutal for them and, accordingly, less likely to arouse indignation from the public.

Nevertheless, like their male counterparts, female teams competitively represented schools, businesses, neighborhoods, and religious organizations in the 1920s, 1930s, and 1940s. With the 1950s, we find considerably less publicized female basketball, because athletic-minded women were largely persuaded to channel their athletic passions in post–World War II America into more approved sporting activities—golf, tennis, bowling, and aquatic sports.[8]

Forging Communities in American Colleges

As we noted in the introduction, a sense of community can tie people together in places other than urban neighborhoods or small towns. Interestingly, some of the earliest reports of organized teams composed of Asian people in the United States came out of mainland college campuses. The nativity of these college students is hard to establish. Some of the participants were, no doubt, foreign-born and intended to return to their homelands. Yet some of the participants could have been born in the United States, or at least set on settling in the United States. In the early 1900s, terms such as Chinese American, Japanese American, or Filipino American were not used, with or without the hyphen. Rather, some people, regardless of birth, were usually viewed as Chinese, Japanese, or Filipinos. Yet no matter their nativity, these young people experienced white-dominated and often very large educational institutions; they sought in basketball and other activities ways to rise above the isolation many of them felt.

After America claimed the Philippines as a colonial possession in the late 1890s, a good portion of the earliest Filipino migrants to the United States were *pensionados*. That is, they were dispatched to the United States in order to attain a higher education and return to the Philippines with enhanced skills and knowledge. In the early 1900s, Illinois' DeKalb University enrolled enough

Filipinos that they could consider forming a basketball team, which the *Rockford Star*, in 1905, predicted would oppose the local high school team.[9]

Reed College, a liberal arts school in Oregon, had a Chinese Student Alliance as early as 1916. This organization hosted festivities for other college students of Chinese ancestry in the Pacific Northwest. Basketball competition reportedly excited substantial interest among participants. The *Portland Oregonian* informed readers that Chinese students from Oregon Agricultural College had beaten a team from the University of Washington during one of the get-togethers.[10]

Stanford and Cal have long been considered rivals when it comes to athletic endeavors. Students of Asian ancestry at these esteemed institutions took seriously that rivalry as early as the 1910s. The physical education publication *Mind and Body* reported in 1916 that Chinese students at both Cal and Stanford developed their own basketball teams. In March 1918, the *San Francisco Evening News* claimed that Captain Chin of the Stanford Chinese basketball team challenged the "Oriental" five from Cal for a game scheduled at the Olympic Club in San Francisco.[11]

In 1919, the Chinese Student Alliance met at Cal. The *Oakland Tribune* maintained that basketball competition was a feature of the get together. In one game, UC's Mon Kwok Club beat the Berkeley Congregation five, 30–19, at the old Harmon Gym. Ed Chew starred for the winners, while teammate and Cal varsity gridder, Son Kai Kee, performed well, too. The *Tribune* noted that the game was entertaining. Subsequently, the Mon Kwok Club downed the San Francisco YMCA Chinese Club, which had, according to the somewhat biased *Tribune* account, claimed "the championship of California, but they certainly don't know what championship means." Ed Chew once again stood out, making 12 baskets for the winners. Yar Chew deserved special mention for his defense. And Lee Chung proved the most effective San Franciscan. At the end of the festivities, the Mon Kwok aggregation was rewarded with a silver trophy.[12]

College students of Asian ancestry competed in both intercollegiate and intramural basketball in the early 1920s. In 1922, the *San Jose Mercury* informed readers that "Japs" were playing basketball at Stanford and the University of Southern California (USC). Apparently, the "Nipponese hoop ringers" from Stanford had thumped their Southern California opponents, 43–3. Fred Koba, who once played for the Stanford varsity team, scored 20 for the victors. In 1923, Stanford's *Daily Palo Alto* reported that the Japanese Club was doing quite well in intramural basketball at the university. In one game, it defeated the Encina Hall First Floor five, 11–4. The *Daily Palo Alto* testified, "The large Encina men seemed to have the edge in guarding but the Japanese players were much faster and more clever with their passes and shooting."[13]

East of the Mississippi, college students of Asian descent also took up basketball in the early 1920s. In New England, Massachusetts Institute of Technology (MIT) could boast of an all-Chinese basketball squad. According to the *New York Times*, this team was composed of former members of the Tsing-Hui quintet that had played intercollegiate basketball in China. In the early 1920s, these MIT students were achieving a near perfect record, although the *Times* did not disclose the squad's opponents. Meanwhile, according to a Wisconsin newspaper, Beloit College Chinese students were trying to organize a basketball team in 1921.[14]

In the 1930s, Asian American college students continued to assemble ethnic squads. In 1936, the University of Washington won the Northwest Chinese Basketball Tournament championship. Playing were Edwin Luke, Butch Luke, Frank Nipp, Robert Wong, James Mar, Tom Sing, Vincent Goon, and Art Louie. In 1937, Stanford's Japanese Club still competed in intramural basketball. Around the same time, a Japanese American five from Cal toured the West Coast. In Seattle, the Cal Japanese Americans beat a team of local Nikkei, 53–31. Center Kayo Senzaki scored 18 for the Berkeley contingent. Forward Obizairo tallied a team high of eight for the losers.[15]

Chinese American Ethnic Teams

The Chinese comprised the first Asian immigrant group to migrate to the U.S. mainland and Hawai'i in significant numbers. Chiefly possessing laboring-class backgrounds, early Chinese immigrants seemed too intent upon earning meager wages and, if they owned their own businesses, meager profits to organize the kind of athletic organizations out of which basketball might bloom. Moreover, immigration restriction and anti-miscegenation laws combined to play a strong role in minimizing a second generation of youthful Chinese Americans that could more readily embrace basketball. Yet by the second decade of the twentieth century, a second generation did emerge on the mainland and, despite its relatively small numbers, American-born Chinese enthusiastically supported basketball. As early as 1918, the San Francisco Chinese Students Association reportedly assembled a representative basketball team of high school–aged boys. According to a wire story, team members would wear "attractive red and black uniforms."[16]

Hawaiian Chinese proved very resourceful at assembling ethnic teams. Maui Chinese put together a male basketball team at least as early as 1919. In the early 1920s, the *Maui News* printed an advertisement announcing a benefit for the "Chinese-American Basketball Team" at the Lahaina Armory. It promised "four hours of real jazzy music" played by Eddie Tam and his orchestra. In 1922, the *Maui News* reported that the "Chinese-Americans" had beaten the Asahi five at Wailuku. Paul Low was one of the stars for the winning team.[17]

Honolulu sportswriter Loui Leong Hop argued that basketball was popular among Hawaiian Chinese. He pointed out in the late 1920s that only baseball exceeded basketball in luring the participation and backing of Hawaiian Chinese. Later, Hop wrote about Hawaiian Chinese hoopsters: "While small in most cases, they utilize superior speed and teamwork to attain victories and championships. The ACA's (All Chinese Athletics) always enter title contending quintets in local senior leagues." In 1927, Lin Young managed the ACA squad, while Chong Hong served as captain. Other members of the team included "the speedy and ever dangerous forward" Tai Sun Yim, as well as Tom Koop, Pung Afo, S. U. Won, K. C. Yuen, Loo Soo, M. K. Ching, Frank S. Tyau, Archie Ho, Peter Yee, Mathew Chang, Arthur Yee, William Chan, Robert Chung, Bunny "Pake Tourist" Chung, and Walter "Chocolate" Chung.[18]

In the late 1920s, the *Honolulu Star-Bulletin* hailed the ACA Dragons after they downed the University of Hawai'i five. They did so, according to the daily, "with a display of team work and shooting seldom seen on a local court." In the mid–1930s, the ACA squad was still competing effectively. By this time, the Chinese Hawaiians who excelled in hoops included Kwai Fong, "Maggie" Chow, Francis Wong, Wrinky Wong, and Q. C. Lum, who many asserted was the first Hawaiian to shoot one-handed.[19]

Hawaiian Chinese in the late 1920s also organized a basketball league on Oahu. One of the teams represented the Mid-Pacific School. Peter Yee captained the squad. Aside from the Mid-Pacifics, fives representing the Wah Mun School and Mun Lun School were in the league, as well as the Young Chinese Athletic Club and the Chinese Amateur Athletes. Loui Leong Hop also pointed out that a Chinese Hawaiian YMCA team competed in the 1920s.[20]

Chinese Hawaiians on Hilo forged a formidable basketball team in the 1920s. Hop declared that this team won senior league championships on the Big Island and did well in interisland matchups. One reason why the Hilo squad excelled was that it included island legend Ung Soy Afook.[21]

Well to the east of the islands, basketball flourished among Chinese San Franciscans in the years before World War II. The *Chinese Digest's* Frank Hee claimed in 1938 that the first Chinese San Franciscan five was formed from a contingent of Chinatown Boy Scouts in 1919. The construction of the Chinese Playground in Chinatown gave a decided impetus to Chinese San Franciscan hoops. According to sociologist Kathleen S. Yep, San Francisco authorities were pleased with the playground's attraction to Chinatown's youthful denizens. They "believed that basketball taught Chinese American kids to perform and embody American themes of democracy, discipline, and hard work." Chinese San Franciscans were pleased, too, although many considered the one playground insufficient for their needs. Yep quotes Felton Suen, who shot hoops on the Chinese Playground in the early 1940s. Suen maintained, "We didn't have no place to go. That's why we always went to the Playground."[22]

The Chinese Playground bred highly competitive and frequently able hoopsters. In 1936, according to Yep, the Chinese Playground boys' basketball teams won all five of the division championships for the city's youth squads. Often quite fiercely, Chinese Playground girls' squads took on other youth teams, as well as engaging in intramural contests. The playground, Yep declares, "was one of the few spaces where girls could strengthen their athletic skills."[23]

Whether boys or girls, Chinese Playground athletes developed into quick and agile basketball players, well-versed in aggressive defense. The leading scholar on Chinese American basketball in San Francisco, Yep writes,

> Basketball offered these youth a structure in which they could exercise spontaneity as well as agility, free from the constraints of the crowded physical spaces in their homes and work.... On the court they could challenge socially determined limits to their achievement and stake a place in the world as Chinese Americans and as mostly working class youths.[24]

Yep concedes that basketball could not erase "racial and class hierarchies" but still inclined Chinese American youth in San Francisco toward challenging social and economic inequality. Significantly, Yep contends, Chinese San Franciscan youth basketball players did not perceive or necessarily desire a route through basketball to assimilation in American society. Instead, the sport allowed them to assert their class and ethnic distinctiveness. Ethnic community teams such as those that emerged in San Francisco's Chinatown demonstrate the usefulness of the concept of cultural citizenship.[25]

For much of the twentieth century, the Bay Area hosted an annual tournament pitting the best amateur fives in the region. This competition was held under the aegis of an organization variously called the Pacific Athletic Association or the Pacific Association (PA), and it was often sponsored by the *San Francisco Examiner*. In 1928, a Chinatown team won the 88-pound division of the tournament. This was, according to the *San Francisco Chronicle*, the first time "Chinese boys" had entered the tournament. When the tournament was held in 1930, two Chinese San Franciscan squads participated: the Nam Wahs in the 100-pound division and the Chinese Telegraph Exchange in the 120-pound division. On January 8, 1930, the *San Francisco Chronicle* reported that in the tournament the Chinese Telegraph Exchange had been taken down by the Central YMCA squad. However, the Nam Wahs edged the Red Shields, 26–25 in overtime. To get to the finals of the 120-pound division tournament, the Nam Wahs narrowly defeated a team representing the Japanese Reformed Church, 24–23.[26]

Chinatown squads earned some mainstream publicity for playing outside of the Pacific Athletic Association tournament as well. In 1931, the *San Francisco Chronicle* told readers about a local contest between Chinese American fives. The "Namwah Chinese Cagers" and the "Tahmies-Chi-Fornia" squads were spotted practicing for an upcoming game at San Francisco's French Court. The Namwahs, according to the *Chronicle*, "claim[ed] the distinction of the best Chinese lightweight cage squad west of the Rocky Mountains." Around the same time, an aggregation called True Sunshine, with a roster entirely composed of athletes with Chinese surnames, played in the city's Episcopal League. In 1932, "Chinese boys" copped playground championships in the 95- and 110-pound divisions. In the fall of 1936, a San Francisco High School Chinese League competed with Galileo and Commerce lads leading the way. Around the same time, a Chinatown YMCA 80-pound team devastated a YMCA team from the Mission district, 64–0. In 1939, San Francisco State's 145-pound team lost to a Chinese YMCA squad. Early in 1941, an all–Chinese American team sponsored by the St. Mary's Mission in Chinatown took part in a Catholic Youth Organization (CYO) tournament at Kezar Pavilion, situated on the edge of Golden Gate Park and near the city's famed Kezar Stadium.[27]

The San Francisco–based *Chinese Digest* offered readers plenty of details on community basketball from the mid- to late 1930s. The "Chinfornian" five encountered a Boys Club team at the latter's home court. The Chinese Americans drew ahead at half by a healthy 17–8 margin. However, the referees stopped the game because the Boys Club engaged in "rough house tactics." Subsequently, the Chinfornians lost a game to the Evening School of Commerce, 60–47. Among the young men playing for Chinfornia were Victor Wong, Richard Wong, Jack Lee, Ted Lee, James Hall, Fred Woo, Jack Lock, and Francis Mark.[28]

It was not only non–Chinese Americans who roughed up Chinese American hoopsters. Early in 1936, the *Chinese Digest* rebuked community basketball players for fighting each other. It complained that such brawls reflected badly on Chinese Americans and that those involved should act like "gentlemen."[29]

The Chinese Troop Three Scouts team and the Shangtai five emerged as superior San Francisco Chinatown squads in the mid–1930s. Managed by a former athlete at Commerce High, Don Lee, the Scouts had also barnstormed Southern California. In Los Angeles, for example, they beat two Japanese American fives and one Chinese American squad. Playing for the Scouts were Frank Wong, Frank Lee, Captain Earl Wong, Herbert Tom, Philip Chinn, Hin Chin, Bing Chin, Henry Kan, Silas Chinn, Edward Leong, Ted Moy, Albert Young, and Francis Chin. The Scouts won the 1936 Wah Ying Tournament, established in the mid–1930s to inspire more enthusiasm for Chinatown basketball. In the meantime, they edged a fine team of Chinese American hoopsters from Los Angeles's Lowa Club. The game ended 24–23 with Earl Wong leading the way with 15 points, while George Tong managed eight for the losers.[30]

The Shangtai five comprised another strong team. To the *Chinese Digest* in January 1936, it was "potentially the greatest cage team of Chinese ever mustard [*sic*]." Coached by Joe Chew, it included several players with high school experience. Charlie Hing hailed from Polytechnic (Poly) High. Gerald Leong played for Commerce. And Fred Gok, called the best guard in San Francisco Chinatown, competed for Galileo. Hing, one of the better all-around Chinese American athletes in the Bay Area, was, according to the U.S. census manuscripts in 1930, the son of a single mother and telephone operator, Rose Hing.[31]

The Namwahs played well against Chinese and non–Chinese American competition. In the spring of 1938, they beat Young China, an Oakland five, 29–23. Leading scorer for the victors was the gifted Robert Lum, who tallied 11 points. Al Lee chipped in nine for the Namwahs.[32]

These pre–World War II teams usually held their own against non–Asian American fives. Late in 1935, the Shangtais barely lost to Golden Gate Junior College, 43–39. Taking part in San Francisco's Recreation League, the Shangtais downed the Joan of Arc five, 43–26. Then they lost to Sunset Majors, 34–32. The *Digest* complained that bad refereeing made the difference. In any event, Allen Lee Po, Charlie Hing, and Fred Gok stood out.[33]

The previous paragraphs have detailed male basketball. However, female Chinese San Franciscans gained some citywide publicity via the sport. In 1934, the *San Francisco Chronicle* announced that the "St. Mary's Chinese Sextet" competed in the Catholic Girls League. Meanwhile, according to historian Judy Yung, San Francisco's Chinese Young Women's Christian Association (YWCA) constructed facilities for basketball.[34]

In the late 1990s, Florence Chinn recalled growing up in San Francisco's Chinatown in the 1930s. She remembered a basketball team coached by a young woman who had played the sport competitively and was attending the University of California at the time. Known as the Catholic Daughters of America (CDA) in Chinatown and sponsored by the church, the CDA hoopsters also played at the "Chinese School," where apparently they learned the game from competing with the older boys. Chinn recollected that the team occasionally went to Oakland to contest a "Chinese girls' team" there. According to Chinn, the players either took public transportation to the East Bay or their parents would drive them. Scholar Susan Zieff underscored the passion Chinese American females expressed for basketball. She cited a study of athletic predilections of San Francisco school children in the 1930s. This study showed that basketball was overwhelmingly the favorite sport of Chinese American youngsters, regardless of gender.[35]

The most notable Chinese American women's squad competing in San Francisco before World War II represented the Mei Wah Club. This squad, Yep insists, generally consisted of young working-class women. Among the members were Josephine Chan, Rachael Lee, Mae Fung, Mary Lee, Camille Wong, Ella Mark Chan, Mabel Choy, Susan Lee, Franche Lee, Peony Wong, and Erline Lowe, who was "Chinatown's foremost all around girl athlete," according to the *Chinese Digest* in the 1930s. Their parents, Yep informs us, were often garment workers or labored in grocery stores and restaurants. Franche Lee was probably unusual, however. Her family moved to San Francisco from West Virginia. Moreover, according to the biographer of one of her sons, writer Laurence Yep, she "saw nothing wrong with playing basketball against the boys—much to the disgust of old-time Chinese." While in high school, Franche Lee and her sisters cleaned houses for pay. Teammate Peony Wong, according to the San Francisco City Directory of 1935, lived on Stockton Street and worked as a clerk. The U.S. census manuscript schedules tell us that Erline Lowe in 1940 was a 21-year-old playground director. She lived with a mother and older sister, both of whom worked in a dress factory.[36]

According to Yep, Mei Wah could mean, depending on the Chinese characters, American Chinese or Beautiful Flower. However, as hoopsters, the Mei Wahs were hardly shrinking violets as they practiced against Chinese American boys and opposed other Chinese American teams, such as the arch rival from Oakland, the Wa Ku aggregation, as well as Japanese American squads. The *Chinese Digest* maintained that the Mei Wah girls were just as athletic as their boy counterparts, and the young boys even regarded them as their sports role models. Even though some of their parents were upset that they were playing aggressive basketball, the Mei Wahs continued to terrorize opponents. Yep writes that "[e]ven while playing within girls' rules, the Mei Wahs were tough—using their elbows, tripping players, and posting up.... To them, women realized themselves as women through their strength, stamina, and toughness. These working-class Chinese American women found gratification using their physical power, agility, and endurance."[37]

The Mei Wahs fearlessly took on white teams. Using a "brand of basketball [that] involved speed, under the bucket shots, and physical aggression," they might have been shorter than their European American opponents, but they were, according to Rachael Lee, "quicker." Consequently, the Mei Wahs won two San Francisco Playground championships in the 1930s. Playing eight p.m. weeknight contests at the San Francisco's Girls' High and French Court, they encountered little racial integration in city basketball. Save for one Japanese American contingent, all their opponents were European Americans.[38]

Journeying outside of Chinatown, the Mei Wah hoopsters not only left their comfort zone but often faced hostility. They understood, Yep asserts, the limitations of basketball. Playing the game would not cure racism, sexism, and economic inequality, but the sport offered the Mei Wahs an opportunity to assert their agency in the face of injustice.[39]

In May 1936, the *Chinese Digest* hailed the Mei Wahs' copping of the Police Athletic League (PAL) championship. In the process, the young hoopsters had lost but one game. Franche Lee ranked as the team's top scorer. The *Digest* credited Jo Chan as a top foul shooter. The versatile Rachael Lee could hold down both the guard and forward positions. Captain Peony Wong, Janet Hoo, and Mary Chan were good guards, while Erline Lowe worked well as a forward. Two years later, the Mai Wahs, coached by Thomas Tip, still excelled in San Francisco's PAL. In a PAL game against the First United Church, the Mei Wahs won 33–27, with Franche Lee notching 16 points.[40]

Meanwhile, the Mei Wahs of San Francisco trekked down to Los Angeles, where they took on another Mei Wah squad. The *Chinese Digest* reported that a large crowd watched on Memorial Day, 1936, as the San Franciscans dumped the host team, 36–6. Erline Lowe proved the big star as she "tossed the ball into the basket from all angles."[41]

While heavily stressing male hoops, the *Chinese Digest* offered glimpses of female basketball as well. In the spring of 1936, it reported that the Chungwah squad had beaten Portsmouth, 29–19. In the spring of 1937, the *Digest* hailed the St. Mary's Junior CDA aggregation as the "undisputed champ of Chinatown" after beating the Girl Reserves, 19–4, and Chung Wah, 22–6. On the CDA roster were young women such as Norma Wong, Wawona Tang, Hattie Chew, Charmaine Tang, Catherine Chu, May Lo, Blossom Tang, Rosemary Gee, and Patricia Yee, who bucketed 13 points against the Girl Reserves. The CDA not only took the championship of the A division, but the Chinese Baptists won the B division crown. The next year, the Baptists downed the CDA for the B division championship in the Chinese Playground Girls' League. In the A division championship, CDA beat the Mei Wah Juniors before 200 cold but excited spectators at the Chinese Playground, 20–16. Mei Wah standouts Mary Chan and Erline Lowe coached all four teams vying for supremacy. Chan handled the Baptists and Mei Wah Juniors, while Lowe mentored the CDA hoopsters. Games in the Playground League took place on Friday evenings and Saturday afternoons. As for some of the individual athletes, the American-born Wawona Tang came from a relatively good background, according to the U.S. census manuscripts for 1930. Her immigrant father was head of Chinatown's

Chamber of Commerce, and her mother was born in California. May Lo's background seemed not so privileged. Born in California, her parents were immigrants and her father was described in the 1930 census manuscript schedules as a general laborer.[42]

Prior to World War II, Chinese San Franciscans seemed fairly pleased with the growing popularity of basketball among themselves and Chinese Americans in general. The *Chinese Digest's* Frank Hee asserted in 1938, "Chinese in America have been growing in leaps and bounds toward the betterment of sports and this is especially so in basketball." As the twentieth century's fourth decade began, the *California Chinese Press* hailed San Francisco's Chinatown as "the hotbed of city basketball." In calling San Francisco's Chinatown "one of the bright spots of basketball in San Francisco" in 1940, the *Press* proudly acknowledged that the community sent 300 children to Cow Palace, then the Bay Area's version of Madison Square Garden, to watch the great Hank Luisetti in action with the Olympic Club five against his alma mater, Stanford. To see Luisetti perform, the Chinese American young people arrived early—five p.m. for an eight p.m. game. Accentuating further the *California Chinese Press's* pleasure in Chinatown basketball, it reported that a St. Mary's boys' team, led by the young Willie Wong, had beaten the Mission Delores contingent in a CYO championship game. Meanwhile, the *San Francisco Chronicle* published a "photograph of Chinese cagers"—the boys' 80-pound team. The *Chronicle* added that St. Mary's entered four teams in all for the 1941 CYO tourney. Not only did the 80-pounders participate but 90-, 100-, and 110-pound boys as well. As it turned out, all four would win CYO championships.[43]

East Bay Chinese Americans did not ignore basketball. Berkeley's Chinese Congregational Mission Club sponsored a 110-pound team in 1920 that shined against other East Bay members of the same weight division. A couple of months later, the Wa Ku contingent won a game at Oakland's Lincoln School, 35–13. The *Oakland Tribune* observed that a large crowd attended the game— a crowd mostly consisting of enthusiastic Chinese Americans who cheered in both "Chinese and English." The *Oakland Tribune* reported in 1927 that a "Chinese team" from the Lincoln Playground clobbered a squad from the Durant Playground. In January 1932, the Wa Sung Club's basketball decidedly defeated the Boeing School, 28–16. Chin scored 16 for the winners. The next month, these Chinese Oaklanders, members of a prominent Chinese American athletic organization, downed the New Century Olympic Club in the East Bay Basketball League, 24–23. A few years later, a couple of Chinese American fives took part in Oakland's All-Nations' Basketball League, sponsored by the city's Jewish community center. Early in February 1934, the Young Chinese Juniors edged the Alexander Community House five, 19–18. A young man called Lew Shane by the *Oakland Tribune* was high scorer for the winners. Meanwhile, Gum Wong tallied 16 for the Chinese Presbyterians when they took the measure of the East Oakland Community Center's Ramblers, 34–21. Also in Oakland, the Wa Ku Auxiliary forged a Chinese American women's team, which competed throughout Northern California in the late 1920s and into the 1930s, playing, as mentioned earlier, San Francisco's Mei Wah contingent. In 1938, the Waku Auxiliary Juniors thumped the Young Ladies' Institute aggregation, 39–3. According to the *Chinese Digest*, Captain Stella Lew stood out on defense, while Laura Tom proved effective on offense. Early in 1936, Oakland's Young Chinese Club traveled down to San Jose, where they downed the San Jose Chinese, 27–23. The next year, the Young Chinese copped the crown of the All-Nations League 110-pound division. Moreover, the Young Chinese had a female "auxiliary" squad competing in the late 1930s. In 1940, the *Oakland Tribune* pointed out that a group of Chinese American boys had won the basketball championships at the city's Lincoln Park.[44]

Proffering evidence for the exuberant support for Chinese American basketball on both sides of the Bay, the *California Chinese Press* reported in December 1940 that ten teams were to compete in the Wah Ying Bay Regional tournament. This was supposedly the largest turn out ever for the tournament. From San Francisco and the East Bay, teams such as the Nam Wahs, Buccaneers, Cathay, Berkeley Athletic Club, Nulite, Dragoneers, Chinatown Merchants, and Lucky 13 were expected to participate.[45]

Chinese California communities to the north and south of the San Francisco–Oakland area organized fives. In Marin County, the unlimited or varsity San Rafael High School lost to the North Bay Chinese Athletic Club, 34–29. In Palo Alto, the Chinese American Palicjique Club had a hoops team in the mid–1930s. The San Jose Chinese invaded Watsonville in January 1936 to take on a Watsonville Chinese American five. The visitors won, thanks to the Lee brothers, Jimmy and Harry. Earl Goon managed to score 12 for the losers. Later that month, Harry Lee tallied 14 of San Jose's 24 points to help his team beat a squad of barnstormers from St. Louis, 24–20. The San Jose Chinese were downed by the "Stanford Chinese," 27–23, at San Jose's Roosevelt Recreation Center in early February 1936. Several days later the "Chinese boys," as the *Mercury* called them, lost to the Trojan Athletic Club, 71–61. "S. H. Lee," perhaps Harry, led the vanquished with an impressive 34 points. The *Chinese Digest* informed readers that this team represented the San Jose Chinese Students Club and included, besides Harry and Jimmy Lee, Gaius Shew, James Chow, and Steve Chow. The latter, the 1940 U.S. census manuscript schedules tell us, was the American-born son of a Chinese immigrant father who clerked in a clothing store. His mother, also American-born, worked in a cannery. Like his father, Chow was a clothing store clerk. Gaius Shew was the son of a California-born father and a Hawaiian-born mother. The father, according to the 1920 census, owned a store.[46]

To the south of San Jose, Salinas was home to a Chinese American five in the 1930s. Earl Goon and Parker Chan starred for the Watsonville Chinese in the late 1930s. In nearby Monterey, a Chinese American contingent lost to the Monterey Young Men's Institute five. The losers had to play, according to the *Chinese Digest*, without star Benson Choye. Paul Mark did his best to make up for the loss by pitching in 17 points.[47]

Chinese Americans in California's Central Valley busied themselves with basketball. The Chinese Athletic Club installed a team of adult males in Sacramento's Playground League in 1923, participating in the 135-pound division of Sacramento's Municipal Basketball League in 1929. Sacramento's Wah Yen Club won a city basketball championship in 1937, going undefeated in the process. Managed by Woodrow Louie, the team's big stars were brothers Edmund and Walter Yee. The latter was a physician in Sacramento. According to the census manuscript schedules of 1940, the 28-year-old American-born Walter headed a house in which Edmund, who was a 22-year-old railroad worker, lived. There was a Chinese American five in Sacramento's Church League in 1938. This five lost to the Oak Park Baptists, 34–28. The Chi-Nettes was a women's team out of Sacramento. Locke, which served as a historic haven for Chinese Americans, embraced community basketball in the decade before World War II. Late in 1936, the Locke Chinese School five came from behind to down a Chinese American team from Sacramento, 54–44. In December 1938, a lightweight boys' five from Sacramento High downed the Marysville Chinese, 46–21. Fresno's Fay Wah Club five won the Playground League's championship in 1937. Described in the *Chinese Digest* as "small but fast and elusive," the Fay Wahs knocked off the taller Woodsmen of the World team, 25–17. Among those playing for the Fay Wahs were Toy Wong, Irwin Chow, Hiram Ching, George Chan, Harry Tom, Ed Fong, George Wong, and Floyd Sam, the team's big star, according to the *Digest*. Albert Chinn and Henry Ching served as managers in the late 1930s. In Bakersfield, the Chinese Athletic Club organized a five that competed in the town's recreational league.[48]

At least one matchup between Chinese American fives in Northern California and the European American communities suggest the limitations of basketball as a cosmopolitan canopy. In 1937, a *Chinese Digest* reporter lambasted the *Willits News*'s narration of a game between a Chinese American YMCA five and the Willits Lions, won by the latter, 77–73. Apparently, Willits' spectators rooted for the Chinese Americans, who were the underdogs. They even booed a referee's decision that apparently favored the ultimate victors. Yet this reporter understandably took exception to the *News*'s generous use of the term *Chinks* to describe the Chinese American hoopsters. The *Digest* reporter insisted, "We did not know there could be such an ignorant editor in America as the man who edits the Willits' 'slander-sheet.' For an editor to let this get into public print constitutes a disgrace to the journalist profession. Moreover, [it] is an insult to the Chinese race…. We just blew up (and so would you protest vigorously if you had read it)."[49]

Moving down to Southern California, one of the first Chinese American teams in Los Angeles was composed of young women, who formed their own Mei Wah squad in the 1920s. The Mei Wahs played a game in 1931, according to historians Emery and Costa, against a team of Japanese American women attending Lincoln High School. The *Chinese Digest* reported that they were set to play a team of "Korean girls" in 1936. The latter, however, failed to show up. Thus, to buck up disappointed fans, the Mei Wahs engaged in a "hard fought" intrasquad game. Playing for the Los Angeles Mei Wahs were Dora, Mary, and May Tom, Cleo and Betty Chow, Esther Lew, Eleanor Soo, Florence Ung, Barbara Jein, and Dorothy Lung.[50]

The Lowa men's team competed against Asian and non–Asian American fives in the 1930s. According to the *Chinese Digest*, the Lowas were managed by Taft K. Cheung in the mid–1930s. Their ranks included Richard Hong, Ken Ung, Captain George Tong, George Lee, and Donald Sue. Competing as the only Chinese American contingent in the Southern California Basketball League, the Lowas handled the Nikkei Spartan five, 33–22, and then beat a team representing Columbia Studios, 40–28, thanks to George Wong, an arrival from San Francisco who poured in 18 points. The *San Diego Union* reported that Lowa hoopsters journeyed down to Southern California's second largest city in 1936. There, in mid–November, the Lowa first team upended the YMCA 145-pounders, 42–37. Doc Wong wound up with 20 points for the winners. However, a local Chinese American five, the Yingwas beat the "Lowa seconds" convincingly, 51–24. Subsequently, the Lowa first team subdued a Japanese American five called the Bears, 42–32.[51]

In the late 1930s and early 1940s, the Lowas seemed to dominate Chinese American community hoops in Southern California. In the spring of 1936, the *Chinese Digest* reported that they had prevailed as champions of the Southern California AA Division Basketball League. To do so, they had to struggle past the Croatian Club five in three overtimes. The final score was 46–44. In 1937, the Lowa men's five challenged for the championship of the Southern California Open Tournament. The *Los Angeles Times* maintained that the team was composed of "Orientals" over six feet tall and quite accomplished at beating white opponents with varsity college experience. A USC graduate, George Tong was described as a "scintillating center" who confessed he was not good enough to play for the Trojans' varsity. Four years later, the *California Chinese Press* acknowledged the Lowas as "the tallest and biggest quintet in Chinese basketball." George Tong captained the 1941 squad. He was reputedly six foot two and a county engineer. Five-foot-eleven Frankie Dong was supposedly the smallest player on the squad. Dong, 21 years old at the time, hoped to become a professional boxer and fight as Ah Wing Dong. The 200-pounder drove a truck for a wholesale grocery store and had, according to the *Press*, played for Belmont High School. In addition to the Lowa five, the Chinese Guardsmen were represented by a five in Los Angeles in 1941. Lowa was also represented by a women's team. Founded in the mid–1930s and coached by Elsie Wong, the Lowa women did not have any formal sponsors. They practiced at the Twenty-first Playground and Poly High.[52]

In May 1938, the *Chinese Digest* observed that the Federation of Chinese Clubs in Los Angeles organized a basketball tournament to which Chinese and non–Chinese American teams were invited. The "Wah Kue" male five was downed by the Korean All-Stars, 29–24. The Lowa five beat the Twin Dragons, a squad from San Francisco. George Tong led the victors with 16 points, while Johnny Wong, Allan Lee, and Chauncey Yip performed admirably for the San Franciscans. And a Chinese American contingent of women, assembled from the Mei Wah and Lowa teams, defeated the "Independent Colored Girls."[53]

Outside of Los Angeles, Chinese American hoopsters were active in Southern California. Santa Barbara's Sun Wah Club hoopsters competed in the city's Boys Basketball League in 1937. Down in San Diego, Chinese American teams or one team, publicized under different names, appeared in the 1930s. A "Chinese Mission" five competed in 1933. In 1936, the "Chinese Eagles" used a "balance attack" to vanquish the Delta Sigma Fraternity, 31–25. Then, a few weeks subsequent, the Eagles downed the Schrages 41–23. Late in 1936, the Yingwas easily triumphed over the Lowa's second team. A couple of years later, four members of the Chinese Mission team scored in double figures as the Chinese San Diegans beat the Ryans, 54–39. The Mission five then defeated a YMCA dorm team, 33–20. In early December 1938, the Chinese Y team was humbled by the Chula Vista Y, 53–30.[54]

Chinese American basketball thrived in the Pacific Northwest. The Chinese Lions took part in the Spalding League in Portland in 1922. Teams called the Chinese Eagles and Chinese Dragons competed in city leagues in the early 1930s. In 1933, the Chinese Eagles took two overtimes to edge the First Presbyterian team in Portland, 18–17. The Wah Kiang Club five emerged as one of the teams affiliated with the YMCA in Portland in the mid–1930s. In Seattle, the China Club participated in the city's municipal league in the mid–1920s.

Late in 1926, the *Seattle Times* reported that good team work propelled the Chinese Club to a victory over the French Service Station squad, 20–14. During the next decade, the Chinese Students played competitive hoops in Seattle. Early in 1937, the five won their fifth straight game in the class B recreational league by edging the Sons of Italy, 28–27. The next year, the Chinese Gardens five lost to American Auto, 29–25, at Garfield High. And a "Chinese Community" five participated in the All Nationals Basketball Tourney at Seattle's Central YMCA early in 1941.The latter took the measure of the Sons of Italy five in January 1941, 36–33. The *Seattle Post-Intelligencer* hailed the game as a "Melting Pot Court Event."[55]

Historian Shelly Sang-Hee Lee offers us a heady glimpse of Asian American community basketball in Seattle prior to World War II. In the 1920s, Chinese American fives did well in citywide competitions in Seattle. In 1929, the China Club won seven straight games en route to winning the "Class B South Division." During the next decade, several Chinese American teams competed in the Courier League, sponsored significantly by the *Japanese American Courier*. In 1935, China Club, Young China, and Chinese Students excelled in the Courier League, fostering some interethnic friction, largely because Japan and China were at war. When the China Club defeated the Japanese Black Hawks, 21–14, at the Garfield High Gymnasium, the *Courier* invoked the tragic Asian conflict by remarking that the "game renewed 'basketball hostilities' between the two groups." As for the Chinese Students squad, it played in the AA division of the Courier League in 1936 and was led by Kaye Hong and Edwin Luke. Still, a writer for the *Japanese American Courier* expressed the hope in 1937 that Chinese Americans would continue to compete in the Courier League despite the emotional spillovers from the bitter warfare embroiling Asia. That writer wished, moreover, that Chinese American hoopsters would "have a good time with us again. It is unfortunate that there should be so much trouble in the Orient, but I believe that is not going to spoil the friendship that has grown up between the Japanese and the Chinese second generation of this city."[56]

The Courier League sponsored competition for females as well as males. In the mid–1930s, the Chinese Girls five competed in the league. The Chinese Girls' Jesse Duong was named to the league's first team all-stars. And a couple of her teammates also achieved postseason honors.[57]

Thus, Courier League basketball contributed to a certain amount of Asian American interethnic cooperation. By 1937, it could boast of 37 teams. The strength of the Chinese American fives fueled ethnic rivalry but also respect. Clarence Arai, manager of the Japanese Hi-Stars, publicly admired the Chinese Athletic Club team. Another fine Chinese American five in the Courier League was the China Club aggregation. In the late 1930s, the team's coach, Stanley Louie, bragged that his team had garnered the "mythical Oriental Basketball Championship of the Pacific Northwest."[58]

Indeed, interethnic competition in Seattle continued as the United States moved closer to December 7, 1941. In February 1940, the Japanese Vandals conquered the China Clippers, 35–28. Their game was a preliminary, staged before the barnstorming House of David five was to play a local team. However, ethnic tensions also surfaced. A Walla Walla sportswriter recalled after World War II that a Chinese American five had won a Courier League championship before the war, "when," he wrote, "feelings between the two races ran high." Accordingly, when the Chinese Americans represented the league at an otherwise Nikkei tournament in Portland, the team was forced to withdraw after local Japanese Americans voiced opposition. Moreover, a game pitting Japanese Americans against Chinese Americans—a game scheduled for tip off before the Harlem Globetrotters took the court against a Seattle five—was cancelled for unspecified reasons in January 1941.[59]

The aforementioned China Club received some interesting publicity from the *Seattle Times* in 1930. The daily told readers that team members largely came from three families—the Chinns, Louies, and Mar Hings. The roster in the fall of 1930 included Nuey Robert Chinn, Clarence Mar Hing, Howard Mar Hing, Junie Mar Hing, George Stanley Louie, and Washer Wong. The team was coached by Claude Norris. A look at the U.S. census manuscript schedules from 1930 reveal that Robert Chinn was an American-born son of Chinese immigrants. His father was an import merchant. Howard Mar Hing was also American-born and the son of Chinese immigrants. His father operated a grocery store, and Howard drove a delivery truck for his father. Philip Mar Hing, who would be a prominent participant in Chinese American community basketball, was a brother.[60]

Six years later, China Club subdued Young China, 16–11, at Rainier Playfield Gym. Playing for the losers at the time were Tommy Sing, Mosey Kay, Wally Lew Kay, Jimmy Mar, Raymond Wong, Lucas Chinn, Clifton Goon, and Vincent Goon. One of the team's stars, Art Louie, appeared to be missing in action.[61]

Readers of the *Seattle Times* could come across a photograph of the Chinese Girls' Athletic Club basketball team in October 1934. The occasion was a benefit dance staged in Seattle's Chinese community in order to buy the team uniforms and finance possible trips to Portland and even San Francisco. The young women in the photo included team manager Mabel Gon, who, according to the 1930 U.S. census manuscript schedules, was the daughter of an American-born father, described in the census as a laborer, and an immigrant mother.

Others in the photo were captain Lilly Chinn, Mildred King, Josephine Chinn, Mamie Locke, Jessie Duong, Rose Woo, and Mary Luke.[62]

Six years later, the *Times* reported on another basketball-related dance in the city's Chinatown. The "Chinese Meteorites Club," described as an "all-Chinese girls basketball team" sponsored the dance, presumably as a fundraiser. It was supposed to take place at the Chung Wah Association, located at Seventh and Weller in Seattle. The newspaper informed readers that "among those organizing the dance were Rosie Louie, team captain, and Marjorie Low Key, team manager."[63]

In the 1930s, the *Portland Oregonian* paid relatively considerable attention to the Chung Wah women's sextet. On Christmas Eve, 1934, the daily told readers that the "Chung Wah Aces, a group of Chinese girls" were scheduled to take to the floor of Turn-Verein Hall to oppose the Turnerettes. The Manley Aces topped Chung Wah, 29–21 in January 1935. Ann Chin and Lalun Chin scored 13 and 8 points respectively in the game. In February 1935, Chung Wah edged the Willamette five at the Willamette Evangelical Church. The score was 25–23, with Anne Chin accumulating 15 points. Later in February, the St. Andrews aggregation topped the Ching Wahs easily, 54–28. One of the St. Andrews women scored 44 points. For the losers, Ann Chin scored 19, while Lalun managed 9. The next month, the Sunnyside Methodists fell to the Chung Wahs, 31–16, despite the fact that apparently Lalun Chin was unavailable. In any event, Ann Chin took up the slack with 22 points. In December 1935, the Chung Wahs decisively downed the Highland Congregation team, 49–33. Presumably mishmashing Ann Chin and teammate Eva Moe, the *Oregonian* reported that "Ann C. Moe" scored 32 for the victors, while Lalun Chin totaled 17.[64]

The Chung Wah squad also took on other Chinese American teams in the region. Late in December 1934, the Portland sextet met the Chinese American female hoopsters from Seattle on the Oregon city's Salvation Army gym floor. The hosts dominated, 33–14. Lalun Chin scored 17 and her sister, Anne, tallied 16.[65]

The *Oregonian* did not just publish accounts of Chung Wah games. On December 23, 1934, it displayed a photograph of Lalun Chin and Eva Moe. The photograph was entitled, "Oriental Dames Play Occidental Games." A caption embracing Orientalism added, "It's a long way from the far east to a west coast basketball floor but a number of Chinese girls have negotiated the distance with ease." One could not only find reporting on the Chung Wah hoopsters in the *Oregonian* sports section, but in the women's section as well. In February 1933, readers of the women's section discovered that the Chinese American women practiced basketball every Thursday night.[66]

The Portland female hoopsters attracted the attention of the *Chinese*

Digest, down in San Francisco. Late in 1935, it hoped that the young women would journey sometime to the Bay Area to take on local teams. In January 1936, the *Digest* told readers that the Chung Wahs had made a triumphant trip to Seattle, where they once again tripped the Seattle Chinese Girls Club team at the YWCA gym, 22–16. After the game, "the fair maids from the City of Roses" were treated to a dinner at the local Chung Wah Hall. They subsequently proved rude hosts, at least on the basketball court, as they drubbed the Seattle hoopsters in Portland, 35–15. Early in 1937, the *Digest* published a photo of Lalun Chin and pronounced her one of its athletes of the month. It added that the Chung Wahs had not lost a game in two years. Indeed, the *Digest* praised the Chung Wahs as "undisputed champions of the Northwest" and that no "Oriental team" had taken their measure.[67]

Another Pacific Northwestern Chinese American female team was known as the "Portland Girl Reserves." In 1935, the Reserves took second place in the city's YWCA league. Betty Hole coached the team, which included Phyllis Lee, Dorothy Lee Hong, Nellie Lee, Ada Lee, Vivien Wong, Maxine Chu, Lorraine Sun, Isabelle Lee, Nymphia Lum, Irene Chin, Maxine Chin, and Jessie Lee. In February 1937, the *Chinese Digest* reported that this team had lost a "heart-breaker" to a Seattle Chinese American contingent at the Portland YWCA gym. The "one armed" shooting of Jessie Lee helped keep the Portland hoopsters in contention, but three quick baskets by Ruby Mar put the game out of reach.[68]

Portland male Wah Kiang hoopsters were not as dominant as the Chung Wahs. Late in 1936, they managed to stifle a Japanese Athletic Club team on a YMCA court, 14–8. Then, they barely lost to the Neighborhood House aggregation, 22–21. Consequently, readers of the *Chinese Digest* learned they were good on defense but ragged on offense. Another Chinese American male team competing in Portland was the Eagles, captained by Eddie Luke.[69]

Chinese Americans living beyond the Pacific Coast did not neglect community hoops. In the Southwest, where Chinese Americans were not known to live in great numbers before World War II, at least some community basketball took place. In Phoenix, the Chinese Lions' Club backed a quintet in 1940. In mid–February, the Chinese Lions participated in the Verde Park Boys Basketball League. In the process, they beat a team called Central Park, 48–39.[70]

East of the Rockies, Chinese Americans formed and supported basketball teams. As early as 1915, the *Brooklyn Daily Standard Union* informed readers that the Nonpareils had downed the "Chinese basketball team," 33–18. The account of the game asserted that "[t]he Chinese were clever passers but did not measure up well in caging baskets." A fellow supposedly named "Wishee" was the best player for the losers. In 1918, the *New York Herald* reported that, inspired by American entry into World War I, the city's Chinatown was set to stage a Liberty Loan Rally. The *Herald* predicted that the "Chinese Basketball Team" would march in the parade with other Chinatown organizations. Around the same time, readers of the *New York Tribune* could learn that a "Chinese YWCA" team was decidedly defeated by an "American" squad. Three years later, the *Philadelphia Public Ledger* announced that the "only Chinese basketball team in the city" beat N. Snellenberg, 15–11 before a large crowd. The victors were praised for their defense and ball handling. A couple of weeks later, the *Public Ledger* displayed a photograph of Sing Yet Lou, describing him in the caption as captain of the Chinese Boys Basketball team that would play in a benefit for the Chinese Famine Fund. A wire story published in the *Miami Herald* declared that an "all-Chinese team" played in a church league in Lafayette, Indiana, in 1923. In 1934, Brooklyn sportswriter Bill McCulloch formed a team of "Chinese-American" boys in his borough. In the mid–1930s, New York City's Chinese Athletic Club sponsored a basketball team. Its roster included Captain Charles Young, Danny Low, John Doshim, Scotty Hing, Foo Chu, Louie Jung, Tommy Chu, Ralph Kimlau, Woot Moy, and Eddie Lee. At the end of the decade of the 1930s, Georgia's *Augusta Chronicle* reported that the Chinese Club competed in YMCA basketball. And at the beginning of the next decade, the *San Antonio Express* published a photograph of an "all-Chinese" boys' team.[71]

The mid–1920s, meanwhile, witnessed the emergence of a Chinese American five in Cleveland. A columnist for the *Buffalo News* incorrectly averred that the Ohio city had the only "all-Chinese basketball team" in the nation. In any event, the team was coached by Paul Lee, reportedly a former star athlete at Crane Technical High in Cleveland and the University of Chicago. Representing the Chinese Students' Club, Lee's squad of 17-year-old or older males was scheduled to take on the Irish Caseys as a preliminary to the Rosenblum–Fort Wayne professional game.[72]

In Baltimore, the Chinese Wonders, later known as the Peiping Athletic Club five, competed in the 1930s. The *Chinese Digest* hailed it as the only Chinese American team in the mid–1930s east of the Rockies and west of New York City. The *Digest* informed readers in late 1935 that the team had just beaten a good Jackson Jewish Club contingent. James Wong, William Lee, Herbert Lew, Hockwee Doy, Leonard Wong, and Henry Hom were on the team, coached by James Wong. James and Leonard Wong were apparently brothers. The 1930 U.S. census manuscript schedules tell us that they were dwelling with their mother, a Chinese immigrant owner of a restaurant. The 1940 U.S. census indicates that James Wong was living with his wife. He repaired radios for a living while his wife worked as a hostess. Leonard, younger than James by five years, was still living with his mother, who still owned a restaurant. Interestingly, she was married to her Filipino chef, while Leonard worked as a chef's helper. Henry Hom, according to the 1930 U.S. census manuscript schedules, was the son of a Chinese immigrant father, who worked as a cook, and a European American mother.[73]

In New England, Boston's Dennison Settlement House, situated in the city's south end and for a while directed by legendary pilot Amelia Earhart, was represented by a comparatively well-publicized female "all-Chinese basketball team." In early March 1928, the *Boston Herald* published a photograph of the "Chinese girls at Dennison House." These young women were, according to the caption, "very fond of basketball and play an excellent game." A "Negro Girl Five" from Morgan Memorial, the *Herald* announced, decisively defeated the Dennison House squad, 21–3 a few weeks later. Forward Margaret Chin scored the only points for the losers. Fifteen years old, according to the 1930

Representing the Dennison Settlement House in Boston, a Chinese American girls' team not only played hoops quite well, but gained national publicity in the late 1920s and early 1930s. Courtesy Schlesinger Library, Radcliffe Institute, Harvard University.

U.S. census manuscript schedules, Chin's California-born father owned a laundry in Boston, while her mother was a supposedly unemployed Chinese immigrant. The *Herald* informed readers that the squad had been practicing for two months under the direction of Miss Mildred Towle at Beacon Hill's Bullfinch Gym. The next year, the *Herald* reported that the "Dennison House Chinese girls" continued to compete. The daily pointed out that the young hoopsters were able to practice at an "outside gym," located in the rear of the settlement house. Marjorie Chin, probably the Margaret Chin mentioned earlier, was the elected team captain at the time. The Dennison House team had, the *Herald* proclaimed, achieved a record in recent weeks of four victories, five defeats, and one tie. Early in 1930 the *Herald* announced that the team elected Mabel Wong as captain. Nettie Dow served as both a player and team manager. To the *Herald*, the Dennison House congregation was a "unique team." In March 1930, the "Dennison House Chinese girls" easily won a game against East End Union at the loser's gym in Cambridge. Marjorie Chin led all scorers with 26 points. Five years later, the Dennison House squad was still active, although the *Herald's* Dorothy Lindsay claimed the "Chinese girls" were devoting more time to track and field than basketball.[74]

Meanwhile, the Dennison House hoopsters achieved attention outside of Boston. In April 1928, the *New Orleans Times-Picayune* displayed a photograph of the team. The caption asked, "Are they the Only All-Chinese Girls' Basketball Team in the U.S.?" The players photographed were then-manager Susie Woo, Alice Eng, Helen Eng, captain Marjorie Chin, Helen Wing, Mabel Wong, May Jeong, Rose Chin, Alice Chin, Esther Wong, Minnie Wong, Winne Eng, Lillian Goon, and Elizabeth Moy.[75]

Japanese American Ethnic Teams

Nikkei in the United States were taking up community basketball as early as the 1900s and 1910s. In Bellingham, Washington, during the first decade of the twentieth century, the Japanese American community sought to accelerate interest in sports such as baseball and basketball. A local newspaper entitled its 1910 story, "Japs Decide to Follow Up Sports," while it asserted that the "local Japanese society" anticipated sports such as baseball and basketball would render young men in the community more well rounded. In 1916, the *San Francisco Chronicle* reported that the Nikkei Spartans, a 110-pound team, caused a stir in city basketball circles. The Spartans' fast floor play, in particular, proved impressive. The next year, the *Oakland Tribune* published an article purporting that a contingent of youthful Japanese Americans, playing out of

Berkeley's Live Oak Park, sought opponents. The "little brown men" were 12 to 15 years of age and weighed from 75 to 115 pounds. Moreover, they were, the *Tribune* pointed out, products of Berkeley's effective recreational department, in that they not only competed successfully against "members of their race" but against white players as well.[76]

Japanese Hawaiians were represented in island basketball before World War II. In 1921, a Kauai publication, *The Garden Island,* announced that the "Japanese boys have organized a basketball team that is showing up in good form." Traveling to Lihue, they played "interesting games" against Filipino Hawaiians and "they think they can play anybody 15–18 [years of age] on the island." On Maui, the Japanese American Asahi five was downed by a squad of Chinese Hawaiians in December 1922.[77]

The San Francisco Bay Area, nevertheless, proved a productive incubator of Japanese American community hoops. In the late 1990s, historian John Christgau discussed the beginnings of Japanese American basketball in San Francisco. Christgau maintained that early in the twentieth century the Japanese American community converted an old mansion into a gymnasium overseen by the Japanese YMCA. However, the gym had a ten-foot ceiling that became five feet by the time it reached the court sidelines. Thus, Nikkei hoopsters had to learn to launch flat shots that bounced off the backboard into the basket. Later, wealthy San Francisco philanthropist John Mott helped fund a new Japanese YMCA on Buchanan Street. This gym furnished a more desirable home to a myriad of Japanese American recreational leagues in the 1930s, including a highly competitive male contingent, called the Greyhounds because of their swiftness.[78]

The late scholar Harry Kitano argued that community basketball was important to *Nisei,* or second generation, San Franciscans in the 1930s. Participants, he wrote, got much out of athletic competition because they were able to assert a bit of independence from their parents, travel, and interact with other Japanese Americans. Competitive basketball supplied Nisei with self-esteem, because Japanese American players could become, according to Kitano, "big fish in a little pond." The first generation, or *Issei,* Kitano insisted, were not that much interested in basketball. Thus by playing basketball the Nisei could claim a certain amount of generational autonomy. Moreover, teams like the San Francisco Mikados were highly respected throughout the city's vibrant basketball world. Indeed, the five left a Nisei League to compete in a citywide league. Yet this distressed other Nisei hoopsters, who effectively pressured the Mikados to return to the fold.[79]

Throughout the 1930s, Japanese San Franciscans fiercely competed against non-Nikkei and Nikkei. In 1930, the Japanese YMCA team humiliated a Boys Club five in San Francisco, 58–1, in the 80-pound division. In 1933, the Mikados downed a visiting five from Meiji University. The score was 43–23, and Ted Ohashi, who had previously played for Cal, almost won the game singlehandedly, according to the *Berkeley Daily Gazette*. Ohashi tallied 18 points and characteristically defended fiercely. In 1934, the *San Francisco Chronicle* informed readers that the San Francisco Japanese YMCA team was to oppose a University of California Nikkei students' squad led by Ohashi. Also in 1934, the Japanese Reform Church 120-pounders took on a Chinese American quintet in a PA game. In 1936, the 110-pounders from the Japanese YMCA in San Francisco lost to the Boys Club in the PA tournament. As for female Japanese Americans, the *San Francisco Chronicle* noted in 1930 the presence of Nikkei women's teams in the city.[80]

Japanese Americans in the East Bay took up basketball in the years before America's entry into World War II. The All-Nations' League in Oakland included a Nisei Japanese Club five in 1934. The *Berkeley Gazette* announced, in 1940, that the California School for the Deaf's "Silent Five" was scheduled to oppose the "Nissei Club" in Berkeley City League play. Around the same time, a Nikkei five called the Blues competed in Berkeley's Playground League. In Alameda, a female Young Women's Buddhist Association team garnered championships in the 1930s.[81]

Down in San Jose, Japanese Americans formed a team called the Zebras in 1930—a team initially coached by a European American named Everett Roseveaux, who played interscholastic hoops for San Jose High in the 1920s. San Jose's Young Men's Buddhist Association supported the contingent. And Roseveaux apparently supplied the Zebras with striped uniforms and, perhaps inadvertently, their team name.[82]

The Zebras played good basketball. In 1934, the *San Jose Mercury* called them "a high-powered Japanese team" when they beat Santa Clara High School, 32–28. Informing readers that the Zebras were about to participate in the Northern California Young Buddhist Association's basketball tournament, the *Mercury* described them as hoopsters who had played for San Jose High School and various community fives. The daily added, "The mighty mites, lightweight in proportion, but experts in ability" used their teamwork to good effect. In 1937, one can find in the *Mercury*'s pages references to the Zebras participating in San Jose's City Basketball League. Meanwhile, San Jose's Buddhist Church also supported a team of female Nikkei. They were called the Purplettes, because they donned uniforms that were purple and white, the colors of the Buddhist Church. Aside from the Zebras, a team composed of players with Japanese surnames competed in San Jose's Burnett Cadet League in 1936. In nearby Palo Alto a male five called the Hinodes played hoops prior to December 7, 1941.[83]

Nikkei in California's Central Valley put up competitive teams. In the late 1930s, the Stockton Young Women's Buddhist Association's Busy Bees embarked on a three-state, 2500-mile tour of the Southwest. Coached by George "Pop" Suzuki, the team had been in action since the late 1920s. According to one source, the Busy Bees played 236 games from 1928 to 1940 and lost but four. Upon her death, Teruko Terao Yamauchi was remembered as "a proud member of the 'Busy Bees.'" Likewise, Yoshi Grace Hattori's obituary recalled her as a young woman for whom "basketball was [a] passion," while growing up in Stockton. She therefore became a member of the "Stockton Busy Bees, a touring basketball team that traveled throughout the western United States." Another female team called the Cherry Blossoms played out of the small town of Cortez. To the south, the Japanese Athletic Club five competed in Bakersfield Recreational League in 1940. Indeed, the *Bakersfield Californian* reported that the "classy Japanese athletic club" had handily beaten Bakersfield High's B team, 41–12. Based on one account of the game, the "Japanese" displayed "dazzling speed and agility."[84]

Northern California, in general, presented a beehive of Japanese American basketball between the world wars. In January 1937, the *San Jose Mercury*

Japanese Americans were quite active in forming pre–World War II community teams and leagues in California's Central Valley. This is a photo of the Florin Bluettes 1940–1941 squad. Courtesy Japanese American Archival Collection, Department of Special Collections and University Archives, California State University, Sacramento.

announced an impending Northern California Young Men's Buddhist Association tournament. It claimed as well that "a girls' exhibition will open" the tournament. The A teams invited included not only the local Zebras, but the Stockton Cardinals and the San Francisco Protos. Among the B teams participating were the Sacramento Zephyrs, the San Francisco Gales, and the San Jose Bees.[85]

Early in 1938, the *Sacramento Bee* reported on a set of basketball games taking place at Vacaville High. The Young Women's Buddhist Association team out of Vacaville barely downed a squad from Sacramento, 25–24. In another game, in which the gender of the participants is unclear, Sacramento's Crimson Tide beat Manila Rose, 28–13. The San Francisco Protos, a male five, then took the measure of the Vacaville Roughriders.[86]

One evening in Lodi in February 1940, three Japanese American teams won games against visiting squads. The Lodi Young Men's Buddhist Association five humbled a team from Woodland, 50–27. Shet Iwamura was high scorer with 14 points. The Young Women's Buddhist Association aggregation downed a Cortez squad, 24–19. Terry Oga was high scorer for the winners with nine points, while Peggy Taniguchi tallied 17 for Cortez. In the third game, a squad called the Lodi Babes barely beat an unnamed opponent, 16–15.[87]

In Southern California, Japanese Americans embraced basketball no less lovingly than their Northern California counterparts. Southern California's Japanese Athletic Union staged basketball tournaments and games at Chapman College in Orange, California, in the 1930s. The teams participating included the Utes, Wanjis, Bruins, Boyle Heights Cougars, Long Beach Asahis, Golden Bears, Crown City, Carson City, Tartans, Argonauts, and Cardinals. In April 1939, Chapman College hosted an interstate matchup between the San Francisco Mikados and the Utes. The San Franciscans won, 37–27. Meanwhile, the all–Japanese American Queen Esther team competed in an industrial league for women in Los Angeles in the 1930s.[88]

Early in 1932, the *San Diego Evening Tribune* reported that Los Angeles's Japanese Bruin squad had visited Tijuana. There, they had downed a junior high school team, 37–16, at the Tijuana bull fight ring before a good size crowd. Led by Dr. Tetsuyo G. Ishimoto, the Bruins were shown around town by their hosts, among whom were members of the Tijuana Japanese Association.[89]

Outside of Los Angeles County, Nikkei in Southern California swished baskets. In Riverside in the mid–1930s, the Japanese Mission squad participated in a church league. To the south, the *San Diego Union* reported in February 1927 that there was much interest in a scheduled game between the Occidental Comrade Club, representing Los Angeles's Japanese Congregational Mission, and the San Diego Japanese. This was to be the third encounter between the two fives. A year earlier, the San Diegans won by an unspecified score. The previous December, the Angelinos eked out an 11–10 victory.[90]

Throughout California, the Japanese Athletic Union staged tournaments. In 1929, the Northern California–based Japanese American Athletic Union was organized, with a basketball division emerging in 1931. A year later, the Southern California Japanese Athletic Union was assembled with basketball competition starting in 1933. The first statewide championship was held in San Francisco in 1934. The Los Angeles Spartans, champion of the Southern California Japanese Athletic Union, met the San Francisco YMCA Soko Greyhounds, the Northern California Japanese American Athletic Union title holder. The San Franciscans triumphed over the Southern Californians, 33–15. In 1938, the Los Angeles Cardinals beat a Nisei squad from Cal, 56–49, in overtime. The next year the San Francisco Mikados took the crown away from the Cardinals.[91]

Of course, not all Japanese American mainland fives competed in California. Japanese Americans in Seattle organized several community fives. In 1924, a five called the Broadway Tigers downed the "speedy Nipponese," 31–22. The *Seattle Times* pointed out in 1925 that the Eatonville Lumber Company's "Japanese basketball team" had challenged the Seattle Nippon Athletic Club's five. The winner would play a visiting YMCA team from Japan. That same year, Seattle's municipal league embraced fives from both the Nippon Athletic Club and the Japanese Athletic Club. In 1926, the Taiyo Athletic Club five was overwhelmed by the Red Devils in class B league competition in Seattle. Hoopsters with Japanese surnames competed for an organization called the Bachelor's Club in Seattle in 1928. In October 1932, the "Japanese High Stars" were beaten by the Secretarial School five, 30–20. Late in 1932, the *Portland Oregonian* announced that "the best and fastest Japanese basketball team in the Northwest" had arrived in Portland from Seattle. The Waseda five, the *Oregonian* maintained, was in town to oppose a team of locals. Early in 1933, the Meiji University five from Japan showed up in the Emerald City, where it beat the "Japanese All-Stars," 40–34. Art Sasaki led the losers with 16 points. The preliminary to the Meiji game was a matchup between two Nikkei squads—the Tacoma Crusaders and the Taiyo Club. The latter barely won, 22–21. As mentioned earlier, the *Japanese American Courier* sponsored a league in which several Japanese American fives participated before World War II. As part of league action, in mid–February 1939, the Munson Midgets defeated the Lotus Troys, 37–24 at the Seattle Prep Gym.[92]

In 1939, a team from Auburn, Washington, copped the Courier League's women's championship. The team roster included Mitzie Fujii, Esther Mae Kawa, June Nakagawa, Chiyoko Nakaso, Toshiko Nakaso, Mary Natsuhara,

Soyono Natsuhara, and Haruco Okura. A male named Connie Shimojima is also pictured in a photograph of the victorious team.[93]

Portland saw plenty of Japanese Americans shooting hoops. Late in 1932, the "Japanese" lost to the Colts, 31–11. In January 1932, the St. Mary's five easily eclipsed the "Japanese High Stars," 52–23. When the *Portland Oregonian* publicized the arrival of Seattle's Waseda five in December 1932, it also pointed out that a team of locals called the Nippons would tip off against Waseda's second team in a preliminary game. A month later, the *Oregonian* published an account of the Softwood Colts downing the "Chinese Nippons," a team curiously possessing Japanese surnames. A couple of days later, the *Oregonian* reported that "Osei's Japanese Basketball team" had beaten the YMCA Koala five, 24–16. And an Asahi Basketball Club participated in Portland's Columbia League early in 1941.[94]

Somewhat to the east, Japanese Americans took to the courts. In 1939, the *Salt Lake Tribune* displayed a photograph of the Salt Lake Nippons, victors

Japanese Americans in the Pacific Northwest also organized community teams and leagues. This is the Girl Reserves squad from Portland, taken around 1940. Courtesy Oregon Nikkei Endowment, Portland, Oregon, photo number ONLC 00536.

in the Intermountain Japanese Basketball Tournament. By edging the Murray Taiyo, 28–27, the Nippons copped the third consecutive tournament championship.[95]

Korean American and Filipino American Community Basketball Before 1941

Filipino Americans and Korean Americans organized community teams. Filipinos on Kauai had a basketball team in the early 1920s. The Oahu All-Star Filipino squad competed on the islands in the mid–1930s. Marcus Sibalon, Jesus Caballero, Teadro Ballasteros, and Vicente Rausa ranked among some of the team's better players. Hawaiian Ernest Richardson told researchers that a Filipino basketball team played on the Lanai Ranch in the 1920s and 1930s. When Filipinos on the islands celebrated Jose Rizal day, one of the sports they enjoyed was basketball. Meanwhile, Marie Booty reported that in the mid–1930s, Korean Hawaiian girls played basketball. Moreover, Korean Hawaiian male basketball in Honolulu was represented by the Delta Frats, starring S. A. Kim, P. Kim, and C. Park. On the mainland, the *Seattle Times* pointed out in 1926 that a "strong Filipino club" participated in a local church league. And the "Korean All-Stars male squad defeated a Chinese American five in Los Angeles in 1938."[96]

While World War II started in Europe, a group of Filipino San Franciscans decided to form the Mango Athletic Association. Ernie Bala, Julian Calagos, Ben Marcelo, Chris Punzal, and Cepy Villanueva claimed that the purpose of their organization was "[t]o interest and develop the Filipino youth of our community in a better understanding of friendship and good citizenship." The Mango Athletic Association would, subsequently, put together a formidable basketball team.[97]

World War II

The aftermath of the early December 1941 attack on Pearl Harbor shadowed the 1941–1942 basketball season for all Americans, but probably for Japanese Americans the most. After Executive Order 9066 was issued in February 1942, which led to the internment of over 100,000 West Coast Japanese Americans, the Japanese YMCA team in Salinas lost easily to the Salinas High lightweights, 33–14. Around the same time, the Zenimura basketball team in Fresno played the Roosevelt five and lost, 28–17. This team was coached by Kenichi

Zenimura, an Issei who made his way to Fresno by way of Hawai'i. Known better as a Japanese American baseball pioneer in California's Central Valley, Zenimura had two of his sons on the team.[98]

Despite the tensions wrought by the devastation of Pearl Harbor, Hawaiian Japanese forged basketball teams. The Varsity Victory Volunteers (VVV) was a paramilitary Hawaiian Japanese organization that took on many necessary tasks in wartime Hawai'i, thus helping to dispel some of the fears non-Nikkei Hawaiians entertained of the islands' largest ethnic group. Sports such as basketball became an important way for the VVV participants to enhance group morale. The VVV basketball team included Walter Okumoto and Hirochi Tomita as forwards, center Claude Takekawa, and guards Sus Yamamoto and Toshi Nakasone.[99]

In California, where anti–Japanese zealotry was most pronounced and where Japanese Americans faced internment in the spring of 1942, famed San Francisco columnist Herb Caen reported that the "good neighbor policy" existed at Watsonville's YMCA. There, in early March 1942, a contingent of Chinese Americans took on Japanese Americans. A seemingly none-too-pleased Caen summarized the event: "The Japanese won, hm...."[100]

Japanese Americans on the East Coast could enjoy a certain amount of freedom. More than a year after the attack on Pearl Harbor, New York City hosted a game between Japanese Americans and Chinese Americans, won by the former, 24–20. Previously, the *Pacific Citizen* had reported that a Japanese American five, affiliated with the city's Young People's Christian Federation, had started practicing at the Church of All Nations. Among those turning out for the practice were Min Arita, Asao Inouye, Kiyoshi Inouye, George Buto, Aki Yamasaki, Jack Hata, Toge Fujihara, and young man named Eddie Cook.[101]

The game was held at the Church of All Nations' gym, which had been used by the Chinese American hoopsters representing the Chinese Athletic Club for years. As for the Nikkei team, the *New York Times* reported, they were "all American citizens" from the Young People's Christian Federation, composed of three New York–based churches. About 200 people, many of them female, watched the game, according to the *Times*. The referee was an Italian American who insisted that he called them as he saw them. Captains Dan Wong and Tojo Fujihara said there were no hard feelings after the game and hoped future contests between the two teams would be scheduled. Once the dribbling and shooting ended, the *Times* mused that the court was turned into a dance hall with "zoot-suited young Chinese" dancing with Japanese American girls and "vice versa."[102]

Two Japanese American federation squads developed over the next couple of years in New York City. The A team, the *Pacific Citizen* announced in the spring of 1944, won the Church of All Nations' league championship by downing the previous champions, the Dukes, 33–14. Located on the Lower East Side, the Church of All Nations had assembled an eight-team league, composed of not only the champion Japanese American A team, but a B five as well. The As wound up with 11 victories in 14 games, while the Bs landed in seventh place. The rest of the league was composed of aggregations of Italian, Jewish, Russian, Polish, and Chinese American hoopsters.[103]

The champion A team was built around several internment camp evacuees who had chosen to resettle in New York City. One of the stars was Shig Murao, described as a former internee at the Minidoka camp in Idaho and all-city standout from Seattle. Others who had come from the Minidoka camp were Juggo Hata and Norman Sato. Once interned at Heart Mountain in Wyoming were Willie Mori, a three-year letterman from Chapman College in Southern California, and Hideo Furukawa, who played for the Palo Alto Hinodes in Northern California. From Colorado's Granada camp came George Karatsu, Grove Yoshiwara, and Min Arata. New Yorkers Asaho Inouye and George Buto rounded out the five. The A team was managed and coached by Tojo or Toge Fujihara, who had lived in Seattle. As for the B team, it included Topaz evacuees Archie Hirahshima, Jack Mizono, and Kaz Nomura. From Rohwer internment camp came Gunji Watanabe and Mas Matsuoka. George Sakamoto had been interned at Tule Lake in California, George Tamaki at Heart Mountain, and Bob Suzuki at Granada.[104]

At the same time, the *Pacific Citizen* reported that the two federation Nisei teams were to blend in several Chinese American players to form the Oriental American All-Stars. This team was scheduled to take on the Caucasian All-Stars in a benefit game in late March. Proceeds of the game and the subsequent dance were to go toward sending "underprivileged children of the lower east side to summer camps."[105]

Almost half way across the country from New York City, Nisei soldiers, training at Camp Crowder in Missouri, created a basketball league and a team to oppose other military fives. In late December 1942, the Camp Crowder five vanquished the Sunny Jim Candy Store team, 33–19. Played at Joplin, the game was, the *Pacific Citizen* reported, well attended by fans vocal in their support for the Japanese Americans. The Camp Crowder hoopsters "display[ed] a well-rounded attack." Private First Class Tomo Kanzaki, described in the *Pacific Citizen* account as a "diminutive forward," took the scoring honors with 12 points. Within weeks, Kanzaki and his teammates upended two more opponents. They barely beat the Seventh Regiment five, 23–21 and then the 804th Midwestern Signal School, 30–26. The five-foot-four Kanzaki proved the big star once again and "the nisei put on a spectacular show of passing and fast-breaking."[106]

In the assembly centers, in which West Coast Nikkei were gathered in the spring of 1942 before they were dispatched to the camps, evidence of basketball enthusiasm went on display. The *Santa Anita Pacemaker*, a publication put out by internees forcibly residing at the Santa Anita racetrack, noted in early June 1942 that "a miniature basketball net catches your eye when you pass behind Bar 28, Ave. D." It was "put up by three boys who wanted to play basketball but couldn't and decided to do something about it." Fourteen-year-old Masayoshi Nagamoto, 15-year-old Masa Taketoshi, and 13-year-old George Yamada engaged in what the *Pacemaker* described as "tennis basketball." And the boys said they would be content until given an opportunity to "put up a real cage." Meanwhile, basketball courts were being readied, and by late July, internees

In the spring of 1941, West Coast Japanese Americans were initially dispatched to assembly centers, often located in fairgrounds and horse racetracks. Conditions were often fairly primitive for youthful hoopsters, but this young lady was able to make do. Courtesy Flaherty Collection, Japanese Internment Records, MSS-2006–02, San Jose State University, Special Collections and Archives.

were playing recreational basketball. Assembled at another racetrack in the Bay Area, Japanese Americans engaged in recreational basketball. The *Tanforan Totalizer* pointed out that John Oshida, Sei Adachi, and Jiro Nakamura were particularly good Nikkei hoopsters.[107]

Much has been written about Japanese American internees using baseball to sustain community ties in the camps. However, basketball performed something of the same function, although difficulties often arose. Because of the cold weather at the Heart Mountain Camp in Wyoming, the winter season of basketball had to be cancelled in 1942, because internees were not furnished with an indoor gym. In January 1943, George Kinoshito reported to readers of the *Heart Mountain Sentinel* that the gym was not yet built: "This means you'll have to don your pea coats, invest in some earmuffs, scars, snowshoes, and some cough drops before going out and cavorting on the [outside] courts."[108]

Heart Mountain was the destination for many Japanese Americans from the San Jose area. Thus, Zebra players were able to keep themselves together as a team in the camp. Indeed, in 1943, the Zebras were accused of running up scores against camp opposition. *Heart Mountain Sentinel* writer, Jack Kumotomi, lamented, "This seems to reflect poor judgment on the part of the coach and also of the Zebras' partisans, who clamored and agitated for such an incident." Described by camp officials as an internee capable of managerial and office occupations, Chi Akizuki was a key member of the squad. After the Zebras won a game, the *Sentinel* observed he "stole the show" with his "demon ball handling." When the Zebras copped the camp championship in the spring of 1943, the *Sentinel* hailed the Zebras' "team coordination and high spirit."[109]

The Zebras were not the only five worthy of note at Heart Mountain. Moreover, camp hoopsters not only engaged in internal competition but also represented Heart Mountain in games against outsiders. Indeed, several fine Japanese American basketball players were imprisoned at Heart Mountain: Wally Funabiki, who played Stanford freshman hoops; Babe Nomura, who had been top scorer in Japanese American community hoops in Southern California; and Tosh Shiotake, who had been one of the best players on the San Francisco Greyhounds. Moreover, former Hollywood High luminary Art Kaihatsu served as the camp's athletic director and, in the spring of 1943, coached the Heart Mountain High School five. Angelino Babe Nomura, who excelled in football and baseball as well as hoops, was one of Kaihatsu's best players. When the high schoolers lost to Lowell High, Nomura was high scorer for the vanquished with nine points. In April 1943, he led the Heart Mountain High School in a losing effort against a local five with 14 points. Another squad representing the camp was the Heart Mountain All-Stars. In February 1943, they visited Lowell, where they lost to the Lowell West Ward Indians, 46–26. Wally

Funabiki proved the big star for the losers. Despite the loss, Kinoshita said things went well, because the athletes were treated with respect in the "little Mormon town." Not confining his basketball duties to coaching, Art Kaihatsu was one of the top players on the Heart Mountain All-Stars in 1943, tallying 15 in a victorious contest. In 1944, Nomura stood out for the All-Stars when they took on the Red Lodge Squad, a five out of Montana consisting of former college players.[110]

In the late winter of 1944, Heart Mountain was visited by the San Kuo Low Bears from Denver. Praised in the *Heart Mountain Sentinel* as one of the finest Nisei teams in the United States, the Bears edged the Zebras, 42–41. Effie Kawahara scored 22 for the winners, while Akizuki popped in 20 for the losers. The Zebras won the rematch, 43–41. Akizuki led the winners with ten and Kawakami topped all scorers with 11. Captain Kayo Senzaki added nine to the Bears' total.[111]

Females at Heart Mountain took up basketball, too. The young women engaged in a free throw contest at the camp, and they did more than just toss free throws. Coached by Babe Nomura and another Southern California Nisei, Ets Yoshiyama, the Lil' Yokums won the camp championship in 1943 and 1944. The *Sentinel* praised Ay Fujioka, Bernice Hinaga, and Jane Nakamoto as three of the better players on the squad. According to camp records, Jane Nakamoto had finished four years in high school but was still considered maid material. Jane's sister Flo was another adept hoopster, praised by the *Sentinel* as a high-scoring "diminutive ... forward." Among the other top female players in camp were Yukiro Sugiura, Kaoru Emi, Mitsuko Kataoka, and Lucy Matsunaga.[112]

Heart Mountain High School had a Girls' Athletic Association (GAA). We will discuss GAA basketball in a future chapter. The *Heart Mountain Sentinel* reported that the Heart Mountain GAA squad downed Powell High, 27–19. Chi's sister, Agnes Akizuki, led the way with nine points, while Flo Nakamoto garnered eight.[113]

Like Heart Mountain, the Rohwer camp interned many California Japanese. The camp's physical education staff early in 1943 included George Yamasaki, who, according to the *Rohwer Outpost*, played lightweight hoops at Norwalk High in Southern California. Also on the staff was none other than "amiable Ted Ohashi ... the pride and joy of Stockton." Meanwhile, *Rohwer Outpost* sportswriter Fred Oshima informed readers of the impending arrival in January 1943 of "King basketball ... relocation style ... minus the rafters, glossy hardwood floors, bleachers, and indirect light."[114]

A contingent of male journalists calling themselves the Casaba Musketeers claimed to be impressed with the play of females at Rohwer. After their first look at female basketball for the season, they asserted, "One impression brought into our minds is that these girls can take care of themselves." They admired the performance of Mary Ito of the Blue Babes. The left-handed hoopster "showed the fans how to make baskets in 3 easy lessons." Standing out for the Billantees was Terrie Otsubo, "whose fakes had many players baffled an' [*sic*] some of the fans too." According to the *Outpost*, Rosey Tsukumoto ranked among the better female hoopsters at the camp.[115]

Japanese American internees sought basketball joy at other camps. Located in Utah, the Topaz camp was represented by a five that beat the Hinckley Mustangs twice by sizable numbers in January 1943. The first game was won 38–18 and the second, 33–7. Meanwhile, a six-foot-tall Kiyosuki Nomura led a team of Topaz internees to a not-so-easy victory over Delta High School, 38–36. A Poston camp aggregation in Arizona fared poorly against an American Indian five, led by "Sunshine Willie" Fisher's 28 points. The victors from Parker, Arizona, ran up a 71–35 score against the Nikkei.[116]

Outside of the Pacific war zone, Japanese Americans in western states engaged in community basketball. In Arizona early in 1943, the Arizona Athletic Club won a doubleheader at Peoria High School. One of the Arizona Athletic Club teams, the Esquires, barely got by the Matsumoto All-Stars, 19–18. Lindy Okabayashi scored a game-high six points for the winners. The next week, the Mesa All-Stars, coached by former Arizona State football great, Bill Kajikawa, triumphed over the Arizona A.C. Esquires, 30–26. Kajikawa's squad, according to the *Pacific Citizen*, "used smooth floorwork." Kat Ikeda was high scorer for Mesa with nine points. In Utah in February 1943, the *Ogden Standard-Examiner* reported that the Ogden Ramblers had downed the Hill Field Aces. All the surnames on the victors' team were Japanese, save one. The Japanese American Citizens League (JACL) organized teams in Salt Lake City, Pocatello, and Idaho Falls. In Idaho in January 1943, the Idaho Falls Nisei five easily got by another Japanese American squad from Pocatello. The score was 56–35, and Jun Ueda led the way with 25 points.[117]

Denver was a beehive of wartime Japanese American hoops. In early 1943, Japanese Americans, mainly émigrés from the Pacific Coast, competed for a team sponsored by Cary's Malt Shop. According to the *Pacific Citizen*, "Due to their aggressiveness and speed, they've been able to win their share of games against taller competition." A year later, the *Pacific Citizen* told readers that the Denver JACL had formed a league with teams like Littleton, Brighton, San Kuo Low Bears, San Kuo Low Cubs, and the Denver Bankers' Union. The Bears, managed by onetime San Jose Zebra manager Clark Taketa, also competed in a city league and, according to the *Heart Mountain Sentinel*, consisted of some of the best Nisei hoopsters around. Sponsored by San Kuo Low Cafe, the team's better players included brothers Yuke and Effie Kawahara, as well as Kayo

Senzaki. The *Rohwer Outpost* praised Yuke Kawahara as "one of the greatest nisei basketball players to come out of the coast." And while Yuke starred for the San Francisco Mikados before the war, Effie stood out for the San Francisco Protos. The five also won Denver's Amateur Athletic Union (AAU) class B tournament during the war. During the war's last year, *Rocky Shimpo*, which published out of Denver, pointed out that Clark Taketa was managing a five called the Manchu Bears in Denver, adding that "rangy Soapy Miyashima" was a team star. A month later, the *Rocky Shimpo* complained that Nisei basketball faced a "manpower shortage" because of the draft. In any event, the Japanese American publication pointed out that the Japanese American Downtown Merchants cagers had beaten the Castle Rock five in the opening round of Denver's AAU class B tournament early in 1945.[118]

In the Midwest, Japanese Americans, many of whom had either left the West Coast before the region's Nikkei were rounded up or relocated from the camps, mustered basketball teams. Early in 1944, the *Rohwer Outpost* reported that a Nisei five in Mt. Clemens, Michigan, had defeated a white squad in three games out of five. In Cleveland, Japanese Americans formed the city's first all-Nisei five in the spring of 1944. The team was called the Cal-Jays, an abbreviation of California Japanese Americans. According to the *Pacific Citizen*, the Cal-Jays participated in the city's municipal A league, which included top-flight amateur squads. Their first victory was over the Cleveland Buckeyes, an "all-Negro squad." The 35–33 score was hardly a stunner, but it was impressive enough. The *Pacific Citizen* reported that the Buckeyes, probably named after a famous Negro League baseball franchise, comprised one of the better fives in Cleveland and had previously won the league championship. As for the Cal-Jays, the *Pacific Citizen* told readers that they were "originally formed to show Cleveland sports fans a scrappy squad with good sportsmanship." In February 1945, *Rocky Shimpo* reported that a contingent of Japanese American women in Milwaukee had organized a team called the 442nd, in tribute to the brave World War II Nikkei regiment. The 442nd competed in the Women's Municipal Athletic Association and James Yamaguch served as team manager. That same month, *Rocky Shimpo* published a short piece that described a six-team Nikkei league forming in Chicago under the auspices of the First Baptist Church. According to the piece's author, Bob Okizaki, Tosh Oakamura had scored 18 points to lead his Southside Bears over the Chicago Miks in a 40–39 overtime triumph.[119]

Other Asian American groups engaged in community basketball during World War II. In Salinas less than a month after the Pearl Harbor attack, the *Salinas Index-Journal* reported that the Chinese demolished a team called the All-Stars, 32–0, in the heavyweight division of a YMCA tournament. Subsequently, they lost the championship game, with Grove Wong leading the scoring with five points.[120]

A few months after the United States entered the war, the *San Francisco Chronicle*'s Art Rosenbaum tied Chinese American basketball to Chinese military advances reportedly made in Asia. He wrote, "The Chinese are advancing on the C.Y.O. front, too…. There are six Chinese teams entered this year, and it may be remembered they won four titles last year." Indeed, the *Chronicle* eventually reported, "Chinese youngsters from the St. Mary's mission" won CYO championships in the 90- and 110-pound boys' divisions. In the fall of 1942, the YMCA in San Francisco had organized a "Chinese basketball league."[121]

China's alliance with the United States inspired some Chinese Americans to hope that assimilation was not far off. The *San Francisco Chronicle* seemed to support such a hope by giving a guest column to local journalist William Hoy during the war. Hoy alerted *Chronicle* readers to the Americanizing of Chinese Americans by pointing out their enthusiasm for coffee and basketball.[122]

As the war wound down, Chinese American hoopsters gained publicity in the Bay Area press. Early in 1945, the Chinese Falcons competed as a Boys Club five in San Francisco. And the Chinese American CYO teams still excelled in the months before V-E Day. Late in January 1945, Albert Fong bagged 12 points as his 100-pound team of "Chinese lads put … on their usual pressure" to down St. Ann's, according to the *Monitor*, a weekly serving the Bay Area's Roman Catholics. In early February 1945, the *Monitor* reported that "William Wong" led his 120-pound CYO team against Epiphany. The young Wong tallied 36 points, 23 of which he scored in the third quarter alone. Subsequently, Wong, captain of his team, tied his CYO scoring record set in 1944 with 45 points and then followed up with a 43 point effort. Wong continued on his hot streak. The *Monitor* pointed out that "Billy Wong was his usual shot maker for the Chinese Missions with 30 to his credit," as his team downed St. Elizabeth's of Oakland. Moreover, in an 80-pound division game, Oakland's St. Bernard's five jumped off to a lead, but "the always relaxed, never excited Chinese youngsters [from St. Mary's] came back to win," 20–15. In the spring of 1945, the *San Francisco Examiner* reported that the "Chinese Playground Girls" beat the "Douglas Playground Girls" in the Senior Girls' Basketball League conducted by San Francisco's recreation department.[123]

Korean Angelinos shared in wartime community basketball. A few months before V-J Day, Virginia Chung reported in the *Korean Independence* that a Korean Christian Association female basketball team had just edged a "colored girls team combined from Poly and Manual Arts High Schools," 15–12. The game was played at a gym on Whittier Avenue. And after it was over, the losers sought a rematch from the "Little Foxes." Chung then urged readers to "[c]ome and see the only Korean girls team ever to be organized." A prominent voice of Southern Californian Korean Americans hoping for an independent Korea in the wake of the war, the *Korean Independence* advertised the impending game between the Korean Christian Association hoopsters and the Sportettes at Patriot Hall on South Figueroa. Ticket prices were 35 cents apiece.[124]

Embattled Asian American ethnic groups forged vibrant community institutions before World War II. Basketball proved potent in welding together Asian Americans, while representing their desire to build bridges to other communities and share in American civil and cultural institutions. In the process, basketball's ability to appeal to ordinary Asian Americans across class and gender lines exemplified its democratic potential. At the same time, the need for such separate teams and leagues reveals a profoundly troubling feature of American and sport history.

CHAPTER 2

Asian American Community Basketball, 1945–1965

World War II brought changes, good and bad, to Asian Americans. At its end, many Asian American ethnic groups, because they were connected with nations friendly to the Allies' cause, were seen in a better light. Japanese Americans, however, were still distrusted. Nevertheless, it was hard for even the most persistent bigots to deny the valor of Nisei military personnel during the war, nor eventually the United States' need for a friendly Japan as the Cold War loomed over Asia. Thus, by the 1950s, all Asian American ethnic groups were seemingly groomed for assimilation. Yet as Asian Americans were supposedly heading for the melting pot, they asserted their cultural citizenship by holding on to their ethnic community institutions and practices, such as their basketball teams and leagues, perhaps because they understandably perceived the racially inequitable execution of assimilation in American life.

442nd Basketball

Stationed in Europe, the 442nd regiment of the U.S. Army organized a postcombat basketball team. In early January 1946, the regimental report declared that the team, composed of enlisted men, performed well: "Smooth coordination, team play, plus rabid rooting, on the part of Regimental supporters contributed to much of its success on the court." Several months later, the regimental report continued to praise the five which had barnstormed northern Italy: "The speed, the smooth performance, and the dogged fighting spirit that carried the 442nd basketball team to victory over towering opponents won it

66

a reputation among U.S. Army personnel throughout Europe." Interestingly, 442nd officers formed their own team, refusing to let the enlisted men get all the glory.[1]

The aforementioned trek into northern Italy inspired journalist John Ito to pen a two-part account in the *Pacific Citizen* during May 1946. In the first part of his story published on May 4, Ito maintained that the 442nd basketball team was welcomed generously by the northern Italians, although team members were still anxious to return to the United States. The first game of the tour, according to Ito, was an exhibition to benefit a British sport center in Udine in northeastern Italy. Apparently, the instructors for this center wanted to introduce basketball to British soldiers and hoped the Japanese Americans would exemplify the North American sport. The game was essentially an intrasquad matchup between the first and second teams. About 300 British soldiers not only attended but were expected to listen as a British warrant officer, knowledgeable in basketball, "explained the finer points of the game to the soldier audience." Ito wrote, "The diminutive bucketeers of the 442nd brought rounds of applause from the well-mannered spectators as they skillfully worked the ball around the court while one of their comrades broke to make clean and accurate set-up shots, giving a perfect example of how basketball should be played."[2]

The next day, the 442nd hoopsters played their first real game on the tour. The opponent was an all-star squad of Italians from Udine. Ito estimated that about 400 British soldiers showed up to cheer for the Americans, who won the game 44–37. Ito wrote, "It warmed the heart of each and every man on the team to hear the British soldiers cheer, 'Go it Yank,' 'Atta boy Yank.'" Perhaps, the warm feelings were accentuated by the hoopsters' knowledge that many fellow Americans wrongfully dismissed them as not actually "Yanks." In any event, the game was as close as it was, Ito pointed out, because the second team played much of the remaining minutes after the first team romped off to a big lead. To the Nisei athletes, "[i]t was a secret pleasure ... [when] the team watched one of their comrades bottle-up an Italian center who stood six-feet-five inches off the floor." After the game, the British spectators offered both teams "three rousing cheers, then they all retired to the club nearby and exchanged ideas about basketball over tea and crumpets."[3]

On May 11, Ito's story of the 442nd squad's journeys in northern Italy was continued. Ito told readers that the Japanese American hoopsters had little trouble with the U.S. 88th Medics team. The Nisei "slapped" the losers, 67–35. Furthermore, according to Ito, nearly all the rooters, including Italians, cheered for the "agile Nisei cagers."[4]

A three game series with the notably taller 349th Infantry team proved more challenging. Playing in Trieste, the Nisei put on a display in the first game that proved "disheartening" to their taller opponents, winning 64–53. For the second game, the 442nd team had to play without two of their better hoopsters, who were involved in a military all-star game. This time the 349th won handily, thanks largely to the efforts of their tall center. However, the 442nd seemed to have beaten the odds by prevailing in the "rubber match" by 12 points. In so doing, the Japanese Americans bottled up the center who had caused so much damage in the previous game. Referring to tensions between Hawaiians and mainlanders in the regiment, Ito, in celebrating the 442nd's triumph, pointed out that it proved Nisei mainlanders and Hawaiians could play as one.[5]

Thomas Harimoto was one of the better hoopsters on the 442nd. According to his enlistment papers, Harimoto was born in Hawai'i in 1920. While a U.S. citizen, he was racially identified as Japanese in those papers. The Japanese American veterans organization possesses an online photo archive in which one can find a shot of Harimoto with teammates Conrad Kuhahara, Lavern Kuhahara, Allan Kobata, and James Tsuha. One action photo shows Conrad Kuhahara trying to gather in a pass from San Franciscan Frank Ichimoto in a game in Italy lost by the Japanese American soldiers, 49–43. Another photo snapped during the same game displays Tom Harimoto jumping for an errant pass from James Tsuha. Roy Suzuki, a hoopster from Seattle, is in the picture, too.[6]

Aside from the 442nd, the 552nd Japanese American brigade was stationed in occupied Germany after V-E Day. The 552nd put together a league that enticed 98 men to the basketball courts. The *Pacific Citizen* revealed in September 1945 that Shiro Takeshita from Salinas, California, was the league's high scorer.[7]

Postwar Japanese American Basketball

After World War II, Japanese American college students organized teams. In 1948, Nikkei students in the Rocky Mountain area launched a basketball tournament in Colorado. In the 1950s, the *Pacific Citizen* reported that, replicating the historic sports rivalry between UCLA and USC, the Nisei Bruins Club had beaten the Nisei Trojans Club, 51–31, at Hollywood High School for the California Intercollegiate Nisei Organization Championship. Frank Chong bucketed 11 points for the Bruins, while Yoshi Nishimoto managed 11 for USC. Before the game, a squad of Nisei females from Fresno State edged East Los Angeles Junior College, 13–12, for the women's title.[8]

Determined to make their presence known in a positive way throughout all of island life, Hawaiian Japanese stood in the forefront of community basketball on the islands after World War II. In late summer of 1948, a team called the "Nisei-All Stars" by the *Pacific Citizen* hosted the Philippines' Olympic team in Hawai'i. As it turned out, the Hawaiians topped the visitors, 58–53.[9]

A few months later, the All-Nisei quintet hosted a substantially more challenging game with the Oakland Bittners, a powerful amateur team affiliated with the AAU and led by the legendary Don Barksdale. A former UCLA star, Barksdale pioneered basketball's racial frontiers by being the first African American to play on the U.S. Olympic team in 1948 and one of the first African Americans to suit up in an NBA uniform. The Hawaiians lost easily to the Bittners, 93–44. However, the *Honolulu Star-Bulletin* passed along some praise for the losers: "Although dwarfed and outclassed by the Bittners ... the local cagers put up a spirited battle all the way." Five-foot forward Dick Shimomura managed 15 points for the vanquished Hawaiians.[10]

The Americans of Japanese Ancestry (AJA) was an organization fashioned to represent Hawaiian Japanese after World War II. Deeply committed to sponsoring athletic teams and leagues, the AJA organized a senior basketball league in Honolulu after World War II. It also formed other basketball leagues. For example, an AJA league operated in rural Oahu with teams playing out of Wahiawa, Ewa, Pearl City, Waipahu, Waialua, and Aiea in the early 1950s.[11]

In the late 1940s, the AJA attracted so many skilled basketball players that it could afford to ship one team to Japan, while launching another to the mainland. Unfortunately, the Hawai'i AAU was not happy about the Japanese journey, because the departing Hawaiian Japanese would leave the Honolulu AAU bereft of basketball talent. Moreover, the national AAU claimed only a "championship caliber team" should journey to Japan and "not just any group of players who band together." At any rate, Japan had not been readmitted to the World Basketball Federation; hence, it was widely believed that international competition was banned as a result of the nation's responsibility for World War II.[12]

Eventually, the AAU and the World Basketball Federation relented and, according to the *Hawaii Herald*, a large aggregation of Nisei GIs greeted the Hawaiians upon their arrival in Japan. Subsequently, a noteworthy crowd of 10,000 watched the AJA quintet defeat a team of Japanese college all-stars, 64–48. A Hawaiian Japanese publication, the *Herald*, contended that many Nisei GIs were in attendance, mainly to root for the Hawaiians.[13]

An AJA team spent extensive time competing after World War II. In January 1949, the Hawai'i All-Stars split two games in Salt Lake City. The AJA five was downed by the Brooklawn Creamery squad, 59–46, but managed to take the measure of the Salt Lake Nisei All-Stars, 52–40. In March 1950, the AJA team once again toured the West, beating the San Francisco Japanese, 48–41, while in the city. Five years later, a team called the Islanders by the *Pacific Citizen* was on the mainland. Coached by Stanley Kudo, a JACL publication reported that this aggregation would compete in the Chicago Nisei tournament and oppose Japanese American fives while touring the mainland. The AJA squad also, as we will discuss later, competed consistently in post–World War II pan–Asian American basketball tournaments on the mainland.[14]

Elite AJA hoopsters could hold their own with anybody on the islands. They included Herbert "Gunner" Sumida, who earned a basketball scholarship to the University of Utah. In 1948, Sumida was the Most Valuable Player (MVP) in interscholastic basketball on the islands. John Holi Tome was another strong AJA contributor. In Honolulu, Wally Yonamine, the great all-around Hawaiian athlete, competed in the AJA league during the winter of 1950–1951, making the Honolulu Nisei All-Star squad as a guard. Yonamine had been the top scorer for the Russell Squad. Other all-stars were Wally Tome and Charlie Hamane as forwards, Harold Tome as a center, and guard Reggie Aisaka; Ray Oyama made the team as a utility player.[15]

Better known for his baseball and football exploits, Yonamine was a good basketball player. Yonamine was chosen to play on a team that opposed the Harlem Globetrotters. He also organized an all-Oahu Nisei team that trekked to Hilo, where it won all of its games. Among the formidable Japanese Hawaiian athletes who journeyed with Yonamine were Herbert Sumida, who had left the University of Utah for military service; Jimmy Miyasato, who quarterbacked the Weber College football squad on the mainland; Chico Miyashiro; and John Honda Holi.[16]

Since AJA basketball consisted of numerous teams and leagues throughout the islands, it did a fine job of training youthful Hawaiian hoopsters, according to the *Hawaii Herald*. In 1951, the publication noted that young Fred Furukawa was developing into a strong player under AJA mentorship, despite a bout of awkwardness while playing for the Farrington AJA team. Furukawa would later star for the University of Hawai'i, performing well against mainland opponents. The *Herald*'s Eddie Tanaka noted, "AJA basketball players need no longer take a back seat to other nationalities any more. Gone is the day when their numbers were limited in the senior league," although "as Japanese are a small race, the going was tough and only a handful were able to compete in the top-notch division." Meantime, other Hawaiian Japanese leagues were organized in the 1950s. In the mid–1950s, the Honolulu Nisei Basketball League had teams such as Nippon Theater, Ebisu Caterers, and Aiea JAC.[17]

In California after the war, the returning Zebras remained highly competitive in San Jose and beyond. Playing in the San Jose City League, they beat a team sponsored by Rosendin Motors in January 1946, 40–33. Furusho was high scorer with 14. In 1947, the Zebras copped the first half championship of the San Jose City League. Among the Zebras standouts were Southern California native Babe Nomura, who also starred in football for San Jose State, and Chi "T. Bone" Akizuki, who in 1953 labored as a clerk while living in San Jose's Japantown. Early in December 1949, the Zebras roughed up an opponent 50–25, and Akizuki led the way with 16 points. Around the same time, the Zebras took the San Francisco Nisei Invitational championship. Chi Akizuki, Hide Kashima, and Eichi Adachi were the big stars. A week later, readers of the *San Jose Mercury* learned that the "San Jose Zebras, classy local Nisei team" won a tournament in San Mateo. Akizuki and Kashima led the way. In February 1950, the Zebras won the championship of the Western Young Buddhist League. However, they had to subdue the Sacramento Maroons in the process, 66–51. Akizuki was the big scorer for the victors. In the spring of 1950, the Zebras took part in Santa Clara County's Youth Basketball Academy (YBA) tournament. Aside from the Zebras, the Hawaiian AJA all-stars, the Berkeley Nisei, the Los Angeles Nisei Vets, the Sacramento Stags, and the Madrone Athletic Club participated. Meanwhile, the Zebras continued to take part in San Jose's City Adult Basketball League. Akizuki was one of the top scorers in the league in 1949.[18]

The Zebras represented a larger experience. Throughout the Pacific Coast, Nisei leagues and teams thrived after World War II. Sharing San Jose with the Zebras, the Cardinals played hoops in an adult basketball league in the late 1940s. In mid–January 1948, they edged Memory Post, 38–37, with Yosh Nishimura contributing ten points to the cause. Aside from the Zebras, the Bay Area had its share of talented squads. The Berkeley Nisei won the Nisei Athletic Union (NAU) championship in 1948 and 1951. The San Francisco Drakes in 1948 put together a formidable team led by Lips Miyahara, who had previously put in time with the Zebras. Another consistent winner in post–World War II Bay Area hoops was the San Francisco Associates. A female team, the Sacramento Saints, was coached by Yoshiro Matsuhara, father of future college coach Colleen Matsuhara. In Fresno, a Nisei team competed in the city's National League along with the Fay Wahs, Club Gaona, and the American Yugoslavs.[19]

Focusing on Southern California, the region's Nikkei could certainly root for excellent community fives. Based in West Los Angeles, the Lucky Doks took home the NAU title in 1952. The team included standouts such as Herb Isono and Dickie Nagai. The five representing the Nisei Trading Company was often called the Trading Lords. This aggregation excelled in Nikkei hoops on the West Coast. In 1962, it won the NAU championship. Outside of Los Angeles, Frank Gotori scored 13 for Riverside's Japanese Union in 1949, when the five lost decisively to the First Baptists, 58–35.[20]

Nikkei in the Pacific Northwest remained steadfast in their involvement in community basketball. From Seattle, a Nisei squad sponsored by Tokuda Drugs barnstormed the western states from Utah to California, winning many tournaments in the process. One of the key members was Frank Fuji, who would later gain notoriety as a high school coach in Seattle. The Tokuda Drugs five was formidable. According to the *Pacific Citizen*, Manabu Fujino, standing over six feet tall, was the team's best player. He reportedly averaged 12 points a game for the Seattle outfit. Eighteen-year-old Shobo (Frank) Fuji was another stellar performer. He was named the outstanding player at the 1947 Salt Lake City tournament. Chuck Kinoshita was good, too. While Fuji was MVP, Kinoshita was named to the all-tournament team. Stanley Karikomi coached the Tokuda Drugs five. Several years later, Seattle's Japanese All-Stars were organized to play a visiting team from Hawai'i. Iso Nishimura and Ray Saito were two of the better hoopsters on this five.[21]

In the Southwest, an Arizona Nisei League existed after the war. The *Pacific Citizen* reported that the TNT five decisively took the measure of the Panthers, 31–16, for the league championship. Played at the Alhambra Gymnasium in Glendale, TNT's Shoji Teraji was the game's big star.[22]

Journeying toward the Atlantic, we could find postwar Nisei fives in the Rocky Mountain and Great Plains regions. Idaho Japanese American hoopsters met in a game in 1948. An Idaho Falls team upended a Pocatello five, 41–27, in a contest benefiting polio victims. Denver, the *Pacific Citizen* reported in 1950, hosted 17 Nisei basketball teams. Three years later, the *Pacific Citizen* informed readers about the six-team Colorado Nisei League, centered in Denver. In one game, the California Street Methodist Church five decisively defeated the Johnny Down team, 49–29. Tak Tsutui scored 25 points for the victors. In 1951, the *Pacific Citizen* announced the third annual Nisei Basketball Tournament scheduled for Scottsbluff, Nebraska. In 1956, the *Provo Daily Herald* informed readers of a looming contest between the "all-Japanese" Salt Lake City All-Stars and the Riverside Stake M five. Both teams, the *Daily Herald* maintained, were expected to play in the "Nesei" tournament slated for Salt Lake City.[23]

Chicago provided venues for Japanese American community basketball. After leaving the camps, thousands of Japanese Americans moved to the city. To help ease the transition from the camps to city life, often a half continent away from the communities in which they were raised, the Chicago Nisei Athletic Association (CNAA) was organized. According to the Chicago Japanese American Historical Society, "the CNAA developed into a hub of activity within the Chicago Japanese American community during the postwar era." Basketball, softball, volleyball, bowling, golf, and tennis, were offered to participants. Historian Ellen Wu wrote that the CNAA organized basketball and other leagues for Japanese Americans in Chicago to divert young people from trouble, while acknowledging the limitations of assimilation for Nikkei.[24]

In 2006, Alec Yoshio McDonald interviewed former participants in post–World War II Nikkei athletic endeavors in Chicago. They talked about Nisei gathering at the North Side's Olivet Institute to watch teams like the boys' Broncos and Collegians and the girls' Debonaires and Silhouettes in action. They remembered "hanging out at the soda fountain after a lengthy slate of action wrapped up on game days." And they went on to describe how CNAA squads on occasion traveled to tournaments across the country in search of fresh opposition.[25]

By the early 1950s, Chicago's Nikkei community was seeing many of its denizens returning to the West Coast. Thus, the CNAA announced a cutback in its basketball program in 1952. There simply were not enough players for an elite double A league. It would, however, continue to sponsor single A, B, and women's leagues, as well as a team that would compete in Chicago's municipal league.[26]

In Chicago, therefore, and other eastern urban centers, postwar Nikkei community basketball thrived for at least a while. The Chicago Huskies constituted a notable postwar Nisei team. In the late 1940s, they appeared at Chicago Stadium to compete in a preliminary game before the professional Chicago Stags and Rochester Royals took the court. When this squad traveled to San Jose in December 1949, the *San Jose Mercury* observed that it was the first "simon-pure non-college team from East of the Mississippi to play in San Jose." In 1952, the *Pacific Citizen* informed readers that the Japanese American Chicago Romans contingent was heading to Denver to oppose Nisei squads in the Mile High City. Also in the urban Midwest, a Twin Cities Nisei basketball team competed in the Minneapolis-St. Paul area and the Detroit Dukes participated in a Nisei tournament in Detroit in 1953. The *Pacific Citizen* noted, however, that the team had a couple of "Chinese stars," Al Chang and Al Chin, in addition to "an erstwhile Californian," Herbie Sugiyama. In 1947, the *Pacific Citizen* announced the advent of the first Nisei basketball team to play in New England. The Boston Nisei Club took part in the Cambridge municipal league and possessed several players with prior experience on the Hawaiian Islands and the Pacific Coast. The New York Bears and the Philadelphia Nisei Athletic Club performed on the East Coast in the early 1950s. The *Pacific Citizen* reported in 1951 that Sam Nakaso of the New York Bears starred in a Nisei tournament at McGill University in Montreal.[27]

Mainland Japanese Americans passionately organized leagues after World War II. In California, the Central California Young Buddha Association (YBA) sponsored a girls' league for the winter of 1947–1948 in Fresno. The games were held at Fowler's Gym, where three contests would be played on Saturday evening, while one was held on Sunday. That same year, Japanese American communities operated a Northern California league with two divisions. The first included the Zebras, San Francisco Drakes, San Francisco Vets, Berkeley Nisei, Richmond Athletic Club, and Sacramento Rockets. The second comprised the Sacramento Micks, Alameda Acorns, Harlem Athletic Club of San Francisco, San Mateo Russets, Oakland Paramounts, and Florin Athletic Club. When the Zebras took on the Drakes in January 1948, however, the preliminary was a female game between players from San Jose and San Francisco. In 1954, the NAU Double Aye League in Northern California included teams such as the Zebras, Sacramento Stags, San Francisco Protos, and Alameda Acorns. Other aggregations involved came from San Lorenzo, as well as one sponsored by Berkeley's Bob's TV—a five evolving out of the Berkeley Niseis.[28]

In the Rocky Mountain region, the JACL forged an eight-team basketball league in Salt Lake City in 1948. Among the members were the Salt Lake Seagulls, Pagoda Zephyrs, City Cafe, Sleepy Lagoon, Orem Utah Auto Club, University Niseis, and Good Laundry. In 1950, a Japanese American Athletic Union league appeared in the area, with teams in Ogden, Honeyville, Davis, Corinne, Syracuse, and Garland. In 1952, the *Pacific Citizen* observed that a former University of Utah basketball star, Wat Misaka, was tied for top scorer in his league while suiting up for the Salt Lake Harlems. Averaging 16.3 points per game, Misaka shared the scoring leadership with Tad Hideshima of the Salt Lake Zephyrs.[29]

With all of these teams and leagues active, postwar Nisei on the West Coast engaged in plenty of basketball tournaments sponsored by Japanese American communities. Yet notable non-Nikkei teams like the San Francisco Chinese Saints were often invited. In 1947, the *San Jose Mercury* promised "local fans ... a real treat" if they attended a male eight-team Nisei tournament to settle the championship of Northern and Central California. The Zebras would be there, as would the Sacramento Maroons, Berkeley Nisei, Presidio All-Stars, Reedly YBA, San Francisco Drakes, Oakland Paramounts, and San Mateo Athletic Club. The *Mercury* further announced a featured women's game pitting Japanese Americans from Mountain View against Sacramento.[30]

Around a year later, a YBA tournament was held at Los Angeles City College. In publicizing the event, the *Pacific Citizen* announced that an adroit female team from Los Angeles would go up against a squad called the Sacramento Saints. Reportedly, the Los Angeles crew had previously won the Japanese American Women's Athletic Union title in 1947. The tournament would feature, however, a contest between the Los Angeles Bucs and the San Francisco

Protos. The latter was described by the *Pacific Citizen* as the "kingpins of the Bay Area."[31]

In the spring of 1949, the Wah Kues, a Chinese American five, copped the Japanese American championship of Southern California. The Wah Kues had to defeat the West Los Angeles YBA five to get the crown, which brought with it the honor of representing Southern California in games against two of Northern California's Japanese American finest—the Berkeley Nissei Greens and the San Francisco Drakes.[32]

In 1952, the Lucky Doks took down a YBA five from Oakland in a Northern California tournament in San Jose in front of 3000 spectators. For the winners, Dick Nagai and Hiro Kubo scored 19 and 17 points, respectively, while Yun Akinaga and Sat Harada led the losers with 12 apiece. To get to the championship game, the Lucky Doks had to overcome the Zebras. They were able to do so thanks largely to Nagai's 22 points, while Danny Fukushima scored 20 for the losers. Prior to the game, two female teams vied for basketball supremacy. The San Jose Alphas barely beat the Sacramento Saints, 48–46. Alice Nishijima led the victors with 26 points, but Lai Fong of Sacramento wound up with 31. At tournament's end, Dick Nagai was chosen as "most outstanding player," and Hiro Kubo was named MVP.[33]

The Sacramento YBA squad took the California Bussei Championship in 1951 upon defeating the Los Angeles Lucky Doks. To get to the championship game, the Sacramentans upended the Zebras, who were defending champions. The victors were spearheaded by the play of Tosh Matsuhara, who scored 52 points in the semifinals and the championship game. Other standouts for the Sacramentans were Jimmy Yokota and Vic Nakamoto. Herb Isono sparkled for the Lucky Doks with 18 points in the championship game. Later in the 1950s, the Young Buddhist League in Central California staged a tournament in Lodi. In 1957, 17 squads, male and female, were invited from Central California municipalities: Lodi, Florin, Marysville, Walnut Grove, and Sacramento. North of the Golden State, the Nisei Northwest Invitational Championship was held in Seattle in the early 1950s. The Chinese American Cathay Post 186 squad wound up winning the tournament by beating the Seattle Lancers.[34]

Japanese American tournament basketball seemed to thrive in Utah after the war. In 1948, the *Seattle Times* notified readers that the local Tokuda Drugs five had won the thirteenth annual Intermountain Nisei tournament in Salt Lake City. To do so, they had to beat the Harlem Seagulls of Salt Lake City, 35–24. The consolation championship was a triumph for the Ogden Loboes when they beat the Daisy County Comets from Farming, Utah. As mentioned earlier, Seattle's Chuck Kinoshita was chosen as the tournament's MVP.[35]

Tournaments were staged in other parts of the West. In March 1946, Idaho

Falls hosted an invitational Japanese American tournament. Utah's Murray Taiyos copped the JACL-sponsored event by beating the Salt Lake Busseis, 48–36. Additional teams in the tournament included the Idaho Falls Russets, Cache Valley Eagles, Rexburg Bombers, Salt Lake Buffs, and Davis County All-Stars. Davis's Tom Akimoto took away scoring honors in the tournament by pumping in 44 points. In 1950, the Salt Lake City Zephyrs beat the Idaho host squad to win the tournament championship. Other teams participating included the Murray Taiyos and Ogden YBA. Two years later, the Idaho Falls tournament featured an abundance of exciting action, according to the *Pacific Citizen*.[36]

Western Nebraska was the site of a Nisei tournament in the early spring of 1951. The Lyman, Nebraska, Nisei five hosted the tournament at a local high school. However, all the rest of the teams came from Colorado—places like Rocky Ford, Sedgwick, Las Animas, Fort Morgan, Ordway, Brighton, and Denver.[37]

Midwestern Nikkei organized tournaments after World War II. In 1949, a Nisei tournament was held in Chicago. Journalist Robert Cromrie reported that the Chicago Huskies beat the Berkeley Nisei, 53–46, in front of 2700 at Lane Tech. Ted Hiyama and Shig Murao sparked the Huskies. In the consolation game, the AJA Hawaii All-Stars topped Salt Lake City. Six years later, the Chicago Nisei tournament attracted fives such as the Toronto Mustangs, Minneapolis Stars, and the Midwest Chinese Americans. Proceeds from the event were to benefit the CNAA's basketball and softball programs.[38]

One of the most prestigious events in post–World War II Japanese American basketball was a national Nisei tournament, which, for many years, was held in Salt Lake City. In the 1950 national Nisei tournament, the Zebras beat the AJA Hawaii All-Stars, 61–48, behind the inspired play of Jiro Nakamura. In 1953, Salt Lake City hosted the eighteenth annual Nisei tournament. The event was won by the San Francisco Chinese Saints, who had victimized the defending champions, the Magna Hellenics, in a championship game. A Nisei team from Chicago, perhaps the Huskies, won the consolation game.[39]

The Salt Lake City tournament, then often referred to as the National Oriental Basketball Tournament, was held throughout the 1950s. In 1956, the *Idaho Falls Register* asserted that the "San Francisco Chinese" were the favorites to fend off Nikkei rivals for the championship. Still, the Hawai'i Nisei five was expected to contend as well. The daily reported that George Ishihara, who coached the Hawaiians, would present a key to the city of Honolulu to Salt Lake City's mayor, Adlai Stewart, on behalf of Honolulu's mayor, Neil Blaisdell. Other teams competing were the Zebras, the Rexburg Idaho Ramblers, the Seattle Main Bowl Savoy, the Los Angeles All-Stars, and the Salt Lake All-Stars.[40]

In 1957, Utah's *Deseret News* announced, "Basketball giants will have to take a back seat in the local hoop buggy," as "oriental cagers, which make up for height in speed and agility take over University of Utah's Einar Nelson Fieldhouse." The occasion was the twenty-second "Oriental tourney." The 1956 defending champs, the San Francisco Chinese Saints, would not show up, the *News* advised, but the talented Trading Lords from Los Angeles would. "Dick Nagel [*sic*]," according to the *News*, led the Lords. The *News* also published a photograph of Virginia Uyeda, who had been crowned queen of the tournament.[41]

In 1958, the Zebras claimed the Salt Lake City title by upsetting the Los Angeles Travelers, 70–68. Yosh Kumagai scored the winning basket. In the battle for third place, the Oakland YBA quintet dumped the Salt Lake All-Stars, while the Los Angeles Kow Kwongs won the consolation round title by beating the Seattle Nisei Baptists. A onetime prep star for Palo Alto High, Kumagai was named the tournament's MVP.[42]

A year later, the *Seattle Times* reported that California teams like the Los Angeles Kow Kwongs, San Jose Zebras, Los Angeles Kono Travelers, and the Oakland YBA dominated the tournament. For example, thanks to Myron Chong's 25 points, the Kow Kwongs beat Seattle. The *Hayward Daily Review*, moreover, reported that the Los Angeles Travelers downed the Zebras, 85–58, during the Salt Lake City festivities.[43]

In 1960, the Salt Lake City tournament was replaced by Southern California's Gardena F.O.R. tournament. The F.O.R. stood for "Friends of Richard"—Richard Nishimoto, a promising Japanese American hoopster who played basketball for Gardena High School before dying in 1959. The tournament continued to draw female and male teams, as well as the San Francisco Chinese, for years.[44]

Meanwhile, California Nikkei staged state championships. The Berkeley Nisei won the NAU championship by beating the Southern California Appliance Saints, 49–32. In 1951, the Berkeley Nisei barely got by the West Los Angeles Lucky Doks. The next year, the Lucky Doks were luckier, downing the Zebras, 65–57. In 1955, the Southern California NAU five beat the Northern California representative. Yet the Los Angeles Lords–Local 299 needed an overtime to edge the San Francisco Protos, 47–46. Kaz Shinzato, hailed in the *Pacific Citizen* as the first all-city prep Nisei in Los Angeles, led the way, although Kengoro Yamamoto was high scorer with 14 points. Previously Shinzato had tallied 31 points in a semifinal game against the Zebras. As for the Protos, Eichi Moromoto scored a game high of 15 points, while Tosh Suto put up 14. In 1962, the Nisei Trading Lords downed the San Francisco Associates, 71–65, for the state title.[45]

To be sure, males got most of the press attention from publications like the *Pacific Citizen*. Still, the weekly did report on a matchup between community female teams in 1955. At that time, the *Pacific Citizen* informed readers that the Reedley Manjiettes had conquered the Lucky Doks from Los Angeles. Michi Nishimoto's 20 points led the victors to a 39–26 triumph.[46]

Chinese American Community Hoops after World War II

Hawaiian Chinese continued to take part in community basketball in the years after World War II. A Chinese basketball league competed in Honolulu in 1951. One of the teams participating in the league was sponsored by a business called Jongshi Express. However, if one wanted to see Chinese American community hoops abuzz, it was necessary to head to the mainland.[47]

To the east of the islands, San Francisco remained a stronghold of Chinese American basketball after World War II. In December 1945, the *San Francisco Examiner* asserted that a Chinese American squad was involved in the YMCA's junior division. Yet the most famous post–World War II Chinese American fives were male and female teams sponsored by the St. Mary's Mission in Chinatown and were thus dubbed the "Saints" and the "Lady Saints."[48]

The male Saints five seems to have evolved, in part, out of an all–Chinese American squad, representing a San Francisco–based business, Mierson Products. In 1946, this aggregation competed in the San Francisco Pacific Athletic Association tournament. The press noted that the team's tallest player was five foot nine and the smallest five foot six. Significantly, the Mierson five was the first all–Chinese American aggregation to vie in the PA tournament in the unlimited weight division.[49]

When the Mierson quintet conquered Autera of Palo Alto in the first round of the tournament, the unsubtle title of the *San Francisco Chronicle's* story was "Wongs Tong Score 47–43." The *Examiner's* Harry Borna exclaimed, "Eight little Chinese boys got the thirty-eighth annual *San Francisco Examiner's* Pacific Association cage tournament away to a sensational start in Kezar Pavilion." The Palo Alto five, according to Borna, tried to rough up "[t]he little men from Chinatown," but it could not restrain the victors from using their crowd-pleasing dribbling and passing to good effect.[50]

Taking over where the Mierson five left off, the Saints participated in the 1947 PA tournament in the unlimited division. In the first round, the Chinese American five demolished the Golden Gate Athletic Club Golds, 74–47. Already developing a reputation as a local hoops wizard, Willie Wong scored

37 points, setting a PA record. In the second round, the Saints beat the Chabot Athletic Club five, prompting the *Examiner's* Bob Brachman to call the Chinese American hoopsters "the scrappy fleet Chinese." "Billy 'Woo Woo' Wong" tallied 16, and the headline writer to Brachman's piece claimed the Chinese San Franciscan was on "another spree." When the Saints lost to San Francisco State in the third round, the mission's "All-Girl Drum Corp" performed at half time. Meanwhile, the Chinese YMCA had also entered a team in the unlimited division. However, this five lost in the first round to the Allen Redshirts, even though Charlie Lum scored 18 points.[51]

Unfortunately, the 1947 PA tournament was marred by San Francisco State's controversial defeat of the Saints. Willie Wong scored 23 in the losing effort, but that was not enough. The Saints, however, complained that San Francisco State had used ineligible players in the game, and Bob Brachman was convinced their grievance was justified. Yet demonstrating "graciousness" to the *Examiner*, the Chinese American squad inexplicably did not pursue the matter.

The next year, the San Francisco Chinese continued to impress in their PA tournament performances, as did Willie Wong. Indeed, Wong notched 29 points to help the San Francisco Chinese beat the Calinco Social Club five, 54–47. Subsequently, the Saints were bounced from the tournament when they were edged by the Stockton Amblers, 46–43. The game was part of a double-header at Kezar Pavilion and, according to the *Oakland Tribune*, Willie Wong and his teammates, "stole the show," despite their defeat. Wong tallied 19 points, but the Saints could not match their opponents' size and experience.[52]

To Bob Brachman, who was a truly dedicated if sometimes patronizing booster of Chinese American basketball in San Francisco, the Saints were "San Francisco's famed and colorful Chinese squad." When they performed, the young men put on "an artistic display of short, jolting passes and stop and go dribbling." They were, moreover, "clever little Chinese." Another *San Francisco Examiner* writer described the Saints as "darting little Chinese, who, because of their nimbleness, have been accused of coming up out of holes in the floor." Known as both the San Francisco and St. Mary's Saints, the five also competed in predominantly European American basketball leagues in the Bay Area.[53]

Saints' star Willie "Woo Woo" Wong was celebrated in the *Examiner* as "the 5–4 Chinese flash." Furnished with the nickname of "Woo Woo" by Brachman, Willie Wong, according to Kathleen Yep, grew up in poverty in San Francisco's Chinatown—a son of a garment worker and store clerk. The U.S. census manuscripts of 1940 describe the Wong family, with at least four children capable of playing good basketball, as living on Grant Street. Gong Wong, Willie's father, was a janitor in a public building, while Willie's mother, Lee Shee, had no apparent occupation outside the home. After Willie Wong died in 2005,

San Franciscan Willie Wong starred on probably the best post–World War II Asian American community team—the San Francisco Chinese Saints. However, he also played a season of big time college hoops for the University of San Francisco. Here is Wong's 1949–1950 University of San Francisco squad. Wong is in the front row, second from left. Courtesy University of San Francisco Archives.

San Francisco sportswriter Dwight Chapin told readers that the hoopster and his family lived in a "spartan ... Chinatown flat that was across the street from the Chinese playground." At the playground, Wong learned basketball, often the hard way. He remembered, "I used to stand and watch, and I was always the last guy picked for teams.... When I got to play, they always yelled at me not to shoot, because I couldn't. That became motivation for me."[54]

Willie Wong's brothers, Hank and "Wee" Wong, were teammates on the Saints and good hoopsters themselves. Bob Brachman described the latter as "just about as spectacular a shot" as Willie. Pete Lum, at five-feet-eleven, was the squad's tallest player. Coaching the five initially was Kenny Kim. During the early 1950s, Willie Wong, by this time hailed as Chinatown's "Mr. Basketball," was coach. The *San Francisco Examiner*, perhaps motivated by a desire to generate interest in the Pacific Athletic Association tournament it co-sponsored, was won over enough to describe Wong as "the biggest little man in basketball" and "one of the greatest box-office players in San Francisco history."[55]

Willie Wong's reputation as a hoopster transcended San Francisco's Chinatown. Preparing for the 1948 Olympiad, China declared an interest in recruiting Chinese Americans to boost its performances. According to the press, Chinese Olympic authorities considered recruiting Willie Wong, "the sensational young San Francisco basketball star." Since both of Wong's parents were immigrants, he was apparently eligible to represent prerevolutionary China. Wong, as it turned out, did not play Olympic basketball for China.[56]

The St. Mary's Mission, meanwhile, sent younger and smaller boys into Bay Area competitive basketball. In 1945, Willie Wong, playing for the St. Mary's 120-pound quintet, set a CYO record of 43 points in one game. In February 1948, the *Monitor* informed readers that the Salesian 80-pounders had won the "League C" championship by edging the St. Mary's five, 17–15. Still, the weekly hailed the losers as "courageous little Chinese lads" and praised Tommy Ng, who "played a great defensive game." Later in February 1948, the St. Mary's 80-pounders subdued a Mission Delores five, 44–11, while the 110-pound five beat Sacred Heart, 40–26. In March 1948, the 110-pounders decisively downed the St. Paul's five, 33–14. George Wong and Robert Lew were the big stars. Meanwhile, Willie Wong was coaching the 110- and 130-pounders. As the 1950 CYO tournament began, the *Monitor* hailed the 105-pound contingent as "the swift Chinese cagers from St. Mary's."[57]

Chinese American female squads also shined in Bay Area basketball. Affiliated with St. Mary's Church, the "Holy Family Chinese Mission" put together a formidable female squad right after World War II. Comprised of athletes the *Monitor* called "swift Chinese girls," the team's most famous player was Helen Wong, Willie's sister. In 1946, the Holy Family sextet was favored to win the CYO tournament but lost 29–24 to St. Cecilia. The next year, the Holy Family team seemed better than ever. Thanks to what the *Monitor* described as "the sensational play of Helen Wong," Holy Family routed one opponent in late November 1947, 48–17. Wong scored 28 points in the game. A couple of weeks later, "the amazing Helen Wong stole the spotlight" and led Holy Family to a CYO championship. She set a CYO record of 32 points, which the *Monitor* claimed was "by far the best individual effort seen in parish section competition." The *Chinese Press*, in January 1949, hailed the "Outstanding Chinese Girls Cagers" on its front page. In December 1949, the young women won the CYO crown. Helen Wong and Lucille Chong, a United States–born daughter of working-class parents, scored 12 each to help the "St. Mary's Chinese" beat St. Patrick's, 32–20. Helen Wong's free throw put her team in front after a nearly game-long struggle to overcome the girls from St. Monica's. In the relatively low scoring game of 17–16, Wong tallied 12 points.[58]

Eventually named to San Francisco's High School Sports Hall of Fame, Helen Wong could play. Her brother Hank said of her, "My sister was a natural athlete ... had a good sense of the court. She knew how to move and had a good eye." Yep asserted she averaged 20 points for the female Saints. Helen Wong told the *Asian Week* in the early 2000s that it was the Reverend Father Donal Forrester of the St. Mary's Chinese Mission who inspired in her a passion for basketball. In school, the young Helen found out that there was not much interest in girls' sports. However, Forrester organized a girls' team at the mission and paid for the team's uniforms.[59]

The Reverend Forrester's role in supporting San Francisco Chinese American basketball was acknowledged by the national press. In 1948, a wire story on Forrester portrayed the priest as a teacher of English and Mandarin. The priest told the press he believed it was useful to teach both languages because "it helps the Chinese make the transition from that of foreigners in a strange country to real Americans." He added, "We try to indoctrinate them in their native heritage as well and we believe that this has kept the Chinese from feeling the bitterness so many foreign groups feel. The parents, when we teach Chinese, feel that the children are not being estranged from the racial culture and the child is equally at home." Forrester also expressed pride in the performances of Willie and Helen Wong, as well as their reportedly bilingual teammates. Forrester, according to the wire story, "smilingly admits that Chinese can be effective in basketball. Neither the umpire nor the other team knows whether they are being insulted or whether instructions are being shouted to the floor in violation of rules."[60]

The late 1940s and early 1950s saw the St. Mary's elite male and female squads quite busy, tipping off against a variety of non–Chinese American teams. In December 1947, the Fasler Athletic Club five beat the San Francisco Chinese males, 61–48. "Bill Wong," however, contributed 17 points to the losers. In early January 1948, the *San Francisco Examiner* announced that the "Chinese Champion Cagers" would participate in a doubleheader at Kezar Pavilion. According to the Hearst daily, the "SF Chinese" would take on the freshman team from the University of San Francisco (USF) and would feature the "sensational Willie Wong." In the preliminary game, the "Chinese Saints CYO girls" were scheduled to oppose a team of U.S. Navy women from Treasure Island. On January 9, 1948, the USF freshman five drubbed the "Chinese boys," 58–26, before a crowd of 1400 at Kezar Pavilion. Yet the "Chinese girls" even more decisively defeated a squad of Navy Waves, 41–15. Competing in the Metro Cal League a week later, the male Saints lost to the Golden Gate Athletic Club, 46–38.[61]

As the decade of the 1950s dawned, Chinese San Franciscan hoopsters retained a spot in the Bay Area's sports limelight. The *San Francisco Examiner* announced that the "St. Mary's Chinese Girls Saints" won another CYO championship. On January 5, the *Examiner* reported that the "Chinese Girls' Cage

Team" had chosen Helen Thompson of the Holy Redeemer Parish's sextet "as the most sportsmanlike opponent." Around the same time, the males, minus Willie Wong because he was then playing for USF, encountered the Treasure Island Electronics at Kezar Pavilion. The game was preliminary to a contest between the College of Pacific and the Olympic Club. George Wong led the way with 14 points, and the Saints wound up barely on top, 56–55. The male and female Saints then traveled to Hamilton Field in Marin County. There the Chinese American males defeated their Hamilton Field opponents, 53–47, while the "Chinese Girls' Saints" had an easier time of it, conquering a Women's Army Corps team, 43–10. On January 18, 1950, the "San Francisco Chinese" downed a team representing the Young Men's Institute. Wee Wong tallied 24 as the Saints won, 72–58, in the game at Kezar Pavilion. In 1952, the Saints, described in the *Pacific Citizen* as the "best Oriental American basketball team," won a first-round PA tournament game against the Salesian Club. Although the Chinese San Franciscans were without Willie Wong, who was playing AAU ball for an Oakland five, they managed to win easily, 81–52. Jimmy Wong led the way with 17 points. Also on the team were Earl Gee, Eugene Wong, Cliff Wong, and Hanson Quock.[62]

Meanwhile, San Francisco's Chinatown hosted an annual basketball festival. In 1949, the event was held at Kezar Pavilion. The *San Francisco Examiner* predicted, "There won't be a lantern hung at Kezar Pavilion this afternoon but the annual Chinese Basketball Festival won't lack color." The Filipino national team downed the male Saints, 53–42. While the latter was without Willie Wong and talented Pete Lum, who reportedly was at college in Southern California, Percy Chu, Jimmy Wong, and Charley Lum played well for the losers. Chu led the team with ten points. As for the "Chinese girls," Helen Wong's 18 points pushed her team to victory over St. Vincent's. And Franklin Wong's nine points prodded an 80-pound team to dump the San Francisco Boys Club, 20–5. The next year, San Francisco's Chinatown again hosted the Chinese basketball festival at Kezar Pavilion. The Saints defeated the Hawaiian AJA team, 50–40. And the female St. Mary's squad beat a team from Oakland's Sacred Heart, 43–28.[63]

San Francisco's Chinese Playground remained a magnet for eager, if underfunded, basketball players. Phil Whang, who coached a playground team after World War II, told Kathleen Yep that the playground had no funds for uniforms. Better financed, generally European American teams wore nice uniforms, but, Whang proudly proclaimed, "We won." Lillian Yuen, who directed the Chinese Playground in 1950, boldly asserted the importance of Chinese Playground basketball. She declared, "When the pool-halls are empty the basketball league at the playground must be underway." Without playground basketball,

Chinatown's young people might engage, Yuen cautioned, in "puncturing tires, breaking windows, and jamming parking meters."[64]

As the 1950s progressed, male Chinese Americans remained competitive in San Francisco basketball. In 1953, Willie Wong, back with his old team, scored 17 points as the Saints handily defeated the USF freshman team, 56–43, in the PA tournament. In 1955, the squad lost to the USF freshmen, 82–60, as a prelude to a game between the Bill Russell–led Dons and the Cal Bears. Chinese San Franciscan hoopsters traveled to Asia as well. In 1956 they won a game in Hong Kong, 65–55.[65]

The game in Hong Kong was undoubtedly part of a tour arranged by the U.S. State Department and described in Ellen Wu's *Color of Success*. Wu writes that the U.S. government's handpicking of Chinese Americans, such as writer Jade Snow Wong, artist Dong Kingman, and the San Francisco Chinese hoopsters, to tour Asia in the 1950s "reflected the nexus of racial liberalism, cultural pluralism, and anti–Communism that opened up possibilities for national inclusion" for Chinese Americans.[66]

Wu reminds us that the Cold War could work in varied ways for racial minorities in the United States. It suppressed dissent in the name of a supposedly united front against Communism, but it also moved American institutions to moderate their longtime flirtation with, if not outright embrace of, racism. American policy makers, that is, may have wanted to do the right thing for historically aggrieved racial minorities, but they were just as concerned about winning the propaganda war against Communists, who insisted to people of color throughout the world that American democracy was a sham and American capitalism, an exploitative economic system knee-deep in racism and nativism. And the problem for American policy makers was that the Communist propaganda machine did not have to lie all that much. America's historical record regarding race and ethnicity was, in itself, an indictment.

Thus, by dispatching people of color who had achieved a certain amount of success and respect in the United States to third-world lands was a potentially powerful way for the United States to combat Communist propaganda. In terms of sports, famed African American tennis star Althea Gibson and Korean American Olympic gold medal diver Sammy Lee toured the third world on behalf of the United States. And while not as famous as Gibson or Lee at the time, the San Francisco Chinese hoopsters could serve the same purpose by touring Asia.

Nevertheless, the U.S. State Department, according to Wu, was troubled by the racial homogeneity of the San Francisco Chinese. If racial barriers were breaking down in the United States, an Asian could well ask, why wasn't this basketball team more racially integrated? Thus, the State Department told its people on the ground to promote the team as American rather than Chinese in the hope that Asians would get the idea that America was both inclusive and pluralistic. In particular, the State Department hoped the hoopsters would win over people of Chinese descent living in Asian countries other than China.[67]

The team played games and put on basketball clinics in Tokyo, Taipei, Hong Kong, Singapore, Kuala Lumpur, Penang, and Bangkok. In the process, the San Franciscans won the Overseas Chinese Presidential Cup Tournament in Taipei. Generally, the tour went smoothly, except for a "minor riot" that ensued during a game against Bangkok in Taipei. Moreover, the Chinese Americans rebelled against using squat toilets in Thailand.[68]

San Francisco's Chinatown, meanwhile, had been caught up in the Cold War. Organized on the basis of districts from which members could trace their Chinese ancestry, the powerful Chinese Consolidated Benevolent Associations, generally known as the "Chinese Six Companies," had long been a source of political and cultural conservatism in various Chinatowns in the United States. Even before the Cold War, they had battled left-wing unionists and activists within Chinese American communities, and they continued that struggle with a great deal of effectiveness after the Cold War started. Moreover, the Chinese Six Companies sought to represent Chinatowns to mainstream America as unified in their opposition to Communism. The San Francisco Chinese basketball team's tour on behalf of the U.S. government was, therefore, greeted enthusiastically by the Chinese Six Companies and the San Francisco Chinatown's Anti–Communist League. Both organizations praised the hoopsters as "goodwill ambassadors."[69]

Percy Chu coached the team and Marshall Lee served as team manager. The players included Harvey Y. J. Fong, Sherman Fong, Douglas Hom, Chew Jeong, David Ap Lew, Victor Low, George Chew Lum, Donald Fong, Hanson Quock, and Clifford Wong. Still sponsored by St. Mary's, the team continued to compete in CYO tournaments into the 1960s.[70]

Outside of San Francisco, post–World War II Chinese American community fives performed on various, mainly West Coast, courts. The "Oakland Chinese" male five took part in the city's Industrial Athletic Association League in 1946. In 1950, East Bay Chinese played for the Chinese Young Adults squad in Oakland, as well as the Oakland Chinese Center team. To the east, in Sacramento in 1946, the YMCA Senior Basketball League included one Chinese American quintet. In Fresno in 1946, a Chinese American squad called the Dragoneers participated in a league with the Sons of Italy and Club Gaona, consisting of players possessing Spanish surnames. Also in the late 1940s, the Chinese Baptist Juniors five competed in Fresno. An elite Chinese American five in Fresno, moreover, continued to represent the Fay Wah Club. In Los

Angeles, the Cathayette Girls Club formed a basketball team in the mid–1940s. Elsie Wong, who had formerly mentored the Lowa female squad, took charge of the Cathayette team. In the mid–1960s, the Chinese Presbyterians competed in Los Angeles.[71]

In the Pacific Northwest, Chinese American communities were represented by basketball teams in post–World War II America. A Chinese American five, sponsored by American Auto Sales, competed in Portland in 1948. To Portland's north, a Seattle team called the Chinese Stars was assembled to play against the Hawaii All-Stars in the spring of 1956. Former college standouts Al Mar and Ray Soo suited up for the five. A Chinese American team of adult males operated out of Seattle in 1960. Identified as barely five feet tall, Willie Chin served as team captain. The *Seattle Times'* Robert Heilman wrote that several members of the team were "dragonmen" operating the large Dragon that wound its way through Chinatown streets during special events.[72]

Not all post–World War II Chinese American squads were assembled on the West Coast. In September 1952, the *Brooklyn Eagle's* Jimmy Murphy announced that *Eagle* sportswriter Bill McCulloch was set to coach an "all-Chinese" team. Practice would start at the Church of All Nations in Manhattan. About 30 were expected to try out for a team that scheduled approximately 25 games against quintets representing Brooklyn Poly and the Brooklyn Friends. The New York City's Chinese Athletic Club sponsored the squad. Later in 1952, the *Brooklyn Eagle* reported that the Bishop Yu Pin Club of Philadelphia planned an "all-Chinese" tournament in the City of Brotherly Love. Bill McCulloch brought a team to the tournament. Squads from Boston, Washington, D.C., and of course, Philadelphia would participate. On the Brooklyn squad, the *Eagle* informed readers, were some talented hoopsters, such as Timmy Tsang, Fong Wo, and Herb Leong from Brooklyn Poly; Stuart Mock from Brooklyn Auto; and Alden Lee from Hofstra University. As it turned out, McCulloch's New York City team won the tournament staged at La Salle University. The team along with coaches McCulloch and Hong Wu were honored by a banquet in New York's Chinatown. Toward the end of the 1950s, the *Boston Herald* displayed a photograph of the Chinese YMCA five then participating in the city's Interagency League. Bruce Wong was team captain. A few years later, a Chinese American tournament was held in Washington, D.C., in 1962.[73]

Filipino and Korean Americans

Filipino Hawaiians seemed to rival Japanese Hawaiians in their enthusiasm for post–World War II basketball. The Hawaii Fil-Vets sponsored a squad after the war. Many of the players were former members of a valiant Filipino infantry regiment. Other Filipino American squads competing on Oahu included Waialu Fils and Waipahu Fil Americans. Moreover, Filipino Honolulans assembled their own league. And in the fall of 1948, an interisland Filipino American tournament took place. Competing were fives such as the Maui Fil Americans, the Hil-Fil All-Stars, Waialua Fil A.C., Lanai Filipino Youth Organization, and Hollywood Custom Tailors. Coached by Marionel Lunasco, the Waialua Fil A.C. five won the interisland championship. Saburo Fujisaki, who wrote for the *Honolulu Record*, a voice of the postwar militant, multiethnic Hawaiian labor movement, called the Waialua five "crack ... Filipino cagers." The Filipino Hawaiians further demonstrated a fervor for basketball in a diasporic Filipino community. Early in 1949, the Honolulu Filipino Civic Associates sponsored the visit to the islands of the Manila Industrial Commercial AA All-Stars.[74]

Formed in San Francisco's Filipino American community before the United States entered World War II, the Mango Athletic Club sponsored a formidable basketball team. Frank Fuji remembered that when his Tokuda Drugs team encountered them, they were stylishly adorned with green satin warmups, while wearing chartreuse green shoes. The Mangoes were organized by Filipino American young men, who generally lived in San Francisco's Western Addition. They practiced at the Buchanan Street YMCA, taking pride in their Filipino heritage while taking on white teams. Initially, community elders held back support, but when the Mangoes started to win games, the elders became more forthcoming with offers of financial aid. The Mangoes, however, decided to go it on their own without the help of the elders. Indeed, they turned out to be expert money raisers. The great jazz musician Cal Tjader performed at one of their benefits. In the process, the Mangoes became the best-known Filipino American basketball team in Northern California. According to Clemente Joe San Felipe, the Mangoes did well against Filipino foes because they had taller players who were "mestizos like me." He admitted, however, that some "full-blooded" hoopsters were relatively tall as well. The Mangoes also sponsored a female team called the Mangoettes.[75]

The U.S. census manuscript schedules reveal a bit about a couple of Mango hoopsters: Ed Campos and Rudy Calica. The 1930 census data shows a five-year-old Edward Campos living in San Francisco. Born in California, he was the son of Filipino immigrants. His father was an apartment house janitor, while his mother claimed no occupation. Rudy Calica, according to the 1940 U.S. census manuscripts, was the seven-year-old son of Filipino immigrants in San Francisco. Neither parent had an occupation, but the family was living with relatives and boarders.[76]

Throughout California, Filipino community basketball proliferated after the war. Frank Padin, a Filipino Hawaiian war veteran who settled in the Central Valley town of Livingston, was inspired by the Mangoes to launch a similar organization in his adopted town. With the help of Herb Jamero and Trongkilino Dacuyan, Padin organized teams for Filipino American boys. In nearby Stockton, the Saga five was a team of Filipino American vets coached by Manuel Cantino in 1946. The Salinas Filipino Young Catholics beat the Stockton Filipino Catholic Youth five in 1948. Stockton had not only a Filipino Catholic Youth basketball team but also a Filipino Youth Association squad. Stockton High School hosted a tournament sponsored by the Filipino Catholic Youth Organization. Led by high school standout Eddie Chavez, a team from Vallejo won the tournament. Down the peninsula, a Filipino American tournament was held in San Jose in the spring of 1950. Games were played at the city's Civic Auditorium. The Mangoes participated, as well as squads from San Francisco, San Jose, Livingston, Livermore, and Oakland. Filipino American tournaments in California attracted participants from not only the areas already mentioned but Los Angeles, San Diego, Delano, Lodi, and Walnut Grove. Peter Jamero has described Filipino American hoops tournaments as "treasured memories" for competitors. Tournament "experiences developed a special camaraderie with our own club members and those from other communities as well." Moreover, they were "healthy outlets for many Filipino Americans—who, because of their short statures and socioeconomic circumstances, were not always able to compete on their high school teams."[77]

Women's teams and tournaments developed as well. In California's Central Valley, the Isleton LVM (Luzon, Visayo, and Mindanao) female basketball team was active in the early 1950s. Other female squads included not only the Mangoettes, but the Sacramento Static Six, the Fremont Boloeettes, the Livingston Dragonettes, and the Bay Area Bay-O-Nets. Peter Jamero argues that female tournament play drew participants because they "sheltered Filipino girls from overprotective parents, who might be willing to let their daughters go away because of the numbers involved."[78]

In January 1949, the Mangoes hosted a relatively well-publicized "Filipino Tournament" at Kezar Pavilion. The *San Francisco Examiner* told readers that among the fives participating would be the Stockton Padres, the Stockton Filipino Youth Association, the Salinas Filipino Youth Club, the Livingston Fil-Americans, the San Francisco Filipino Youth, and the Vallejo All-Stars, led by "Eddie Chavez, star of the Santa Clara Frosh team." The Mangoes triumphed, beating the Salinas Filipino Youth Club, 37–24. The Mangoes' standout Babe Samson was named the tourney's "outstanding player."[79]

Author Peter Jamero demonstrated the importance of community basketball to many second-generation Filipino Americans—members of what he

After World War II, the San Francisco Mangoes stood out as the best-known Filipino American basketball squad around. Courtesy Peter Jamero.

calls the "bridge generation." The noted Filipino American activist and writer Fred Cordova expressed pride in being a sixth man on the Stockton Padres as a youth. Sam Catiel Garcia played for the Salinas Filipino Youth Council five. Gregory Bautista Bomba joined the Salinas Filipino American Youth Club five sponsored by the Sacred Heart Church. He loved going to tournaments, "where I formed some lifelong friendships that continue until this day." Jose Oriarte starred for several Filipino American squads representing Vallejo, Stockton, and in Southern California, Wilmington. Playing for the Wilmington Papayas in the 1950s was Hildo "Sonny" Pomicpic Jr., who, according to Jamero, was one of the best of the bridge generation athletes. A skilled ball handler, the five-foot-eleven Pomicpic played for years for the Livingston Dragons. Among female hoopsters, Jamero points out Nina Dublin Gonzales, who played for the Livingston Dragonettes, winners of many Filipino American tournaments. However, Jamero also interviewed Virginia Garcia Randall, who told him she joined the Salinas Filipino American Youth Club before it sponsored female basketball. Accordingly, Randall expressed disappointment because she claimed she was good hoopster who could hold her own with males.[80]

The Filipino community in Seattle also supported basketball. In 1948, the Filipino Catholic Youth team won the 17-year-old division championship of the park department's Queen Anne Lions Marine Reserve Tournament. Jamero writes about the Seattle Cavaliers who drove all the way to Stockton to compete in a postwar tournament but were too tired to do well. In 1961, Seattle's Filipino Youth Activities organization sponsored a basketball tournament to highlight Filipino Youth Week.[81]

The relatively small population of mid-twentieth-century Korean Americans assembled basketball teams after World War II. In 1946, the *Korean Independence* published a notice from Mary Lyou, who wrote that the Kon Wa Girls composed a "sports loving group whose desire it is to have a victorious basketball team this season." A male by the name of Paul Schoo coached the team. A Korean Basketball League existed in post–World War II Honolulu. The teams participating represented Moililli Realty Company, Makiki Nursery, Delta Frat, and Radio Appliance, coached by one of Hawai'i's most important contributors to island hoops lore, Art Kim.[82]

The Oriental Basketball Tournaments, 1947–1949

Community fives participated in multiethnic Asian American basketball events and tournaments. They may have helped, perhaps in a small way, to forge an Asian American identity that transcended the ethnic distinctions dividing Filipino Americans from Japanese Americans and Chinese Americans. In 1948, the Catholic Bishops' Relief Fund sponsored a game in San Francisco between the victorious AJA Nisei All-Stars from Hawai'i and the Saints, led by Willie Wong. The latter managed 15 points while closely guarded. At the same event, the female Saints, with Helen Wong scoring 24, downed a Nisei squad called the Rogues, 34–20.[83]

The "Oriental Basketball Tournament" emerged as a national gathering of Asian American community teams in the late 1940s. In 1947, the tournament was held in Seattle.

In preparation for the tournament, the Hawaiian AJA Nisei All-Stars arrived early from the islands, subsequently losing to the Budnick Cleaners in Seattle, 41–34. Soon after the Hawaiian Nisei appeared in the Emerald City, Seattle's mayor officially greeted them. The Hawaiians, in turn, gifted the mayor with leis. The mayor quipped, "All I need now is a grass skirt." Perhaps joking about the presumed lack of height of the competitors, the *Seattle Post-Intelligencer* declared that the tournament was "[a]ppropriately called the season's biggest little tournament." Its purpose, according to the daily, was to raise funds for disabled and needy veterans, while fostering interethnic competition and community harmony. Teams from as far away as Salt Lake City and even New York City and, of course, Honolulu were expected to take part.[84]

Among the teams gathering in Seattle was the five representing San Francisco's St. Mary's Mission. Spearheaded by the Wong brothers, the Saints won the tournament's championship. Previously, however, Willie Wong and his brothers had to persuade the mission's Father Forrester to sponsor their trek to the Pacific Northwest.[85]

According to sports columnist Jack Hewins of the *Walla Walla Union Bulletin*, the Oriental Tournament reflected a growing postwar rapprochement between Seattle's Chinese and Japanese American communities. Hewins wrote that tensions had resulted in anti–Chinese mob action at a Portland tournament put on by Nikkei before the war had subsided—a position sustained by local Chinese American basketball players and supporters Phil Mar Hing and Art Louie.[86]

The opening night of the 1947 tournament was, the *Seattle Times* told readers, highlighted by the performances of "little Tetsuo Odo" of Hawai'i and "highly touted Willie Wong." A crowd of 2000 watched Odo score the winning basket against the Berkeley Nisei, while Wong, as expected, put up a game-high 20 points to lead the Saints to an easy 45–24 victory over the Chicago Huskies. Al Mar, who had played stellar college basketball for the University of Washington and Whitman, made the winning basket for Seattle's Cathay five when it edged a Nisei team from Salt Lake City. Phil Mar Hing was high scorer for Cathay with six. F. Kasai was the losing team's high scorer with five.[87]

Eventually, the Chinese San Franciscans downed the Hawaiians for the tournament's first championship. Willie Wong proved as good as advertised. His performance at the 1947 tournament helped persuade the *Pacific Citizen* to describe him several months later as "fabulous." An overly sanguine Royal Brougham believed that the Oriental Basketball Tournament proved something wondrous about sports. He declared in a column for the *Post-Intelligencer*, "Athletics knows no race, color, or creed and there was nothing but the best sportsmanship when Japanese, Chinese, and Hawaiian teams from over the Pacific played their basketball tournament this week."[88]

The *Seattle Times*' Alex Shults identified Art Louie as one of the prime movers behind the tournament when it reappeared in Seattle a year later. Shults described Louie as a 30-year-old member of the five representing Cathay Post No. 186. An owner of a sporting goods store in Seattle, Louie counted upon teammate Phil Mar Hing to serve as co-organizer of the event.[89]

The theme of Shults' piece was that this basketball tournament bred good will among historically antagonistic "oriental" groups. It also seemed to do well financially. In 1947, according to Shults, the tournament made nearly $5000. Yet Shults found it curious that the Filipino American Mangoes were invited to trek up from San Francisco. He could only guess that the Filipino hoopsters offered a little variety to a generally Japanese and Chinese American fare.[90]

The way the tournament matchups were arranged intrigued Shults. He wrote that the early rounds assured that Nikkei squads would play Chinese Americans, while the Mangoes, of course, would have to play one or the other. "Old timers" among Seattle's Asian Americans, Shults advised, shook their heads, fearing trouble. However, he reassured readers that the "younger generation" knew how to move beyond historic animosities. Invitees, Shults moreover maintained, had to pay their way to Seattle on their own. The one exception was the Hawaiian AJA squad. Traveling the greatest distance, the Hawaiians were offered a $350 guarantee.[91]

Seattle Post-Intelligencer's sports columnist Royal Brougham was no less optimistic than Shults when he hailed the 1948 tournament in Seattle as an "athletic event fostering good will." To promote the hoops affair, Brougham's newspaper displayed a photograph of three athletes participating in the tournament and representing different ethnic groups—Berkeley's Harlan Sano, Phil Mar Hing of Seattle, and the Mangoes' Babe Samson. According to the *Seattle Times*, the tournament was co-sponsored by the Chinese American Cathay Post 168 and the Seattle Nisei Veteran's Committee. Japanese American Shiro Kashino and Chinese American Phil Mar Hing served as co-chairs of the event. Once again, the Hawaiian Nisei basketball team was on hand to bestow gifts on Seattle's mayor—this time, a lei and a "Kanaka" shirt. In doing so, the AJA squad had to trudge through snow, which, the *Seattle Times* reported, was the first they had seen in any U.S. city.[92]

Once the 1948 tournament began, the *Walla Walla Union Bulletin* reported, the Hawaiian All-Stars edged the Seattle Cathay five, 36–34. Richard Asato and Ritchie Shimomura were the big stars for the winners. The next day the Berkeley Nisei beat the Hawaii All-Stars, while the Saints defeated the Seattle Nisei. Hiro Higashi shined for Berkeley, while Willie Wong was top scorer for San Francisco, albeit he was held to a mere nine points. In the championship game, a near-capacity crowd of 2000 saw the San Franciscans, led by "Speedy Willie" with 16 points, beat the East Bay five.[93]

The 1949 tournament shifted to San Jose. To prepare for the festivities, the Seattle American Legion Cathay Post merged seven players from its basketball team with seven players from the Nisei Veteran's Committee to give their city better and multiethnic representation. The *Seattle Times* published the roster, which included the very adept Ray Soo, Ray Saito, and Frank Fuji. Pretournament publicity embraced the *San Francisco Examiner* observation that the "all-Nisei" Chicago Huskies would rank among the favorites to win the championship. It also acknowledged that the San Francisco's Filipino Mango A.C. would show up.[94]

The *San Jose Mercury* covered the reception accorded by the city to the AJA's Hawaii All-Stars at San Jose's Civic Auditorium. It published a photograph of San Jose's mayor greeting the Hawaiian Japanese as they presented him a gift from Honolulu's mayor. The daily appeared more than willing to promote the tournament, claiming that "some of the most colorful basketball games of the season" would eventuate and that the tournament marked "one of the most outstanding sports events in the history of San Jose." Indeed, San Jose hoops fans were "due for a treat." They would find the participants "specializing in fast-breaking attacks that employ the wizardry of ball handling and sharp shooting, scoring from all angles, excelled only by the professional Harlem Globetrotters and House of David teams." The *Mercury* also informed readers that "Ray Saito, Wyoming State All-Prep, plays for the Seattle Oriental All-Stars." It added that the Zebras would host the tournament, and Zebras star Chi "T. Bone" Akizuki had once stood out for San Jose High School and remained a "great favorite with local fans."[95]

In an early round, the "Seattle All-Stars" upended the Zebras, 55–52. Eddie Wong led the way by scoring 15 points. However, Chi Akizuki notched 17 as high scorer for the Zebras. The San Francisco Chinese Saints rallied from behind to beat a team sponsored by the Southern California Appliance Company. George Wong was the big star for the victors, who were without the services of his brother, Willie Wong, then playing for USF. A few days later, the Zebras avenged their earlier loss to the Seattle five, 51–33. Frank Yoshioka was high scorer with 11 points.[96]

A crowd of about 2500 witnessed the Hawaii All-Stars end the Chinese Saints two-year championship run. Manifesting "fast action," according to the *Mercury,* the game was a nail-biter, but the Hawaiians came out on top, 42–39. In the consolation game, the Zebras topped the Huskies.[97]

Even though Asian Americans constituted a relatively small portion of America's mid-twentieth-century ethnic mix, their commitment to community basketball should strike the modern reader as impressive. Composed of generally second-generation participants, Asian American community basketball in the middle of the twentieth century demonstrated the sport's vitality and democratic promise. To be sure, many of these hoopsters could not escape ethnocentrism and racism. Institutional discrimination continued in the shape of the American government's refusal to grant easy entry for Asian immigrants in the 1940s and 1950s. For Japanese Americans, in particular, community basketball no doubt meant many things, but clearly they hoped was that it could bring Nikkei together after the onerous conditions that many had faced during World War II. Significantly, liberalization of U.S. immigration laws in the mid–1960s and the subsequent and often harrowing journeys of Southeast Asians to the United States in the wake of war would change Asian American communities dramatically, as well as the ethnic composition of Asian America basketball.

CHAPTER 3

Crossing Sidelines

Asian Americans
and Intercultural Basketball
to 1945

Basketball lured Americans of Asian ancestry across difficult cultural terrain in the earlier decades of the twentieth century. Some played on competitive and recreational teams as adults and youth. As children and young adults, some played for elementary, middle, and high school teams. Indeed, as high schoolers, they even attained recognition and honors. To be sure, basketball, as have other sports, carried the banner of bigotry. Yet gyms from Honolulu to Boston could serve as cosmopolitan canopies, allowing basketball to abet democracy a bit by lowering, but sadly not shattering, well-constructed racial and ethnic barriers.

Multiethnic Teams in Hawai'i

If basketball were going to thrive on the islands, it would have to do so under the auspices of racial and ethnic diversity. Representing a majority of the islands' population by the early twentieth century, Asian Hawaiians had to play if neighborhood, company, and school teams and leagues were going to operate. Indeed, Asian Hawaiians such as Ah Chew Goo not only dribbled, shot, and defended on courts throughout the islands but in many ways symbolized basketball in Hawai'i to others.

Significantly, one of the primary motivators of multiethnic basketball in Hawai'i was the use of recreation to ostensibly improve the lives of children with parents from working-class, immigrant backgrounds. While active throughout urban America in the early twentieth century, the Progressive Era's recreational reform movement acknowledged the need to spread the gospel of healthy physical recreation to the ethnically mixed, working-class neighborhoods of Honolulu—neighborhoods such as Kalihi, Kaako, and Palama, where settlement houses were established. Nor were recreational reformers in Hawai'i shy about putting basketballs in female hands. Thus young women played for multiethnic, multiracial teams representing these neighborhoods, as well as other teams, in the first two decades of the twentieth century. In 1912, the Kalihi Girls basketball team beat a squad from the Palama Settlement House. Among the young women competing was A. Sing for the victors, while Mabel Doo played for the losers. On Maui, Ah Choy was one of the stars of the Wailuku team. A few years later, the Maui women's basketball team was coached by Achoy Ahou. Playing for the Kalihi Camp Fire Club was Rose Chung. Around the same time, Marilyn Goo competed with the Kakaako contingent. In the late 1920s, the Palama women's team hosted a squad from Kauai. The home team won, 31–18. However, hoopsters surnamed Chang and Hing competed for the visitors.[1]

The blossoming multiethnic Hawaiian local culture seemed at work as not only Hawaiian females but Hawaiian males played plenty of interethnic basketball with Native Hawaiians and *haoles* in the 1910s. Moreover, since basketball could be played in the evening if indoor gyms were available, participants could run around a court after a day at school or work. In the 1910s, all sorts of teams with Asian Hawaiians on their rosters appeared on local courts. Chinito Moriyama, who was also a famed baseball player in Honolulu, played for Palama. Kong Lam played for the Diamonds. The Athletics had Che Hoy, Wah Soon, and Tai Leong. The Giants' captain was Ah You Chong, who competed on the same team with Kam Lee, Tin Choh Wong, Thomas Wong, Charles Kee, and You Chou. The Pirates had Minoru Sokata, Moy Hee Chong, and William Chung. The Dodgers had S. Ling and Shorichi Hashimoto. The Cubs suited up Allen Mau, Joseph Tseu, Kong Mau, and Kim Too Ho. F. A. Sing, Tay Loy, Cheong, and Wang Pui were on the Washington squad. The Kailunas included a hoopster surnamed Morita along with Ah Cheong.[2]

During the interwar years, interethnic basketball teams and leagues thrived on the islands. An Employed Boys League consisted of squads named after Ivy League schools. Ho, Kwock, and Kudo played for Cornell, while Sakata played for Princeton. In August 1919, reports on basketball on Maui disclose Ah Fong as a substitute for the Lahaina squad. Kahului had an E. Apau as a substitute and F. Hamamoto subbed for the Rubes. Later in 1919, a Maui five beat a visiting team from the island of Hawai'i handily, 30–8. The *Maui News* contended that the largest crowd ever to watch a basketball game on the island was in attendance. Local dignitaries even showed up to watch Apau compete for the winners and Ah Fook, Ah Soy, Lai Hip, and Okino for the losers.[3]

The 1920s witnessed a notable presence of multiethnic basketball on Hawai'i's less populated islands. In the late summer of 1920, Maui basketball enticed F. Tsuda, a forward for Lahaina. Around the same time, Bunn Hee guided the Kapaa five to a victory over a picked team in Lihue on Kauai. Early the next year, a five from the island of Hawai'i was in Lahaina to edge Maui, 21–18. Ching, Ah Pung, Higuchi, and Suzukawa comprised part of the Hawai'i roster. Meanwhile, the *Maui News* announced that the Scouts from Hilo were on the island to take on local aggregations. It asserted that the Hilo male five was comprised of equal parts Japanese, Chinese, and *haole*. Warning readers that the visitors were good, the *Maui News* averred that they had previously beaten a team visiting from the University of Nevada. Early in 1922, a box score in the *Garden Island* reveals that the Waimea aggregation had Oyama, Akama, and Yoshimitsu in the lineup. In December 1922, the *Maui News* reported that a good crowd turned out in Wailuku to see the Maui Alerts humble the Pals, 51–9. Hangai stood out for the victors, while H. Ah Chee provided some of the few good moments for the losers. On Kauai in 1922, Nakashima, Ohama, Watase, Kaohi, and Moura played for the Hanapepe team, while Waimea was represented by Oyama and Yoshimatsu. Managed by H. Horio, the Horio's Eight squad took part in the Paaia League on Maui. Its roster included K. Muroki, K. Toyota, T. Nagata, S. Higashi, and S. Shegeto. Also on Maui, a boys' league for 120-pounders competed in 1927. And playing for the Olympics were S. Suezaki, P. Moikeha, S. Yokuchi, J. Tokunaga, and G. Matsue.[4]

A plethora of multicultural squads and leagues competed on Oahu during the 1920s and 1930s. The National Guard five suited up Takeguchi and Hohu in 1927. Suzuki was a starter for the Honolulu Athletic Club around the same time. Meanwhile, the Central Y five suited up center Buck You Wong. The Central Y also organized a junior team with players such as R. Y. Egamo, Ted Ching, Herbert Omura, and Ah Sum Hee. The Nuunu Y had its own league. One of the teams was named the Spartans, a five composed in part of Howard Pang, Rueben Lee, Muu Soo Song, Konichi Murata, Tokio Hirokawa, and Young Sung Hinn. The Palama Settlement House contingent was led by Lee Chong, Hong Yim, Lefty Chow, Ernest Iaea, Lum Goo, and Francis Wong.[5]

Some of the best of Honolulu's hoopsters graced the Bankers League in the late 1920s and early 1930s. Early in 1927, Chinese Hawaiian sportswriter Loui Leong Hop told readers that Edward "Duke" Way, S. Leong, H. S. Ching, and F. S. Dung played for the First National five. Alexander and Baldwin had Frong Mau, Walter Aki, and captain Morris Chang. Charlie Dung played for the Treasury quintet. Bishop Trust suited up S. Sugama, Ah You Wong, and

Mun On Chun, while W. Chun played for the Bank of Hawaii. Teams representing two of Hawai'i's most powerful economic entities opposed one another in mid–January 1927; Alexander and Baldwin defeated the Bank of Hawaii, thanks largely to Morris Chang's 14 points. In 1933 William "Spike" Nakayama was one of the stars for Bishop Trust. Goro Moriguchi, one of the best Hawaiian basketball players of the 1930s and 1940s, teamed up with Nakayama, Kugiya, Ouchi, and Ching on the Bishop Trust team.[6]

In the early and mid–1930s, plenty of basketball was played in and around Honolulu. Dr. Clarence Lee Ching coached the Palama five, while Tuck Chong was one of Palama's best players. Visiting Honolulu, Lahaina was coached by Norman Oda and had Leong at forward. In 1934, the Pearl Harbor Boys basketball team was coached by Henry Wong. It included athletes such as Francis Wong, Chin Lo, Joe Wong, Chin Chun, and the adept Swanee Pang. Competing in Honolulu's Businessmen's Basketball League was Bernard Wong for the *Honolulu Advertiser* five, while Kats Nakamura suited up for Liberty House. In 1936, the Palama men's squad included players such as Tuck Chong and Kumashiro. The James Chong Clothiers team suited up Richard Tom and Walter Wong, who later gained notoriety on the islands as a high school coach. The University of Hawai'i alumni were represented by a squad that had players such as Irving Maeda. Coached by Hong Wai Chong, the Nuunu Speeders consisted of young men such as the highly able Chew Chong Ching, Kam Chong Yuen, and Gene or Goro Moriguchi. The latter was, according to the U.S. census manuscript schedules of 1940, the son of Japanese immigrants. His father at the time worked as a laundryman while he was described as a clerk.[7]

As Hawai'i edged closer to World War II, Hawaiians did not stray from multiethnic basketball. Twenty-nine teams and 390 athletes participated in the Recreation Outdoor Basketball League, sponsored in the spring of 1940, by the Recreation Commission and Playground Association. Coached by Matsuo Katayama, the Hall Street Babes won the league's 100-pound crown.[8]

In the months before U.S. entry in World War II, the *Dallas Morning News* published an article praising Hawaiian plantation life. Author Mrs. E. P. Reppert proclaimed that the plantation operators encouraged "good fellowship" through sports such as basketball. She described an Oahu plantation five from Waiahua Plantation as represented by a team of players of Scottish, Portuguese, Chinese, and Japanese descent. However, as Takaki has pointed out, plantation operators may have been concerned about the welfare of their often overworked and underpaid employees, but they were just as concerned, if not more so, about diverting workers from unionization and strikes. They hoped that encouraging sports on the plantation would discourage worker militancy.[9]

The attack on Pearl Harbor cast a pall over Hawai'i, but did not necessarily dim Hawaiian enthusiasm for competitive sports such as basketball. During World War II, the Honolulu Senior Basketball League engaged the athletic talents of Francis Sing, Jimmy Koo, Harold Tome, and Bill Choy. The league was represented by an all-star team coached by Art Kim. There was also a women's league in which Rose Kaulukukui, who belonged to a famous Hawaiian family of athletes possessing mixed Chinese and Hawaiian ancestry, was one of the participants.[10]

Ah Chew Goo was Hawai'i's most famous basketball player before World War II. He was a son of a Chinese immigrant father, who worked in a Hilo auto garage in 1930, and a Native Hawaiian mother. As a youth growing up in Hilo, he persistently worked on nurturing his basketball talents. According to *Honolulu Advertiser* writer Lelia Wai, Goo started playing basketball at seven but with a volleyball. Hilo then, Goo recalled, "was a pretty good basketball town" but did not have much in the way of basketball courts and had but one gym. With little access to the more conventional trappings of basketball, Goo set up a "basket" that was actually "a wooden carton with an open top nailed to one of the walls in an empty apartment." To avoid provoking the ire of neighbors of the empty apartment, Goo refused to let the ball bounce against the walls or on the floor after taking his shots; when he shot, he "had to make it." Moreover, while walking the streets with a ball, Goo practiced his passing by trying to hit telephone poles. This all must have worked, because while barely over five feet tall, Goo led Hilo High School to three straight interisland championships from 1934 to 1936. All the while, Goo remembered, "There's always someone better than you. But I was always trying to be better than someone else."[11]

Goo's ball handling skills became vital to Hawaiian basketball lore. Red Rocha, a Portuguese Hawaiian and onetime University of Hawai'i coach, said Goo's reputation was that "he did everything with the basketball that people weren't doing at the time." He added, "He was unusually quick and a really good passer." Rocha claimed that as the only Hawaiian-born and -raised player to suit up in an NBA uniform, Goo should "have to be considered one of the better basketball players in Hawai'i history. He was way ahead of his time." Sportswriter Andrew Mitsukado once wrote of Goo, "He did everything with the ball except make it talk back to him." Goo, according to Mitsukado, was known as a "hardwood magician [who] perfected the cross-over dribble long before it became popular," while "his circus passes became the stuff of legend."[12]

His son, Vince Goo, recalled for sportswriter Dave Reardon that Ah Chew Goo "played against the Globetrotters in the 40s, and they didn't want to play against him the next year." Abe Saperstein, who ran the Globetrotters, even wanted to sign the Hawaiian. Vince Goo asserted that his dad was "offered a chance to play for the Globetrotters on the mainland, but he turned it down. He had heard about some of the prejudice across the country and didn't want to be a part of that." Nevertheless, Ah Chew Goo remembered with some pride that he had inspired some of the Globetrotters' illustrious showmanship. He said he went to Abe Saperstein, asking the famed basketball entrepreneur if he could put a rubber band on the ball when he shot a free throw. Saperstein responded that he did not think that was a good idea. "So I asked him," Goo continued, "if I could call a time-out and switch the ball [in the huddle] to a flat basketball." Saperstein again responded in the negative. "The next year," writer Bob Hogue contended, "when the Globetrotters returned to Honolulu, they were doing Ah Chew's tricks as part of their regular comedy routine."[13]

A year before the United States entered World War II, noted syndicated sportswriter Robert Edgren journeyed to the islands. One of the things he was anxious to do before returning home was catch a glimpse of a "Chinese named Ah Chew Goo in action." Edgren had heard that Goo was "[o]ne of Honolulu's basketball stars." Unfortunately, Goo took ill and could not play while Edgren was in Hawai'i.[14]

The illustrious Hank Luisetti admired Ah Chew Goo's ball handling so much that he declared that the Hawaiian would have excelled on the mainland. Indeed, when Luisetti visited the islands in the spring of 1941, he helped lead a team representing Coca-Cola to a victory over the touring University of Oregon five. However, according to one press report, Luisetti was aided "by Ah Chew Goo, speedy Chinese star." Subsequently, a Utah sports columnist told readers, whom he expected to be befuddled, that someone named Ah Chew Goo had played with Luisetti in Hawai'i. Trying his hand at sarcasm, the mainlander added awkwardly, "We don't know the answer but Goo almost matched Luisetti in scoring during the games." Luisetti himself told a Hawaiian newspaper, "I never had so much fun in my life, don't know if Stanford will ever want him, but [Goo] certainly can play for my club any day."[15]

Press Maravich, a famed mainland coach and father of the even more famous Pete Maravich, encountered Ah Chew Goo while serving in Hawai'i during World War II. The "Mandarin Magician," according to Press Maravich, was "the best ball-handler I've ever seen." The elder Maravich was persuaded that he needed to teach his son to handle a ball like the Hawaiian if Pete was going to become a star. Thus, Press put Pete through a complex array of ballhandling drills inspired by Ah Chew Goo; these basketball drills helped forge "Pistol Pete" into one of the greatest offensive players in NCAA and NBA annals.[16]

Hawaiian Traveling Teams

In the early 1920s, the multiethnic Hawaiian All-Stars toured the mainland's West Coast. This was not the first time Hawaiian athletes had trekked to the mainland to compete. Mainland sports fans in the 1910s grew accustomed to seeing Hawaiian baseball players and swimmers in action. From 1912 to 1916, a baseball team considered on the mainland as entirely composed of Hawaiian Chinese barnstormed the mainland, playing against college and semi-professional teams, as well as African American and white professional nines. In the process, they won a majority of the games while frequently stunning opponents and spectators with their athleticism and baseball IQ. Initially, the team was "all-Chinese," but over the years it became more representative of Hawai'i's emerging local culture, with players possessing a mixture of racial and ethnic backgrounds. While this ball team gained some fame for Hawai'i, water athlete Duke Kahanamoku seemed to best represent the islands to many mainlanders. After winning Olympic gold as a swimmer in 1912 for the United States, Kahanamoku regularly competed on the islands along with other Hawaiians. While he dazzled mainlanders with his swift swimming, Kahanamoku also brought along his surfboard, on which he amazed mainlanders with exhibitions of balance, agility, and strength, thus helping to pioneer the sport of surfing on both coasts of the mainland.[17]

Upon the Hawaiian hoop team's arrival on the West Coast, the local press revealed a certain amount of confusion as to the athletes' ethnic backgrounds. In early January 1923, the *Oakland Tribune* described the visitors as "full-blooded Hawaiian" and informed readers that two of them, Chung and Matsunaga, played for the University of Hawai'i. As for the *San Francisco Chronicle's* Hamilton Hintz, he declared that there were four "Japanese boys with the outfit and one Hawaiian." Expected to tour the mainland for two months, the team was managed by a Honolulu *haole*, Percy H. Nottage, who was a prominent member of the generally white Outriggers Club.[18]

The visitors held their own against California fives. In the Bay Area, the Hawaiians edged the Young Men's Institute of San Francisco, 25–24. Apparently, "Bunny" Chung hit a game winning basket with six seconds left. A few days later, Petaluma, a town north of San Francisco, hosted the Hawaiians. The local five, called the Spartans, won 45–28 before "one of the largest crowds" to see a game in the north bay. Within a week, the *Chronicle* displayed a photograph of Bunny's brother, "Chocolate Chung." The daily called him the "smallest star player on the islands. He makes up for his lack of size by his speed and aggressiveness." The Hawaiians subsequently conquered the Agnetian Club in San Francisco, 19–9.[19]

The island five headed then into California's Central Valley. Publicizing an upcoming game between the Hawaiians and the Sacramento American Legion five, the *Sacramento Bee* pointed out that "Chocolate Chung, a Chinese forward, is said to be the real star of the outfit and has been making impressive showing in games played by the team." Others on the squad included not only Bunny Chung, according to the *Bee*, but Shigi Matsunaga, as well as Native Hawaiians Abe Kaleikuu and Herman Clark, an athlete of indigenous Hawaiian ancestry who would father two NFL standouts. In late January 1923, the team barely lost to the Sacramento American Legion five, 28–26. The game, however, was marred by extracurricular violence. One Sacramento player was thrown out for hitting "Matsunaga, the little Japanese, on the All-Stars." Early in February 1923, the California Aggies' five downed the Hawaiians despite Chocolate Chung's good showing. The score was 23–22, and apparently a missed free throw by Chocolate Chung proved crucial.[20]

In early February, the Fresno State College squad had to come from behind to beat the Hawaiians, 26–22. The *Fresno Bee* contended that the visitors' speed and deception surprised the Fresnans. The key to Fresno State's victory was that the Californians were eventually able to "smother ... diminutive Choc Chung," who, the *Bee* acknowledged, possessed "remarkable shooting and ball handling skills."[21]

After barnstorming California, the team was scheduled to journey to the Pacific Northwest. However, the *Portland Oregonian's* L. H. Gregory announced that the Hawaiians had to cancel their remaining games because of mounting injuries. Gregory regretted that the barnstormers were beset by one broken nose, one broken ankle, one sprained thigh, one cracked wrist, and bruises too numerous to mention.[22]

Significantly, team star Chocolate Chung was more formally known as Walter M. S. Chung; he would subsequently attend medical school at the University of Chicago and show up in the 1930 U.S. census manuscripts as a physician. A census taker in the Windy City found a Hawaiian-born "Chinese" physician named Walter M. S. Chung at Chicago's Memorial Hospital. Walter M. S. Chung must have soon thereafter moved back to Hawai'i, where his name would appear in the manuscripts as a physician in Honolulu, living with his Chinese immigrant parents.[23]

Ostensibly amateur barnstorming Hawaiian squads toured North America in the late 1930s. In November 1936, a team of Hawaiian hoopsters set sail for Vancouver. Swanee Pang was one of these athletes. The ship's manifest described him as a 25-year-old "Corean," working as a laborer for a naval shipyard. Chew Chong Ching, Wah Chan Goo, Edward Akau, and Walter Wong were also on board. All were identified as "Chinese" and thus subject to particular scrutiny, even though they were U.S. citizens. Chew Chong Ching was described as a 24-year-old clerk. Wah Chan Goo, probably Ah Chew Goo in actuality, was an 18-year-old laborer. The 24-year-old Wong was a bus operator, while Edward Akau labored as a 22-year-old clerk. The fact that all these young men possessed lower-, middle-, or working-class backgrounds suggest that they perhaps did not compete over an extended period of time, quite a long way from home, without some kind of renumeration.[24]

After arriving in Vancouver, the Hawaiians made their way down to the states. In December 1936, the *Portland Oregonian* reported that the city's Mantle Club downed the visitors, 51–47. Walter Wong led the losers with 18 points, while Goro Moriguchi racked up 16. The next month saw the Hawaiians in San Antonio, where they decisively beat the Simpson aggregation, 50–36.[25]

Acknowledging the team as the "Hawaiian All-Stars," the *Chinese Digest* recognized them among its athletes of the month in January 1937. The *Digest* pointed out that the Hawaiians had done well in the Pacific Northwest, downing a Portland Y team, 30–20. The *Digest* praised the performances of not only Chinese Hawaiians such as Captain Walter Wong, Ah Chew Goo, and Chew Chong Ching, but Nikkei Goro Moriguchi.[26]

In 1937, Ah Chew Goo, Chew Chong Ching, Takeo Goya, and Goro Moriguchi got in trouble with the AAU for extending their tour beyond 30 days after their Hawaiian contingent arrived on the West Coast. To be sure, the Hawaiians kept fairly busy in the Southwest. In December, the Hardin-Simmons five barely beat the visitors, 33–29. Before the game, an Abilene newspaper published a photograph of Chew Chong Ching. The caption described Ching as a forward and assistant coach. To prove the Hawaiians were good, the *Abilene Reporter News* informed readers that the Hawaiians had just downed the University of New Mexico Aggies, 52–45. The promotional piece depicted the visitors as "clever natives from the Pacific isle." Yet it also emphasized the lack of size on the squad. Goro Moriguchi was but five foot seven; at five foot three, Ah Chew Goo and John Wong were even shorter, while Takeo Goya was a relative giant at five foot seven. After the game, the *Reporter News* expressed admiration for the Hawaiians. Ah Chew Goo was "especially clever" and led the team in scoring with 11 points. Goro Moriguchi hit a key basket to tie the score and wound up with eight points, as did Chew Chong Ching.[27]

Chew Chong Ching and his name seemed to inspire Orientalist efforts at perhaps gentle wit. In January 1937, columnist Hugh Bradley remarked, "Among the stars of a Hawaiian basketball team now touring the states is a gent prettily entitled Chew Chong Ching." In December 1937, the *Albuquerque News* reported to readers that Chew Chong Ching and his teammates were heading their way. Alluding to the New Deal's Civilian Conservation Corp, the *News*, moreover, assured them that the hoopster "doesn't represent a C.C.C. camp."[28]

The Mainland

Adult Asian Californians dribbled, passed, and defended for various levels of amateur basketball in the Golden State. J. and D. Gibino were teammates of Ichishita on an aggregation sponsored by San Jose's Gibino Meats in the early 1930s. In Southern California, Kim played for the Press-Enterprise five in Riverside in December 1932. Identified as a "former [Cal] Bear star" by the *Berkeley Daily Gazette*, Ted Ohashi performed for an East Bay squad sponsored by J. F. Hinks and Son. The occasion was an upcoming game between the Hinks and St. Mary's College. Early in 1936, the *Chinese Digest* disclosed that June Lau was the only Chinese American female taking part in the Southern California Basketball Tournament. She played on a team sponsored by Southwest Cafe. According to a list of registered voters in Los Angeles, June Lau worked as a secretary in 1938, lived on Lucretia Avenue, and was a registered Democrat. A quintet called Numbers participated in the Sacramento Church League in 1938. Several Anglo names appear in the box score of the game in which this team conquered a Chinese American squad, 51–29. However, the Numbers could also boast of two Lums and one Fong on the roster. Interestingly, a fellow surnamed Nakamura refereed a Sacramento Church League game between the Chinese and the First Baptists. In January 1942, the *Fresno Bee* reported that H. Zenimura tallied 12 points for the Artistige Club a month before Roosevelt's Executive Order 9066 was issued.[29]

Outside of California, Asian American hoopsters crossed racial and cultural barriers to play independent amateur basketball. In New England in 1909, Ah Chung gained press attention as a "Chinese ... basketball star" for the Peabody Athletic Association. The *Boston Journal* reported that Peabody had lost a game to the Winthrop Yacht Club team, but Ah Chung impressed with his shooting. In 1923, the *Brooklyn Standard Union* informed readers that "Hus Song, the well-known Chinese forward from San Francisco," had joined the local Devil Dogs squad.[30]

While in the military, Asian Americans played intercultural hoops during World War II. A couple of months before the Pearl Harbor bombing, the *Rockford Morning Star* revealed that "players of Japanese descent can beat Americans in basketball, strictly an American sport." That is, two Japanese American soldiers, Tahoe Suzita and Frank Arawaka, had taken first and tied for second place, respectively, in a free throw shooting contest. Suzita had won, nailing 42 out of 50 shots. Arakawa made 41 shots. Ruth Chan Jang was a Chinese San Franciscan stationed with the Women's Army Corps in Georgia. There, she competed on a service team. She recalled for historian Judy Yung, "I was the only Chinese on the basketball team and all the other teams we played were white...."

I was very active and loved playing basketball." The remarkable Buck Lai Jr., a son of a Chinese Hawaiian father and a European American mother, played basketball for Pensacola Naval Station in Florida during World War II. Lai had previously gained notoriety as a baseball player for Long Island University.[31]

While in New York City, Japanese American hoopsters encountered something of a cosmopolitan canopy during World War II. Yet they were not so lucky in nearby Seabrook, New Jersey, where the Seabrook Farm employed 20 Nisei, three of whom played for the farm's basketball team in 1944. When the Seabrook five showed up to play in Bridgeton, New Jersey, local authorities halted the game when the Nisei were inserted into the lineup.[32]

For much of the twentieth century, Asian American children did not regularly compete with non–Asian Americans on the mainland. Yet it did happen. As early as 1905, the *San Jose Mercury* reported that a "Japanese student" played for Fremont Grammar School in San Francisco. In the Oakland area, Wah Lo was on the Prescott School team in 1927, while Edwin Wong competed on Lincoln High School's eighth grade squad. In the early 1930s, Yan played for Moore Junior High School in the San Jose area. Around the same time, Chan took the court for the 100-pound team representing Burnett Junior High School in San Jose. When the San Pablo All-Stars knocked off Washington for the Berkeley Playground Championship in 1933, Yamamoto played for the victors. Lincoln Junior High in the Sacramento area put out a team in 1938 that included several players with Japanese surnames. In 1944, Myron Lien, Loy Chiu, and Edward Chow competed for an after school team in San Mateo called the Turnbull Pygmies.[33]

Asian Americans played school basketball outside of California during the early decades of the twentieth century. In Helena, Montana, in 1930, Wong performed for Hawthorne School, while Central School was represented by George Wong and Gar Ken Wong. In Ogden, Utah, a young man named Wataru Misaka stood out for Central Junior High in the late 1930s. In mid–February 1939, Misaka scored 16 points against Mount Fort. Moreover, coach Al Worden called Misaka and fellow forward Pete Ramirez "two of the cleverest ball hawks on tap."[34]

Secondary School Hoops on the Islands

On the islands, secondary schools were hard pressed to put together athletic teams without at least a few Hawaiians of Asian descent. There simply were not enough *haoles* and Native Hawaiians around to fill roster spaces. Thus, many Asian Hawaiians and part–Asian Hawaiians made their way on to secondary school basketball teams on the islands.

Like their contemporaries on the mainland, Hawaiian females played interscholastic basketball in the 1890s. An educational institution established for students of indigenous ancestry to propel them out of perceived primitiveness, Kamehameha (Kam) claimed students who were not just "full blooded" Hawaiians but indigenous young people possessing European and Asian ancestry as well. Kam took up athletic competition seriously and, significantly, sponsored girls' basketball before and after the turn of the century. In 1903, the Kam girls' squad beat the YWCA second team. Playing for the victors was Lani Wonghong. In 1905, the *Honolulu Evening Bulletin* claimed that "two Chinese girls" competed for Kam. These girls were Ah Moe Akui and captain Ah Chop Ahui. At other schools, Hawaiian females competed throughout the early decades of the twentieth century. Playing intramural girls' basketball at Kauai High School in the early 1920s were Chiyo Dobashi, Daisy Chang, and Esther Tseu. And later in the 1920s, Rose Ah Ho starred at Kona before she left school.[35]

To be sure, Hawaiian males played secondary school basketball when girls' hoops blossomed in the early twentieth century, and they would continue to play competitive interscholastic basketball when female participation in the sport underwent marginalization. In 1915, Honolulu's St. Louis Preparatory suited up Lam Wing. When St. Louis downed Punahou in early February of 1917, Lam Wing led the way. In the fall of 1917, intramural competition at St. Louis included players such as Lam Wing and King Tan for the sophomores and Fan Luke and Ah Chong for the freshman. In late 1917, the *Star-Bulletin* reported on intramural basketball at Honolulu's Mills Institute. It stated that among the top participants were Kan Leong, Charles Woon, Wah Han, Kelly Kim, and Young Yuen. In June 1921, the Kauai's *Garden Island* reported that two of the islands' sons had lettered in basketball for Mid-Pacific Institute in Honolulu. These young men were S. Kawakami and Kum Lun. In 1922, the Kauai High School squad included two players surnamed Nishimoto, while Hilo High had players such as K. Ching and P. Ching. During the 1940–1941 school year, Maui's Leilehua High had Masao Fukumoto, Koji Ito, Stanley Kim, Jerry Lee, Lionel Lim, Haruo Saifuko, George Shibano, and Tsutae Tomia on the varsity squad.[36]

A public school with a largely working-class and lower-middle-class student body, Honolulu's McKinley High School went up against generally private secondary schools for years. In 1917, an intramural tournament took place at the school and the first-year students came out on top, after beating the seniors for the title. Bob Chung was one of the first-year students' big stars. In 1927, McKinley High School was led by Bert Itoga. At that time, the "Micks" were able to journey to Hilo to play a series of games. Bert Itoga, according to the *Honolulu Star-Bulletin*, served as acting captain. Also on the traveling team were Sik Kum Tsai, Whang Wanj, and Quong Sun. In McKinley's losing effort to

Kam in early February 1927, Dung was high scorer with seven. Itoga and Kim also contributed to whatever success the Micks had.[37]

McKinley High yearbooks in the 1930s reveal the importance of Asian Hawaiians to the school's basketball prowess. The 1931 McKinley yearbook shows a squad with players such as Soo Bok Kim, Earl Lew, Nobu Chiya, and John Sur, as well as Walter Wong and Chew Chong Ching, both of whom would illuminate Hawaiian basketball for many years to come. In 1936, the McKinley varsity five included players surnamed Loui, Sudo, Shimizu, Terado, Matsura, Ohara, Sing, Koo, Kim, Harada, Hosea, Wong, and Izumi, who served as team captain.[38]

Originally founded for children of elite *haoles*, Punahou retained something of a white upper-class bias but became more multiethnic and multiracial in the twentieth century. In Honolulu, Punahou students could play for a Hi-Y team in 1930. Satoru Nishima participated on that squad in addition to playing varsity baseball. The band also organized a basketball team, on which Albert Fong competed. Punahou girls played basketball, too. Marie Achong, the yearbook claimed, played basketball, baseball, and volleyball her first two years but switched her passions to "Home Ec" as she entered her third year. The yearbook wondered what that meant.[39]

Other Honolulu secondary schools were represented by Asian Hawaiians. Originally known as St. Louis College, St. Louis Preparatory, long affiliated with the Catholic Church, was a secondary school that attracted prominent, culturally diverse athletes. When St. Louis downed Mills in early February of 1927, Quan starred. As for Mills, which was once Mid-Pacific Institute, its best players in the game were Eddie Han and Sambo Takahachi.[40]

Hilo High School has long been a repository of legendary Hawaiian basketball. For example, we have already discussed Ah Chew Goo's contributions in the 1930s. Tommy Kaulukukui, a magnificently versatile athlete of mixed Chinese and indigenous descent, played for Hilo High in the 1930s as well. Coached by "Beans" Afook, a revered figure in Hawaiian hoops history, the Hilo five was hailed in the school yearbook for winning its third territorial championship in a row in 1941. Playing for Hilo at that time were Nobu Yamauchi, James Tsui, Harry Hong, Sung Bok Kim, George Izumi, Joe Apao, Shigeo Imada, and Hiromus Doi.[41]

Secondary School Hoops on the Mainland

While housing segregation generally victimized Asian Americans on the mainland before World War II and even after, social spaces existed where they could encounter people from other ethnic groups. High schools served at times as cosmopolitan canopies, especially those schools in urban neighborhoods relatively integrated in terms of race and ethnicity. This hardly meant the high school was a den of sport democracy. Looking beyond the bigotry of many coaches who might have kept Asian Americans off their teams or on their benches, gender and class privileged some over others in prep athletics. By the 1930s, gender served as an effective source of athletic segregation in the high school. For at least half of the twentieth century, males dominated interscholastic basketball, while females were contained within a structure encouraging generally less physically strenuous and intramural basketball. At the same time, working- or lower-middle-class youths in many immigrant communities were less likely to be allowed to participate in school-sponsored extracurricular activities when their parents needed them to help out financially or look after younger siblings.

To be sure, there were perhaps other factors limiting Asian American participation in high school basketball. In 1950, the *Pacific Citizen* lamented that because of their lack of height, few Nisei had competed for high school varsity squads, although the weekly conceded that numerous Nisei had suited up for lightweight and junior varsity teams. Much the same could have been said for other mainland Asian American hoopsters in mid-twentieth-century America. And though unacknowledged at this time by the *Pacific Citizen*, racism played a role. There is no way of knowing how often racially biased coaches discouraged Asian American participation, but we do know that racialized immigration restriction meant that there was a limited number of Asian Americans to take up roster spaces on high school squads compared to European American hoopsters.[42]

Varsity Hoops

The kingpins of high school basketball were the boys who made the varsity team. Earlier in the twentieth century, the term *unlimited* was used to distinguish these hoopsters from those who competed for teams composed of smaller or less skilled players. While Asian American varsity competition was relatively circumscribed for many years on the mainland, it was prolific enough to force me to geographically organize these and other sections regarding secondary school hoops. I will start with San Francisco and then work my way throughout California. Then, I will move eastward toward the Atlantic Coast.

Well before World War II, Asian Americans in San Francisco and Oakland took part in varsity high school hoops. Indeed, even before World War I the *San Francisco Evening Post* told readers about "Fujita, the plucky little Japanese" who played forward for Lowell High School. This was probably Henry Fujita, who subsequently became a champion flycaster in California. He informed the *Tanforan Totalizer*, a newspaper published in the Japanese American assembly center in the Bay Area during the early months after Executive Order 9066 was issued, that he made "all-state" while playing for Lowell. In 1919, the *San Francisco Chronicle* reported that Hasegawa starred for Poly High against Lowell as well as against Lick-Wilmerding. In December 1930, Leong performed well for San Francisco's Commerce High against San Mateo's Sequoia High. The *Chronicle* complimented Walter Tong, forward for St. Ignatius High School, as "a capable scorer" in 1931. In Oakland in the early 1930s, Chin was a forward for Oakland's McClymonds High and Saito played for University High. San Francisco's Poly High had guards Min Ichiyasu, Nishamura, and Hong Wong on its varsity teams in the mid–1930s. Indeed, Hong Wong, in 1936, was praised by the *Chronicle* and named third team all-city.[43]

The first half of the 1940s witnessed more Asian American varsity hoopsters in San Francisco. Jimmy Wong and Mits Kojimoto played for Commerce High School. When Commerce dumped Lincoln, sportswriter Bob Stevens said Kojimoto's provided the needed momentum. Stevens, moreover, called Jimmy Wong the "stocky … Chinese sharpshooter." Playing with Wong during the 1941–1942 season was a Japanese San Franciscan, "slender Tommy Yoshitomi." When, in early March 1942, Commerce barely lost to Sacred Heart, Yoshitomi came off the bench to spell an injured Wong. He wound up racking up 14 points to help Commerce. Meanwhile, "tiny Tommy Lew, 118-pound Chinese forward" stood out for Lowell against Commerce in January 1941. A couple of months later "tiny Tommy Lew, Lowell's half-pint," according to Stevens, hit three long shots and scored eight points to keep his team in the game against George Washington. During the 1941–1942 season, Lowell suited up "little Pete Lum." Also during World War II, Galileo played Kay Wong and Willie Chang.[44]

South of San Francisco, Asian Americans took up varsity hoops. In 1930, Palo Alto High was represented by Saito as a forward, and Frank Ichishita played forward for San Jose High. The *San Jose Mercury* dubbed Ichishita "the Japanese boy." A few years later, M. Takata was on San Jose High's unlimited squad. Around the same time, Inagi was on Salinas High School varsity in the early 1930s and Nakayama competed as an alternate on the Palo Alto varsity team. The school's yearbook said he played as much as the starters. San Mateo High suited up Kay Yama in the early 1930s. The San Mateo High School's 1933 yearbook described "Captain Yama" as "the most elusive, dynamic player on the San Mateo squad." He was a unanimous all-league choice. In 1935, Kawamoto competed for Campbell High in Santa Clara County, while at nearby

Fremont High in Sunnyvale Takaki played varsity basketball during the 1936–1937 season.[45]

California's Central Valley has long been the site of extensive Asian American male varsity high school competitors. In the late 1920s, Ted Ohashi starred for Stockton High School before heading to Cal. An all-around athlete who was eventually named to the Stockton High School's Hall of Fame, Ohashi helped lead the school to a state championship in 1928. Nevertheless, because of Ohashi presence on the team, one opponent refused to play Stockton. Ohashi's coach, Pete Lenz, insisted that his team would not participate without him. As it turned, the game was played with the Nisei in the lineup.[46]

Ohashi may have been the most famous of Central Valley Asian American prep hoopsters before World War II's end, but there were several others. Foon Kai Kee performed for Dinuba High School in Tulare County in 1919. Ray Wong played for Stockton High a few years after Ohashi. In 1930, the *Oakland Tribune* informed readers that Sacramento's Courtland High was not only good but "cosmopolitan." Its lineup included two Chinese Americans and one Japanese American to go along with an "Irishman" and a "Swede." Forwards George Chew and Fred Gunn were the Chinese Americans, while Ted Shironaka played guard. In 1934, Grass Valley High School had William Wong on its basketball roster. In 1935, George Kawamura played varsity basketball for Courtland. Jack Oshita started at guard for Sacramento High in the late 1930s. Charles Mayeda also started for Grant High around the same time, while George Mayeda came off the bench, and Frank Kebo played varsity hoops for Fresno High. Livingston High had H. Kajioka on varsity during the 1940–1941 season, and Fresno's Washington High could claim the services of Tokomoto during the 1941–1942 season.[47]

The vast Los Angeles County nurtured several Asian American varsity competitors before World War II. Gardena High's varsity squad had a Morita during the 1928–1929 season. During the 1929–1930 season, Onishi suited up for Lincoln High. Fremont High School played Sato in 1935. That same year, Murakami and Wong were varsity starters for Lincoln High, while Fukuyama played for Los Angeles High in 1936. The starting lineup for El Monte High on January 22, 1937, included Inouye. Poly had Kawabe on its roster in January 1937, while Okada starred for Narbonne. And Frank Dong and Eddie Kwong were regulars on Belmont High School's team in the late 1930s.[48]

Art Kaihatsu and Tatsuro Kaku were probably the best of Japanese Americans cavorting on Los Angeles High School basketball courts in the years immediately preceding U.S. entry into World War II. According to Hollywood High School's 1940 yearbook, Art Kaihatsu was a "speedy forward" and Nishibayashi was his teammate. The five-foot-eight Kaihatsu made all-league first team, averaging over ten points per game in league play. The Helms Athletic Foundation's press release noted Kaihatsu was known best for his scoring, but it was his all-around skills that made him an all-leaguer. The 1940 edition of Hollywood High's yearbook traced some of Kaihatsu's contributions. When Hollywood High beat Wilson, he led all scorers with 13. Notching 17 points, he was high scorer as Hollywood conquered Belmont. Against Marshall, Kaihatsu's 15 points contributed to Hollywood's victory. The *Los Angeles Times* tried to pay tribute to Kaihatsu's performance against Marshall, calling him a "Nipponese ace." The newspaper admired the "ball handling and smooth floor … work and relaxed shooting of catlike Art Kaihatsu." And when Belmont beat Hollywood, Kaihatsu tallied 11 points. Tatsuro Kaku shared all-league honors with Kaihatsu. The five-foot-seven guard from Lincoln did not score much, averaging two points per game in league play. But the Helms' press release maintained, "Kaku, although small, was a thorn in the side of every team that he faced. The little Lincoln guard held many of the best scorers in the Northern League in check." During that same season, "Taji Hirayama, diminutive Gardena forward" led all scorers when his team lost to Tarzana. Subsequently, Hirayama scored 13 for Gardena High in a losing effort to El Segundo.[49]

Southern California Asian American varsity hoopsters bobbed up outside of Los Angeles. Kim played for Riverside High School in 1932. In Orange County, K. Sahara was on Garden Grove's varsity team in 1935. Down in San Diego County, Sweetwater High beat La Jolla High in overtime, 17–14, in 1934. Playing for the losers was Yamaguchi.[50]

Asian Americans participated in boys' varsity basketball in other regions. Indeed, maybe some of the more respected names in the history of Asian American basketball belong to non-Californians. For example, few Asian American athletes of the past merit more esteem than Bill Kajikawa. During the early 1930s, Bill Kajikawa captained the Phoenix High School squad in Arizona. Also playing football and baseball at Phoenix High, Kajikawa later remembered, "Sports was a great vehicle for me because I could meet people and fit in…. I was the first Japanese-American to play sports at Phoenix Union and I enjoyed it."[51]

In the Pacific Northwest, Garfield, located in a relatively multicultural area of Seattle, was well represented by Asian American varsity hoopsters. Art Louie, according to the *Chinese Digest* in late January 1936, was one of the few Chinese Americans to play "unlimited basketball" when he starred as a forward for Garfield. In 1938, George Okamura played for the school. A few years later, Garfield's Al Mar and Phil Mar Hing were called by Seattle's *Post-Intelligencer* "two clever Chinese maple courters" in the early 1940s. When Garfield downed

West Seattle, 25–15, in January 1941, the *Post-Intelligencer* pointed out that "little Al Mar" tallied ten points. A week later, "little Al Mar bombarded the Roosevelt basket with uncanny accuracy," winding up with 15 points. On January 25, the *Post-Intelligencer* acclaimed "little Al Mar's ... left wing howitzer" that heaved in 15 points and helped Garfield edge Lincoln. In March 1941, the *Seattle Times* honored Al Mar as one of the best prep performers of the week. Mar's 16 points aided Garfield in conquering Ballard High. Bill Yanagamachi and a young man surnamed Wong, moreover, played on the same five as Mar and Mar Hing.[52]

Historian Shelly Sang-Hee Lee points out that even though Mar, Mar Hing, and Yanagamachi played on the same team, the *Seattle Post-Intelligencer* unfortunately connected them to the bitter war taking place in Asia between Japan and China: "With the Japanese and Chinese at each other's throats in the Orient, there's also an 'all-out' fight on being staged right in the high school basketball league." Yet the *Post-Intelligencer* also published a photograph of Garfield's coach giving tips to his team. The players, including all three Asian Americans, had their arms around one another. By the 1941–1942 season, Mar and Mar Hing had graduated, but Suzuki and Hata joined Yanagimichi in the Garfield five.[53]

Other high schools in the Pacific Northwest and West used Asian American varsity hoopsters. In Seattle, a hoopster surnamed Kono played for Franklin High in the early 1920s. Paul Hiyama was on Seattle's Queen Anne five before Nikkei evacuation. In a losing game against Lincoln, Hiyama still managed to score 13 points. A few days later, Hiyama left the court with 15 points against West Seattle. According to the school's 1941 yearbook, Hiyama was the team's second-highest scorer. Around the same time, Shig Murao played for Broadway High in Seattle. After Broadway dumped Cleveland in mid–January, the *Post-Intelligencer* observed, "little Shig Murao ... held down taller opponents." When Broadway downed Queen Anne in late January, the *Post-Intelligencer* praised Murao's contribution. John Okomoto also played for Broadway. After he notched 18 points against Roosevelt, he made the *Seattle Times'* honor roll. Seattle's all-city team for the 1940–1941 season, indeed, reflected Asian American contributions. Al Mar was on the first team, but Phil Mar Hing, Shig Murao, and Paul Hiyama received honorable mention.

In the Portland area, Paul Wong was on Commerce High's five in 1918. Also in Portland, Tokomoto suited up for St. Johns in 1941. An adept Chinese American hoopster named Fred Lee was a standout for Astoria High during the early years of World War II, and George Saito lettered for three years at Salem High. Somewhat to the east, Shake Ushio was on a championship South Cottonwood High team in Utah during the early 1930s. Also in Utah, Wat Misaka stood out on the Ogden High squad. During the early stages of his varsity career, Misaka scored one point against Weber in a game in mid–January 1940. The next year, Misaka earned recognition as second team, all-divison.[54]

Young men of Asian ancestry played secondary school hoops east of the Rockies during the first decades of the twentieth century. Early in 1915, the *Philadelphia Public Ledger* asserted that Kohl Am Wee illuminated Leonia High School hoops. Described as a popular student and an all-around athlete, he scored 16 points in a game against Hackensack. During the mid–1920s, Illinois' *Rockford Republic* announced that Toy Kwan, "full-blooded Chinese star" was on Wheaton High School's squad. The *Republic* pointed out that he had been in the United States for three years but "surpasses many of his Anglo-Saxon companions" academically and athletically. Reportedly, he had learned basketball while living in Tientsin. In the late 1920s, an athlete named Nakagawa competed for Roosevelt High in New York City. During the mid–1930s, Lum Yee, who apparently hailed from San Francisco, played forward for Richmond Academy in Augusta, Georgia. The *Augusta Chronicle* described him as a "Chinese youth." In Cleveland, Central High School suited up a lineup in 1939 comprised of a "Chinese, a Negro, an Italian, a Serbian, and an Irishman."[55]

During World War II, Japan's brutal occupation of the Philippines and Filipinos' valiant resistance elicited a sometimes patronizing sympathy from Americans. Thus, the *Boston Herald*'s Ralph Wheeler proclaimed that "Johnny Paredes gallantry in making varsity at Cambridge Latin reflected the courage of Filipino people." To Wheeler, Paredes was a "little Filipino" who became the first freshman to win a spot on the varsity. In the process, "little Johnny" showed the courage of his "race" when he continued to play a game after receiving a kick in the face. The next year, the *Herald* displayed a photograph of Paredes along with his Cambridge Latin teammates. The caption hailed Cambridge Latin for stopping Brookline's six-game winning streak.[56]

Nonvarsity Hoopsters

In the previous section, we explored the participation of Asian American boys in varsity or unlimited basketball. However, those boys either too young, too short, too slim, or too incapable of playing elite high school basketball had opportunities to represent their schools in basketball, especially during the middle third of the twentieth century. And wherever one found a large concentration of Asian American students, one could find them playing nonvarsity basketball, and frequently very well.

San Francisco nurtured an abundance of nonvarsity Asian American basketball players before the end of World War II. Three schools, Lowell, Commerce, and Galileo, especially suited up several of such athletes, many of whom were quite good despite their lack of size. In 1913, the *San Francisco Chronicle* noted the presence of Aoki on Lowell High School's 100-pounders. Six years later, *Chronicle* readers could come across Koba and Tagasaki on Lowell's 110-pound team and Tegesawa on the 100-pound squad.[57]

Not far from San Francisco's Chinatown, Commerce High suited up plenty of Asian American lightweights. The 1916 yearbook of the High School of Commerce declared that a young man named Wong was one of the stars of the 110-pound team. In the mid–1920s, Harry and Willie Wong won letters on Commerce High's 110-pound team. Eng competed on the lightweight squad in the late 1930s. In 1941, the Commerce High School yearbook asserted that Vince Shijo was the 110-pound squad's highest scorer and Cyril Jeung was team captain, while George Yamamura, Billy Louie, and Albert Yee did well for the 120-pounders. When Commerce dumped Sacred Heart in March 1942, Filipino Frank "Babe" Samson scored 14 points for Commerce. Furthermore, he was named to the all-city lightweight team in 1942. Samson, one of the league's scoring leaders, gained some fame later with the Mango five. And as the war was heading for a bloody resolution on both fronts in February 1945, "little Sau Chin" helped Commerce beat Lincoln by hitting key baskets. "Slim Gil McDougald," future infielder for Casey Stengel's New York Yankees, was Chin's teammate.[58]

Galileo High, also not too far from Chinatown, enrolled several Asian American hoopsters. Future Hong Wah Kue professional Fred Gok was on the 130-pound team in 1933. Kaneko also played lightweight hoops for Galileo in the mid–1930s. When Galileo's lightweights clubbed Balboa, 38–18, in 1937, Bob Stevens praised the play of Wong and Lee, whom he described as "two little Chinese boys." Stevens, in 1942, identified "little Richie Tong" as one of Galileo's 130-pound stars. The leading lightweight scorer in San Francisco in 1942, Tong was named to the all-city team. When his team took down St. Ignatius, 30–24, Tong scored 13 points. His teammate, Miyahara, added nine. George Lum was a 120-pounder in 1944. The next year, Frank Chui and Frank Lum were 120-pounders for Galileo.[59]

At other San Francisco High schools, smaller Asian American boys also enjoyed interscholastic basketball. In the late 1930s, Frank Yano and Fee Yee were 130-pounders for Poly. In early March 1941, Bob Stevens told readers that Charlie Chin tallied 11 points to lead George Washington to a victory over Lowell. A few years later, Percy Chu stood out on the 110-pound squad for Washington. At Mission, Michie Yoshimura was a lightweight in 1941, making the all-city five for his weight division.[60]

In the fog-bound city, lightweight basketball in the 1930s was illuminated by the supreme performances of Robert, often known as "Benny," Lum. Competing as a 120-pounder in the fall of 1937, "Robert Lum, Chinese star" led Sacred Heart to a victory over South San Francisco High. Early in 1938, the *San Francisco Chronicle* acquainted readers with "little Benny Lum, Sacred Heart's Chinese sensation." Indeed, one suspects that few lightweights anywhere got the press attention accorded Lum, especially by the *Chronicle*'s Bob Stevens, who, in mid–January 1938, called the Chinese American "the latest sensation of the courts." A venerated San Francisco sportswriter in the mid- to late twentieth century, the then youthful Stevens, upon watching the "105 pound ... five-foot-one-inch Chinese forward," proclaimed that he "jumped higher, sank baskets further out, and passed harder than any player on the court." Called "Egg Foo Lum" by Stevens, the hoopster consistently inspired the sportswriter's praise: "It is seldom a lightweight basketball star stands a crowd on its ear with a sensational court effort but when a wee little mite of a Chinese boy ... took the court ... the exception to the rule was born." After Sacred Heart scored a lightweight victory over Mission, 33–24, Stevens wrote of Lum, "To say he is the most remarkable little player in the lightweight loop this season is putting it mildly. Even taking the unlimited division into consideration, Lum stands out as the find of the season."[61]

Some years later, Willie Wong shook up San Francisco's lightweight basketball in the months before V-E Day. In mid–January, the *Chronicle*'s Bob Marcus informed readers that Polytechnic's "Bill Wong" had made the *San Francisco Chronicle*'s lightweight honor roll. Late in January, Marcus wrote, "Bill Wong, the clever Parrot forward, set a new high in the division, hitting nineteen points," as Poly beat St. Ignatius, 31–19. Bob Stevens, moreover, extolled "Willy Wong, tiny Poly lightweight, leading 130-pound scorer." A highlight of Wong's season had to have been the game in which he outdueled his rival for league scoring honors in late February by racking up 14 points to his rival's eight.[62]

In counties surrounding San Francisco, Asian American nonvarsity hoopsters crossed cultural sidelines to compete with and against young men of other racial and ethnic groups. The *San Francisco Evening News* reported in 1918 that "Iki a Japanese boy ... has developed into a star" for Berkeley High's 120-pound team. When Napa High School's lightweights defeated Berkeley High in 1926, "Chew, a Chinese player" was the big star for the losers, according to the *Oakland Tribune*. In 1931, Yamamoto led all scorers with ten points as his Berkeley High B team downed Richmond, 25–21. A couple of years later, Hiro Katayama was hailed as the MVP of Berkeley High's B team in 1933. To the south of San Francisco, San Mateo High School's 130-pound team was captained in February 1933 by Sike Yama. In defeating Sequoia High, a San Mateo newspaper reported, the San Mateo High team was sparked by Yama, who seemed involved in every key offensive play for the victors. In 1942, the *San Francisco Chronicle*'s Douglas Guy identified John Young as "the fighting Chinese" star of Burlingame High's lightweight five.[63]

In Santa Clara County, Mountain View and San Jose High Schools consistently suited up several nonvarsity Asian Americans in the 1930s, 1940s, and beyond. Yoshida was a lightweight player for Mountain View High School during the early 1930s. Harry Kiyomura played for Mountain View in 1937. As thousands of Japanese Americans faced relocation on the West Coast, Izu and Hoshita still managed to represent Mountain View early in 1942.[64]

Across the county, Asian Americans played nonvarsity hoops for San Jose High. Yoshioka was on B squad during the 1930–1931 academic year, while Okagaki was on the C team. Sakamoto captained the D team, which included Chow and Ichishita. A couple of years later, Jio, Kifune, and Kita played D hoops, while Yoshioka, Lee, Ichishita, and Captain Sakamoto were on the C squad. In the mid–1930s, James Okita and George Yamaoka were on the B team. Harry Lee captained the C team, which included Mitsu Ishikawa and star George Hinaga, who also excelled in baseball. The D team was captained by Vic Hirose. Sal Jio, at the same time, captained the lightweight team in 1935. In 1940, Wong starred on the 110-pound squad, while Chi Akizuki led the 120-pounders. And during the 1941–1942 basketball season, Frank Mouri, Fred Morita, Shioki Hioki, and Ed Hagihara competed for the 110-pounders, while Frank Yoshioka and Yoshi Minato starred on the 120-pound team, on which Izumi Kawakami, William Morita, and Shig Suyeishi also played.[65]

Other Santa Clara County high schools were represented by Asian Americans in nonvarsity hoops. Nishita was on Campbell High's B team in the mid–1920s. Fremont High School in Sunnyvale suited up Higuchi during the 1932–1933 season. Two hoopsters named Imamura played as 130-pounders for Los Gatos High in the early 1930s. In 1937, Imada, Yoshioka, and Kawayoshi dribbled and passed for San Jose Tech's 130-pound team. Fuji suited up for Campbell High in the late 1930s as a 130-pounder, while Live Oak was represented by Jimmy Nishioka and Okida. And during the 1939–1940 school year, Ray Kawamoto played junior varsity hoops for Campbell, while the school suited up lightweights Kazuo Uchiyama, Roy Uyeda, and Tom Tomihara .[66]

In Santa Cruz and Monterey Counties, Asian Americans played lightweight hoops for Salinas High. According to the school's 1941 yearbook, Kay Matsushita captained a lightweight five, while. T. Nakasaki and D. Chinn also played lightweight hoops. In the months after Pearl Harbor was attacked, Tony Nakasaki co-captained the lightweights. Also on the team were Dick Yee and Henry Chin. After the 1941–1942 basketball season ended, Santa Cruz High's

Tom Otsuki was honored as a member of the league's first team. Takamoto from Monterey and Kong from Watsonville earned second team honors. Salinas High School's 1945 yearbook points out that Filipino Sammy Garcia co-captained a lightweight squad and made the all-league team. G. Fong was Garcia's teammate.[67]

California's Central Valley high schools had numerous Asian Americans on their nonvarsity fives. In the late 1920s, Sacramento High suited up Eugene Nakagawa and Donald Kitazumi on the B squad. Wong wore a Stockton High uniform on the B team in 1929. Livingston High's C squad had Yenokida in 1932. In 1935, George Kumamoto won a letter for playing B basketball for Sacramento's Grant High School. In the same city around the same time, B basketball performers D. Sato and T. Mizuno won letters, while H. Kusunoki earned a letter for C basketball at Galt High. Sukumoto and Yasukawa competed for Elk Grove's B team in the late 1930s while Lincoln High's C team possessed K. Hada, S. Hada, Kaneko, and "Fugioka." At Lodi High toward the end of the 1930s, there were two Hiramotos on the B team and one Hiramoto on the C team during the same school year. Vacaville High's B team had Furuya, Inai, and Fujimoto. Inouye played for Stockton High's B team. Woodland High, meanwhile, suited up Yorio Aoki and Michio Nagasaki, as well as Tanaka. S. Yamada and M. Yamada competed for McClatchy High's C team. In the Fresno area in the late 1930s, Tsurukoa starred on Fresno High's B team. Tachino, Chingkow, Sandongi, Kunitaki, and Kuwamoto played C hoops. A few years later, Fong was on Fresno High's B team. According to the school's 1941 yearbook, Okawara and Nakamoto played on the C team as well. Meanwhile, Livingston High's B team had J. Hamaguchi, J. Kimoto, A. Noda, and F. Kajioka during the 1940–1941 season. In the 1941–1942 season Kinoshita and Goto played "middleweight" basketball for Madera High School, while Ichiba did the same for Fresno High.[68]

In nonvarsity basketball, Southern California proved just as inclusive as Northern California. In 1923, Iwamizu played lightweight basketball for Polytechnic in Los Angeles. Gardena High School was represented by Japanese American lightweights during the 1928–1929 academic year. Tateshi Yamaguchi stood out for the C team, while Nakayama came off the bench. Sam Ishihara was a stellar performer for the D team, on which Ito and Tsunami also played. The next year, Lincoln High's C team included Kenneth Ung, Paul Yazaki, Joe Mitsuhashi, and Joe Itano; Frank Takahashi competed on Long Beach's Poly High B team. During the mid–1930s in Los Angeles, Jack Tagawa was on Roosevelt's B team. F. Hirota and S. Hirota played B basketball for Franklin, along with Ito. Shigekawa, meanwhile, was on Jefferson's B squad. At Downey High, Umemoto suited up as a lightweight. Kashiwagi played C hoops for Los Angeles's

Belmont High in the early 1930s, and in the late 1930s "Itch" Taniguchi starred on Belmont High School's B team. Kenji Taniguchi and James Urata were on the C team, while Tara Mishima, Geoge Harada, and Isao Hara were on the D team, captained by Takashi Senzaki. Eddie Okisaki played C basketball for Hollywood High School in 1939. Moreover, the Hollywood High yearbook called Art Kaihatsu a "high scoring guard" for the C team. The next year, Art Kaihatsu was promoted to the B team, for which he made a last-minute shot to dump Dorsey. Perhaps not coincidentally, the Hollywood High yearbook called him once again a "high scoring guard." Wayne Tokuhisa also lettered on the Hollywood High C team.[69]

Outside of California, smaller, younger, or less skilled Asian Americans played interscholastic basketball. Seattle's Broadway High had Isaac Yamaoka and Bennie Eng on its sophomore team, while Toshi Tsukono played for the freshman squad in 1924. Four years later, the school's yearbook pronounced Okada and Sasaki as stars on the sophomore five. In 1934, Siquo Oshide lettered for Broadway's second team. Captain Stan Karikomi and Ray Obazawa led Broadway's second team in the 1936–1937 season. Pete Yoshitomi and Bob Nakasoni were also on the squad. Frank Watanabe, Toshi Hirabayashi, and Ikuo Yoshino played for the sophomore five, while Yukio Imada suited up for the freshmen. Also in Seattle, Garfield High's 1933 freshman-sophomore squad included Kazuko Tokoyama and Tsumeko Yorita. Bob Hosokawa and Art Louie competed on the "second team." Ken Louie and Tochiyuki Nishimura were on Garfield High's second team in 1938. In Oregon, the talented Fred Lee apprenticed on Astoria High's junior varsity five during the 1940–1941 season.[70]

Girls' Basketball

Whereas boys could compete in interscholastic basketball for much of the twentieth century, young women, often organized into athletic associations, partook of intramural basketball typically formed along school class lines. To be fair, however, female hoopsters frequented "Play Days," organized competition against other schools. They mostly played the six-on-a-side game created to limit female exhaustion and injuries. A photograph of Gardena High's championship girls' team in 1929 displayed several Asian faces, but no names. Playing for Livingston High's senior intramural team in 1932 was a young woman named Eiko Masuda. San Francisco's Galileo High School was home to many Asian American female hoopsters in the early to mid–1930s. Among those listed as basketball players in the 1932 yearbook were Toshiko Kitano, Seo

Kikuye, Kimiko Amano, Toshiko Shikuzawa, Bessie Kitano, May Morioka, Agnes Kusimine, Shizuko Moto, Chiyo Takatochi, and Misako Kitano. The 1934 Galileo High School yearbook reveals that in the fall of 1933, basketball was the most popular girls' sport. May Morioka and Agnes Kusimine participated on the senior class team. During the same academic year, Yamada played advanced basketball at Fresno High. In Chico, California, a young lady surnamed Matsura played GAA basketball during the 1934–1935 academic year. The next year at Chico, Wakayo Miyasako and Satsuko Suyehiro competed in GAA basketball. In San Jose in the mid–1930s, Helen Tokunaga managed the senior GAA basketball team, while Leah Tokunaga and Tatsuye Suyeishi served as team captains. Later in the decade, Bernice Hinaga, who belonged to a Japanese American family well known for their athletic proclivities, played basketball at San Jose High School. In Sacramento, a couple of unnamed young women with Asian faces appeared in photographs of girls' basketball teams displayed in McClatchy High School's 1939 yearbook. During the 1939–1940 school year, Lilly Takemoto, Evelyn Yoshida, and Mary Nakagawa were active hoopsters at Campbell High. According to Fresno High's 1941 yearbook, Ono played "intermediate basketball." San Jose High's 1942 yearbook is interesting, given that Executive Order 9066 was proclaimed in February 1941. It shows photographs of girls' basketball teams competing in the fall of 1941. Several Asian faces appear in these photographs. However, the photograph of the spring teams displays only a couple of Asian faces.[71]

Outside of California, Asian American girls participated in secondary school basketball. In the 1930s, the *Chinese Digest* pointed out that Lalun Chin had captained and starred for Beaverton High School's girls' team. Hasegawa competed in GAA basketball at Seattle's Broadway High in 1937. Basketball attracted the efforts of Minnie Yokoyama, Amy Hidaka, and Tayeko Kurimura at Seattle's Garfield High in the late 1930s. A couple of years later, M. Miyauchi, M. Kumagi, Y. Akagi, M. Matsumoto, and N. Sikiguchi took up the sport at Queen Anne High in Seattle.[72]

Many of us like to think we are substantially more cosmopolitan today than those who came before us. However, the experiences of Asian Americans in intercultural basketball more than 70 years ago demonstrate that people were able, at least occasionally, to look beyond racial and ethnic distinctions. Asian Americans were given a chance to participate in varsity and nonvarsity hoops. A few were even honored as team captains and all-leaguers. "Racism's traveling eye" still stalked Asian Americans. But if they were good enough and their teammates and coaches at least willing to put aside bigotry in the hopes of victory, they might find themselves smiling in basketball uniforms on the pages of some American high school yearbooks.

CHAPTER 4

Crossing Sidelines, 1945–1965

Thanks to World War II and the Cold War, as well as the efforts of the Civil Rights Movement, institutionalized racism and nativism took some jarring hits in the 1940s, 1950s, and 1960s. Thus, Asian American hoopsters were, if anything, more prominent in basketball than before World War II. Still, the decades witnessed the male domination of the game, most notably at the secondary school level, where highly competitive, interscholastic female basketball was generally but, as we will find out, not totally shunned.

Hawai'i

After World War II, Ah Chew Goo continued to influence Hawaiian basketball. In 1948, he coached the Bank of Hawaii quintet. In 1950, he and Bill Choy ran a Young Buddhist Association Basketball Clinic in March. The *Hawaii Herald* dubbed Chew and Choy "two cage artists." In 1951, Ah Chew Goo headed up an all-star team to oppose the visiting Harlem Globetrotters. Described by the *Honolulu Star-Bulletin* as "once the darling of Hawaiian basketball," Goo would also play in the game along with other Hawaiian notables, such as Bill Choy, Alvin Chang, Harry Chang, and Sunny Lee. Two famous mainlanders also played with Goo—football stars Marion Motley and Glen Davis. The Harlem Globetrotters won an exciting game against Goo's five, called the Balfour All-Stars.[1]

After World War II, there was a great deal of basketball action in and round Honolulu. The Honolulu Senior Basketball League in 1947 could boast of coaches such as Walter Wong, who headed the Whitey's Athletic Club five. King Song Wong and Francis Sing played for the Police Athletic Club, while

Sonny Chang performed for the Mid-Pacific Trotters. Bert Chan Wa, in 1948, coached the Liberty House five, which competed in Honolulu's Commercial League in the fall of 1948. He also coached the National Photo Supply aggregation. Indeed, the former University of Hawai'i forward was store manager. Bobby Kau, who once starred for the University of Hawai'i, suited up for another participating team, the John Hancock Life Insurance five.[2]

In the 1950s, the University Invitational Conference included a variety of Hawai'i's most elite amateur basketball teams, one of which represented the University of Hawai'i. Arthur Kim coached the Service Center 5 squad in 1951. In that capacity, he could call upon the services of elite Hawaiian performers, including Robert Kau, Ed Loui, Larry Sato, and Robert Wong. Japanese American Dr. Shunzo Sakamaki was president of the league in 1954.[3]

Coached by Chew Chong Ching, the Universal Motors team was one of the best in the conference. Several of the best players on the squad were Japanese Americans: Wally Tome, John Honda Holi, and Chico Miyashiro. In 1951, Ching's Universal Motors squad beat a visiting Cal five. Early in 1952, Universal Motors lost to the visiting St. Mary's of Moraga squad, 63–44 and 83–46. In the latter game, John Honda Holi led the losers with 11 points. Later in 1952, the Universal Motors five toured the West Coast, although it had to cancel its trek to the Pacific Northwest due to mounting costs. Meanwhile, a wire photo of Ching and one of his *haole* players doing the hula was published on the mainland. Early in 1953, Universal Motors downed the Pearl Harbor Marines, 65–59, with Wally Tome scoring a team high 11 points. In 1954, Universal Motors hosted the Santa Clara University five, led by powerful big man and future New York Knicks standout Ken Sears. The Hawaiian squad lost, but Chico Miyashiro and Wally Tome more than held their own.[4]

On the lower levels of multiethnic Hawaiian basketball, teams and leagues flourished after World War II. In Honolulu's Police Athletic League, the Kapalana Athletic Club suited up Ronnie Hozaka and Gene Okazaki. Early in 1953, the *Honolulu Star-Bulletin* reported on the Honolulu Amateur League. Heading this league was "hard working" George Ishihara, who formerly led the post–World War II AJA fives.[5]

Women's basketball existed in post–World War II Hawai'i. In the fall of 1949, Honolulu was home to a Hawai'i Senior Girls Basketball League. The league featured athletes such as Gwen Kam, Louise Kipi, Bobbie Dela Cruz, Dorothy Dung, and Annette Akana. Unlike most of the female basketball played on the mainland at this time, this league competed under men's rules. In a preliminary game before the Harlem Globetrotters took the court against the Balfour All-Stars, two women's squad vied for supremacy. Among the starring athletes were Miriam Wong and Doreen Leong.[6]

A multiethnic team called the Hawaiian All-Stars toured the U.S. mainland after World War II. Art Kim, who was then coaching at Honolulu's Roosevelt High, was in command of the aggregation that was reportedly sponsored by the Hawaii Tourist Bureau, the Honolulu Chamber of Commerce, and the territorial government. Hawaiian business and political elites hoped that through sports such as basketball they could promote Hawai'i as a future state, as well as tourism to the "land of Aloha." If basketball was not enough to curry mainland favor, Hawaiian musicians and dancers who accompanied the hoopsters would hopefully close the deal.[7]

When a Pan American plane brought the troupe home in March 1947, the "Air Passenger Manifest" disclosed that most of the individuals who had been representing Hawai'i in basketball on the mainland claimed white-collar, but lower-middle-class, occupations. Art Kim, Harry Chang, Clement Ching, Peter Chun, Thomas Harimoto, and Hawaiian entertainer Barbara Holt were clerks. George Lee was a police officer, and *hapa haole* Anthony Morse, a probation officer. Paul Kim, however, was a laborer.[8]

Wishing to make the most of the commercial and political potential of sending Hawaiian hoopsters to the mainland, financial backers of the 1947 team recruited Abe Saperstein to handle the bookings for the "colorful" Hawaiian five. Writing for the *Los Angeles Times* in late January 1947, Braven Dyer informed readers that the team had arrived in San Francisco accompanied by hula dancers, including the famous Barbara Holt and a Hawaiian entertainer named Miki Lani. The team was slated, according to Dyer, to take on the Harlem Globetrotters during their journey. Dyer advised the Globetrotters to be wary because Hawaiians had proven quite adept at sports. Proud of the contribution of Tom Harimoto, a veteran of the 442nd, the *Pacific Citizen* hailed the team, claiming the Hawaiians "showed a good brand of ball, although they lost ... games to taller and heavier teams."[9]

Among those who played included Kim himself, who was a five-foot-seven-inch forward. Tom Harimoto was described in the press as a 25-year-old, five-foot-seven "Japanese league star" and war veteran. Paul Kim Kahele was a 19-year-old "Hawaiian-Korean." Standing at five foot nine, he had graduated from Kaimuki High. Harry Chang was another 19-year-old and the tallest member of the team at six foot ten. A "Chinese-Portuguese guard," Peter Chang was a five-foot-nine-inch graduate of St. Louis Prep. Clem Ching was called an "all-star forward from Palama." Thirty-two-year-old Robert Lee was a five-foot-six-inch guard from McKinley High, while George Lee was a six-foot-seven inch Korean Hawaiian from the University of Hawai'i. Curiously, while the press identified Lee as Korean, it also dubbed him "the world's tallest Chinese cager."[10]

In 1947, the Hawaiians won games as long as their opponents were not the Globetrotters. In February 1947, the Hawaiian All-Stars lost to the Harlem Globetrotters, 65–40 before a crowd of 6000 at Los Angeles's Shrine Auditorium. Prior to the game, the *Los Angeles Times* asked readers to keep an eye on Harimoto, because he was a "dead shot." The legendary Goose Tatum scored 20 points for the victors. For the losers, the box score indicated that Harimoto and one of the Changs scored ten. In the Midwest, the Hawaiian All-Stars defeated the B and A Knacks at a local high school gym. The *Dixon Evening Telegram* reported that "the islanders impressed with slick ball handling, plenty of drive, and a skillful passing technique." Paul Kim, Peter Chang, and Harry Chang stood out for the visitors. When the squad headed for Utah in March, the *Ogden Standard-Examiner* exhibited a photograph of "Paul Kahele Kim," with a caption describing him as a "colorful forward." To the *Portland Oregonian*, Kim was a "high scoring forward."[11]

In 1948, the Hawaiians continued to excel against local fives. An upstate New York daily publicized the impending arrival in January of the "Hawaii All-Stars" by displaying a photo of Nisei Wally Tome and describing the aggregation as "made up of Chinese, Japs, and Koreans" and "an interesting unit to watch because of their unique native antics." In March 1948, the Hawaii All-Stars were in Benton Harbor, Michigan, where they beat a Veterans of Foreign Wars team, 28–22. Reportedly, the game was dreary and the 300 fans in attendance were not much excited by the goings-on. Still, a local newspaper contended that the Hawaiians compensated for a lack of size with a good fast break and sterling defense.[12]

Kim's all-stars continued to tour the mainland in the 1950s. When they showed up in Utah to play Weber College in late January 1952, the *Ogden Standard-Examiner* promised spectators an exhibit of hula dancing to accompany the game. Paul Kim was still on the team, as well as Ronald Kim, the high-scoring son of Art. The *Standard-Examiner* revealed that the team had gone 73 and 7 since coming to the mainland the previous November. In publicizing the visitors as the "Surfriders," a mainland newspaper in 1953 noted that the team included George Makini, "Chinese-Hawaiian"; Robert Akeo, "English-Hawaiian"; Harry Bento and John McGuire, possessors of Hawaiian, Portuguese, and English ancestors; and Ronald Kim. Also on the squad was Chico Miyashiro, five foot four and "clever as a frisky frog."[13]

Not all of the traveling Hawaiian fives were necessarily mentored by Kim. In the spring of 1956, while Kim seemed to be busy elsewhere with the Surfriders, the *Provo Daily Herald* announced that a team called the Hawaii All-Stars would take on the Wilson Ward M squad in the Utah town. It promoted Rupert Chung as "Honolulu's top player," as well as Isao Tomita.

Meanwhile, coached by Chew Chong Ching, a Hawaiian all-star five also competed in Asia.[14]

Art Kim's Hawaiian Surfriders not only continued to visit the mainland in the mid- to late 1950s, but often toured with the Harlem Globetrotters, typically as patsies for the antics of the highly talented and entertaining team. The Surfriders also journeyed the southern United States to oppose a contingent called the Boston Whirlwinds, which featured Bevo Francis, a legendary high-scoring college star of the 1950s. Interestingly, two European American NBA standouts, Clyde Lovellete and Joe Grabowski, joined the Surfriders. Readers of an upstate New York daily learned in November 1955 that the Surfriders were made of "players ... selected from among the Hawaiian Islands' foremost college and high school players. Mainlanders augment the roster, adding height to an otherwise small unit." The "scrappiest" hoopster on the 1955 squad, according to the *Amsterdam Evening Bulletin*, was five-foot-six Frankie Sunn, who, the daily reported, possessed Chinese and Japanese ancestry. When the Surfriders were in the West to play the Globetrotters in 1957, the local newspapers announced that members included Donald Ho, a Chinese Hawaiian who was in his third year with the five. This Don Ho stood at six foot three and did not become the relatively celebrated singer who recorded "Tiny Bubbles." Japanese Hawaiian Frank Muramoto was a smaller, five-foot-seven hoopster. Possessing Spanish, Portuguese, and Korean ancestry, Ronald Kim was nearly six feet. And Korean Hawaiian Taddy Song was reportedly one of the team's best players.[15]

The Mainland

On the mainland, skilled Asian American adults who craved to play basketball could find themselves competing on a variety of elite, ostensibly amateur teams affiliated with the AAU. This may have been especially the case in the West, where professional basketball foundered. AAU teams were sponsored largely by businesses—often, but not always, large-scale businesses. For example, Oklahoma's Phillips 66 Oil Company was represented by many powerful fives. Athletic clubs such as San Francisco's Olympic Club also backed AAU teams. Indeed, the great Hank Luisetti played for the Olympic Club five after graduating from Stanford, and later he played for the Phillips 66 squad. Many other college stars were lured by the offer of jobs with the sponsoring businesses.[16]

Willie Wong played on a team called the Oakland Atlas Engineers in 1952. According to the *Humboldt Standard*'s Scoop Bean, the Engineers comprised a "good AAU team." At the same time, Bean used dismissive language such as the "honorable Mr. Wong" while referring to the adult athlete as a "China boy."[17]

Wong did not star for the Oakland five. In an article describing the Engineers, the *Oakland Tribune's* Ray Haywood said that "Willie (Woo Woo) Wong, the diminutive San Francisco Chinese player who is famous for his set shot," would be on the bench. In a game against Artesia, Wong got off the bench long enough to score one point. After the Engineers downed San Francisco's Stewart Chevrolet for the PA championship, the coach was allowed to take but ten players to the national AAU tournament. Wong was in consideration for the tenth spot. But even though he wound up not getting it, Wong did accompany the team to the national tournament. And though he did not see any action in the AAU tournament, Wong's basketball acumen was considered sharp enough that he was tasked with helping scout an opponent for the Atlas Engineers.[18]

Readers of post–World War II California sports pages could encounter Japanese and Chinese surnames suiting up for independent amateur teams. In 1947, Yamamoto played for the Madison All-Stars in San Jose's city basketball league. In the same league, Nakamura competed for the Bueno Bulldogs and Nishimura for the Pappa Swishers. Another Nakamura played for a team in the Fresno City League. In the early 1950s, Yasukawa was on the Eagles, a team that participated in San Jose's Prep League, and Wu played for the Retail Clerks' five while Wong played for the Y Greens in the city league. Moving down to Southern California, Tanaka competed for the Canoga Park Community Church team in 1946. In the mid–1950s, Asian Americans participated in the Long Beach city basketball league. Homada suited up for Harvey's Canteen and Kagagama played for Richfield Oil. The Jet Propulsion Lab was represented by a team in Pasadena's Industrial League in 1956. Hiroshida played on that team.[19]

In the Pacific Northwest, Asian Americans competed on multiethnic fives. Al Mar starred in amateur basketball circles in the Seattle area. He suited up for a team called the Collins Fieldhousers. In February 1946, Mar scored 16 points to lead the team to a victory over Alki Fieldhouse. In 1946 and 1947, the multiethnic Collins five won "interleague council titles" before advancing to the Pacific Northwest AAU championships.[20]

The Collins Playground, on which the aforementioned field house stood, served as a magnet for hoopsters possessing various Asian American ethnic backgrounds. Shelly Sang-Hang Lee traced the existence of Asian American basketball on the playground to the 1920s. Collins Playground teams were multiethnic, possessing Jewish, African, Chinese, Japanese, and Filipino ancestry. A decade before Al Mar played AAU hoops for the Collins Fieldhousers, he took up playground hoops as a child at Collins. Moreover, in the 1950s, a five representing the multiethnic Yesler Terrace area of Seattle included players sur-named Soo, Wong, Yee, and Chinn.[21]

In the Rockies and on the East Coast, Asian American women played intercultural hoops. Nancy Ito, a truly versatile, magnificent athlete, joined a squad sponsored by the Denver Industrial Bank. In 1948, her team had made it to the AAU's national tournament, but she could not play because at 14, Ito was too young by a year. Interestingly, the *Pacific Citizen* revealed that the Bankerettes were coached by an unnamed Japanese American from Hawai'i. Ito starred for a team called the Denver Hudsonettes in 1950. When the Hud-sonettes took on a male team from Sedalia, they not only won, 36–28, but Ito scored 22 points to spearhead the victory. Later, Nancy Ito played for a nation-ally powerful AAU's women's squad, the Denver Tillers. In the spring of 1952, the Tillers participated in the national AAU championship. Sparked in part by Ito's 13 points, the Tillers triumphed over the Atlanta Peaches in the tourna-ment's first round. Subsequently, the Tillers lost to the Dallas Hornets, 33–31, in the quarter finals of the national women's tournament. Ito, however, scored 13 points in the game. Ito later gained repute as a women's baseball and softball player in the 1950s, 1960s, and 1970s. She also worked as a computer program-mer for the Federal Aviation Agency. Meanwhile, in Boston, Violet Wong was declared the star of the Pepsi-Cola team by the *Boston Herald* in the early 1950s.[22]

Asian Americans participated in post–World War II military hoops. In the late 1940s, Danny Fukushima and Johnny Oshida played for the Fort Snelling five. Air Force captain John Kashiwabara, who had played junior col-lege hoops in Northern California, coached a military team in the early 1950s called the Johnson Gunners. A hoopster surnamed Koto played for the Camp Cook five in the Fresno area in 1951. Filipino Sonny Pomicpic told author Peter Jamero he joined an otherwise all–African American team competing out of March Air Force Base in Riverside, California. He remembered that the military closed the team down because it had no European Americans.[23]

Asian American children played hoops with non–Asian Americans in California during the post–World War II era. A Boy Scouts tournament was staged in the mid–1950s in Lodi. Newton Iwamiya, according to the *Lodi News-Sentinel*, was one of the event's outstanding performers. Meanwhile, the Lodi Recreation Department sponsored a basketball tournament for elementary school children. Tom Fukumoto played for one of the participating teams—the Meteors. The *San Jose Mercury* named Chris Yasukawa, Bryan Uyemura, Gary Morikawa and Allan Kawabata among the outstanding participants in San Jose's Junior Basketball Program in 1960. And in Southern California, a young man surnamed Yamoto took the court for McKinley Junior High in

Pasadena. Meanwhile, Bob Hayashi served as a referee for the YMCA's boys' basketball league in Sacramento in the 1950s.[24]

Not known as a state with a large population of Asian Americans, South Dakota provided a home for Asian American boys crossing cultural lines to play basketball. In 1952, the *Aberdeen Daily News* published a photograph of the Aberdeen Gra Y team, which won a championship in Sioux City. Ronnie Wong and Byron Wong were on the triumphant squad. The latter, furthermore, played for his seventh grade Simmons Junior High five. And on the East Coast, Al Wong suited up for Wally's Boys, a team that competed in the Connecticut Valley League.[25]

Hank Luisetti's Basketball Clinic and Helen Wong

For many years after his remarkable playing days ended, Hank Luisetti ran an annual youth basketball clinic in the Bay Area—a camp often sponsored by the *San Francisco Examiner*. This clinic offered something of a cosmopolitan canopy for participants, many of whom were Chinese American young men and women. In mid–December 1948, Bob Brachman reported for the *Examiner* that 125 girls had enrolled in Luisetti's camp. However, the heaviest enrollment was "of girls from Chinatown where the sport is having a big boom." One of these girls was Helen Wong.[26]

Helen Wong's shooting skills took center stage at the clinic. On December 22, 1948, a free throw contest was held at Luisetti's camp. Helen Wong sank 49 of 52 shots. Amazed onlooker and Washington University star Jack Nichols declared, "I've seen a lot of girls shoot basketballs ... but in all my life I've never seen any girl shoot like that." Bob Brachman added that "the young Chinese miss's" exhibition was astounding. On December 26, the *Examiner* published a photograph of Helen Wong with Hank Luisetti and another female hoopster, Shirley Tochini. The caption described the "Queen of Chinatown" as the "sister of the redoubtable Woo Woo Wong." Don Selby of the *Examiner* raved about Wong's "easy, co-ordinated style of ... shooting." He added, "She could put many men cagers to shame in that department." Aside from Wong, Maureen Chan, a Commerce High student, and Elizabeth Chong from San Francisco's Star of the Sea Academy shined at Luisetti's camp. Unfortunately, Wong lost in the finals of the camp shooting competition for her age group. Brachman blamed her downfall on nervousness.[27]

Early in December 1949, the *Examiner* again promoted Luisetti's clinic. It informed readers that "[a]s usual, one of the most enthusiastic groups is the gang from St. Mary's Chinese Boys Club." Director Hank Wong, Willie and Helen's brother, had requested 100 entry cards. A week later, Brachman pointed out that Cynthia Wong of the Catholic Chinese Social Center wrote that she wanted to enroll "our girls from the St. Mary's Chinese basketball team." To Brachman that meant "sensational Helen Wong, who coaches the Chinese girls will be in there pitching." The sportswriter reminded readers that Wong "gave an amazing exhibition of shooting" at the previous Luisetti clinic. On December 21, 1949, the *Examiner* reported that of all the participants only Helen Wong seemed able to command Luisetti's "one handed push shot." It added that Wong is "perhaps the most graceful student in the school." Three Chinese Americans copped shooting prizes in the finals at Luisetti's clinic—Helen Wong and Elizabeth Chong of San Francisco and Berkeley's Billy Wong.[28]

High School Varsity Males in Hawai'i

After World War II, interscholastic football on the islands garnered a great deal of attention. But interscholastic basketball was hardly forgotten. During the 1952–1953 season, Baldwin High School in Honolulu was represented by a team with Doarel Fujitani, Robert Takitami, Allan Yamamoto, and captain Tadashi Sakamoto. Yamamoto was, at six feet, the tallest player on the team and a standout performer. The five-foot-six Fujitani was another outstanding player. When Roosevelt beat Kaimuki in 1954, Johnny Chong was the leading scorer for the victors. George Fujiwara of Farrington and Ron Kakuda of McKinley, according to sportswriter Bill Miller, also illuminated Honolulu basketball in the mid–1950s. In the meantime, Pahoa High School, on the Big Island, had a girls' basketball team in the late 1940s. It was led by player-coach Kimmie Hayashikawa.[29]

The 1956 McKinley High School yearbook informs us that Frank Minato was head coach of the varsity five. On the team were Kenneth Takeyasu, Harold Teramae, Herbert Hew Len, Chester Yuen, and David Yoshino. According to the yearbook, Teramae and Hew Yen were the team stars, while Chester Yuen was co-captain.[30]

Hilo High continued to put on the court some of the better squads on the islands. In 1953, the *Honolulu Star-Bulletin* expressed admiration for a team that included "Richard Shigekane, cane-sized southpaw speedster." Teammates included Louis Hao, Al Takahata, and future University of Hawai'i, Hilo coach Jimmy Yagi. When Hilo beat Farrington in January 1953, Takahata was the big star for the victors. In 1957, Hilo lost the territorial championship to St. Louis. However, Guy Ichinose scored 20 points for the vanquished.[31]

Asian American coaches pervaded the Hawaiian Islands after the war. On the island of Hawai'i, Ung Soy Afook earned a legendary reputation as a high school coach at Hilo High from 1935 to 1948, winning, in the process, several territorial championships. Indeed, Hilo's Afook-Chinen Auditorium is partially named after him. Afook was born in 1901. As a child he fostered a love of basketball, as well as other sports such as baseball, football, track, and swimming. While attending high school in Hilo, Afook decided he wanted to become a coach. At Hilo High he coached not only successful teams but other Hawaiian basketball luminaries such as Ah Chew Goo and Tommy Kaulukukui. The 1940 U.S. census manuscript schedules describe the 37-year-old Ung Soy Afook as a "public school teacher" in Hilo. The racially "Chinese" Afook was married to a part-Hawaiian, Elizabeth, and made $2500 a year. After Afook departed from Hilo High, Achong Young coached Hilo High in the 1950s.[32]

During the mid-twentieth century, Walter Wong emerged as a victorious high school coach on Oahu, although other Asian Hawaiians ran high school basketball programs on the island. After graduating from McKinley in 1932, Wong starred in Hawaiian basketball circles. The 1940 U.S. census reveals a racial designation for him as a "Hawaiian-Asian." Working as a clerk-typist for the U.S. Army, Wong was married to Etta, with whom he had a one-year-old child, Walter Jr. Wong coached various independent and community teams before taking over the St. Louis Prep basketball program—community teams such as the Palama Settlement House five. Starting at St. Louis in 1947, Wong's teams won several league titles, including the first Hawai'i High School Athletic Association Championship in 1957. Former player Mike Chow told the press upon Wong's death that his old coach was a stickler for fundamentals. Chow, who played on the 1961 state champion team, recalled, "He knew how to motivate the players and get the best out of you.... He was hard-nosed. He was an old Palama Settlement guy. Everybody wanted to play him." His 1958–1959 team was captained by Dennis Wong, and the starting lineup included not only Wong but also John Low. In the early 1960s, David Dung starred on Wong's five. The versatile Dung was team captain in the 1960–1961 season. Also on Oahu, Joe Tom, a former quarterback for the University of Oregon, coached McKinley's varsity in the mid–1950s. And in the early 1960s, the Roosevelt High School yearbook praised coach Stanley Chung's "versatility and know-how." The yearbook, furthermore, hailed the shooting of Wallace Miyasaki as crucial to the success of Chung's five.[33]

Varsity Males on the Mainland

Several Asian Americans appeared on varsity squads in San Francisco in the late 1940s and early 1950s. Ralph Yakushi played for Galileo, as did Joe

Hong. In January 1950, the *San Francisco Examiner* published a photo of Yakushi battling for a loose ball against Balboa. Commerce High was represented by talented Chinese American hoopsters after World War II. Henry Chin starred on the Commerce five. The school yearbook described Chin as a "dead-eye forward ... good faker," while the *Chronicle's* Bob Marcus dubbed him the "little Chinese cager." After the 1946–1947 season, Chin took second place in a write-in contest to name Northern California's most popular prep player. During the contest, Bob Brachman averred that Chinese San Franciscans were working hard to push Chin to victory, the prize for which would be an all-expenses-paid trip to Denver. Early in 1948, the *Examiner* pointed out that Chin and Francis Lai helped keep Commerce close to Lowell, who eventually won. Called the team's "Chinese ace," Chin hit 21 points against Balboa—the most scored by a San Francisco prep hoopster thus far during the 1947–1948 season.[34]

Stan Mock, Harry Mock, and "Tiny" David Lew also played for Commerce in the late 1940s and early 1950s. The 1949 Commerce yearbook described Harry Mock as a "good rebounder" with a "fine eye." In other words, "Handsome Harry Mock" was a "stellar guard." Don Selby told *San Francisco Examiner* readers that Mock and Lew keyed Commerce's narrow victory over Lowell, 31–30, in mid–January 1950. A few days later, Selby commended Mock for keeping Commerce in the game against Lincoln, scoring 16 points in a 37–26 losing effort.[35]

In the 1950s and into the 1960s, Asian Americans maintained a steady presence as varsity hoopsters in San Francisco. During the 1953–1954 season, Calvin Tam and Chew Jeong played varsity hoops for George Washington. Performing for the same high school in the late 1950s, "diminutive Norm Owyoung," according to the 1959 George Washington High School yearbook, was one of the varsity five's best players. Indeed, he won the MVP award at a tournament in Gridley, California. Meanwhile, T. Gong played for Lowell during the 1957–1958 season. Doug Yoshimura starred on Lowell's 1960–1961 squad and was named second team all-city. Ken Uyeda was on the Lowell five in the early 1960s, as well as Warren Doo, Cedric Goo, and Andy Jew.[36]

High schools in Alameda, Solano, and San Mateo Counties suited up varsity Asian Americans. In Alameda County, Jiro Nakamura competed for Fremont's Washington High School in 1946, along with Nishioka. Castlemont played George Moy during the 1959–1960 season. And, in the mid–1960s, Barry Ng was on Newark High School's team. Ng, the *San Jose Mercury* proclaimed, was a "high scoring center." Meanwhile, Gene Chin suited up for Oakland Technical during the 1965–1966 season. In Solano County, northeast of San Francisco, Filipino American Eddie Chavez starred for St. Vincent's High.

In 1947, Chavez was the leading scorer in the California Catholic League. According to the *Monitor*, Chavez was the star of the St. Vincent's team when it lost to St. Mary's of Berkeley. Chavez tallied nine points and handled the ball well for the losers. To the south of San Francisco, Tekawa, Wong, Takeshita, and Hamada played for San Mateo High in the early 1950s.[37]

Varsity Santa Clara County high school basketball lured the services of many Asian Americans. In mid–January 1948, Willie Yoshimoto's 11 points paved the way for a Fremont triumph over Santa Clara, 29–28. Ray Matsunaga and Ben Yoshihara performed for San Jose High during the 1949–1950 season. In the mid–1950s, five-foot-six Yosh Kumagai was an all-league selection from Palo Alto High. Palo Alto's "Little Ko Abe" was good, too, scoring 15 points to lead his five against Carlmont in a game in December 1956. Bob Tsukuda sparked Mountain View's Ayer High School to a victory over Amador in early January 1960. Around the same time, Sammy Liu was the game's high scorer with 14 points when his Mountain View High five lost to Sunnyvale, 46–43. In 1961, Campbell High School's varsity team had a B. Yoshida and R. Taniguchi. Sammy Lio, Pete Shimizu, and R. Nakamoto competed on Mountain View's squad in the early 1960s. Tom Uchiyama played for San Jose's Andrew Hill in 1963. And a few years later, Dave Maruyama joined the Campbell High varsity.[38]

Terry Maruyama was a special varsity performer for San Jose High. Maruyama had a particularly great 1959–1960 season. Early in January 1960, Maruyama's 25-foot jump shot beat Campbell High with three seconds left. Maruyama scored nine and "displayed," according to the *San Jose Mercury*, "a fine floor game." A few days later, "[d]iminutive Terry Maruyama" popped in 25 against James Lick. Within a week, Maruyama garnered praise from the *Mercury* for his 16-point effort against Santa Clara High. When San Jose downed Logan, the *Mercury* hailed Maruyama as the five's "sparkplug." Maruyama, by the way, scored 20 in the game. According to the *Mercury's* Rob Kohn, Maruyama was known for his "outstanding floor game and peerless scoring."[39]

In the counties just to the south of San Jose, Watsonville High suited up some Asian Americans, as did other high schools in the region. The 1949 Watsonville High yearbook depicted Johnny Wong and captain Roy Kusumoto as two of the varsity's better players, along with future NBA star Kenny Sears. During the previous year, Wong put up 13 points to lead Watsonville to a 28–24 victory over Los Gatos. Around the same time, Kishomura and Hori competed for Gilroy High in the late 1940s and early 1950s.[40]

Several varsity Asian Californians performed for Central Valley schools. Also a fine football player, Tommy Yagi suited up for Livingston in the late

1940s and early 1950s. During the 1950–1951 season, Tosh Minamoto played at Madera and Tom Dajoga at Lodi. In early February 1952, the *Pacific Citizen* reported that Wheatland High's Ray Fukui had recently scored 14 points to top all scorers as his team downed East Nicolas in the Sacramento Valley League. The talented Harvey Fong performed for Sacramento High during the early 1950s as well. In the late 1950s, Terry Fong performed for McClatchy High and Howard Shinitaki suited up for Rio Vista High. During the early 1960s, Gary Yamada was a five-foot-seven inch guard for Lodi High.[41]

In the nearby Sierras, Japanese American prepsters often stood out. Jim Yokota and Vic Nakamoto were exceptional performers at Placer High after World War II. Yokota captained Placer during the 1949–1950 season. Averaging 13 points a game and making a very impressive 90 percent of his free throws, Yokota was named Northern California Basketball Player of the Week by the *San Francisco Examiner*. Nakamoto, the *Pacific Citizen* boasted, tallied 15 against Lodi. Around the same time, Herb Yasumoto and Ike Yamagata, according to a 1950 *Pacific Citizen* piece, starred at Sanger and Reedley High Schools, respectively.[42]

After World War II, Asian Americans, especially Japanese Americans, populated varsity basketball rosters in and around Los Angeles. Herb Isono starred as "a sharp shooting forward" for University High School in Los Angeles. In December 1951, the *Pacific Citizen* hailed Isono as one of the finest Nisei athletes ever in Los Angeles. It reported that Isono had been named to an all-tourney team after a citywide tournament was staged. The weekly declared, "Isono's accurate shooting guided University to the finals of the consolation round."[43]

Herb Isono was not unique. Herbie Kubo competed for Leuzinger High after World War II. Early in February 1950, the *Los Angeles Times* reported that Kubo had scored 11 points against the Long Beach Jordan quintet. Dickie Nagai and Kazuo Shinzato illuminated Roosevelt High hoops in the early and mid–1950s. Dickie Nagai was a second team all-league for the 1951–1952 season. Averaging 15.7 points per game in the 1954 league season, Shinzato was named to the second team all-league squad. The 1954 Roosevelt High yearbook noted that Shinzato's teammates included Yoneo Inouye, and Eddie Kikuchi and the offense used the "Shinzato Shift" to take better advantage of his skills. The next year Shinzato was even better. Averaging over 20 points per game, the five-foot-eleven standout was named his league's player of the year. And his coach claimed he was even better than Nagai, who would ultimately play varsity hoops for USC. Meanwhile, Lelan Wong was a second team all-leaguer for Poly during the 1953–1954 season. Playing guard for Alhambra's Keppel High early in 1957 was a young man surnamed Lin. In the early 1960s, Kenji Tanaka and Kay Oda stood out for Garfield. A five-foot-eight forward, Tanaka averaged nearly 17 points per game and was a first team all-leaguer. A second team all-leaguer, Oda was a five-foot-five guard who averaged 11 points per game. Meanwhile, Y. Shimizu was named MVP in the Western League, pouring in 26.7 points per game. Outside of Los Angeles County, Nob Kitada played for Garden Grove, George Maeda for Citrus, and Harry Yasumoto and George Kubo for Sanger during the early 1950s. And Newport High suited up Tamura during the 1955–1956 season.[44]

Pacific Northwest Asian Americans crossed basketball and cultural sidelines after World War II. In Seattle, Ray Soo starred in the late 1940s for Garfield High. Early in 1948, the *Seattle Times* reported that "little Ray Soo" sparked Garfield's victory over Ballard. He subsequently earned honorable mention in all-city honors. Early in the 1948–1949 season, Bob Schwartzman identified Soo in the *Times* as "a little five-foot-six-inch senior and outstanding ball handler." The daily also published a photograph of Soo flanked by two white players. All three were dribbling. In February 1949, Soo rang up 16 points as Garfield vanquished West Seattle. The 1949 Garfield High yearbook identified Soo as an "inspirational all-city" performer and pointed out he was on the second team in the all-state tournament.[45]

Later in February, Bob Sutton wrote an admiring piece on Soo, accompanied by a Jack Winter illustration of the prep star—an illustration that was realistic and respectful. However, a side illustration of Soo would strike most modern readers as stereotypical and was captioned "a little dynamo." Sutton dubbed Soo a "diminutive Chinese," born 18 years earlier in California. His parents returned to China with him when he was a child, but Soo came back to the United States with his sister when he was ten. Sutton told readers that the Garfield senior was at the time living alone and worked as a waiter at a cafe, where he got his board. Soo apparently earned enough on weekends to concentrate on his basketball and school work during the week, both of which, Sutton assured readers, he did well. Soo, according to Sutton, originally attended Broadway, where he ran track. After transferring to Garfield, Soo concentrated more on basketball, in which "he's quick, a great ball handler, and a fine shot from all angles." If he could find the financial means, Soo hoped to go to college in order to major in electrical engineering.[46]

Soo was just one of several Asian Americans often excelling in Pacific Northwest high school hoops in the postwar era. As league play was set to begin in Seattle in 1950, Bob Sutton pointed out that "two little Chinese lads— Frank Yee, 5–6½ and Jim Hino, 5–5" started for Garfield. Joining these two, described as exceptional ball handlers by Sutton, was Kai Lim Eng. During the 1954–1955 season, Ed Tanaka started at guard for Garfield, while Ken Watanabe was also on the five. Arthur Kono, meanwhile, made third team all-city for Garfield. Around the same time, Ken Sakamoto played for O'Dea in Seattle. Royal Brougham, in 1955, called the O'Dea five "a real United Nations team— a Chinese boy, a Japanese, an Indian, a Negro, a Jewish player, and, oh yes, an Irishman named Kelly." Near Portland, Jimmy Tsugawa starred at Beaverton High School in the early 1950s, while Benny Morinaga played for Ontario High in Oregon.[47]

East of the Pacific Coast, Asian Americans appeared on other varsity teams in the United States after World War II. Niboru Iwami played for Tooele High in Utah after World War II. In 1965, Utah's Carbon High School yearbook praised the five-foot-ten Billy Yamaguchi as a good defender, playmaker, and "hard driver." In New England the *Lowell Sun* reported that the Roslindale High School team in 1948 had a couple of Chinese American players possessing "southern accents." It called this a "weird combination."[48]

Nonvarsity Hoopsters

Lightweight and lesser experienced and skilled Asian American boys helped fill high school rosters in San Francisco after World War II. In the late 1940s, Francis Lai, Norman Lai, Hoover Wong, and top scorer Cliff Wong competed for Commerce High's 130-pound team. In late February 1947, the latter scored 13 points to lead Commerce over Galileo. The 120-pounders were led by the "sensational guard Howard Lim." Jim Hom and David Kwan were also on the team. At the same time, Louis Kwock, Bill Lee, and Tom Yuen were 110-pounders. In 1949, David Lew was described as the "sharpshooting Commerce center." Late in January 1949, Lew was named lightweight player of the week, while topping the league in scoring. In January 1950, Hanson Quock player center for Commerce and tallied 13 points against St. Ignatius. Subsequently, Don Selby praised Quock's performance against Lincoln when the center scored 14.[49]

Galileo High had spots for Asian American lightweights. Dong Hong led the league in scoring and made all-league as a Galileo lightweight in 1953. In the late 1950s and early 1960s, Galileo High had Herb Chan, Cal Gon, Fred Joe, Larry Chew, Percy Mim, Herman Chan, Victor Quan, Tom Chee, Ben Yim, Art Kikugawa, Archie Wong, Jerald Tom, Ken Chung, Wilson Lue, Evin Huie, and Terrence Lee on its lightweight squads. The school's 1957 yearbook pronounced James Fong as one of the stars on the 112-pound five. During the early 1960s, Harry Yee and Tony Lyau were 130-pounders.[50]

Lowell High School nonvarsity hoops embraced Asian Americans.

According to the 1958 school yearbook, Donald Takahura starred on the 130-pound team, as did Randy Chin and Doug Yoshimura for the 120s and 112s, respectively. The 1960 school yearbook acclaimed Wayne Tado as a luminary on the 130-pound team. Gary Hiroshima, Mel Kumagai, Nick Wada, Bennet Tom, and Hideki Ota were regulars on the 112-pound five. And John Leong and Corey Gin performed well for the 120-pounders.[51]

George Washington High and St. Ignatius were represented by Asian American lightweights. Sherman Fong made third team all-city while representing George Washington High in 1951. According to George Washington High School's 1954 yearbook, Victor Low was one of the top scorers on the 120-pound team. Others on the squad were Kinya Matsuma, Larry Lum, Adolphus Wong, Bob Leong, and Don Miyamoto. Johnny Leong starred on the 110-pound team. Joining him were Marshall Uyeda, Tommy Lee, Henry Yee, and William Low. William Chun, at the same time, competed on the "reserve" squad. The next year, Washington High lightweights included Bob Wong, Russell Wong, and George Yee. And during the 1958–1959 season, Art Yoshihara became the city's lightweight of the year. As for St. Ignatius, Thomas "Spikey" Yep was an all-leaguer as a lightweight in the mid–1950s. Yep, by the way, was one of Franche Lee's sons.[52]

Nonvarsity Asian Americans were, in the meantime, less visible in Alameda and San Mateo counties. Still, in 1946, George Matsumoto played B basketball for Berkeley High. During the 1951–1952 and 1952–1953 seasons,130-pounders Kaneko, Sato, and E. Ikeda suited up for San Mateo High. Around the same time, Nakanishi played for Menlo-Atherton High's 130-pound team, while a few years later, Odo did the same.[53]

In Santa Clara County, Asian Americans pervaded nonvarsity squads. In the first school year after the end of the war, Ernie Inouye competed for San Jose High's 130-pound squad and Sho Yamashita was proclaimed in the school's yearbook as one of the best players on the 120-pound squad. Playing for San Jose's 110-pound squad during the 1950–1951 academic year was Ken Sakamoto. Johnnie Kimura and Dickie Wong were 120-pounders. And the 130-pound squad included M. Fukumura, W. Jeu, R. Matsunaga, J. Lowe, and T. Sakamoto. During the 1953–1954 school year, James Lick High's C team had Akira Ouchida and B. Nakamura. Playing for the D team was Jerry Ikegemi. In the early 1960s, Dennis Taku played D basketball for Campbell. Around the same time, Art Mori was a standout lightweight hoopster for Los Altos High School. At East San Jose's James Lick High, Al Taira co-captained the B team in 1964 and Steve Itatani captained the D team. In the early 1960s, Randall Nakamoto starred as a lightweight for Mountain View. During the 1965–1966 school year, Mountain View's junior varsity squad included Curtis Nakamoto and Cliff Kitayama. And the school's C and D teams suited up Ray Tashitune, Dennis Chan, Harry Chew, Bob Nakano, Brian Nakamoto, Douglas Chew, Douglas Chan, Bob Watanabe, and Garry Miyahara.[54]

Asian American prepsters competed in nonvarsity hoops in San Benito and Monterey counties. F. Jue and J. Jue played for Watsonville High's 130-pound squad right after World War II. Fujimoto and Chinn were Gilroy High lightweights in January 1950. In 1954, Hiromi Takemoto captained Watsonville High's lightweight five and Gordon Iwanaga was also on the team. Around the same time, Yamanishi and Kodani played for Monterey High, while Gin and Mar suited up for Salinas High.[55]

California's Central Valley seemed ripe with Asian Americans playing nonvarsity hoops after World War II. In 1950, Sacramento High School's championship C squad had Steve Matsumoto, Ted Miyagawa, and Sam Okubo, as well as Maeda, Nakota, and Yamashiro. Two years later, Steve Matsumoto was on the B team with Ted Miyagawa and Joe Ikami. The C team included Sam Noguchi, Henry Din, Lewis Sasaki, Masaki Kobayashi, Sammy Okubo, and Harvey Yamasaki. Ken Sakoda started at guard for Lodi High's B team in 1957. B. Lee performed for Sacramento High's B team during the 1957–1958 season. The next year, Sacramento's B team suited up Muramoto, Yung, and T. Kojima.[56]

Asian Southern Californians competed on a variety of nonvarsity squads. Los Angeles's Poly High D team in the early 1950s suited up George Nakamura. The C team included Kinji Koro, Ray Fujimoto, and Taxon Yoshida. The B team included Bill Kobayashi and Aubrey Yano. During the 1953–1954 season, Karl Kato performed for Roosevelt High's junior varsity squad. Playing for the C team were Glen Yoshimoto, Dave Matsui, Jerry Nagufuji, Sam Kawakami, and George Uyemura. Tom Miyakawa, Frank Nagano, and Hal Kawakami made the B team. In 1954, Clifford Arakaki competed on Lincoln High's D team. In the early 1960s, Los Angeles's Garfield High suited up M. Miyamoto and A. Lui on the B team, while H. Mori and J. Shiohowa performed for the C team. A couple of years later, C. Ogawa was on Long Beach's Polytechnic High's junior varsity team. And down in El Centro County, where a relatively large number of immigrants from the Punjab had settled, Steve Singh and Freddie Singh were on Calipatria High's B team in 1950.[57]

In the Pacific Northwest, Seattle's Garfield High was a repository of Asian American nonvarsity hoopsters after World War II. During the 1954–1955 school year, B. Sawaya performed on the junior varsity squad. The Garfield High yearbook proclaimed D. Kawahara an outstanding player on the C squad, on which S. Tanaka played as well. Also in Washington, Norio Takayama and Sam Nishi played B hoops for Wapato High in the early 1950s. And halfway across the continent, Gene Sue, a "plucky Chinese," competed in Canton, Ohio, on Lehman High's freshman five right after World War II.[58]

Girls' High School Basketball

In mid-twentieth-century America, secondary schools generally marginalized girls' basketball. Young women took part in intramural hoops and occasionally interscholastic basketball under the jurisdiction of the GAA and similar organizations. However, secondary schools operated by the Catholic Church seemed to offer more competitive opportunities for female hoopsters. Asian American girls experienced marginalization while availing themselves of the opportunities. Thus, Berkeley High School's 1947 yearbook details the varsity boys' season. However, it also displays a photograph of Berkeley High's girls' basketball club. The photograph reveals no names of participants but also several seemingly Asian faces. Competing in GAA basketball in 1947 for San Francisco's Commerce High were young women surnamed Quan, Wong, Leong, Kawasaki, Chew, and Ching. May Yasumoto, S. Sukekane, and A. Yasumoto competed for what Watsonville High School's 1949 yearbook called the "Girls All-Stars." During the fall of 1950, Betty Jean Inouye and Lillie Ishizaki played competitive basketball at San Jose High. Inouye displayed her shooting form in a photograph printed in the school's 1951 yearbook. At Monterey High School, during the 1952–1953 school year, R. Tsoubouchi, S. Honda, M. Maegi, and H. Chan were female hoopsters. At San Francisco's George Washington High School in 1954, Barbara Wong and Marion Wong competed in basketball. In 1959, the *Seattle Daily Times* reported on Wilma Eng, the then newly crowned "Miss Chinese Community," adding that the young woman also played basketball at Franklin High.[59]

Female students attending Roman Catholic high schools were more likely to compete interscholastically in basketball than public school athletes during the mid–1900s. The talented Helen Wong played for San Francisco's Star of the Sea school in the late 1940s. Indeed, Wong's prep athletic career led her into the city's high school hall of fame. However, she was not the only Chinese American to perform well for Star of the Sea. The *Monitor* praised Helen Wong, Jenny Chong, and Anita Lew when Star of the Sea humbled St. Bridget's in February 1947, 43–23. Wong and Jenny Chong stood out as Star of the Sea downed St. Paul's, 22–18, in early March 1947. After Star of the Sea edged St. John's, 31–30, a week later, the *Monitor* enthused over the duel between Wong and St. John's Betty Spaulding—a duel won by the former who tallied 21 points to Spaulding's 19. Wong scored 18 to lead Star of the Sea to a 30–18 conquest of St. Peters' in April 1947. A year later, Wong finished a game with 16 points, but Star of the Sea lost 31–29. Later in March 1948, Wong's Star of the Sea fought St. Vincent's to a 32–32 tie. A crowd of 600, according to the *Monitor*, watched Wong make 26 points on mostly long shots. Among other Chinese American hoopsters at Star of the Sea was Lucille Chong. When, in mid–March 1950, Star of the Sea got by St. Bridget's, 35–34, the eventual victors were struggling until, according to the *Monitor*, "forward Lucille Chong started tanking long and short ones, besides hitting four out of four foul shots." In the early 1950s, Lillian Ong and Jackie Yee competed for Star of the Sea. Later in the decade, Norma Lee and Terry Lee were on the school's five.[60]

High School Coaches on the Mainland

Postwar high school hoops saw a handful of Asian American coaches. Nisei Dan Fukushima started coaching at James Lick High in San Jose in the 1950s. Another Nisei, George Goto, coached at Roseville High in California's Central Valley from 1955 to 1962. Filipino Eddie Chavez began a long career of high school coaching at Tamalpais High in Marin County in the late 1950s. In 1959, he guided Tamalpais to a league title. His teams, according to journalist Brian Bainum, were frequent visitors to Northern California's Tournament of Champions. Bainum wrote that "Chavez would usually put on a calm face on the sidelines and save all of his outwardly vocal coaching for practice."[61]

If one were an Asian American male with some skill in basketball, mid-twentieth-century Hawai'i and many Pacific Coast communities were relatively decent places to live. Non–Asian American teammates and coaches, even if bigoted, might overcome their prejudices if Asian Americans could help them win games. Height was obviously important, but it did not pose an overwhelming barrier to Asian American boys seeking to play competitive basketball because high schools typically assembled multiple interscholastic basketball teams, based on size and skill differentials. In places like San Francisco, San Jose, Los Angeles, or Seattle this meant that five-foot-tall Asian American hoopsters could see their surnames in the box scores of local newspapers. On the other hand, Asian American females competed in the comparative anonymity of GAA–sponsored hoops, although exceptional athletes such as Helen Wong were able to gain some notice knocking in shots in Roman Catholic interscholastic hoops. Meanwhile, of course, the very exceptional Nancy Ito could manifest her skills at the highest level of pre–Title IX women's basketball by shining in the national AAU tournament.

CHAPTER 5

Asian American College and Professional Hoops to 1965

America's most elite hoopsters have performed at the college level and, as we will explore later, the professional level. College basketball was, for years, played well in the shadows of "King Football." In the 1920s and 1930s, college basketball crawled out a bit from that shadow, thanks to exciting performers such as Hank Luisetti and the emergence of New York's Madison Square Garden as the sport's premier venue. The latter's luster diminished somewhat due to a point-shaving scandal we will examine later, but by the 1950s college basketball fans could enjoy the sport from coast to coast. And by the 1960s, the sport had become more accessible to African American hoopsters, several of whom, such as Bill Russell, Wilt Chamberlain, Elgin Baylor, and Oscar Robertson, dominated the game.

It is true that college basketball programs have largely ignored Asian Americans as participants and coaches. However, historically, hoopsters of Asian ancestry managed to grace college basketball rosters, and some of these athletes were considered standouts. Yet before the 1970s, these intercollegiate hoopsters were all males; female college students were generally confined to the rules and anonymity of their high school counterparts.

College Basketball in Hawai'i

The University of Hawai'i began on Oahu as a land-grant institution in 1907. For years, it operated as the College of Hawai'i until it was renamed the University of Hawai'i (UH) in the 1920s. During this time and for many years after, the school was represented by basketball squads which typically opposed independent, amateur island teams because postsecondary schools were few and far between on the islands. In 1922, for example, the UH team journeyed to Kauai to take on a local five. Among the visitors were the Chung brothers, Chung Wong, and Matsunaga. In 1927, UH lost to the ACA Dragons, 37–29. However, "Kanky Chun" scored five for the losers. Chun, during the 1927–1928 season, served as team captain, and a hoopster named Ching played with him.[1]

In the 1930s, UH could boast of some fine local talent. On the 1931–1932 squad, letter winners included Soo Sun Kim, Kusonoki, and I. Maeda. In the mid–1930s, the great Tommy Kaulukukui competed for UH. Kaulukukui excelled in football for UH, as well. Indeed, Kaulukukui, who was also a talented baseball player, would eventually head UH's football program for many years. Inspired by Kaululukui's basketball talent, Andrew Mitsukado called Kaulukukui in the mid–1930s the "greatest athlete to come out of Hilo." His UH teammates of Asian ancestry included Hayakawa and Saiki.[2]

During World War II, basketball was decidedly de-emphasized on the Manoa campus. In 1944, Bert Chan Wa coached what the yearbook described as a junior AAU team. On this team were Robert Chuck, Mike Hazama, John Ohtani, Harry Noda, Harry Kurisaki, Jenjo Yasutomi, and Eddie Chock.[3]

After World War II, UH basketball became more competitive and at least the equal of some mainland college fives. Bert Chan Wa coached the five when it appeared at Madison Square Garden in early 1947. On the team's return via Pan American Airways, the passenger manifest listed Bert Chan Wa as a "coach-student," as well as players such as Donald Fong, Robert Kau, Edward Loui, George Malama, Robert Wong, and Vernon Wong. During the 1948–1949 season, UH basketball claimed the services of Asian Americans Ed Loui, Bobby Wong, Robert Kau, George Malama, Charley Hamane, Larry Sato, Bill Young, Allan Yokomoto, and John Tashito. On Oahu, the UH five still continued to generally contest locals. For example, in November 1948, it topped the "All-Nisei" team, 39–36, with Bobby Wong scoring 14 points for the victors.[4]

While UH played mainland teams at Madison Square Garden and other stops in the continental United States, they also hosted mainland college fives during the late 1940s. In February 1948, Pacific Lutheran defeated a "scrappy" UH five on the latter's home court, 65–54. The starting lineup for the home team was Mamiya, Chang, Kahuanui, Malama, and Wong. Ed Loui came off the bench to lead UH with 17 points. When Hamline University decidedly defeated UH in Honolulu, Ed Loui scored 12 for the losers.[5]

In 1951, the *Pacific Citizen* proudly pointed out that three of UH's starters were Nisei—forward Tommy Yasuhara and guards Fred Furukawa and

Allen Yokomoto. The Rainbows also had Satoru Amaki on the bench. The six-foot-four Amaki, according to the *Pacific Citizen*, was the tallest Nisei playing basketball.[6]

UH yearbooks of the early 1950s show the important basketball presence of Asian Americans on the Manoa campus. UH's 1951 yearbook pointed out that Allen Yokomoto captained the 1950–1951 squad. It pronounced William Lee the most improved member of the squad, adding that he was a top scorer against visiting mainland squads such as Bradley and Oregon State. Tom Yasuhara was another invaluable member of the UH five, scoring 31 points in one game. Others on the team included Stanley Chung and Herbert Ching, as well as the aforementioned Fred Furukawa and Satoru Amaki. According to the 1953 yearbook, Stanley Chung, Walter Taguma, Thomas Ida, Thomas Yasuhara, Al Manliguis, William Lee, and Fred Furukawa were on the 1952–1953 roster.[7]

The UH squad of the 1950s still competed usually against amateur fives on the islands. As mentioned earlier, it was a member of the University Invitational Conference. In January 1953, UH pounded the "Nisei All-Stars," 92–68, in Honolulu. Willie Lee scored 32 and Hawaiian Filipino Al Manliguis scored 29 for the victors.[8]

Fred Furukawa and Willie or Bill Lee were probably the two finest UH players of the 1950s. As far as a *Honolulu Advertiser* sportswriter was concerned, Willie Lee was "the greatest center in the University of Hawaii history," averaging 20 points a game in the University Invitational Conference in 1954. Early in 1952, UH upset St. Mary's of Moraga, 62–61, in a double overtime game on the islands. Furukawa's 18 points proved vital for the victors. Several months later, a surprisingly successful UH team toured the Pacific Coast. The Hawaiians barely lost to USC, prompting sportswriter Jack Geyer to pay homage to Willie Lee. Scoring 24 points, Lee was, according to Geyer, a "smoothie with a hundred moves."[9]

In 1953, the UH quintet toured the Pacific Coast again. On December 9, Willie Lee starred as the Hawaiians edged Washington State, 47–45. Later, Bob Brachman touted the imminent arrival in the Bay Area of the University of Hawai'i hoopsters. Calling them "the colorful Rainbows," Brachman said they "have the tallest Japanese cager in the world, a *haole* Chinese, a Filipino, a Korean, and a former University of Pennsylvania freshman." The big stars, Brachman told readers, were Lee and Furukawa. In Monterey County, the UH five found themselves in Watsonville, California, taking on Santa Clara University. The mainlanders won handily, 68–49, behind Kenny Sears's 14 points. Fred Furukawa scored nine for the losers. Then, UH challenged Stanford at its campus pavilion. The home team won 82–74, but Furukawa scored 24 and Lee, 16. Moving on to Berkeley, the Hawaiians broke even against a fine Cal squad. The first game went poorly as the Hawaiians fell to the Bears easily, 77–56. Captain Furukawa scored 14 in the loss. The next game, however, the visitors ignited with Lee's heroics and stunned the Bears in double overtime, 73–70.[10]

There seemed to have been some confusion on the mainland regarding Willie Lee's ethnicity, but not about his skills. The *Los Angeles Times* described him as "a 6 foot 5 inch Chinese center." Over a week later, the *San Francisco Chronicle* asserted he was a "6–5 Korean." Indeed, the *Chronicle's* Darrell Wilson repeated that the Hawaiian hoopster possessed Korean heritage, while praising his ability to haunt the Stanford five: "He is what basketball men would call 'sneaky fast.' Not at all spectacular, he seemed to be always draping those long arms over the bucket for two points."[11]

In 1954, the UH squad showed up again in Southern California. Ah Chew Goo was at the helm. Given how obsessed college basketball coaches seem today, it may surprise the modern reader that Goo was subbing for regular coach Alvin Saake, who, according to sportswriter Jack Geyer, was on vacation. Among the Asian American players Goo brought to the mainland were Walt Taguma and Harvey Lee.[12]

In 1956, Ah Chew Goo once again coached the UH squad. One of his players was another Hilo High School alumnus, Jimmy Yagi, who at five foot six was the smallest player on the team in the 1956–1957 season. Teammate Louis Hao was also a graduate of the school that, according to mainland sports columnist Kerby Kerschull, had previously retired Ah Chew Goo's number.[13]

In the late 1950s, a *Seattle Times'* columnist acknowledged the arrival of the UH basketball team that was set to go up against the Washington Huskies' five. Georg Myers asserted, "For one reason or another known only to anthropologists, Hawaiian basketball players do not run high. Sun, surf, pineapples, and papayas do wonders for swimmers, but most Hawaiians have to stand on a chair to dribble." On the team were Ralph Ichiyama, Norman Ching, Ray Tanimura, Mervyn Chang, Al Mock, and Vernon Oshima; Fred Furukawa served as an assistant coach.[14]

Late in 1958, UH hoopsters revisited Southern California. They opposed USC in two games. In the first, USC romped, 75–56. Vernon Oshima scored four as a starter and coming off the bench, Mervyn Chang tallied two. The next game, the Trojans did even better, clobbering UH, 72–42. Oshima and Al Mock scored two points, while Chang managed three.[15]

In the meantime, UH was also represented by junior varsity squads. Milton Uyehara, Henry Kim, Bobby Kan, Takashi Matsui, and Masaru Hamakawa were on the 1950–1951 team. During the 1952–1953 season, Ah Chew Goo coached junior varsity. Playing for him were Joe Balangitao, James Tanaka, Ralph Ichiyama, and Edwin Fong. Toward the end of the decade, Fred Furukawa coached the junior varsity hoopsters, among whom were Roy Fakuda and Ed Gayagas.[16]

As was the case for most college women on the mainland, women's basketball at UH was confined to six-on-a-side rules in the middle third of the twentieth century. Moreover, women's enthusiasm for the sport was generally sequestered on the Manoa campus. In the late 1940s, for example, UH women competed in intramural basketball.[17]

The 1953 UH yearbook reveals a women's organization called the Heper Club. The women in this organization emerged as basketball champions of the university's Women's Athletic Association. Members of this organization included Keiko Sueishi, Michie Miki, Tamie Yamasaki, Grace Tanaka, Bertha Lee, Janet Matsuda, and Betty Ann Lim.[18]

Male Basketball at Mainland Four-Year Schools

The 1920s witnessed some of the first players of Asian ancestry on mainland intercollegiate fives. In the early 1920s, Fred Koba was a nonstarter for Stanford. The *Daily Palo Alto* described him as a "diminutive forward." Across the continent, Art Matsu, a magnificent quarterback for William and Mary grid squad in the mid–1920s, was capable of mastering other sports. A child of a Scottish immigrant mother and a Japanese father, Matsu participated in basketball for the Virginia school.[19]

Hailing from Stockton, Ted Ohashi was probably the most noteworthy Asian American to appear in big time college hoops before World War II, donning a University of California uniform in the early 1930s. The *Berkeley Daily Gazette* extolled him as "one of the cleverest floormen California ever had" in 1932. A six-foot guard, Ohashi was described by the *San Francisco Chronicle* as a player who "can hold his own with the tallest of them when the play gets rough."[20]

Ohashi's career at Cal seemed to have had more ups than downs. Still, he recalled that many on the Berkeley campus discouraged him from trying out for the basketball team, but Ohashi said, "I figured you can't find out until you try." After making the varsity team as a sophomore, Ohashi's Cal five beat St. Mary's in January 1931. The *Oakland Tribune* sportswriter who provided readers with an account of the game recorded his name correctly as "Ohashi." However, the box score published in the daily showed an "O.Tashi" scoring four points. On January 25, 1931, the Bears fell to USC, but the *San Jose News* reported that "Ted Ohashi, Japanese guard" performed exceptionally. Chiming in, the *Oakland Tribune's* Art Potter said that the Bears failed to jell on a recent jaunt to Southern California, but Ohashi's play was one of the few highlights as Cal lost to USC and UCLA.[21]

The next season was probably not always happy for the Japanese American hoopster. In late December 1931, the *Oakland Tribune's* Milt Phinney called Ohashi "brilliant" and improved over the previous year after a game against Oregon State. In early January 1932, the *San Jose Mercury* informed readers that "Ted Ohashi, the Stockton Japanese" was losing a close competition for time on the court as a running guard with Bill Coughlan, a sophomore a year behind Ohashi in experience. Still, in mid–January the six-foot-tall Ohashi, dubbed in the *Oakland Tribune* as a "fast, little Oriental," made a last-second half-court shot to tie the game against UCLA. Ultimately, the Bears beat the Bruins, 26–25. In February 1932, the *Oakland Tribune* reported that Ohashi was not up to par physically—that the injured "Japanese guard" had been suiting up in practice but was in too poor of shape to play. However, when Stanford's players chose its all-opponent lineup at the end of the 1931–1932 season, they picked Ohashi largely for his defense, claiming "the ability of the giant Japanese to break up offense attacks is outstanding on the team." Moreover, the Stanford yearbook from 1932 identified Ohashi as one of the Bears making life miserable for the Stanford five in a crucial game.[22]

Cal continued to count upon Ohashi's athleticism and defensive prowess in his senior year. In January 1933, the *Oakland Tribune* showed a photo of Ohashi and fellow guard John Crowley. The *Tribune* pointed out that Bear coach Nibs Price wanted the two to "speed-up defense." Meanwhile, the *Tribune* praised Ohashi as a "star guard" and a "stellar guard" who had "broken up more plays this year than any other Californian." After Cal downed UCLA in mid–January, Phinney commended the play of Ohashi, who scored four points in the game. When Cal's coach replaced Ohashi in the starting lineup, Phinney pointed out that many wondered why it was necessary to bench the "Japanese star." Opponents continued to respect Ohashi's performances. UCLA hoopsters named him to their all-opponents team.[23]

Later in his life, Ohashi admitted that some of his college opponents were hostile to the idea of playing against a Japanese American. However, Ohashi contended that he generally tried to stay upbeat about these negative experiences and not let bigotry affect his performances on the court or embitter him off the court.[24]

After graduating from Cal, Ohashi remained involved in athletics. In 1937, Ohashi suited up for a Cal alumni team pitted against the Bear varsity. During World War II, Ohashi was interned at Rohwer, Arkansas. There he met his future wife, Kay. Their daughter Carol subsequently recalled that both her parents were deeply affected by their internment experiences. Like many Nisei, they did not talk about those experiences much, but their daughter declared, "I know they felt very deeply about the injustice of it. But my father didn't ponder on it too much because he met a lot of good people who treated him very fairly."[25]

After World War II, Ohashi served as the physical education director of St. Louis's YMCA. He then took up the same position in Los Angeles before moving on to Oakland, where he continued his involvement with the YMCA. When Ohashi died at the age of 95, he was remembered in the *San Francisco Chronicle* as a "flashy floor performer" who played the first game at Cal's famed Harmon Gym.[26]

Most Asian Americans who competed in college basketball in the decade before Pearl Harbor was attacked did so for less prestigious programs than Cal's. An exception, aside from Ohashi, was Kaye Hong, who, in the mid–1930s, came off the bench for the University of Idaho, which competed in the Pacific Coast Conference. San Diego State suited up Paul Yamamoto in 1930. According to the *Chinese Digest*, Paul Wong played varsity basketball for San Francisco State. Also an effective quarterback for Redlands College, Hawaiian Al Chang was a guard for the Southern California schools' hoops squad. During the 1939–1940 season, Chang came off the bench to play for Redlands. In one game, however, he led all scorers with 13 points as Redlands downed Cal Tech, 52–32. The *Los Angeles Times* said he was one of Redlands' "big guns" in the victory. Around the same time, Harold Ito played for Multnomah College, near Portland.[27]

The problem of confused racial and ethnic identity was raised by the appearance of Wilmeth Sadat-Singh in a Syracuse University basketball uniform in the late 1930s. Famed as a college gridder as well, Sadat-Singh was described in the press as a "Hindoo Hoopster." A caption to a wire photograph published in 1937 proclaimed him "the only Hindu playing intercollegiate basketball this year." However, Sadat-Singh was actually an African American who took the name of his Indo-American stepfather. Many suspected that Syracuse encouraged the ruse in order to escape the controversy of actually having a black athlete performing on its behalf. Sadat-Singh would subsequently play professional basketball and football for all-black squads before dying in World War II while serving as a member of the illustrious Tuskegee Airmen.[28]

During World War II, a few Chinese Americans popped up on mainland college squads. Perhaps the fight for democracy against the Axis powers inspired the lowering of racial barriers in college hoops. Perhaps the movement of white hoopsters into the military rendered coaches more open-minded toward the idea of putting Asian Americans on their college rosters. At any rate, in 1943, the *Brooklyn Eagle* identified James Seto as "one of the few Chinese players in the country" when he played for Rensselaer Polytech. Yet more consequential things were stewing in the Pacific Northwest, where Al Mar and Fred Lee made college hoops more interesting.[29]

After leaving Garfield High School in Seattle, Mar played for Whitman College, and then he jumped to the University of Washington. At Whitman, Mar could be a prodigious scorer. Sandy McDonald, a columnist for the *Seattle Times*, wrote, "A Chinese on a Pacific Northwest basketball team is considered an oddity in some circles, but there's nothing odd about the way little Al Mar ... is clicking at Whitman College." The occasion was Mar tallying 30 points against the University of Puget Sound five. Referring to a city where bloody encounters between Japanese and Chinese military forces had erupted, McDonald said that the former Garfield High star "must have thought he was blasting away at the Japs at Changsa." The *Times* further praised the "diminutive Chinese forward" as a new hero of the Northwest College Basketball Conference. Within a week, Al Mar put up 16 points to lead Whitman over Pacific University. A few weeks later, Whitman traveled to Spokane to play Gonzaga.

During World War II, Al Mar, a Chinese American from Seattle, sparkled as a guard for Whitman College and then the University of Washington. Mar is in the front row, the sixth player from the left, with his Whitman College squad. Courtesy Whitman College and Northwest Archives, WCA80.

The *Spokane Daily Chronicle* said the visitors were "sensational by reason of Al Mar, Chinese forward." Gonzaga played the role of a stingy host by overcoming Whitman. Yet, according to the *Spokane Spokesman-Review*, "[t]he left handed shots of little Al Mar gave Whitman fans something to cheer about, except that he didn't shoot often enough. The little Chinese forward scored four field goals with his peculiar shot." At the end of the 1941–1942 season, players for Pacific University placed Mar on their all-opponents squad, and he was honored as second string all-conference. Early in 1943, however, the *Spokane Spokesman-Review* reported that Mar was leaving Whitman for military service. It declared his departure a blow to Whitman's basketball fortunes.[30]

Instead of entering the military, Mar headed to the University of Washington. Upon Mar's joining the Huskies, the *Seattle Times* informed readers that the Chinese American had previously been an "all-city cager" in Seattle. The *Times* added that Mar was "small of stature, but an excellent floor man and a good ball handler." Mar, moreover, was 4-F (physically unable to serve in the military). Thus, he could travel out of town with the University of Washington squad. Bruce Hamby of the *Portland Oregonian* echoed the *Times* in predicting that Mar would become a "key man" for the Huskies. Hamby enthused that Mar was "a diminutive Chinese lad from Seattle … a fine scorer and an exceptional floor man." His coach Hec Edmondson quipped that Mar was a "flashy little floor man who weighs about eight pounds and six ounces."[31]

Mar proved an asset for the Washington five. He hit a key basket to help his team down Whitman College in overtime. In late January, "little Al Mar," according to the *Bend Bulletin*, sank crucial shots which sank Oregon State's chances to beat the Huskies. When Washington triumphed over Washington State, Mar had a field day. The *Bend Bulletin* told readers he hit 12 of 14 shots, which it insisted added up to 22 points. The *Bulletin*, in any event, seemed right about the point total. The "diminutive Al Mar," according to the University of Washington yearbook, did indeed hurt Washington State with 22 points. The *Seattle Times* dubbed Mar one of the "sparkplugs" of the Huskies' triumph over Gonzaga on February 20. On February 22, Washington beat Idaho and, according to one game account, Al Mar, a "little Chinese boy," was a key factor. Moreover, the University of Washington yearbook for 1944 pointed out he scored 16 against Oregon. Unfortunately, as the Huskies headed into the 1944–1945 season, Mar reportedly had scholastic issues that kept him off the team. After college, Al Mar would remain involved in community basketball, as well as operate a grocery store in Seattle.[32]

During World War II, "little Fred (Happy) Lee" played big time college basketball as Oregon State's "5 foot 4 inch Chinese basketball guard." Lee was the son of a Chinese American father born in Oregon and a Chinese immigrant mother. In 1930, his father labored for a fish cannery while his mother taught Chinese for a living. Ten years later, his father was a foreman while his mother apparently worked at home.[33]

Like Mar, Lee handled the pressure of big time college basketball more than adequately. Before the 1944 Pacific Coast Conference play started for Oregon State, Bruce Hamby described the "Chinese youth from Astoria" as small but fast. Regrettably, Lee had an eventual date with the draft board. His loss to the Beavers, Hamby lamented, would be unfortunate. A photograph of Lee accompanied Hamby's piece. The caption described the Chinese American as "agile." Called the "artful Chinese" by the *Portland Oregonian*, Lee aided Oregon State's victory over Idaho in January 1944. Lingering out of the military, Lee put up nine points in the game. The next month, Lee proved more troublesome to Idaho as he keyed another Oregon State triumph over the Vandals. He sank a clutch free throw and scored 12 as the Beavers triumphed, 52–48. The *Seattle Times'* George Vardell declared that Lee made the University of Washington's all-opponent squad. Indeed, Lee garnered 14 points against Washington in one game, leading the sports columnist to hail him as "dynamite on a basketball floor," while informing readers the Oregon hoopster was one of the leading scorers in the Pacific Coast Conferences' Northern Division. After the 1943–1944 season ended, the *Oregonian's* L. H. Gregory complained that the "midget…. Chinese guard" would serve in the military for the 1944–1945 season.[34]

When Lee's Oregon State confronted the University of Washington, the latter's yearbook noticed. Sadly for Lee, the Huskies trounced the Beavers twice during conference play, 54–30 and 56–29. However, the yearbook observed, "Both games were highlighted by a duel between Washington's Chinese player, Al Mar, and the Beavers' 'Happy' Lee. The two wore the same number, checked each other, and turned in sterling performances."[35]

After Lee was discharged from the military, the Astoria High School grad attended the University of Portland. During the 1947–1948 season, Lee was his team's third-highest scorer. Portland may not have had a big time college basketball program at the time, but it played teams that did. Early in 1948, Oregon State barely beat Portland, 48–44. Lee, the "diminutive Pilot guard" managed 14 points to help keep his team in the hunt against his former squad. Lee, a few weeks later, was on display in the *Portland Oregonian*. A photograph showed "little Fred Lee" snaring a pass. The text described Lee as a "scrappy little Pilot guard" and a crowd favorite when Portland easily downed the College of Puget Sound, 52–34. Lee did not shoot well in the game but managed to end the evening with ten points. Around the same time, Gonzaga vanquished Portland, 47–36, but Lee took his team's scoring honors with nine points. The

Oregonian published a photo of Lee going in for a layup against Gonzaga in January 1949. In the same paper, the daily called Lee a "diminutive ... guard." The next month the *Oregonian* identified him as a "watch charm guard." Late in 1949, the *Seattle Times* described Lee as a "5–5 speedster." When Portland beat Willamette in December 1949, the *Oregonian's* Bill Hulen raved about the "little Chinese slickster" and the "mighty mite from Astoria." Lee, portrayed by Hulen as usually more of a passer than a shooter, hit 11 of 17 shots and scored 24 in all. In February 1950, Portland downed St. Mary's of Moraga, 63–53. Lee led the way with 23 points. The *Oregonian* observed that Lee's father had traveled from Astoria to see his son in action, "and he couldn't have picked a better game."[36]

Meanwhile, Wataru Misaka made it to the center of the college basketball world in the 1940s. Misaka grew up in the lower-class environs of Ogden, Utah. His brother Tats recalled in the early 1970s that the Ogden neighborhood in which he and his brother were raised was "deprived and depraved," although, he insisted, this was so largely because of outsiders coming into their neighborhood to carouse. Misaka's Issei parents, according to the U.S. census manuscripts of 1930, ran a barber shop in Ogden. Subsequently, when Misaka's father died in the late 1930s, his mother, who spoke little English, took over the shop until she died in 1954. At high school, Misaka was a multi-sport athlete who played football and baseball as well as basketball. Fortunately for Misaka and his family, the geographic reach of Executive

Like Al Mar, Fred Lee was a Chinese American who played big time college hoops during World War II. Lee stood out for Oregon State, but after the war he played outstanding hoops for the University of Portland. This is a photograph of Lee when he was a top scorer for the University of Portland. Courtesy University Archives, University of Portland, Oregon.

Order 9066 did not extend as far east as Utah. Accordingly, after Pearl Harbor was attacked, he was free to attend local Weber Junior College, where he was conference MVP, and then head to the University of Utah.[37]

Misaka joined a youthful and lightly respected University of Utah five. Yet the five would become a national powerhouse, competing in both the NCAA and National Invitational tournaments in 1944 while thousands of Japanese Americans languished in concentration camps and the United States was engaged in bitter warfare with Japanese forces. Misaka, Josh and Tres Ferrin claim, was the smallest player on the team but "by far the quickest." Yet for much of the 1943–1944 season, Misaka was a nonstarter who still got plenty of minutes. Consequently, Misaka was a bit discouraged, according to the Ferrins' book about the 1944 Utah five. He wondered if "he wasn't good enough, too short, or had a name his coach couldn't pronounce." The Ferrins write that Misaka's coach, Vadal Peterson, while not personally prejudiced against Misaka himself, did not want to start him. He believed the Japanese American was good enough to start, but feared angering bigoted supporters. Thus, Peterson fretted when Misaka got considerable court time during a game. However, as Utah rolled into postseason play, a teammate's injury put Misaka into the starting five.[38]

Utah had been invited to both the NCAA tournament and the National Invitational Tournament (NIT). However, the team decided to journey to New York City, because at that time the NIT, held at the famed Madison Square Garden, was the more prestigious event. When Utah took the court at the Garden, Misaka stood out, receiving the plaudits of the hard-to-please Garden crowd and much of the press in attendance. Getting Misaka's birthplace wrong, sportswriter Hugh Fullerton Jr. wondered "if there's any place but America where you'd see the kind of sportsmanship the Garden fans displayed when they gave a big hand to Utah's Wat Misaka, Hawaiian-born Japanese? The kid deserved it, too." Despite Misaka's efforts, Utah was bumped from the tournament early. Nevertheless, Utah was asked to compete in the NCAA tournament as a last-minute replacement. Rather than go home, Misaka and his teammates accepted the invitation.[39]

In the 1944 NCAA Western Regional, held at Kansas City, Misaka won over many in attendance. Press coverage was laudatory but not necessarily free of troubling allusions to race. According to notable journalist Bob Considine, "[o]ne of the biggest cheers of the 1943–1944 basketball season went to Wat Misaka, University of Utah's American-born Jap, when he left the floor after his fourth personal foul in the Western NCAA finals." In that game against Iowa State, Utah had to rally from behind. The *Washington Post* reported that Misaka sank three crucial baskets to aid his team's comeback. Yet not everyone was impressed with showing off an America free of bigotry in the midst of World War II. The Ferrins point out that when Misaka reported into the game, he heard boos from spectators, and the referees seemed to have it in for the Japanese American as they quickly called four fouls on him.[40]

Yet the *Kansas City Star* sports editor, C. E. McBride, was moved to the heights of wartime patriotism by Misaka's appearance at the local court. He asserted that Japan's leaders would not understand that Americans applauded the "little fellow." Addressing those leaders in his column, McBride referred to "little ... Misaka, American born representative of your race." McBride conceded that some in attendance may have wondered why Misaka was on the court, but generally chose to keep their concerns to themselves. As for his teammates and opponents, they treated Misaka with respect.[41]

Moving on to the actual game between Utah and Iowa State, McBride declared that the "little Jap" turned things around for his struggling team in the second half. And when Misaka left the game in foul trouble, his coach and team congratulated him, McBride proudly proclaimed, and the fans, generally from Iowa State, cheered him. This would all confound Japan's leaders, McBride advised, but it could happen in a "civilized country where sportsmanship is known and practiced."[42]

After winning the Western Regional, Utah returned to New York City to confront a powerful Dartmouth squad for the championship. Making matters worse for Utah was that the team's regular center had suffered an injury. The five-foot-eight-inch Misaka took over for the injured center and helped spark his team's ultimate victory. After Utah stunned Dartmouth at Madison Square Garden for the NCAA championship, the U.S. military publication, *Stars and Stripes,* praised the performance of the "pint sized Hawaiian-born Japanese-American."[43]

Upon their NCAA victory, Misaka's Utah five was then scheduled to meet the NIT champion—St. John's of New York City. Coached by the legendary Joe Lapchick, St. John's was considered a favorite. Before the game, the *New York Sun's* Wilbur Wood called Misaka "the chubby ball of fire from Hawaii." As it turned out, Utah upset St. John's and Misaka's contributions proved invaluable.[44]

After the postseason tournaments, Ogden applauded its Japanese American hometown hero. The *Pacific Citizen* reported that Ogden was proud of Misaka's accomplishments and "mildly perturbed" by press references to him as a Hawaiian. The *Ogden Standard-Examiner* published a photograph of Misaka in his Ogden High School uniform and another of his mother. The caption to the former picture informed readers that "basketball fans at Madison Square Garden cheered aplenty for Wat Misaka ... of the University of Utah 'blitz kids,' the new national champions." The other photo described his mother as a "feminine barber in Ogden," who "supports her three sons." Subsequently, the Ogden City Council passed a resolution commending two sons of Ogden who made good in Utah University basketball—Misaka and Artie Ferrin, the most talented of the Utah hoopsters.[45]

The seemingly unceasing world conflict interrupted Misaka's Utah education. He eventually served in the Pacific and occupied Japan. And he managed a bit of basketball, playing on the Fort Snelling Language School team. When he returned to the Provo school after the war, Misaka was elected vice-president of the student body.[46]

Despite his achievements a few years earlier, Misaka had to prove himself all over again to his coach. As late as December 1946, he was still not a starter. Yet during the 1946–1947 season, Utah's basketball team reclaimed national fame and the speedy, talented Misaka battled his way back into the starting five. Returning to the NIT, Utah upset West Virginia in the semifinals. The *New York Times* published a photograph of Misaka in action and declared that "little Wat Misaka" was a defensive standout who teamed with Vern Gardner and future pro Arnold Ferrin to power the Utah five.[47]

Utah surprised the favorite Kentucky Wildcats in the NIT championship game in 1947. And Misaka was clearly one of the reasons. A *New York Times* writer attempted to praise "little Wat Misaka, American born of Japanese descent." He described Misaka as "cute" in his play, intercepting passes and generally making life miserable for the Kentucky star, Ralph Beard, who was held to a single point, while Misaka scored two free throws. A UPI account maintained that the University of Utah quintet had several heroes, "but in the final analysis, little old Wat Misaka, an American-born Japanese, who served with the U.S. intelligence units during the war, stood out like a handful of very sore thumbs. Misaka hounded Ralph Beard and tall Ken Rollins on defense." Another UPI report, entitled "Jap Runt Stars in Ute Victory," appeared in a Southern California newspaper. It declared that Utah players "had to stoop down to pat the brunette thatch of little Wat Misaka, the Japanese kid who has improved on the invention of the dynamo." Ogden sportswriter Carl Lundquist asserted, "Misaka, the all-around artist who played tirelessly and who was as fresh as an Easter morning corsage at the finish, with nothing but a defensive record to show for his 40 hard minutes. He did not make a field goal, he bucketed only two free throws, but Utah would have been as far behind as from here to Utah without him." Ned Irish, who ran the basketball program at Madison Square Garden, proclaimed in 1947 that Misaka was one of the best players he had seen in action at the New York City's celebrated indoor sports venue.[48]

A *New York Evening Record* columnist, Leonard Cohen, paid tribute to

Misaka. He wrote, "A chance is all Misaka wants any time on the court or anywhere else." Emphasizing Misaka's lack of height, Cohen went on to call the Utah native "a seemingly tireless bundle of nervous energy, whose catlike speed and court savvy belie his frail and studious appearance," while letting readers know that his performance had fashioned him into a "crowd favorite" at Madison Square Garden. Misaka, Cohen conceded, had found his Japanese ancestry to be a handicap. He advised readers that while serving in the military, Misaka encountered racism. Nevertheless, Cohen declared, the hoopster concentrated on his duties as staff sergeant and tried not to let others' bigotry get to him.[49]

As a Utah hoopster, Misaka had demonstrated to Cohen that he was "[a] well spoken, pleasant chap, he has the courage of his convictions, faith in his own ability and a deep-seated belief that if there is a small chance of reaching any particular goal, he's willing and ready to struggle for the objective." Moreover, he was a "team player." To prove this, Cohen wrote that Misaka's mother had never seen him play college hoops. She went to Utah's game against Brigham Young, but came late. Misaka, by this time, was already out of the game, apparently for good. According to Cohen, the Japanese American could have persuaded Peterson to put him back in the lineup, but he did not want to pressure Peterson into changing his game plan.[50]

Japanese Americans throughout the United States appeared pleased with Misaka's achievements. After the 1947 NIT championship game, a wire photo showed Misaka, called "the hero of the University of Utah victory over Kentucky," receiving a trophy from Yosh Kojimoto, president of the American Nisei Athletic Union. The trophy was inscribed "To Wat Misaka, Utah University National Basketball Champion.... America's Outstanding Nisei Player."[51]

In Utah, Misaka found grateful supporters such as sportswriter Al Warden, who celebrated the hoopster's accomplishments. Writing out of Ogden in the spring of 1947, Warden asserted, "Wat's feats have done much to cement Japanese-American relations. Ogdenites who know the colorful little hoopster stamp him as one of the finest ever to come out of Weber county." Utah's Japanese Americans expressed pride in Misaka's accomplishments. In April 1947, the *Pacific Citizen* reported that the JACL in Mt. Olympus had shown a film of Utah's Madison Square Garden triumph. In late April 1947, Misaka and teammate Arnold Ferrin were feted in Ogden. A banquet held at the Star Noodle Parlor was held in their honor. The gathering was sponsored by the Ogden JACL, the Japanese Buddhist Church, the Japanese Christian Church, Shinwakai, Utah Nippon, and, interestingly, the Wildlife Association. Ogden's mayor, David Romney, was one of the speakers. He proclaimed Misaka a credit to sportsmanship, "not only for Utah, but Japanese people throughout the world." Romney, furthermore, "paid tribute to Japanese Americans and their loyalty to the country."[52]

Meanwhile, Misaka had accepted an invitation to play some basketball in Hawai'i. He joined a team called the Hawaii All-Stars against the visiting Harlem Globetrotters. The All-Stars were comprised of four University of Hawai'i players and the fine Portuguese Hawaiian big man, Red Rocha, who excelled at Oregon State and would later make it to the NBA. The professional troupe won easily, 57–40, but according to the *Pacific Citizen*, Misaka earned admiration for his defense and speed.[53]

Misaka remained a source of pride to Japanese Americans long after his playing career ended. Japanese American high school basketball coach Frank Fuji recalled Misaka as an inspirational figure. When Fuji was in Salt Lake City after the NIT tournament in 1947, he saw a procession of convertibles come down the street. "I was wondering what the heck it was. Then, I saw Wat Misaka, a member of the championship team, in one of the cars, and I was really impressed."[54]

Misaka remembered little hostility from college basketball fans. However, the Ferrins relate that the Japanese American encountered racist taunts and racial discrimination while on the road during the 1943–1944 season. Playing at Colorado College, Misaka heard plenty of derogatory remarks from fans of the home team. When Misaka and his teammates performed at military installations, he was targeted with insults and hostile stares from white soldiers. While the Utah five was traveling by train, a racist conductor kicked Misaka out of his berth to accommodate a white military officer. Nevertheless, Irving Marsh wrote in the *Sporting News* in 1948 that Misaka was one of the best "small players" in recent memory.[55]

Aside from Misaka, several other Japanese Americans played postsecondary school basketball during World War II. Many of these Japanese Americans had lived on the Pacific Coast but either left before Executive Order 9066 was issued or were allowed by the United States to head east for educational purposes. After release from the Topaz camp in Utah, Tuts Tatsumo played for the University of Utah along with Misaka. Unlike Misaka, he saw very little action. Interestingly, when the Utah aggregation headed into postseason play, Peterson decided to take a white player, who had had even less minutes on the court during the season than Tatsumo. Perhaps, the Ferrins speculate, the coach or the school considered two Nikkei on his traveling squad a little too provocative.[56] The College of Idaho suited up two Nisei during the war—George Saito and Roy Hosada. According to the *Pacific Citizen*, Hosada had previously competed for a five representing the University of Idaho, southern branch. Moreover, he was the second-highest scorer on the College of Idaho's team.

Michigan's Kalamazoo College five attained some national publicity as "the shortest basketball team in the nation" because its roster included five-foot-four Tom Sugihara and an equally short, former Seattle prep star, Paul Hiyama. At Hillsdale College, Washington State native Bright Onoto played basketball and football. After release from the Minidoka camp, Kazuo Tada wound up in a Nebraska Wesleyan basketball uniform. Dakota Wesleyan suited up four Nisei—Oliver Takaichi, Bill Marutami, Min Yoshida, and Akira Yukomichi. John Okomoto competed for the University of Illinois Flyers. Huron College suited up Sei Adachi. And Johnny Oshida played for University of Illinois Navy Pier five and Augsburg College.[57]

Postwar American college basketball witnessed continued Asian American participation. We have already noted Wat Misaka's triumphant return to Utah basketball and Fred Lee's efforts in the Pacific Northwest. Additionally, after V-J Day, Seattle's Shig Murao found himself at Springfield College in Massachusetts. During Murao's first year at Springfield, he starred on the school's junior varsity team. When Springfield journeyed west to play the University of Utah, Bill Clegg of the *Salt Lake Tribune* noted in December 1947, that Murao was "a Chicago speedster" who had been performing well off the bench for the Massachusetts five. In one game against Utah, Murao scored nine points. That same month, Springfield journeyed to San Francisco, where it took on the Borlo Athletic Club five coached by Hank Luisetti. Listed in the *San Francisco Chronicle*'s box score as "Murad," the Japanese American managed to notch three points in the game. According to the Springfield College yearbook of 1948, Murao tallied 123 points in all during the 1947–1948 basketball season. A couple of years later, Murao was still making an impact as a role player. The *Portsmouth Herald* maintained, "Shig is very quick and aggressive, resulting in a good many stolen balls which he converts into points."[58]

Thanks in part to the creative machinations of the University of San Francisco's publicity director, Pete Rozelle, Willie Wong surfaced as the most famous Asian American to play mainland college basketball in the late 1940s and early 1950s. In the fall of 1948, Wong entered USF. According to journalist Jim O'Leary, USF coach Pete Newell recruited Wong after he happened to see the San Franciscan in action at the "Oriental Basketball Tournament" in Seattle in 1948. As a freshman, Wong was not, at that time, eligible for the varsity. But he did well as a first-year San Francisco Don. On February 22, according to the *San Francisco Chronicle*, Wong stood out as the USF freshmen beat the Jewish Community Center, 49–32. He also got more publicity than many first-year hoopsters. The *Oakland Tribune* promoted an upcoming game between the USF freshmen and St. Mary's freshmen by pointing out that the former was led by Wong. After his freshman season, one newspaper report, ignoring Al

Mar and Fred Lee, predicted that Wong would stand out as "basketball's first Chinese man of distinction." Indeed, according to Kathleen Yep, Wong averaged a nice 13 points per game with the freshman squad.[59]

Wong's movement to varsity, coached by the legendary Newell, was exploited by the USF publicity mill, overseen by Rozelle. It should be said that the previous year witnessed USF's amazing championship run in the NIT, upsetting more prestigious East Coast fives along the way. Still, Bay Area passion for USF basketball was fairly underwhelming. Hoping to crank up fan interest, Rozelle was probably responsible for an advertisement for the basketball team in a 1949 football program. In the advertisement, Wong was touted as a leading recruit for the varsity team. To further stimulate interest in the Chinese American hoopster, Bob Brachman called Wong "one of the greatest little cagers in the business." The *Monitor* described him as the "five-foot-five-inch Chinese guard sensation." The *Chinese Press* extolled the USF varsity newcomer as "the sharp-shooting sophomore star" and informed readers that Wong would become the first Chinese American to play varsity basketball at Madison Square Garden. The *Press* added that hundreds of Chinese New Yorkers would show up to celebrate Wong's appearance when the Dons took the court in New York City in late December.[60]

Apparently, Newell was not happy about all the publicity swirling around Wong. He dealt with the matter good-humoredly, albeit demonstrating a certain degree of cultural insensitivity. In the process, he targeted Rozelle, who would eventually serve as commissioner of the National Football League and help fashion professional football into the immensely popular American institution it is today. Accordingly, Rozelle, while in his USF office, got a call from someone claiming to be "Cholly Lee, Chinese Press." The caller demanded, "Willie Wong, he play first stling this year." When Rozelle urged some caution about Wong's prospects, the caller said, "What matter? Coach no like Willie." Rozelle responded that Wong was a respected member of the team and would make the traveling squad to New York City. Then "Cholly Lee" wanted to know if Wong would "start the game in Garden in big city of New York." Rozelle said there was indeed a chance he would, transforming "Cholly Lee" into Pete Newell, who complained to Rozelle, "So you're the guy who's been trying to coach my team in the papers."[61]

If nothing else, Wong showed that he belonged on the USF varsity. He made his varsity debut in the last minutes of a game against Nevada. "The sensational San Francisco Chinese," connected on his only shot, according to the *San Francisco Examiner*. Wong did well in USF's subsequent humbling of the Olympic Club five, 80–24.[62]

When USF arrived in New York City, the national press took notice.

Highlighting Wong's relative smallness, the San Franciscan was photographed dunking a ball from on top of six-foot-six teammate Don Lofgren's shoulders. The caption described the adult Wong as "San Francisco's remarkable little Chinese boy." The *New York Times* published a photograph of Wong flanked by Lofgren and another tall Don. The caption referred to "5 foot 4 inch Chinese sophomore, Willie Wong, whose speed may electrify the Garden spectators." Wong got into the game against St. John's, but did not score.[63]

While remaining on the East Coast, USF headed south after New Year's Day. The *Greensboro Record* notified readers that Wong had some gravitas as a hoopster. It published a piece by Newspaper Enterprise Association writer Jim O'Leary, who quoted Newell extensively on the Chinese American. Wong, according to the famed coach, was more fundamentally sound than other smaller players. "Most little guys," Newell insisted, "are merely spectacular chasing opponents." However, Wong on defense did a good job of staying in front of opponents. He also blocked out opponents for rebounds. On offense, Wong had a nice touch on his shots. According to an excessively clever O'Leary, "Woo Woo Wong gives San Francisco a fresh slant on basketball."[64]

Once conference play started for the Dons, Wong too rarely got off the bench, but he and a couple of his teammates' slick ball handing proved instrumental in helping USF ice a victory over Santa Clara. Bob Brachman observed that due to the "nifty" stalling tactics of Wong, Cappy Lavin, and Frankie Kuzara, "[t]he Broncos might just as well have been chasing hummingbirds." At the end of the 1949–1950 season, Wong managed to get into 14 of 26 games and played for two to eight minutes when he did.[65]

Yet, according to Yep, "[c]oaches, competitors, teammates, and journalists recognized Wong's talent as a shooter, playmaker, ball handler, and defender. They also acknowledged his work ethic and drive to compete in the sport." Pete Newell praised Wong's shooting and ball handling ability. Newell remembered, "He had good range ... much farther than a smaller person like him should have had. Because he wasn't as big as most players, he had to learn more about the game, too. He always seemed to make the right pass and never seemed to take a bad shot. And I'll tell you, he was a god in San Francisco's Chinatown." Cappy Lavin, Wong's teammate at USF and father of Steve Lavin, who became a successful NCAA coach and basketball commentator, admired his talent, adding that Chinese Americans in the cities in which the Dons played often honored Wong. Rene Herrerias, a fine Latino guard for Newell and future Cal coach, said "I remember he was the toughest guy to guard, and he fitted in with the team from the first day he came onto it. He was just a great guy."[66]

San Francisco's Chinese community also voiced pride in Wong's achievements at USF, however statistically meager. Yep declares,

Like the popular press, the prominent San Francisco Chinese had a stake in Wong's image. Casting Wong as an ambassador of Chinese America, the Chinatown Chamber of Commerce utilized his fame in white communities as a form of ethnic and economic diplomacy. The Chinatown elite played up Wong's success in non-Chinese contexts to foster their own ethnic pride as well as to increase the exposure of Chinese businesses.[67]

Nevertheless, Phil Woolpert, who succeeded Newell when the latter moved on to Michigan State, was not enamored with Wong's potential contributions to the Dons, and the Chinese American's varsity basketball career at USF ended.

Wong continued to play basketball and exercise an interest in the Chinese American community. Moreover, he worked as a warehouseman in Livermore until his retirement in 1984. Remembering him as emblematic of the strivings of Chinese American young people in post–World War II America, San Francisco's Chinese community named a playground after Willie Wong.[68]

In the Bay Area, other Asian Americans played some big time college basketball in the late 1940s and early 1950s. Eddie Chavez, a multitalented Filipino athlete from Vallejo, surfaced on Santa Clara University's five. During the 1948–1949 season, Chavez emerged as "the star of the Santa Clara frosh team." When the Santa Clara freshman five downed USF, 47–38, in January 1949, Chavez scored 16 points, while Willie Wong led the losers with 13. Chavez joined the Broncos' varsity the next season. Before the 1949–1950 season, the *San Jose Mercury* said "Chavez was a sensation with last season's freshman team and is expected to play great ball" for the varsity. He did not play much, but the Santa Clara 1950 yearbook displayed a photo of Chavez fighting for a rebound against Stanford. In January 1951, Chavez got into a game against San Jose State, but did not score, which seemed to be Chavez's fate while on the varsity five.[69]

In 1951, George Goto played a bit for Stanford. For example, he scored one point in a game against Utah. Goto then moved on to Sacramento State, where he excelled as a hoopster. The Sacramento State yearbook displayed a couple of photographs of Goto in action during the 1953–1954 season. When Sacramento State edged San Francisco State in mid–January 1954, Goto put up seven points. Goto subsequently graduated from Sacramento State, returning to get a MA in 1960. He went on to pursue a career in education as a physical education teacher, coach, and athletic director at Sierra Community College, which ultimately named a basketball court after him. The city of Roseville also honored Goto by naming a park after him. Goto, meanwhile, participated in the "Standing Guard Project," described in a Sierra College website as "a book and CD-ROM that celebrates our region's strong Japanese American heritage as well as educates about the impact of World War II internment."[70]

Dick Nagai played big time basketball for USC in the mid–1950s. According to the 1940 U.S. census manuscripts, Nagai was the son of Japanese immigrants. His father was a produce owner and his mother, a salesperson. Before the 1953–1954 season, the *Pacific Citizen* described the Angelino athlete as a "Boyle Heights lad" who did well on the Trojan freshman team and was expected to contribute to the varsity. During Nagai's first year on varsity, he was often injured, but according to the *Oakland Tribune*'s Bill Dunbar, he contributed valuable minutes off the bench. Against UCLA, Nagai scored six in mid–January. Moreover, he was temporarily moved to the first team because his coach, Forrest Toogood, noticed his scoring potential when he came off the bench. When USC took on Utah in December 1954, the Trojans fell behind early, but according to one wire story, "then seemingly taking on new life with the appearance of Dick Nagai, a 6-foot substitute guard, the Trojans took control of the backboards and started hitting for the first time on drive in shots." While still on the road, the Trojans fell to Wake Forest, but Nagai's 15 points reportedly kept USC from getting blown out. When USC downed Cornell, 77–58, at a tournament in Raleigh, Nagai shined as game-high scorer with 18 points, while demonstrating "fine ball handling" to boot. Still, Nagai often languished on USC's bench. On January 7, 1955, he played but did not score against Stanford. The next year, the *Portland Oregonian* published a photo of Nagai shooting against Oregon. He must have missed, because the two points he scored in the game were on free throws.[71]

After starring at Garfield High in Seattle, Jim Hino and Ray Soo were offered a chance to make Seattle University's five in the early 1950s. Soo was able to stick. The five-foot-five Soo played on a fine squad led by the famed O'Brien brothers, John and Ed. The team was even able to beat the Harlem Globetrotters. As for Soo, he had his moments. For example, he sank the winning basket to beat Montana State in Missoula. The *Pacific Citizen* reported that the people at Seattle University "believe they have the nation's smallest player in the young Chinese American."[72]

Soo did not play regularly for a Seattle five that surfaced as a national power in the early 1950s. During his freshman season, Soo seemed to get plenty of action, although he was not a starter. Early in the season, a photo of him getting a shot off in a game against a prominent AAU team, the Buchan Bakers, was published in the *Seattle Times*. Seattle's freshman team actually won the game in the city's Northwest League and Soo tallied seven points. In mid–December, Soo managed 11 points as his team beat a military five, 86–42. The next month he scored five against Fort Lawson. After his freshman season, Soo was named the "most inspirational" member of his squad.[73]

While not a regular, Soo seemed a valuable member of the Seattle five. In early December 1951, Soo scored three against Pacific Lutheran. The next month, Soo's coach played him more regularly in a game against St. Martin's because he believed the Chinese American could help counteract St. Martin's ball-control offense. Soo wound up tallying five points in the game. As Seattle gained national prominence, sportswriter Jack Hewing noted the contributions of Soo, "a Chinese boy who tiptoes a scant 5–5." And a piece by the Reverend Erle Powell made an interesting reference to Soo's career with Seattle University. Apparently his coach, Al Brightman, encouraged pregame prayers, and Powell found it curious that "Ray Soo, of Chinese origins" joined in.[74]

Asian Americans hoopsters participated in small college programs during the early Cold War years. In the late 1940s and early 1950s, Jimmy Wong took the floor for San Francisco State. In January 1949, Wong tallied ten points as the Gators dumped the Cal Aggies, 56–46. During the 1949–1950 season, he shined and was honored as a second team all-conference player. Wong, furthermore, captained the five. In the early 1950s, Oregon Tech suited up James Minato. When Oregon Tech dumped Oregon College of Education, 77–55, Minato, according to the *Pacific Citizen*, put up eight points on three field goals and two free throws. In Ohio, a hoopster named George Kim played for Wooster College, hitting two key baskets against Otterbein in January 1953. The next season, he scored 15 points against Garden Grove. In the mid–1950s, Al Singh played center for Cal Poly of Pomona. Singh scored 11 when Cal Poly lost to the University of San Diego, 62–41, in January, 1957. Also in Southern California, Raymond Fakuchi competed for Westmont College in Southern California in the early 1950s. Playing for Westmont after Fakuchi, a hoopster surnamed Lum scored eight in a game in January 1954. Following George Goto to California's capital, Jim Yokota played varsity hoops for Sacramento State in the late 1950s. Yokota, who also joined the Hornets' football squad in 1958, suited up in basketball from 1957 to 1959. In January 1958, Yokota tallied five points against the Cal Aggies. And Tanimoto suited up for Los Angeles State in the mid–1960s.[75]

Hawaiian Ken Kimura starred in small college hoops for Southern Oregon during the early 1950s seasons. His 12 points helped his team subdue Humboldt State, 68–44. The *Humboldt Standard-Examiner*, therefore, noticed Kimura's excellence, describing him as "a veteran point getter." In January 1953, Kimura racked up 18 points against Eastern Oregon College. Hitting 12 free throws, Kimura tallied 24 points against Humboldt State in late January 1953. The next month, "tiny Ken Kimura" wound up with 19 against Humboldt in a losing effort. At the end of the 1952–1953 season, Humboldt State, unsurprisingly, named Kimura to its all-opponents five and, more importantly, he was an unanimous all-conference choice. Kimura continued to shine into his senior year. In December 1953, readers of the *Portland Oregonian* learned that

Southern Oregon had beaten Lewis and Clark, thanks in part to Kimura "flashing some classy dribbling," hitting key free throws, and scoring 13. In January 1954, the *Reno Evening Gazette* called six-foot-four Leon Keefe and the five-foot-eight Kimura "the long and short of the Southern Oregon club." The next month, the Hawaiian tallied 22 in a losing effort against Chico State and then pumped in 21 points as Southern Oregon snuck passed Eastern Oregon, 69–66.[76]

Nonvarsity Four-Year Schools and Junior/Community College Hoopsters

In the earlier part of the twentieth century, four-year colleges frequently sponsored lightweight teams for smaller male hoopsters, a few of whom were Asian Americans. Asian Americans also played freshman basketball even if they did not graduate to the varsity. Furthermore, Asian Americans dribbled and passed for business schools and junior, now more commonly called community, colleges.

During the middle decades of the twentieth century, some colleges offered young men diverse opportunities to represent their schools even if they were not necessarily "big time" varsity material. In the early 1920s, Fred Koba starred on Stanford's 135-pound team before going varsity. Koba also played later for the 145-pound team. A Fukada suited up for Healds' Business School in San Jose in 1933, while Fukuyama was a hoopster for Woodbury Business School in Los Angeles. Around the same time, Yamamoto was a top scorer for Cal's 130-pound team, which also included Kamamoto. Earl Wong, by the way, played for Cal's freshman team during the 1930s. When, in 1935, the San Jose State freshman team decimated a squad called the San Jose Fiestas, 60–11, forward Miyamoto tallied 14 points. Wally Funabiki, according to the *Heart Mountain Sentinel*, starred on Stanford's freshman team before the war. The Stanford yearbook for 1940 described Funabiki as "small but tricky." Ted Yano told readers of the *Heart Mountain Sentinel* in 1943 that Art Kaihatsu "sparked the frosh quintet" for UCLA. Unfortunately, according to the UCLA yearbook of 1941, academic problems prematurely ended Kaihatsu's season. Around the same time, Dick Sakamoto and Tosh Ihara participated on the Westwood School's 145-pound team. In the late 1940s, Cliff Wong was the "sharpshooting forward" on the Redlands' freshman squad and Kawashima was on the University of Portland freshman squad. In 1948, a hoopster named Kim played for Multnomah College's physical education department in Portland's Central YMCA League. In 1950, Bill Hirose and John Oshida starred on Cal's 130- and

145-pound teams, respectively. And in the late 1950s, Ikegami was on the Cal Aggies' junior varsity five.[77]

Sal Jio, dubbed a "diminutive Japanese" and "diminutive forward" by the *San Jose Mercury*, performed well for San Jose State's freshman team during the 1935–1936 season. In early February, Jio scored ten points in a game against a Sacramento five. When the Spartan freshman downed Santa Clara, the *San Jose Mercury's* August G. Kettmann observed, "little Sal Jio handled the ball nicely" while he totaled four points. There was another Japanese American playing with Jio whose last name was apparently Sekigahama, although the *Mercury* came up with variations. In any event, he scored eight in the previously mentioned Sacramento game. And in a losing effort against Golden Gate Junior College, "Harry Sakiyama" managed four.[78]

Junior or community college basketball enticed Asian Americans. As early as 1922, the *Riverside Daily Press* observed that "Mino, the little Japanese star football and baseball player" was trying out for Riverside Junior College's basketball team. Before U.S. entry into World War II, Otto Oshida was a "diminutive star" for San Francisco City College and John Kashiwabara played for Placer Junior College. After World War II, Miyamoto was on the Monterey Junior College team. During the 1949–1950 season, Wally Wong made second string all-conference while playing for Hartnell in Salinas, and Babe Samson had some big games for San Francisco City College. Meanwhile, a young woman named Fumie Nishimura had taken up basketball at Fullerton Junior College in the late 1930s and early 1940s. A daughter of a farm laborer, she had previously played basketball at Fullerton High School.[79]

In the late 1940s, San Franciscan Henry Chin showed up on the San Benito Junior College roster several miles south of his home town. Indeed, he seemed to have done quite well, although not without complaint. Early in January 1949, Chin's 13 points aided his team's triumph over San Francisco City College. Later in the month, Don Selby told *Examiner* readers that the onetime league leader in scoring for San Francisco prep hoopsters had put up 33 points in one game. Since several of his points came off of free throws, Chin lamented that junior college ball could be quite rough and sighed, "I think I shall be glad to play in Frisco." Selby quipped, "Imagine a San Francisco lad saying 'Frisco.'"[80]

Early in January 1950, the *Pacific Citizen* called Placer Junior College's George Goto, "probably the first six foot Nisei player to come along since the days of Ted Ohashi." Playing for a school now known as Sierra Community College, Goto was a 23-year-old veteran who had served in Japan during the occupation. The 1930 U.S. census manuscript depicts him as the son of a father who ran a fish market in Placer County. Goto's coach at Placer told the press that he was "basketball smart and shoots well." Moreover, his quickness on defense allowed Goto to intercept many passes. The *Pacific Citizen* informed readers that Goto had been the MVP of the California Junior College tournament, held over the holidays of 1949. According to the *San Francisco Examiner*, Goto scored eight points in the championship game against the favorite Menlo Junior College squad.[81]

Jimmy Yokota played outstandingly for Placer Junior College as well. The *Pacific Citizen* noted that Yokota, who also competed in football for the school, had started the 1950–1951 season as a substitute, but quickly not only won a starting position but was leading the team in scoring. When Placer beat Yuba College, 64–49, Yokota led the way with 15 points. Bob Nakamoto, Ed Miyamoto, and Roy Doi joined Yokota on the Placer five.[82]

Other Asian Americans played junior college basketball in the 1950s. Hiro Kubo suited up for El Camino Junior College in the early 1950s. Junior Singh starred for San Bernadino Junior College in the mid–1950s, while Howard Lum was a top scorer for Hartnell Junior College in the mid–1950s. On January 7, 1955, he put up 11 points against East Contra Costa Junior College. Around the same time, a hoopster named Inouye starred for East Los Angeles Junior College. Against San Diego Junior College, he notched 23 points. And on the East Coast in the mid–1950s, Alfred Wong competed for Holyoke Junior College.[83]

Harvey Fong not only played center for Sacramento Junior College but was a record-setting scorer in the mid–1950s. In January 1954, Fong swished 15 in a triumph over San Francisco City College. In late January, when Sacramento J. C. dumped Stockton J. C., 76–60, Fong ended the game with 23 points. Against San Mateo, Fong accumulated 18 points a week later to help his team win, 71–56. He then scored 29 points against El Camino on January 7, 1955. Fong even managed to pour in 40 points in one game against Santa Rosa. During his years at Sacramento J. C., he averaged 16.5 points per game, ninth in school history as of 2013 and thirteenth in total points.[84]

Bill Kajikawa and Buck Lai, Jr.

The first Asian American head basketball coach of a college five, Bill Kajikawa took over the reins of Arizona State's basketball program after World War II. Born in Oxnard, California, Kajikawa's family moved to Arizona in 1930. In Phoenix, he went to high school and worked in agriculture, while his mother and stepfather cut hair for a living. After attending Phoenix Union High School, Kajikawa headed to nearby Arizona State College in Tempe, where he starred in varsity baseball and football. Kajikawa also played a little hoops as a freshman.[85]

After graduating from Arizona State, Kajikawa's alma mater named him freshman basketball coach. Early in 1940, the *Arizona Republic*'s George Moore hailed the job Kajikawa was doing at Arizona State. In 1941, Kajikawa, described as a "Phoenix Japanese," was named the school's baseball coach. Subsequently, he was honored by the National Japanese Young People's Association "as one of the outstanding young men of his race in the United States." During World War II, Kajikawa fought in the renowned 442nd but happily returned to Arizona State after the war. At the Tempe campus, he helped coach football and baseball, as well as teach physical education courses. In 1946, he was named head coach of the baseball team and two years later was heading up the basketball program as well. The *Pacific Citizen* acknowledged with pride his debut as a college coach as Arizona State headed into conference play in January 1949. Kajikawa, the weekly informed readers, had led his team to a recent tournament triumph and victories in its first two conference games.[86]

As a coach Kajikawa found himself doing the usual things, such as scouting and recruiting, but also sweeping the gym floor for a basketball program that was vastly primitive by today's standards . A true jack-of-all-trades, he also served as an assistant football coach in addition to his coaching duties in baseball. In basketball, he led the Sun Devils to five seasons in the upper division of conference play. Moreover, he was the first Arizona State coach to recruit an African American athlete. Ned Wulk, his replacement and highly respected in college coaching circles in the mid-twentieth century, said of Kajikawa, "Bill is one of a kind in athletics ... and one of the positive kinds. He has the unusual quality of being interested, involved, and concerned about everyone around him, be it player, fellow coach, or anyone else."[87]

At least some followers of college basketball were surprised to see Kajikawa at the helm of any team, however underfunded and comparatively anonymous. Early in 1950, the *Pacific Citizen* observed that Kajikawa's Sun Devils squad had been performing on the East Coast. It cited a Pittsburgh sportswriter, Vince Johnson, who asserted, "Basketball fans ... blinked with surprise when wiry amber-skinned Bill Masao Kajikawa made his appearance with the Arizona State team in the Gardens."[88]

Kajikawa was not exactly the focus of the college basketball world, as was, say, Kentucky's Adolph Rupp. Nevertheless, the press did pay attention to him. In 1951, the *New York Times* observed that Kajikawa was the "nation's only Japanese-American college mentor." In 1952, Kajikawa got caught up a bit in a referee controversy in which his conference was embroiled. After Arizona State played Hardin-Simmons, Kajikawa was somewhat critical of the game's referees. Reluctantly agreeing with those who derided officiating in the conference, Kajikawa admitted that the referees called the game "a little close" even though it was not particularly foul ridden.[89]

While Arizona State did not become a world beater under Kajikawa's leadership, he earned plaudits for his coaching. The 1954–1955 season proved one of Kajikawa's most successful seasons. The team went eight and four in conference play, putting the Arizona State five in a tie for third and helping earn Kajikawa the conference's coach of the year honor. Remembering Kajikawa's fine year, Fred Imhof of the *Oakland Tribune* claimed that the Japanese American stressed character and sportsmanship and was himself involved in community affairs outside of his coaching duties. A proud *Pacific Citizen* pointed out that Kajikawa's squad had to overcome injuries and early losses that season. The *Abilene News Reporter* tried to praise him in 1956 as a "fine little coach." In 1957, Kajikawa announced he was quitting his basketball coaching job for Arizona State, although he would remain an invaluable member of Arizona State's football coaching staff. Fred Sanner, a sportswriter for the *Abilene Reporter News*, remarked, "It would be harder to find a nicer guy than the serene Kajikawa." Sanner said it was a pleasure to watch him direct his team in comparison to the more ill-tempered, demonstrative coaches.[90]

After leaving college basketball coaching, Kajikawa was honored with a membership in Arizona State's Basketball Hall of Fame, as well a spot in the school's Hall of Distinction. In addition, the football program commemorated his career with an award to the top freshman named in his honor, while a practice field was also named after him. Quite understandably, in Tempe, Arizona, the remarkable Kajikawa was considered a "man for all seasons."[91]

A contemporary of Kajikawa's, Buck Lai Jr. was the son of a great Chinese Hawaiian athlete who played professional baseball on the mainland for years. Buck Lai Sr. was, moreover, involved with professional basketball, as we will explore later. Like his father, Buck Lai Jr. was an excellent baseball player who competed for Long Island University (LIU), after attending Ursinius College for a year. Indeed, he attracted some interest from the New York Yankees when he played military baseball during World War II. However, Lai was in love with both LIU and a former student and ultimately long-time employee and administrator of the university, Mary Maneri, to whom he was eventually married for many years. Thus Lai returned to LIU, and in 1947 Clair Bee, the school's athletic director and basketball coach, appointed him freshman basketball and head baseball coach. Meanwhile, Lai earned an MA and eventually a PhD in education from Columbia.[92]

Clair Bee was no ordinary boss. As a basketball coach, he was magnificent. But historians James Olsen and Randy Roberts have portrayed Bee as "a study of contradictions." A scholar, author, and articulate spokesperson for clean living and discipline, Bee was in practice an advocate of victory at any cost. A former player of Bee's once said, "Breathing and winning had the same importance to Clair Bee." Sportswriter Milton Gross revealed that some considered Bee an unhealthy, overwhelming presence on the LIU campus. Gross wrote, "There are those who are unkind to describe LIU as Clair Bee University. Others regard the university as a state of mind perpetuated by Bee and his astounding basketball teams."[93]

While LIU achieved a remarkably successful basketball record under Bee, it became enmeshed in a firestorm when its players, along with other members of East Coast college fives, were accused of taking gamblers' money for attempting to shave the margins of their teams' triumphs in games usually played at Madison Square Garden. To his credit, Bee assumed a large portion of the blame for LIU's role in the point-shaving scandals in the early 1950s: "I was a 'win-em all' coach who helped to create the emotional climate that led to the worst scandal in the history of sports." He maintained that college basketball had become too profitable due to misplaced priorities on the part of many of those in authority, adding "[w]e were basketball playing for money and some boys followed the college's example."[94]

Lai admired Bee and credited him as a generous mentor at LIU. As an assistant, Buck Lai Jr. often seemed to serve as Clair Bee's public relations representative, speaking at various luncheons and press gatherings on behalf of LIU hoops. A *Brooklyn Eagle* sportswriter referred to Lai as one of LIU's "capable, young assistant coaches."[95]

Word of the point-shaving scandal in the early 1950s provoked calls for the resignation of the entire basketball coaching staff. However, Bee and Lai, who was turning his attention to putting together a schedule for his baseball team when news of the scandal broke out, remained at LIU. Eventually, however, drastic measures were demanded. LIU responded by abandoning its basketball program. Clair Bee was kicked upstairs to the University Controller position, while Lai became athletic director. Of all the schools entangled in the scandal, only LIU quit intercollegiate basketball.[96]

Lai not only served as athletic director but continued to coach LIU's baseball team. Yet he and others in the LIU community had not given up on basketball. In December 1955, Lai announced that LIU would reassemble its hoops program, and he would coach the five as well as retain his duties as athletic director and baseball coach. Some expected that LIU would ultimately return to big time basketball. Yet months before he took over the basketball program, Lai denied this, claiming that it was not up to him. The school's Board of Trustees would make the decision. In the meantime, LIU's return to intercollegiate basketball required the school to award only "limited" grants-in-aid to prospective hoopsters. A committee would then determine who merited financial assistance. Before, Clair Bee made those kinds of decisions on his own. Lai, meanwhile, purportedly left the door open to LIU's return to big time basketball.[97]

Yet LIU was not going to do battle under the bright lights of nearby Madison Square Garden anytime soon. In December 1956, the *New York Times'* Howard Tuckner examined LIU's basketball revival. Lai, according to Tuckner, was leading "Operation Rebound" for LIU's basketball program, but was determined at this time to keep LIU out of Madison Square Garden and the lure of the fame and fortune often sought in elite college sports. Tuckner wrote that Lai had felt personally close to those LIU players caught up in the scandal and admitted that he had been in a state of denial for a while about what had happened. Afterwards, Lai conceded he considered quitting LIU and coaching in general. Nevertheless, he declared he could not bring himself to leave a school that had been such an important part of his life since 1937.[98]

Operating on a fairly small time basis, Lai's quintet did not have an on-campus gym, practicing instead at Brooklyn Technical School or the Brooklyn Central YMCA. Still, despite the fact that LIU was competing outside of big time college basketball, Lai was a respected figure in basketball coaching circles. Sometimes he seemed to earn that respect more than other times. For example, Frank McGuire, who coached North Carolina to a NCAA championship in 1957, gratefully recalled Lai's role in perhaps saving his career. McGuire maintained that during the tense championship game against Wilt Chamberlain's Kansas University five, an ice cream vendor blocked his view. An angry McGuire was just about ready to toss the vendor's box at the unsuspecting hawker once the latter decided to put his inventory on the floor. Sensing something was about to go terribly wrong, Lai, sitting near the North Carolina bench, restrained McGuire from making an ill-considered mistake while his team was struggling for survival against the giant Chamberlain and his mates. North Carolina, as it turned out, wound up winning the game.[99]

While LIU rarely faced elite competition under Lai, it did so occasionally. In 1960, LIU beat the "powerful Seton Hall" five. After the game, according to syndicated sportswriter Oscar Fraley, Lai said the line between major and minor college teams was disappearing. The reason was that having a big man, nearer to seven feet tall than six, was a great equalizer, and Lai at that time had an effective big man. Nevertheless, Lai perhaps did not realize that big time programs were more likely to successfully recruit talented and tall hoopsters than a school like LIU.[100]

Meanwhile, Lai penned a well-read instructional book on basketball to go along with a similar book on baseball fundamentals. Serving as the book's illustrator as well, Lai's approach to basketball was fairly conventional. He told readers that the "coach's job is to teach his team the fundamental techniques of basketball.... In general, the coach is responsible for scouting, morale, discipline, strategy, substitutions, and managerial procedure." Possibly a little less conventional, Lai added that the coach should take charge—should not tolerate "interference from parents, students, alumni, or others concerned." As for players, they needed to imbibe the coach's obsession with fundamentals and pay less mind to how much they scored. "A good basketball player," Lai averred, "must know how to pass and guard." Addressing the issue of youth sports, Lai urged moderation between the often conflicting goals of competition and cooperation. He clearly believed that youth sports should avoid the temptation to either overemphasize or underemphasize victory.[101]

As a strategist, Lai preferred using a zone defense. Yet because his team often was short on size and experience, he would switch back and forth between zone and "man" defenses. And while no one would confuse Lai's LIU squads with being national powerhouses, they apparently performed adequately. When Lai resigned as LIU's head basketball coach in 1961, his teams had won 44 games and lost 39 over a six year span.[102]

Remaining on as LIU's athletic director, Lai oversaw the transformation of Brooklyn's old Paramount Theater into a gym set for team practices and home games in the early 1960s. Lai promised, however, that LIU would steer clear of the glare of big time college basketball. As athletic director, Lai of course still kept an eye on the basketball program. In the mid–1960s, he condemned the NIT's selection committee for bypassing LIU for its annual tournament. In 2001, after serving LIU in many capacities, such as chair of the physical education department and acting provost, Lai was named to the LIU Hall of Fame.[103]

There were other Asian Americans taking up college hoops coaching prior to the 1960s. At the junior college level, Dan Fukushima proved a pioneer. Before turning to high school coaching in San Jose, Dan Fukushima coached at Contra Costa Junior College. The former physical education major at Cal and Berkeley Nisei star was announced as the school's head basketball coach in September 1950. Moreover, Fred Lee wound up as an assistant for Portland University in the early 1950s. Upon his appointment, the *Portland Oregonian* praised Lee as a "colorful performer" for his alma mater and a five-foot-five "floor general." And in 1962, George Goto began a stint coaching at Sierra College.[104]

The Professionals

Well before Jeremy Lin popped in nearly 40 points against the Los Angeles Lakers in 2012, Asian Americans played professional basketball. To be sure, their numbers were not great, but hardly shameful given the relatively small population of Asian Americans for large chunks of the twentieth century and the corresponding discrimination they encountered. And while we should remember these Asian Americans as pioneers in basketball history, none reached the acclaim of members of the Original Celtics, the Harlem Renaissance, or the Harlem Globetrotters, let alone NBA legends such as George Mikan, Bob Cousy, Bill Russell, Oscar Robertson, Jerry West, Elgin Baylor, and Jules Erving.

In the early decades of the twentieth century, professional basketball was played by men willing to put their bodies on the line—on courts surrounded by wire mesh to keep the ball from going out of bounds in order to make the game more exciting to spectators, of which there were not that many. Leagues based east of the Mississippi were fairly rare and usually not all that well organized. Thus, professional teams typically barnstormed for pay days in cities and towns across the Eastern Seaboard. Among the most famous of early teams was the Original Celtics, who, in the early 1920s, found themselves playing a role in the history of Asian American basketball.

In December 1921, readers of the *Syracuse Herald* learned that the "All-Chinese" basketball squad, reportedly from Shanghai, was scheduled to play none other than the Original Celtics at Madison Square Garden. The Celtics comprised a New York City–based collection of some of the greatest professional basketball players of the early third of the twentieth century. As for the Celtics' opponents, the *New York Evening World* dubbed the "All-Chinese Collegians of Shanghai" a "novelty in present day athletics." More than just exotic, the five showed to the *Evening World* how much "Far Easterners" wanted to imitate the West. In any event, the *Evening World* pointed out that the "Mongolians" had performed competently in a prior game in Atlantic City.[105]

However the team was not composed of entirely Chinese nationals. One of the stars was a Hawaiian-born athlete of Chinese descent named Buck Lai. Born Lai Tin, he was the father of the LIU coach explored previously in this chapter. Lai was best known as a baseball player who had starred on a then-famous barnstorming Hawaiian team from 1912 to 1916. Afterward, he played a number of years of professional and semi-professional baseball on the East Coast. He was given tryouts in 1918 by the Philadelphia Phillies and in 1928 by the New York Giants. An all-around athlete who was a record-breaking sprinter and long jumper on the islands, Lai must have been a good basketball player, too. Before the Celtic game, the *New York Evening World* displayed a photo of Lai in a basketball uniform. It maintained that "the Chinese cageman is considered one of the cleverest players in the game," adding that he was swift and a good shooter, capable of jumping center but playing guard as well. An article in the *Bridgeport Telegram* pronounced Lai the best player for the "All Chinese Collegians of Shanghai" against the Celtics. Lai held his own with George Haggerty, the Celtics' star center, defending excellently and outscoring the white cager.[106]

In January 1922, the *Philadelphia Inquirer* announced that the Delco Club quintet of Darby, Pennsylvania, would take on the "all-Chinese Collegians" at the Bijou Theater in Philadelphia. Lai played center for his team and scored two buckets against Delco. Moved by Orientalism, the *Inquirer* referred to the visitors as "Celestials" and "Mongolians." About a week later, the East Germantown five beat the "All-Chinese," 35–10, at the Bijou. Very likely the losers were Lai's five, but the box score was not supplied.[107]

A tantalizing bit of evidence can be gleaned from Maine's *St. Alban's Weekly Messenger*. In March 1924, it reported on the imminent arrival of a Chinese five to play a squad of locals. The *Messenger* advised readers that this team had been barnstorming the country and had apparently proved capable cagers. It did no more, however, than identify the team as composed of four Chinese and one Hawaiian, who was perhaps Lai. In any event, a presumably European American surnamed Abair ran the five.[108]

The Hong Wah Kues constituted a more prominent professional basketball team that played out of San Francisco's Chinatown in the late 1930s and early 1940s. Generally, according to Katherine Yep, the Hong Wah Kues came from

Better known as a baseball player, Hawaiian Chinese Buck Lai also played and coached professional basketball in the 1920s and 1930s. Moreover, he was the father of Buck Lai, Jr., who coached basketball at Long Island University. Courtesy Library of Congress, Prints and Photographs Division, LC-B2–3343–5.

working-class backgrounds. Some seem to possess lower-middle-class origins. For example, Fred Gok was born in the United States of Chinese parents, and his father worked as a bookkeeper in San Francisco.[109]

A white San Francisco accountant named James Porter founded the team. He hired six Chinese American basketball players from the city. Each possessed talent, as well as the ability to speak Chinese. Chauncy Yip said, "We went because it was a lot of fun and they were paying us. It's pretty good getting paid when you're having fun." George Lee maintained, "Most of us were just out of high school and we weren't going to college, so we thought we'd see the country." Underlying all this was that the hoopsters faced dead-end economic opportunities in Great Depression Chinatown. Yip told Yep, "We didn't have anything else to do. You know you couldn't go any[where]—we didn't go anyplace. We just stayed in Chinatown."[110]

The Chinese American hoopsters did not travel in style. Fred Gok recalled, "All the [manager] provided was a car, ball, and uniform ... and gas for the car. We had six players and one coach and we were in a Plymouth Sedan. And all the baggage was on top." Porter also bestowed upon the team the name Hong Wah Kues because it supposedly meant "brave Chinese warriors," although "overseas Chinese" seems a better translation. The 1939–1940 squad included Fred Gok, Fred Hong Wong, Albert Lee, George Lee, Robert "Benny" Lum, and Chauncey Yip. In December 1940, the following players, according to the *California Chinese Press*, were packed into a station wagon set to head east—George Lee, Albert Lee, Faye Lee, Robert "Benny" Lum, Arnold Lim, and Douglas Quon.[111]

To furnish them with an exotic, Orientalist aura, Porter implored the athletes to speak Chinese while they were playing. Publicity about the barnstormers pushed the Orientalist theme in often less than respectful ways. Kathy Yep tells us of a promotional cartoon showing a Chinese figure exclaiming, "A basket for washee a basket for the ball." Yep adds, "This phrase reflects and reinforces stereotypes of Chinese as laundrymen who are unable to speak anything other than the pidgin language of fortune cookies and of popular book and movie characters like Charlie Chan."[112]

Furthermore, U.S. newspapers called the Kues "the laundrymen" and a "group of Oriental rug cutters." The press also used terminology such as "Yellow Peril" to describe the Kues, while warning readers about the hoopsters' "invasions" of their communities. Although perhaps vile, in retrospect such journalism probably did not intend to insult people of Chinese descent, given the greater sympathy Americans accorded China in the 1930s due to its conflict with the more hated Japan.[113]

Indeed, Yep argues that the image of the Kues nurtured by the U.S. press was largely aimed at reassuring Americans that their democracy was working out well. Other societies in the 1930s had fallen or were falling to totalitarianism. Other societies seemed to base their national hostility on racial supremacy. By showing a group of young Chinese American men, in stereotypical but yet positive light, the U.S. press claimed that racial tolerance was a cherished American value after all. At the same time, the use of Orientalist-tinged stereotypes worked, Yep claims, to "mollify growing white fears of changes in the dominant racial order." In others words, Americans could tolerate the racial differences without conceding all that much to a true racial democracy.[114]

The Chinese Americans knew that simply because they were playing professional basketball around the country, racial democracy was not waiting around the corner. Spectators often taunted the young professionals as "Chinks." Fred Gok said the team was not bothered: "They told us to talk Chinese only on the court, so we make the spectators laugh. So they don't understand what [we] say, you know…. And you could be telling them to go some place and they don't know the difference." Chauncy Yip asserted, "We weren't in town long enough to protest what was written about us." Not only did the players speak Chinese but they played using Chinese names, presumably the ones given to them at birth, but not necessarily. George Lee, for example, was Lee Bo Chin. The former San Francisco lightweight star Robert Lum was Lee Wah Quong. The reality, missed by many spectators, was that the Kues were not "Orientals," but a product of a blending experience known as Chinese America. As Yep puts it, "Just like the marketing of chop suey, fortune cookies, and egg foo yong, the marketing of the [Kues] offered a supposedly Chinese product that actually originated in the United States."[115]

For working-class and lower-middle-class young men experiencing the Great Depression, the Kues did not do badly in financial terms. The players could earn roughly $200 per month, traveling throughout much of the American heartland while showing up in Canada as well. Yet each was guaranteed about $135 dollars per month, out of which he had to pay for housing, food, and shoes. Porter, in turn, supplied the Plymouth Sedan, gas money, and one set of uniforms. According to Yep, the players divided some of the ticket revenue, but most of it went to the team management.[116]

The Kues did not usually perform in big cities or in front of big audiences. The spectators they did attract typically paid from a quarter to 40¢ for game tickets. The Kues mostly appeared in high school gyms and drew about 100 to 500 fans. The biggest pay days seemingly occurred in more urban settings. Apparently, 700 Vancouver basketball lovers turned out for one of their games, while they lured 2000 in Minneapolis. Fred Gok remembered that the team inspired the most enthusiasm away from the coasts, in areas of North America where the marketing of Orientalism could play best: "The crowd loved us because out in the Midwest they didn't see too many Chinese."[117]

While few would confuse the Kues with the Original Celtics or the Harlem Renaissance in terms of basketball dominance, they did well enough. In their first season, they won 54 of 77 games. Rest assured, victories were hard to come by against the Harlem Globetrotters—a team they opposed about ten times in each of their two seasons. They also competed on the same card as the Globetrotters when they did not take on the renowned traveling squad. Indeed, a columnist for the *Seattle Times* informed readers that Abe Saperstein ran the "San Francisco Chinese" team in January 1940. According to journalist Al Young, "When the Kues played on the Globetrotters' card, exotic hype was the name of the game."[118]

George Lee remembered for Kathy Yep that the Globetrotters treated the Kues with respect. The African American barnstormers rarely tried to humiliate the Chinese San Franciscans as they did white opponents. Moreover, by traveling with the Globetrotters the Kues discovered that some people faced more consistently onerous forms of discrimination than did Chinese Americans in 1940.[119]

Still, Chinese Americans were not welcomed in all the small and midsize towns of mid–America. And the Kues were grateful for the hospitality shown by the often little Chinatowns they encountered along the way. Yep writes, "Barred from some hotels and restaurants, the players found eating food with other Chinese Americans to be a familiar and pleasant respite from uncomfortable race dynamics." To these Chinese American supporters, the Kues represented what Yep calls "icons of racial pride."[120]

Well under six feet, Robert Lum was a crowd favorite who amazed fans with both his ball handling and shooting exhibitions, reminding many of the Globetrotters. A Canadian newspaper reporter said of Lum, "[T]he little chap proved one of the smarter dribblers and ball manipulators seen here this season, and his clowning in the bucket and weaving offense had the spectators in continual laughter." With Lum probably in mind, one newspaper story about the San Franciscans remarked that "the Chinks flashed a snappy and deceptive passing attack."[121]

Although they generally performed in small towns, the Hong Wah Kues actually began their first tour in Chicago. The *Southtown Economist*, in November 1939, announced that "a famous Chinese team from San Francisco" was scheduled to appear in Southside Chicago later that month. Indeed, the first seven games the Hong Wah Kues ever played were in Chicago. The San Franciscans, still new to the idea of performing with one another, played inadequately, but over time they improved, as they made their way to Canada, the

Dakotas, and the Pacific Northwest, confronting not only the Globetrotters but other barnstorming squads such as the House of David five and the Dominoes, a team from Canada. Still, it was a brutal schedule for the professional neophytes, burdened with 80 games in 100 days in late 1939. Additionally, they played with but six players; obviously, they had to play hurt more than occasionally.[122]

An examination of newspaper coverage of the Hong Wong Kues reveals an ambivalent reception—a reception most likely influenced by Porter's Orientalist promotional efforts. In late November 1939, the *Appleton Post-Crescent* announced that the San Franciscans were heading toward the Wisconsin town. It identified the visitors as "leading oriental performers from various high schools and colleges of California," adding that "[i]n recent years, the boys coming out of San Francisco's Chinatown have started to develop a real interest in sports." In promoting an upcoming game in December 1939, Michigan's *Ironwood Daily Globe* actually told readers that several of the Hong Wah Kues were born in China. In any event, the Chinese San Franciscans downed the Ontonagan Legion five in Ironwood, 28–22. A crowd of 250 saw the "California collegians" rally to take the lead in the fourth period. Lee Wah Quong, or Robert Lum, scored 13 points to lead the victors. The next day, the "Wah Hong Kues" downed another Michigan team, 53–47.[123]

In late December 1939, the Hong Wong Kues were in Helena, Montana, for a game against the local Pepper Box team. The *Helena Independent* fervently promoted the impending game. A columnist advised readers to "make a date" to watch the San Franciscans on the day after Christmas. Subsequently, it focused on "spectacular" Ming Gunn Gok, or Fred Gok. The *Independent* asserted that the five-foot-eleven Ming Gunn Gok was "tall for a Chinaman." The daily also displayed a photograph of teammate Wong Buck Hong. In addition, the *Independent* publicized the "brilliant Chinese basketball players [who] mix comedy, showmanship, and genuine ability," insisting the Chinese American hoopsters had won 89 percent of their games—an exaggeration obviously aimed at luring more paying customers.[124]

A few days later, the *Independent* celebrated the visitors as a "clever team" and listed the roster as Lee Wah Quong, Ming Gunn Gok, Wong Buck Hong, Lee Bo Chin, Hang Tai Sun, and Yip Chung Fung. Helena readers were told a great deal about the team. Not all the details were necessarily true, but meant to render the young men as competent hoopsters while orientalizing them as exotic. Thus, the *Independent* declared that Ming Gunn Gok was 23 years old, five foot eleven, and a former teammate of Hank Luisetti's at Galileo High in San Francisco. He was further described as a prep all-leaguer who played basketball at the University of California. Wong Buck Hong was apparently a

24-year-old Polytechnic High School grad. Nearly five foot ten, he reportedly attended Sacramento Junior College and lettered in football, basketball, and track and field. The *Independent* thought it worthwhile to note that he was born in Hong Kong and loved to fly airplanes. The five-foot-eleven Hing Tat Sun was 23 and an all-leaguer from Galileo, for which he captained a basketball squad and scored a "record" 36 points in one game. He, moreover, was an amateur boxer. Lee Bo Chin was supposedly 23 years old and a former all-leaguer for Lowell. Lee Bo Chin, the *Independent* piece pointed out, was born in Canton but came to the United States at an early age. Twenty-one-year-old Lee Wah Quong was five foot eight and an alumnus of Sacred Heart in San Francisco. Readers learned that he was the only person of Chinese ancestry to captain a Roman Catholic high school squad. Lee Wah Quong was further hailed as a "good ball handler" and "very aggressive." He, too, boxed. Supposedly a star at Galileo and a professional singer at San Francisco's Jade Palace, Yip Chung Fung was a five-foot-nine utility player. As it turned out, the San Franciscans could not make the game against Pepper Box because they were in a "bad automobile accident" near Great Falls. Fortunately, no one seemed to have been critically injured.[125]

In February 1940, the San Franciscans were in Butte, Montana. They were scheduled to tip off against a team representing the city's Catholic Youth Organization. A Butte newspaper displayed a photograph of Lee Wah Quong. The caption called him the smallest player on the five but an "exceptional ball handler and clown," thus reinforcing the representation of the Kues as a team that, like the Globetrotters, tried to intermingle humor with serious basketball.[126]

Later in 1940, the Hong Wah Kues spent some time in places like Utah and Idaho. In the fall of 1940, the Chinese American athletes toured with a Utah-based squad called the Ogden Pioneers. The *Ogden Standard-Examiner*, in early November, predicted the "California Hong Wah Kues, All-Chinese basketball team" would oppose the Ogden contingent in three states in subsequent weeks. Early in December, the Hong Wah Kues arrived in Twin Falls, Idaho. A local newspaper averred, "The strong San Francisco club is rated as one of the more clever traveling teams in the west and plays college teams on a par in most cases." The daily added that visitors consisted entirely of athletes of Chinese descent. While in the area, the "world's greatest Chinese basketball team" was slated to take on the Filer Independents and the next day, the Shoshone Redskins. Both games were to start at eight p.m.[127]

The next month the San Franciscans were in Illinois and Wisconsin. Near Chicago, the Arlington Heights Racers downed the San Franciscans, 59–50. The *Cook County Herald* conceded the home team was taller, but added that the visitors put on a better show than either the Harlem Globetrotters or the

Harlem Renaissance. Trying his hand at ethnic humor, Bill Draves of the *Wisconsin Rapids Daily Tribune* told readers that the visiting hoopsters comprised a team called the "Hong Wah Kues (whatever that is)." He asserted that the Chinese Americans were the "smallest exhibition basketball team in the world," assuring his audience that "[t]he Chinks will show their brand of exhibition basketball against the Nepco Comets." The Comets proved "too tall and rugged" for the "Chinese All-Stars." However, according to a press account of the game, "one of the 'Chinks,'" Lee Wah Quang, staged a display of deadeye shooting and adept ball handing. Robert Lum, that is, hit seven of ten shots and scored 15.[128]

In February 1941, the squad crisscrossed the eastern portion of the United States. In Washington, D.C., they lost to the Washington Bruins, a "colored professional five," 52–48. The *Washington Post* described the visitors as "the Chinese Hong Wah Que quintet" and "diminutive." It also informed readers that "wee celestial" Lee Wah Quong poured in 20 points. The team was shortly to arrive in Circleville, Ohio, where it was to encounter a local five. To pump up attendance, the *Circleville Herald* declared of the San Franciscans, "A more colorful aggregation … is not to be found in any sport." The daily also published an advertisement for the upcoming game, which was scheduled for a Saturday night. Adult admission cost 40¢, while children would get in for 20¢.[129]

The onset of U.S. entry into war seemingly put an end to the Hong Wah Kues. But the idea of touring the country with a Chinese American professional team did not die. For example, a *San Francisco Examiner* sports columnist, Prescott Sullivan, reported receiving correspondence from a basketball coach out of Illinois in 1947. Apparently, the Midwesterner wanted to sign "several outstanding San Francisco Chinese players" for a national tour and hoped the sportswriter would help in identifying suitable talent. Nothing seemed to come out of the quest.[130]

Around the same time, the San Francisco All-Nations had emerged as a team of barnstorming professionals. As the name suggests, this aggregation was promoted as multicultural. In February 1945, the *San Francisco Chronicle* reported that the All-Nations' squad was to play a five representing the Mather Field Squadron at San Francisco's USO Club. A few months later, the influential African American newspaper, the *Chicago Defender,* informed readers that the All-Nations five had been accompanying the Harlem Globetrotters on their tour. It claimed that the team consisted of "Chinese, Negroes, Koreans, and Caucasians." On the five, according to the *Defender,* were Bill "Lun," Bill Wong, and Al Lee. An African American named Mahlon Roles had coached the team to a 23 and 7 record over the previous weeks and, the *Defender* added, the San Franciscans had just beaten the Camp John Knight military squad at the

Buchanon Street USO in San Francisco. The All-Nations five won, 45–35, thanks largely to Bob Lum, called "one of the sensational players" and "one of the brilliant players of the season." The *Defender* identified him as a former standout with the "Hong Wah Ques."[131]

The "All-Nations" quintet continued to perform over the next few years. Referring to San Francisco's Chinatown major thoroughfare, the *San Francisco Chronicle* maintained in 1946 that the "All-Nations are paced by Grant Avenue sharpshooter, diminutive Bobby Lum." In the Bay Area, the team performed on the same card as the Globetrotters. Before the Globetrotters beat the House of David five in San Jose, the All-Nations team lost to the Jesse Owens Kansas City Stars. Aside from Lum, called "Bob Lunn" by the *San Jose News*, Bill Wong started for the barnstormers while G. Wong came off the bench. The next day, the All-Nations fell to the Globetrotters before 3000 people at Civic Auditorium in San Jose. The final score was 44–25. Apparently, the Globetrotters played seriously until five minutes were left in the game before exhibiting their internationally known tomfoolery. Within a week, the Kansas City Stars defeated All-Nations, 42–32, in Oakland. The *Oakland Tribune* attributed the Stars' triumph to superior height. In 1947, the Globetrotters topped the All-Nations squad, 50–39, in San Jose. A Yuen was on the losers' roster, along with Bobby Lum and a Wong. Lum managed only two points in the game.[132]

A few months after Wat Misaka's triumphant performance at Madison Square Garden for Utah, Ned Irish declared that the Japanese American standout was one of the best players he had ever seen at basketball's New York City cathedral. Irish, who not only ran the Garden's college basketball program but the new professional franchise known as the New York Knickerbockers, speculated that the Misaka would make a fine addition to the Knicks. Several years later, he reinforced this assertion when asked in 1953 about some of the best players he had seen at Madison Square Garden. He told sportswriter Al Worden, "Wat Misaka may be considered a surprise selection by me, but he was really sensational in his Garden games, a lot of basketball player, especially on defense and ball handling, for a 5–8 boy."[133]

In the summer of 1947, the press announced that the New York Knickerbockers, then a member of the Basketball Association of America, had signed Wat Misaka for $4000. Before that time, neither the Basketball Association of America nor its rival, the National Basketball League, had a person of color on a roster. One wire story called Misaka a "flashy, little Japanese-American" and informed readers that Knicks' coach, Joe Lapchick, was perfectly willing to carry shorter players on his team, presumably if there were not too many of them. Irish, guiding a financially unsteady entity in the Knickerbockers, was probably just glad to have the publicity.[134]

The *Pacific Citizen* celebrated Misaka's venture into professional basketball. Pairing him with Hawaiian Nisei Wally Yonamine, who was crossing racial frontiers to play professional football for the San Francisco 49ers, the weekly said both were exciting "crowd pleasers." Misaka, the *Pacific Citizen* reminded readers, had been the most popular player at Madison Square Garden when Utah upset Kentucky some months earlier. In October, the weekly publicized the fact that Misaka was in the Knicks' training camp at Bar Mountain, a "sylvan retreat on the Hudson River." To those many readers who probably did not know much about the Knicks, the *Pacific Citizen* added that they would host home games at Madison Square Garden, where Misaka had shined most brightly as a collegian.[135]

As the tip off to the professional season drew nearer, the New York media promoted Misaka and the Knicks. The *New York Times* ran a photograph of Misaka with a caption reading "Sensational defensive player and 'ball hawk' on Utah's two national championship teams." The *Times* also published a photograph of Misaka with coach Joe Lapchick, a former six-foot-five-inch center for the Original Celtics, and the Knicks' center, Leo Knorek. The caption pointed out that Misaka was the smallest player on the Knicks' roster and was a foot smaller than Knorek. The *Brooklyn Eagle* speculated that upon the Knicks' opening game "midget…. Misaka may steal the show." Additionally, Misaka appeared on a New York City radio show to hype the Knicks. The *Pacific Citizen* assured readers that Madison Square Garden fans had not forgotten Misaka's NIT exploits the previous April, implying they would support his efforts with the Knicks.[136]

It turned out to be a short season for the Utah hoopster. The *Pacific Citizen* published a wire story on Misaka's first game as a Knick. The New Yorkers beat the Washington Capitals, 80–65 at Madison Square Garden. The story pointed out that "little Wat Misaka of Ogden, Utah" played a bit, scoring two points in that game and five in a subsequent game against Providence. However, after Misaka appeared in but a few games, the Knicks sought waivers on him and Sonny Hertzberg. According to the *Pacific Citizen*, one reason why Misaka was cut was that the National Basketball League had just folded and the Knicks were hoping to sign the great center George Mikan, who had played in the defunct league. Thus, by letting Misaka and Hertzberg go, the Knicks would free up some money for the bespectacled great. Mikan, in any event, wound up with the Minneapolis Lakers and the NBA would emerge out of a marriage between the Basketball Association of America and the National Basketball League.[137]

How much race and ethnicity figured into Misaka's fate as a New York Knickerbocker is an open question. According to at least one account, Misaka felt resentment toward Lapchick. He believed that the coach loaded the dice against him by playing him at forward where he could be posted up by taller players. Misaka was especially displeased by his release just before Christmas. Much later, Misaka declared, "I think I was cut because I was Japanese American. Though I have no real evidence of this, I know that Japanese Americans were not appreciated as fans back then." Misaka, nevertheless, remembered that he did not feel any particular antagonism from fellow players, although "I didn't rub elbows with everyone." Star guard Carl Braun, however, did apparently befriend the Utah star.[138]

In recent years, Misaka has generally deflected charges that racism was responsible for his termination by the Knicks. He articulated this position in a 2010 documentary on his life, although the filmmakers, Bruce Alan Johnson and Christine Toy Johnson, suggest that race still played an adverse role. Meanwhile, *New York Times* sportswriter George Vecsey told readers in 2009 that Misaka did not think race was the reason why the Knicks let him go, although he apparently heard racial insults while he was playing, and he believed his teammates did not always have his back.[139]

Misaka could well have continued to play professionally but chose to concentrate on completing his education and pursuing a career as an engineer. Misaka claimed that Abe Saperstein offered him a job playing with the Globetrotters. The basketball mogul, Misaka remembered, told the young athlete he could not understand why the Knicks released him. Put off by the often grueling, year-round schedule undertaken by the Globetrotters and wanting to get back to Utah to finish his degree in engineering, Misaka turned Saperstein down, but remained active in sports. Back in Salt Lake City in the early 1950s, he bowled in a JACL–sponsored league and played basketball for the Star Coffee five and other local fives. Misaka meanwhile became an electrical engineer and later coached Japanese American community quintets. In the 1990s, Misaka expressed disappointment that the "NBA is not recruiting or encouraging Asian Pacific Americans to be professional basketball players."[140]

In the 1950s and 1960s, we see little evidence of Asian Americans playing elite organized professional basketball in the United States. However, barnstorming teams, composed in part or totally of Asian American hoopsters, continued to surface. In general, these athletes were Hawaiians. Yet in 1959, the "Chinese San Francisco" team traveled with the Globetrotters, accompanying the famous squad to the Soviet Union in the summer of 1959. The *Chicago Defender* hailed this squad as the San Francisco All-Nations. It identified Lelan Wong, a UCLA student, as one of the team members, in addition to Hawaiians Chris Kaniho, Reynold Pretas, Robert Akiko, and Taddy Song. The Hawaiians, according to the *Defender*, had previously played for Art Kim's Hawaii 50

Staters, a team that will be explored a bit in future pages. Like the Globetrotters, the *Defender* asserted, the San Francisco five stressed "showmanship."[141]

A Chinese American, however, came fairly close to making the NBA San Francisco Warriors in the mid–1960s. Norman Owyoung was a high school star in San Francisco during the late 1950s and shined as a playground hoopster. The Warriors gave him a tryout and apparently he proved impressive enough as he was the team's last cut. After Owyoung was released, team owner Franklin Mieuli sent him a letter praising his efforts on behalf of Chinese San Franciscans: "I know many Chinese boys now growing up will take added encouragement from the great strides you made on their behalf."[142]

Buck Lai and Art Kim

In the early 1930s, Buck Lai Sr. took charge of a team called the Hawaiian or Aloha All-Stars. In between spring and summer stints as a semiprofessional baseball player in the early 1930s, Lai engaged in professional basketball promotion while living in Audubon, New Jersey, and working for the Pennsylvania Railroad. Undoubtedly, he sought to take advantage of the interwar years' often positive reception to barnstorming basketball teams marketed as novel and exotic.[143]

Exoticizing promotional literature was the source of information about the Hawaiian five for the East Coast. Readers of Maryland's *Frederick News* learned in February 1932 that players would take time off from their court activities to warble "native" songs, accompanied by hula dancing. The *Gettysburg Times*, early in 1932, announced that "Buck Lai and His Aloha Stars" were in town to play the Fleet-Wing five. It declared, "Buck Lai, the great Hawaiian baseball and basketball star, will bring the fastest basketball club in America" to the Hotel Gettysburg annex. Calling the team a "novelty aggregation," the promotional piece guaranteed that the visitors were able hoopsters by asserting they had won 33 of their previous 41 games against top-notch competition. Lai was identified incorrectly as a former major leaguer with the New York Giants and more accurately as a coach who did not play much, "but directs his speedy players from the bench." Rendering these promotional efforts at least somewhat ludicrous, none of the starters possessed Hawaiian or Asian surnames, although Akuna and Lai were listed as subs. The Gettysburg public was further assured that the visitors would compete in "hula" skirts and leis around the neck during the game's first half. At halftime, moreover, Hawaiian musicians and dancers would entertain spectators.[144]

Lai's team moved up and down the Eastern Seaboard. When Lai's contingent headed to Maryland, a Frederick newspaper promised readers high-class basketball, accompanied by excellent Hawaiian music, "nifty" hula dancing, and tasty chocolate cakes for sale. A photo supposedly of Buck Lai was published alongside the promotional piece. Indeed, a basketball player adorned with a hula skirt was in the photograph, but he was not Buck Lai, who, readers learned, was "one of the best all around Hawaiian athletes ever produced." The next month, the team was in Rochester, where the *Rochester Democrat and Chronicle* insisted that the roster comprised former University of Hawai'i players. Later in the year, Lai's contingent was in Trenton, where the *Trenton Evening Times* pronounced the Chinese Hawaiian a "Jap." The next year, Lai's players competed as the Philadelphia Passons, named after Chick Passon, a noted professional basketball player and sports entrepreneur in the city. However, early in 1934, Lai's "Aloha-Hawaiian" squad was back in business and in Washington, D.C., to play a game at George Washington University. Once again, Lai was represented in the press as a former big leaguer with the Giants and once again his team had just won 33 of 41 games. In March 1934, the *Yonkers Herald* announced that after his team played a game in the New York town, Lai would disband the squad and return to baseball.[145]

Several years later, Lai's basketball team was back on the road. In the meantime, Lai had managed a truly Hawaiian troupe of baseball players on yearly barnstorming journeys across the United States from 1935 to 1937. Returning to basketball in 1939, Lai led the "Buck Lai's Aloha-Hawaiian All-Stars" to Burlington, New Jersey. The hoopsters scheduled to show up in Burlington were called "hula-skirted passers," accompanied by Hawaiian dancers and musicians. According to a confident Lai, the local team was going to be "duck soup" for his five. The *Trenton Evening Times* asserted that Lai's aggregation was composed of Akun and Shrei as forwards, Lolai at center, and Kao and Kato as the guards. Lai was listed as a reserve on a team that on the face of things seemed more Hawaiian than his previous basketball aggregations.[146]

By the 1960s, Art Kim had earned something of a national reputation as a basketball entrepreneur. When Kim brought his traveling Hawaii 50 Staters into Ogden, Utah, in 1958, sports columnist Al Warden called him the "famed basketball coach." In 1960, Art Kim coached the Hawaii 50 Staters against the Globetrotters. Indeed, Kim seemed in charge of Hawaiian teams that, like the more famous of the Globetrotters' opponents, the Washington Generals, regularly fell to the renowned five.[147]

Because of Kim's association with Abe Saperstein, he was given the chance to run the Hawaii Chiefs of the American Basketball League in the early 1960s. The American Basketball League was a league presided over by the Globetrotters' boss and aimed at rivaling the NBA. Yet the American Basketball League was not a financial success. The Chiefs folded after a year in action in 1961 and the franchise moved to Long Beach. Kim still ran the Chiefs when the league collapsed during the 1962–1963 season.

Interestingly, Kim had originally wanted to call his franchise the Hawaii Ali'is. *Ali'i* is a Hawaiian term applied to royalty. Kim changed the name to the Chiefs because, he declared, "members of the Hawaiian royalty had informed him that it was taboo to use the name of Ali'i's [*sic*] in conjunction with ordinary people as it could only be associated with the ancient Hawaiian royalty."[148]

In December 1962, the *Los Angeles Times'* Frank Finch pointed out that the Long Beach Chiefs were not doing well. Finch described the Chiefs' owner as "a Honolulu native of Korean descent and one of Hawaii's most famous athletes." A very sanguine Kim told the press he was not concerned about his franchise's financial miseries. Still, bucking the Los Angeles Lakers, the NBA team that was beginning to root itself in the region, was not easy. Further, Finch maintained that Long Beach fans were tough to please and the Chiefs were hurt by no radio or television contract and no star except for center Bill Spivey, who was hardly Elgin Baylor or Jerry West, the Lakers' two all-time greats. Nevertheless, several years later, Long Beach sportswriter Hank Hollingsworth claimed that the team was starting to entice publicity and fans when the American Basketball League went under.[149]

Interestingly, when the more successful American Basketball Association was formed later in the decade, Kim ran the Anaheim Amigos. According to Hollingsworth, Kim was optimistic about the American Basketball Association's chances in Southern California at the outset. In 1967, Kim scheduled most of the Amigos' home games at the Anaheim Convention Center, but also a few in Honolulu and other Southern California venues. The team did not make much headway with Southern California fans, spoiled in the late 1960s by the Los Angeles Lakers and John Wooden's UCLA NCAA dynasty. Still, the Amigos were hard for some fans to forget, even though the cheerleaders dressed as "Mexican bandits" should have made them forgettable. As owner, Art Kim was hardly above the fray. The son of coach Al Brightman remembered Kim chasing referees into the locker room after they apparently made a bad call.[150]

College and professional sports have never been wellsprings of democracy, despite promotional efforts to characterize them as models of equal opportunity in action. Yet, even though relatively small numbers of Asian Americans lived in the United States, their representation in college and professional basketball before the 1960s appears quite respectable. It is hard to gauge how much racism might have short-circuited the basketball careers of talented Asian American "cagers," as basketball players were often called then. Still, the experiences of Ted Ohashi, Wat Misaka, Al Mar, Fred Lee, Dick Nagai, Bill Kajikawa, Buck Lai Sr., Buck Lai Jr., and Art Kim suggest that elite basketball could occasionally serve as a cosmopolitan canopy. At the same time, opportunities to excel in college and professional basketball afforded Asian American males before the 1960s were denied their sisters.

CHAPTER 6

Asian American Hoops, Cosmopolitan Canopies, and Cultural Democracy Since 1965

When academic and nonacademic analysts of sport and society have looked at the issue of race, they have understandably focused on how, through sport, people of African ancestry have been racialized and have struggled to combat the racial hierarchies erected in the various nations in which they have built and maintained communities. A case in point is an interesting article published in *Sociological Inquiry* in 2011. Written by Daniel Buffington and Tod Fraley, the article is entitled "Racetalk and Sport: The Color Consciousness of Contemporary Discourse on Basketball."

Buffington and Fraley purport that the field of sociology has largely ignored sports, but "a growing number of scholars have begun to theorize sport as one of the more significant institutions for the construction of race in the contemporary United States." What Buffington and Fraley do, however, is stress how basketball has reinforced stereotypes of whites and blacks. They write, "By equating particular racial identities with particular skill sets, racetalk in this context made claims about the content of these categories." The emergence of Jeremy Lin as a professional basketball celebrity and the subsequent attention directed by the media, in all of its manifestations, on Asian American basketball would seem to add another dimension to the interaction of "racetalk" and basketball.[1]

Yet one of the themes of this book is that long before Jeremy Lin heaved his first shot toward a basket, basketball-loving Asian Americans desired a conversation about the racial democratization of basketball. They have often worried about the relative lack of an Asian American presence in elite U.S. college

184

or professional basketball. Respected Japanese American journalist Bill Hosokawa complained in 1948 that Nisei were unable to compete effectively in college hoops because of their size. At six feet, Ted Ohashi could hold his own, Hosokawa admitted, but he exemplified an "exception."[2]

But if we look beyond the relatively elite sites of college and professional basketball, we could find Asian Americans—mainly Chinese American, Japanese American, and Filipino American—running from baseline to baseline on myriad community and high school courts from New England to Hawai'i, even before immigration reform encouraged and diversified the growth of Asian American populations. Beginning then in the 1970s and since, American hoopsters of Asian ancestry have made their presence known in growing numbers, not just as players but as coaches and general managers and even owners of professional franchises.

Community teams still served a purpose for Asian Americans seeking ethnic connections in the late twentieth and twenty-first centuries. Jeremy Lin's rise to NBA prominence inspired many to look, sometimes analytically and sometimes naively, at Asian American basketball. Journalist Jamilah King steadfastly put the Lin story in proper context. She admitted to not knowing how much Lin played Asian American community basketball when he was growing up, but the durable Asian American leagues persuaded her that only our ignorance kept us nonplussed by Lin's racial and ethnic identity. Writing soon after the onset of "Linsanity," King maintained, "Though it is unclear whether Lin played in [an Asian American league] … the fact that his devoted Asian American fan base has been whisked into the spotlight hints at the much larger role that basketball has played in allowing Asian Americans—particularly those of Japanese and Chinese descent—to forge identities and retain their cultural heritage."[3]

Some have argued that Asian American community leagues overly sheltered participants. But such sheltering may have been understandable. That is, there are worse sins than trying to isolate our children from the ignorance of others. Before she became a standout point guard at USC, an adolescent Jamie Hagiya, who competed exclusively with and against Asian Americans until sixth grade, heard when she started playing with and against children from other ethnic groups, "Oh, that Eskimo sure can play." At the same time, basketball has helped to maintain a sense of community among historically aggrieved Asian American ethnic groups. King wrote, "All those close friendships and generations of playing basketball against each other set the groundwork for today's brand of Linsanity."[4]

Well before Lin began his NBA odyssey, filmmaker Tadashi Nakamura told King, Asian Americans had been "die-hard basketball fans." Asian Americans were not only excited about Lin's achievements in February 2012, but Nakamura maintained that many had wished at some time during their lives to do the same. Moreover, Nakamura praised the benefits of Asian American community basketball for women, "noting that girls and women aren't usually encouraged to pursue sports."[5]

For Kathy Yep, Asian American basketball has been about many things, but most notably "race and masculinities, particularly heterosexual masculinities." She asserted to King, "Not only have Asian Americans played basketball forever in the United States but that's especially the case for women who have been redefining femininity throughout the twentieth century."[6]

A February 2012 *New York Times* article echoed King's piece in *Color Lines*. Written by reporter Colin Moynihan, it allied Asian American community basketball on the East Coast to "Linsanity." Moynihan covered the Asian Hardwood Classic, a tournament composed of fives from New York City, New Jersey, Washington, D.C., Boston, and Philadelphia. In particular, Moynihan focused on a game between the Rockits from New York City and the Hard Work squad from Philadelphia.[7]

In the process, however, Moynihan interviewed Mike Mon, coach of the Fastball team out of Washington, D.C. Mon told Moynihan that Asian American teams and leagues surfaced years earlier because the participants had found it difficult to find places on other teams. The leagues continued because they supplied participants with a shared heritage. Moynihan identified Mon as "an official with the North American Chinese Basketball Association" and quoted him as rebuking the notion that contemporary America has left racism behind and embraced "post-raciality." In other words, Mon explained to Moynihan, "Nobody in this gym sees you for your skin color or hair color.... Every single one of these guys at some point dealt with the fact that he has been the only Asian on the court."[8]

Moynihan talked to other participants. He quoted Poon, a 33-year-old from Manhattan playing for one of the two female Rockit squads. For her, Asian American leagues proffered "a sense of camaraderie." Lee, a 26-year-old male point guard for the Rockits, said as a youth he idolized New York Knicks standouts such as Charles Oakley and John Stark. He admitted to Moynihan that the publicity surrounding Lin struck him as "odd," because Lin had become a standard-bearer for all Asian Americans, regardless of their diversity. Still, because Lin seemed to symbolize Asian Americans to non–Asian Americans, Lee rooted for the Californian. Michelle Lam, a 17-year-old Rockits supporter, was no less restrained in her admiration for Lin. She wore an orange Knicks T-shirt bearing Lin's number, 17, and Lin's name. According to Moynihan, she said she was wearing the T-shirt for the first time. "'It's Jeremy Lin,'" she said in a tone that suggested no further explanation was needed. 'He's Chinese and he stands out.'"[9]

Time's Sean Gregory wrote about what happened at a gym near New York City's Chinatown two days after Lin put up 38 points against the Los Angeles Lakers. He claimed to have observed a team of African Americans preparing for a recreational league game against a largely Asian American five. The black hoopsters warned one another, according to Gregory, to "ditch the stereotypes of the Asian dudes as pesky players who nevertheless won't be hard to beat. 'We've got to play these guys,' one of the men barked to his teammates. 'They might have a team full of Jeremy Lins.' The pep talk fell short. The Asian Americans won by a bucket."[10]

Asian American leagues often reflect the different ways in which Asian Americans have perceived community in recent years. That is, some of these leagues seem oriented to a particular Asian American ethnic group. Others mirror the need of many Asian Americans since the 1960s to nurture a pan–Asian American community transcending ethnic boundaries—a need reinforced by the belief that in the minds of numerous non–Asian Americans "all Asian are alike." Asian American community basketball also has mirrored the growing diversity of Asian Americans brought on by the "second-wave" of Asian immigration after the Immigration Reform Act of 1965, an act of New Frontier/Great Society liberalism that eliminated national quotas and opened the United States for Asians and other immigrants based on occupation and family reunification.

In Southern California, the Pasadena Bruins comprise a basketball organization generally aimed at furnishing hoops experiences to Japanese American boys and girls. According to the organization's website, the Bruins consist of 30 youth teams for young people from age seven to high school. The website further claims that many of the children who competed during the organization's early years had children who continued the family legacy by taking part in the Bruins' program.[11]

Squads and leagues composed of young people of varied Asian descent have recently competed in the Bay Area. In San Francisco, Asian American girls' teams like the Enchantees carry on the legacy of Helen Lum nee Wong. In San Jose, the Community Youth Service, operating out of the city's Buddhist Temple, has asserted a commitment to the Positive Coaching Alliance's motto, "Honor the Game." It has hoped to "create a positive environment with effort and improvement, not winning and losing, being our focus." Yearly the San Jose Community Youth Service teams compete against similar squads from Mountain View, Palo Alto, and San Mateo. While these squads must include a core of youthful athletes possessing Japanese ancestry, they have been multiethnic. A Palo Alto Community Youth Service team I coached in the early 2000s consisted of boys of Japanese, Chinese, and Korean descent.[12]

While identified with the San Francisco's Chinese American community, the Bay Area Asian Sports (BAAS) Dragons assembled a summer basketball program, which caught the eye of *Asian Week* in 2010. The program did not require that participants have Asian descent, although many of them did. Journalist Bob Manalo noted that the BAAS had a simple mission: "to develop Asian boys and girls physically, psychologically, and socially through their basketball program." In particular, the BAAS urged participants to learn individual responsibility, get along with others, and "accept praise and constructive criticism … in a safe and positive environment." Parents were, moreover, encouraged to get involved. Interestingly, Elena Wong, niece of Willie and Helen Wong, was on the league's advisory board. She proclaimed, "The Dragons program keeps the kids busy and off the streets…. The program is also family-oriented, where parents are encouraged to support the kids and the program, as well as participate." Recruitment of participants, she added, was enhanced by the Golden State Warriors' signing of Bay Area high school star Jeremy Lin in 2010.[13]

Asian Americans have become more geographically dispersed in recent decades. For example, the Austin Asian Basketball League in Texas claims in its website that "We play for fun, camaraderie, and competition." Norfolk, Virginia, has housed the Asian American Basketball League (AABL). According to the league's website, the AABL began in 2001. The motivation behind the league's formation "was not only to organize an entertaining, competitive, and well-structured basketball league for the entire Asian American community, but one in which fellowship and a sense of community could be developed by allowing people of ALL races, cultures, and backgrounds to participate, whether it be on the court or off." The AABL's mission statement has been "to cultivate fellowship and diversity in the community through basketball."[14]

The inaugural season of the eight-team AABL lasted eight weeks. Games were played at a middle school in Norfolk. Professional referees, affiliated with the Southwestern Virginia Basketball Association, were hired for the games, making the AABL one of the first community leagues to have professional referees. League officials put together a schedule that would hopefully not overly disrupt the personal lives of players and coaches. Moreover, rather than have more than one game going on at the same time, as have other community leagues, the AABL staged one game at a time in order to attract the "undivided attention of fans."[15]

The AABL has handled the issue of ethnicity by ruling that each team must consist of all Asian Americans with the exception of two roster spots. The league website asserts,

This rule has given the Asian American players the opportunity to compete against and alongside players that have experience playing basketball in college, semi-pro, and overseas. This has not only raised the level of competitiveness, but the skills and experiences of the Non-Asian American players has given some of the less seasoned players in the league more basketball knowledge. On the other hand, many Non-Asian American players consider the AABL the most entertaining, exciting, and well-organized community basketball league that they have ever participated in.[16]

Pan–Asian organizations have not necessarily been every one's cup of tea. The Filipino American Community Athletic Association (FACAA) has operated a basketball league in recent years. Aimed at servicing the 20,000 Filipino Americans living in the Philadelphia area, the FACAA, according to *Philadelphia Inquirer* reporter Monica Rhor, assembled a basketball program attracting "college students, doctors, blue-collar workers, salesmen, and insurance underwriters" from Pennsylvania, New Jersey, and Delaware. While varied in occupation and age, the players have had "two things in common: They are of Filipino descent—a requirement for joining the Filipino American Community Athletic Association ... and they are basketball junkies."[17]

To Rhor, the "addiction" these Filipino Americans retain for basketball could be traced "straight back to their roots" in the Philippines, where, "[b]asketball mania" reigned. Rhor maintained,

> The turnout for FACAA games reflects that passion. They have become community socials for local Filipinos, bringing together dozens of fans, families, and other basketball aficionados. The league also serves as a kind of lure to entice younger Filipinos to join community organizations. They come for the basketball and stay for the connection to their culture, FACAA president Jen Omana says. "It's a way to get people involved in the community," she says.[18]

One of the players spotted by Rhor was Dennis Balagtas. A resident of Cherry Hill, New Jersey, Balagtas was recruited by a Filipino talent scout to play eight months of semiprofessional hoops in the Philippines. Earning a living as an automobile salesman at the time of Rhor's interview, Balagtas found in the FACAA a way to preserve his love of basketball and his connection to a diasporic Filipino community. Balagtas told Rohr, "Basketball is life to me .... And when you play in front of your own people, it just makes it more special ... . It made me appreciate my people .... Growing up in the suburbs, where the community isn't large, I didn't really know that much about my heritage. Now, I do."[19]

Forged by war and sometimes calamitous resettlement in the United States in the 1970s and 1980s, ethnic groups with Southeast Asian roots have constructed and reinforced community ties through basketball. Possessing a relatively strong population of Hmong Americans, Minnesota has been the site of an "All-Hmong tournament" in Bloomington. The Hmong Academy in

Minneapolis has launched a boys' team. Moreover, Hmong Coloradans have organized a basketball league.[20]

Athletes of South Asian descent have assembled community basketball teams and leagues in recent years. In 2013, Robert F. Kennedy High School served as the site for New York City's South Asian Basketball League. Scholar Stanley Thangaraj has offered provocative accounts of the community basketball engaged in by many young men of South Central Asian ancestry. Indeed, much of his research was done at the Chicago Indo-Pak tournament, an annual event since 1988. Thangaraj reported in 2010 that it was the oldest such tournament in the United States.[21]

Korean American community basketball went on display at the second annual Korean American Basketball Tournament of North America held in 2012 in Dallas. According to journalist Tony Chai, 300 Korean American hoopsters and team officials descended on the Texas city from Orange County, California; Los Angeles; New York; Toronto; and Vancouver. John Lee, one of the organizers, maintained that the tournament would hopefully bring unity among Korean Americans. He announced at a press conference, "This tournament was first organized to promote mental and physical health through the game of basketball. This tournament symbolizes our desire for unity among the next generation of Korean-Americans."[22]

Chai wrote that the host five, Team Dallas, practiced at the New Song Church's gym on Mondays and Thursdays. As a further demonstration of their dedication, the Dallas athletes used a 24 Hour Fitness Center for workouts on Saturdays and Sundays. And, according to John Lee, the team wanted more practice time. Lee implored, "If any church that has a gym can allow us to use that gym, it would be a great help for the Team Dallas."[23]

Professional teams in recent years have become very well aware of the financial benefits of linking up with the Asian American communities in their areas. This has especially been the case with teams possessing players of Asian ancestry. In 1969, the then San Francisco Warriors had no Asian American on the roster, but they were struggling to find an audience in the Bay Area. Accordingly, the team operated a basketball clinic for San Francisco Chinatown youngsters. Community leaders Thomas Kim and H. K. Wong helped out while Warrior players put in appearances.[24]

In the early 2000s, the recruitment of Chinese nationals by the Houston Rockets and the Dallas Mavericks attracted the attention of Asian American communities in Texas. The Rockets had signed Yao Ming, while Dallas settled for a lesser light, Wang Zhizhi. Writer Sam Le contended that Asian Americans living in the Dallas suburb of Richardson were excited about sending their children to a camp run by the Mavericks.[25]

"Yao-mania" consumed Houston's Chinese American community, leaders of which hoped that the drafting of Yao Ming might change the perception of their community. Gordon Quan, who served as a Houston city council member, insisted that Yao Ming would "help ... break stereotypes.... That has to make you feel proud as a Chinese-American that black kids or Hispanic kids or white kids also want to be Yao." Community leaders hoped Yao would come immediately to Houston after signing with the NBA squad, fatten himself up in the many Chinese restaurants in the city, and hire a Mandarin translator from the community.[26]

The Chinese nationals in the NBA experienced racial taunts and insulting language from fans, players, and commentators, although perhaps some of that insulting language was not always ill-intended. Nevertheless, a diasporic Chinese community seemed to have the backs of Chinese hoopsters. Chinese and, indeed, Asian Americans in general, voiced outrage after superstar Shaquille O'Neal taunted Yao Ming using a stereotyped "Chinese" accent. When former NBA player Steve Kerr referred to the large Chinese center as a "Chinaman," the Organization of Chinese Americans sought and attained an apology from the onetime Chicago Bull. Writing to *Asian Week* in 2004, Raymond Wong, president of the Organization of Chinese Americans, declared, "The use of such names devalues our progress in the struggle for equality. Racial slurs have been used to dehumanize people of color and remind us of a shameful but very real part of American history." Kerr, indeed, apologized.[27]

In 2005, the Seattle Storm of the WNBA had two Chinese nationals on the squad—Miao Lijie and Sui Fei Fei. Ostensibly to welcome the newcomers but probably market them as well to Seattle's extensive Asian American community, the Storm sponsored an "Asian/Chinese Night." The halftime show included a reportedly colorful performance by the Seattle Chinese Community Girls Drill Team.[28]

During the last decade, the Golden State Warriors and the Los Angeles Clippers paid heed to Asian American ethnic communities in their regions. In November 2009 the Warriors staged a "Filipino Heritage Night." A month later, the Clippers hosted a "Filipino Hoops and Heritage Night." Raymond Townsend, a former UCLA star and NBA player of Filipino ancestry, was the prime spokesperson for this event. Proceeds from ticket sales were partially distributed to victims of recent typhoons in the Philippines. In 2011, the Warriors acknowledged the Bay Area's Indo-American community by putting on a "Bollywood Night."[29]

Jeremy Lin has been caught up in the effort of the NBA to market itself effectively to diasporic Asian communities. When the Golden State Warriors signed Jeremy Lin for the 2010–2011 season, many speculated that the Warriors were only trying to appeal to the Bay Area's Asian community rather than employ a truly qualified guard on their roster. The Warriors did, in fact, put on an Asian heritage event at Oakland's Oracle Arena, where the team played their home games. Once the New York Knicks signed Lin the next season, some suspected a publicity stunt in the offing. Subsequently, Lin became a free agent after the 2011–2012 season, and the Houston Rockets attained his services. The Rockets, it was widely believed, were attempting to seek a replacement in the hearts of local Asian fans for the recently departed Yao Ming, whose estimable NBA career was cut short by injuries.

Indeed, *Time*'s blogger Sean Gregory argued that the Rockets sought to extend the franchise's appeal from Chinese Houstonians to China. George Postolos, who ran the Rockets when Yao was on the team, remarked, "The fact that the Rocket brand is a big deal in China makes Jeremy Lin more valuable to the team.... The Rockets aren't starting from scratch. Adding Jeremy Lin to the picture is a natural extension of what they've done." When informed that Lin was heading to Texas, one news report in Houston added, "Without taking a single shot on the court, Lin is already a hero in Houston. So much so, that some are already predicting big things for their favorite team."[30]

Basketball Courts as Cosmopolitan Canopies

After 1965, Asian Americans became more culturally diverse. Thus, non–Asian Americans in the late twentieth and early twenty-first centuries encountered on the basketball court teammates and opponents who were not just Chinese Americans or Japanese Americans, but Filipino, South Central Asian, and Southeast Asian Americans as well. The women's movement in the United States, moreover, effectively broadened the opportunities of females to not only compete in interscholastic basketball but compete under the rules that had been governing male basketball for decades. Citing budgetary concerns, high schools gave with one hand and took away with the other, as lightweight teams for boys were eliminated in the late twentieth century—although to be fair, smaller males could still compete in several other prep sports.

Although it depends upon where one lives, it is not at all unusual to find Asian American youths competing with and against non–Asian Americans today. For example, in California's Silicon Valley, young people of Asian descent might appear with members of other racial and ethnic groups on elementary, middle school, and Y teams. One of basketball's answers to Little League baseball is National Junior Basketball, which has leagues in the region with plenty of contributions from Asian Americans. And Asian Americans also compete on

Silicon Valley–based, multicultural traveling teams, fancied by youthful hoopsters or parents of youthful hoopsters seeking to catch the eyes of college recruiters.

In the 1980s, a team of UCLA sociologists, headed by John Horton, studied racial and ethnic relations in Monterey Park, a Los Angeles suburb noted for experiencing significant and politically traumatic demographic changes brought on by the arrival of a growing population of first-generation Chinese, as well as other Asian immigrants. The Monterey Park Sports Club sponsored a youth basketball league, which, the researchers discovered, was multiethnic. Forty-five percent of the players, 47 percent of the coaches, and 14 percent of the league commissioners were Latino. Thirty-four percent of the competitors, 19 percent of the coaches, and 29 percent of the commissioners possessed Asian ancestry. Anglo participation consisted of 20 percent of the players, 34 percent of the coaches, and 57 percent of the commissioners.[31]

The sociologists also pointed out that at the beginning of league competition, Chinese immigrant parents tended to sit apart from parents identified with other ethnic groups. By the end of the season, the barriers had broken down somewhat. The sociologists contended, "Although new comers and established residents sometimes fought each other in City Hall, in the Sports Club they were members of a team. The link between them was their children. The motive was support and interest in their development. Teamwork and cooperation structured cooperation."[32]

During the 1999–2000 basketball season, I coached a team affiliated with the West San Jose branch of National Junior Basketball, which had been launched several years earlier out of Southern California. Based on the league's 1999–2000 yearbook and my memory, most teams had at least one youth of Asian ancestry. My girls' team, for example, had my *hapa* daughter in addition to an Asian American sharpshooter. Participating in the league were players possessing Japanese, Chinese, Filipino, and South Central Asian ancestry. One of the coaches was a person of South Asian background.[33]

Given the demographic changes taking place in the area, West San Jose National Junior Basketball probably has more players of Asian descent now. Moreover, I recently coached a team for Cupertino Hoops, another organization covering much of the same area as West San Jose National Junior Basketball, and all ten of my fourth- and fifth-grade male players possessed either South Central Asian or Chinese ancestry. And more Asian American youths have taken up roster sports on youth teams throughout the United States. For example, a young woman possessing the Sikh surname of Kaur played youth hoops in Bayonne, New Jersey, in 2009.[34]

Youthful hoopsters who are serious about basketball, or perhaps unfortunately, have parents too serious about basketball, often compete on AAU traveling squads. AAU basketball can start with the fairly young, as a 2007 piece in the *Asian Week* focusing on two middle school–aged girls of Asian descent—Dannika Lugtu and T. J. Breiz Miller—showed. Lugtu was described as descended from Filipinos on both sides of her family, while Miller reportedly descended from African Americans on her paternal side and Filipinos on her maternal side. Both athletes managed to play college hoops later on.[35]

Asian American adults compete in intercultural basketball competition too. In Los Angeles in recent years, the Superstar Basketball League attracted some skilled hoopsters from a variety of racial and ethnic backgrounds. Justin Nguyen, Victor Ng, Greg Harada, and Monica Tokoro have been among the Asian Americans participating.[36]

In not only Hawai'i and California, but increasingly throughout the United States, Asian Americans might have found cosmopolitan canopies on various high school courts. They have played on varsity and junior varsity squads. Furthermore, young Asian American women have gained regional and even national attention for their skills. And Asian American men and women coached high school hoops.

Hawaiian high schools have featured multiethnic teams headed by coaches of diverse Asian descent. For example, Walter Wong remained at the helm of some very good St. Louis fives in the late 1960s. Raymond Lum started on Wong's championship squads between 1966 and 1968, during which St. Louis won 86 games and lost only one—to Bishop O'Dowd in Oakland. In December 1966, St. Louis was in the Bay Area to compete in a holiday tournament. In one game, St. Louis downed San Leandro High with Ray Lum's 14 points leading the way. Lum, according to Wong, was the "best outside shooter in Hawaii." The 1968–1969 season was Wong's last at the school. Among those playing for him were Gary Lau, Mike Chun, Jeff Lum, and Richard He. The school's 1969 yearbook lamented that Wong was about to retire from coaching St. Louis after 22 years. Claiming that the press had dubbed Wong a "magician," the yearbook predicted that "St. Louis will sorely miss Walter Wong and his basketball wizardry."[37]

The best hoopsters in Hawai'i have often possessed Asian ancestry. The first team all-boys squad in 2003 included the talented Derrick Low, a guard from Iolani. When Low was named Hawai'i's "Mr. Basketball" after his sophomore season, a *Honolulu Star-Bulletin* sportswriter proclaimed that while the young man possessed a calm demeanor,

> Derrick Low's game is anything but low-key. The Iolani sophomore and the *Star-Bulletin*'s selection as 2002 Mr. Basketball captured the attention of the entire state with his heroics on the court this season. His deft ball-handling, advanced court savvy and superb body control that allowed him to finish shots many might not even attempt had everyone buying into the hype surrounding one of the state's brightest basketball talents.[38]

In places like California's Silicon Valley, observers have noted the shifting racial and ethnic composition of not only the region but its prep fives in the early twenty-first century. The *San Jose Mercury's* David Kiefer wrote a piece in 2007 entitled, "The Changing Face of Basketball." Kiefer focused on Cupertino's Monte Vista High School boys' squad. He noted that in the past Monte Vista's greatest players were invariably European American. However, Kiefer pointed out that the 2006–2007 Monte Vista boys' team had consistently put on the court an all–Asian American starting lineup. Those hoopsters who had started for the school with a relatively large Asian American student body had at one time or another during the season included Kevin Lang, Erik Lee, Luke Liu, Jon Ou, Marcus Woo, and Sean Brar. All the starters were Chinese American or Taiwanese American except for Brar, who Kiefer described as an Indo-American. Kiefer asserted that all the Asian Americans in Monte Vista's regular rotation learned their basketball while competing in "the South Bay's flourishing Asian youth basketball clubs." Erik Lee, for example, played for the San Jose Zebras traveling team.[39]

Monte Vista's all–Asian American lineup struck Kiefer as groundbreaking. He quoted Kevin Lang's father, Luke, who also served as past president of the Silicon Valley Basketball Club, which generally reached out to Asian American youth. "There are obstacles," Luke Lang admitted to Kiefer. "This is a big man's sport and the fact that there is an Asian starting lineup is encouraging to Asian youth. This tells them that if they work hard, they can compete. But to be fair, this might not happen if the school was only 10 percent Asian."[40]

Meanwhile, Bay Area high school basketball nurtured three hoopsters of Asian ancestry who would find themselves excelling in elite NCAA basketball before playing professionally for the NBA. Part-Filipino Raymond Townsend emerged as one of the top scorers in Santa Clara County history. Playing for a private Catholic school, Archbishop Mitty, and Camden, a public school in West San Jose, Townsend tallied 1296 between 1972 and 1974. Several years later, a *hapa* of Japanese descent, Rex Walters, starred for San Jose's Piedmont Hills High. In the 2000s, a Taiwanese American, Jeremy Lin, led Palo Alto High School to California's Division II championship; this was no small feat given the general dominance of private schools in the tournament. During that tournament, Lin poured in a career-high 33 points against Woodside High. After his senior year was done, Lin was named first team all-state and Northern California's MVP.[41]

Writing for the *Sacramento Bee* in February 2012, Joe Davidson pointed out that long before Jeremy Lin donned a New York Knicks uniform, Asian Americans have been contributing to the rich high school basketball history of California's Central Valley. Robert Fong emerged as a standout hoopster for

Sacramento's Kennedy High in the 1970s. According to Davidson, "Fong lived to play basketball taking on anyone anywhere—the park, the front-yard hoop, the gym—growing up in south Sacramento." In 1975, Fong's 17 points helped spark Kennedy to a 62–59 triumph over Hiram Johnson. Fong would later play community college basketball before taking a hand at high school coaching at his alma mater. Davidson alluded to other Asian American hoopsters for Kennedy High. Ryan Muramoto in the early 1980s and Brian Lee in the early 1990s were fine guards, according to Davidson. Although not a star, Brandon Yung helped lead Kennedy to two championships in the early 1990s.[42]

It was perhaps sad that high school athletic programs largely eliminated lightweight teams for males in the latter part of the twentieth century. These teams undoubtedly gave smaller, often Asian American, boys a chance to represent their schools by playing a game many of them loved and mastered. The flip side is that largely thanks to Title IX, girls could play competitive, interscholastic high school basketball. And some of them could play the game very well, indeed.

The *Los Angeles Times'* Paul McLeod observed the inroads Asian American girls had been making in varsity hoops in Southern California by the turn of the twenty-first century. He contended, "At Alhambra Keppel High, for example, the Aztecs' varsity, junior varsity and freshman-sophomore girls' rosters last season were composed almost entirely of players who have trained in Asian club leagues. And two of the Southern Section's most successful girls' teams last season, Irvine and North Torrance, relied heavily on former Asian club players."[43]

One high school coach pointed out that Asian American girls seemed better able to make it to varsity hoops than their male counterparts. The coach lamented that Asian American hoopsters tended to be short, but this seemingly disadvantaged girls less than boys: "The girls can get by being short because they have the skills, the fundamentals. Whereas with the boys, you just can't teach height and you need that if you're going to play [boys'] varsity."[44]

As the demographics of Asian America changed in the last decades of the twentieth century, fewer people of Asian ancestry were concentrated in Hawai'i, the Pacific Coast, and the Mid-Atlantic East. In the south, *hapa* Atlee Hammaker earned a basketball scholarship to East Tennessee State by playing for Mount Vernon High School in the late 1970s. A son of a Japanese mother and a European American military veteran, Hammaker would spurn the scholarship for a reputable career as a Major League pitcher. Reflecting the relative geographical dispersion of South Asian Americans after the Immigration Reform Act of 1965, Jay Singh surfaced as a top scorer for Augusta Prep in Augusta, Georgia, in the late 1970s. During his freshman year, Singh was honored as the varsity team's MVP. Standing at six foot four, Singh scored 32 points, leading Augusta Prep to a victory over DeKalb Christian. For many years, he held the school's scoring record.[45]

In the late 1900s and early 2000s, Asian American male high school hoopsters have shown up in perhaps surprising places. Alaska's Bartlett High suited up Chang Yi in the late 1990s. According to the *Anchorage Daily News*, he hit 15 points in a summer tournament game in Los Angeles in 1999. Near Dallas, Texas, Thinh Nguyen starred on his high school team in the mid–1990s. In the early 2000s, center Sam Singh lettered at Ozark High in Missouri. During the 1999–2000 season, Duy Nguyen was on Woonsocket High's team in Rhode Island. Cuong Huynh played for Geneseo High in upstate New York. In December 2002, he hit a key three-pointer to help lift his five to a victory over Caledonia-Mumford. Early in the second decade of the twenty-first century, Umar Singh stood out as a prodigious scorer for North Salem High in New York. Singh hit 37 points against Somers High and reached 1000 total points in his high school career.[46]

Yet few prep hoopsters were as vaunted in recent years as *hapa* Lindsey Yamasaki. Her Oregon City, Oregon, five was named before the end of the twentieth century as the best prep girls' five in history. As for Yamasaki, she was only one of the best "all around preps ever." *Sports Illustrated*, early in 1998, honored Yamasaki as "Old Spice Athlete of the Month." Correspondent E. J. McGregor told readers that Yamasaki was nicknamed "Queen Bee." The "affable" six-foot-two-inch forward was a celebrity in the small town of Oregon City, giving basketball clinics and serving as grand marshal at an antidrug parade. Yamasaki was a talented volleyball player but enjoyed basketball more because, she said, "I love how you can take charge of a game. I love that feeling when an opponent scores and you're already running a fast break and scoring at the other end. That's the best."[47]

Of Chinese and African American descent, Saniya Chong became a high school sensation while prepping at Ossing High in upstate New York during the early years of the twenty-first century's second decade. Her achievements against befuddled opponents drew comparisons to Jeremy Lin's tenure as the hottest thing in pro basketball. Chong subsequently was recruited to play for a national powerhouse, University of Connecticut.[48]

Asian American high school hoops coaches have cropped up in the second half of the twentieth century and into the twenty-first century. Dave Shigematsu was a winning coach at Castlemont High School in Oakland in the 1970s. In December 1971, the *Hayward Daily Review* reported that he was readying his team for a campaign to win its fourth straight Oakland Athletic League championship. Former Berkeley High School player, Doug Kagawa, coached at

Albany High School in the late 1970s. In Santa Clara County, Dan Fukushima coached at James Lick High for years. The 1954 Lick yearbook shows a young Fukushima coaching lightweight hoops. In the 1990s, Wendell Yoshida coached at Southern California's Peninsula High School. Basketball experts named his squad in the early 1990s as one of the best girls' teams ever. The Peninsula five went a remarkable 33–0 during the 1991–1992 season. In the 1990s, Karen Bryant, a part-Filipina, coached girls' basketball at Woodinville High School in Washington. In 2000, the *San Jose Mercury* honored Wade Nakamura as its girls' area coach of the year. Nakamura, at the time, headed up the female squad at Homestead High in Sunnyvale. Nakamura then moved on to coach good squads at Leland High. In 2004, the *San Jose Mercury* dubbed him "one of the brightest young coaches in the Central Coast section." Interestingly, Nakamura's father was a very successful coach of Berkeley High's girls' squads in the late 1900s and early 2000s. Gene Nakamura built something of a dynasty in Berkeley, where his teams consistently garnered North Coast Section titles. Former Cal standout Kristin Iwanaga coached young women at St. Francis in Mountain View. In Southern California, Filipina Shawn Berina directed girls' hoops at Bishop Alemany High in Mission Hills.[49]

College Hoops

Since the 1960s, Asian Americans have been represented by some memorable college hoops performers, many of whom, thanks to the women's movement, have been female. It is perhaps disappointing that so few Asian Americans have taken the court for NCAA powerhouses such as Duke, North Carolina, and UCLA on the men's side and the University of Tennessee, the University of Connecticut, and Stanford, on the women's side. But considering the demographic, cultural, and socially constructed restraints based on race, gender, and class, Asian Americans seemingly have done all right as college players and coaches in recent decades.

Given the large population of Hawaiians possessing Asian descent, one might expect the University of Hawai'i to turn out teams with Asian Hawaiian hoopsters. But this has been far truer of the women's squads than the men's squads. As the men's program attained Division I NCAA status, it sought to recruit larger athletes from beyond the islands. Indeed, the UH men's teams typically have suited up white Europeans and Australians to help them compete in elite intercollegiate hoops. However, the *Wahine* teams have often included young women like B. J. Itoman.

The scrappy and popular B. J. Itoman starred as a point guard for the UH five in the mid- and late 1990s. In 1999, she was named Hawai'i NCAA woman of the year. Coach Vince Goo observed, "The crowd likes her best because of how hard she plays. She's the No. 1 enemy for opposing players and the least liked by opposing coaches because of all the problems she causes." Goo added that Itoman was "a student of the game…. She can't wait to borrow the game film, take it home and watch it to dissect her game. She continually tries to improve herself and learn." Teammate Kendis Leeburg asserted, "BJ is everything. She's got the heart of a bear and a lion. She works so hard. She's sweet, smart, and inspirational."[50]

Asian Hawaiians also made their marks as college coaches on the islands. Jimmy Yagi coached successfully at the University of Hawai'i, Hilo, which was represented in the National Association of Intercollegiate Athletics (NAIA), and organization that serves less ambitious, less elite athletic programs than the NCAA. During his many years at the helm, the Vulcans achieved a credible record of 252 wins and 126 losses. Yagi's teams made it to the NAIA national basketball team three times, and he was named the NAIA coach of the year once. One of UH, Hilo's great victories occurred in 1976 when Yagi's five upset a visiting University of Nebraska team before 3000 at Hilo. In 1993, the school named Yagi to its hall of fame in the first year of its operation.[51]

The University of Hawai'i has employed several Asian American coaches for its women's program. Patsy Dung was the first to head an intercollegiate women's team from UH in the 1970s. Several years later, Vince Goo coached the women's team with considerable success. Goo was named conference coach of the year three times. More recently, former UH hoopster Dana Takahara-Dias was in charge. In addition, Asian Americans have been assistant coaches at UH. Da Houl, for example, served under both Goo and Takahara-Dias.[52]

Asian Americans have coached at other Hawaiian four-year schools. Jesse Nakanishi became an assistant coach at Hawai'i Pacific University after coaching prep hoops on the islands for many years. Roger Kiyomura has been another assistant for Hawai'i Pacific University. And Jeff Harada served as head coach for the women's team at Hawai'i Pacific University before moving on to the Naval Academy as an assistant coach for its women's quintet .[53]

On the mainland, Asian Americans have proven capable of making their way onto college rosters. Indeed, a few of them have turned into stellar performers for elite college programs, while others have starred for less elite programs. Meanwhile, Asian Americans have spent considerable time on benches as well.

In the 1970s, hoopsters possessing Filipino ancestry gained national attention. A son of a Filipino American mother and a European American father, Raymond Townsend has been called "the greatest Pinoy to play the game."

After prepping in the San Jose area, he achieved a stellar career at UCLA in the late 1970s. By the time Townsend reached Westwood, UCLA's dynastic reign over college basketball had ended, but the school could still boast of a formidable program. As a freshman, Townsend found help with his shot from the legendary John Wooden, who, while retired as UCLA's head coach, still counseled the Bruins. When Townsend was a junior, Mal Florence told *Sporting News* readers that he was an "accurate shot and defensive specialist." After Townsend emerged as a star, some would claim that he was UCLA's best shooting guard ever, even surpassing the great Gail Goodrich.[54]

Like Townsend, part-Filipinos Ricardo Brown and Eddie Joe Chavez did well in California's college basketball circles in the 1970s. Brown stood out at Pepperdine in Los Angeles. To the north, Eddie Joe Chavez was a slick guard for Santa Clara University. Chavez's father was the Eddie Chavez who played for Santa Clara a generation earlier.[55]

Hapas of Japanese ancestry masterfully played elite college hoops in the 1980s and 1990s. Corey Gaines, a *hapa* of Japanese and African American descent, had an excellent college career, playing for UCLA before transferring to Loyola of Los Angeles. A point guard, Gaines left Westwood for Loyola

Eddie Joe Chavez, the son of Eddie Chavez, was a slick backcourt standout for Santa Clara in the late 1970s. Courtesy Santa Clara University Department of Archives and Special Collections.

when it looked like talented Pooh Richardson would be running in the Bruins offense. In any event, Gaines landed on his feet at Loyola, where he was the trigger of a high-powered offense, which routinely scored 100 points a game during the 1988–1989 season. In the early 1990s, Rex Walters starred as a shooting guard for the powerful Kansas University five. Hailing from San Jose, the *hapa* standout attended Northwestern before transferring to Kansas. He did well at Northwestern but better at Kansas, where he became an All-American.[56]

Meanwhile, other Asian Americans played NCAA men's basketball for respected college basketball programs. The University of Portland suited up a point guard of Filipino ancestry named Erik Spoelstra in the late 1980s and early 1990s. He was the team's starting point guard for three years. Larry Steele, a former Portland Trailblazer and his coach at Portland, said of Spoelstra: "He was dedicated to doing things correctly.... He spent many, many hours honing his basketball skills. He was destined to become successful." In the mid–1990s, Pakistani American Kamran Sufi was an assist machine as a point guard for the St. Mary's Gaels. He averaged 7.5 assists per game, which lasted as a Gael record for many years. Moreover, he led the conference in assists and steals for two years. And part-Korean Tony Rutland played regularly for Wake Forest in the 1990s.[57]

As the twenty-first century tipped off, Asian American male hoopsters seemed more prevalent in college ball, albeit less so at the elite Division I level. Called Hawai'i's greatest basketball player by none other than Ah Chew Goo, Derrick Low was an outstanding backcourt performer for Washington State in the 2000s. When Washington State came through with a scholarship for the Hawaiian prep star, Low's family celebrated because his father, a bus mechanic for Oahu Transit, could not afford to send his son to a four-year school. Derrick Low expressed gratitude to the officials at the Spokane university: "They've provided me with an opportunity to play for a Division I school.... Now, I have to keep my end of the bargain ... playing as hard as I can, studying as hard as I can and just always giving nothing less than 100 percent to the goal I set in the beginning—to play Division I college ball."[58]

Harvard's Jeremy Lin surpassed Low in fame as an Asian American college hoopster, partly because he performed closer to East Coast sports media centers. After leaving Palo Alto High, Jeremy Lin headed to Cambridge, Massachusetts, where he became a top-flight guard for Harvard, which, notably, played against elite competition but offered no athletic scholarships. Curiously, even though he was a well-honored high school star and an excellent student, Lin received no Division I recruiting scholarship offers. Lin admitted that "I do think [my ethnicity] did affect the way coaches recruited me. I think if I were a different race, I would've been treated differently."[59]

Lin became an effective backcourt performer for Harvard, evoking comparisons with the slick professional ball handler Steve Nash. Despite his success at Cambridge, Lin was very much aware of the racial shadows clinging to his sport. While on the road with his Harvard team, Lin listened to more than his share of racial taunts. "I hear everything: 'Go back to China. Orchestra is on the other side of campus. Open up your eyes….' They're yelling at me before, during and after. I'm an easy target because I'm Asian. Sometimes it makes me uncomfortable, but it's part of the game."[60]

Basketball, it seemed to the Harvard backcourt star, was a "sport for white and black people. You don't get respect for being an Asian American basketball player." He acknowledged that as a relatively famous college basketball player he had a role to play: "Especially now that there are lots of Asian Americans growing up and playing, I have to try to hold my own in college.… It's definitely motivational and it gives me a chip on my shoulder."[61]

Reflecting the changing demographics of Asian America, more South Asian American hoopsters have played intercollegiate hoops in recent years. Sam Singh was a six-foot-nine forward/center for Bradley in 2008. Born in Fiji Islands, Singh grew up in Ozark, Missouri. His career at Bradley was, however, hampered by injuries. Dipanjot Singh suited up for the University of Massachusetts at Lowell in 2011. The six-foot-three-inch guard from Evanston, Illinois, impressed his coach as a defender and ball handler and got plenty of floor time. Previously, Singh had played a couple of years at the University of Illinois in Chicago. In mid–America, Nusrath Khan played guard for Missouri University of Science and Technology, and Sarwan Khan was a center for Tiffin University. Gokul Natesan, raised in Silicon Valley, made his way to the roster of the Colorado School of Mines during the 2013–2014 season. He proved to be a deadeye shooter from the perimeter.[62]

Emil Kim was certainly not the best Asian American Division I hoopster in the early twenty-first century. But he was good enough to suit up for University of California, Irvine. After growing up in nearby Santa Ana, the Korean American was a walk-on for the Anteaters. That is, he received no scholarship offer. The six-foot-five Kim's love of basketball did not entirely warm the hearts of his family. His mother, he remembered, preferred he concentrate more on the books than the hoops, "[b]ut she let me do what I wanted in the end, and I managed to end up at a great school. She's on board now."[63]

Kim also perceived a "culture clash" with his teammates. Perhaps, he suggested, this was due in part to his own memories growing up Korean American. "Sometimes," he said, "you feel a little different, a little uncomfortable … it's really two different cultures." However, Kim eventually won over teammates and vice versa. At the same time, Kim "notice[d] a few extra cheers from his fellow Asian-Americans. They can relate to his living out the dream."[64]

While he did not play often, let alone become a star, Kim expressed little regret as he ended his final year of eligibility. He demonstrated pride in playing Division I basketball as a Korean American. He declared, "You kind of feel like you've made it as a player when you play Div. I ball," adding, "I'm definitely thankful ... not many people get to take it this far."[65]

More than a handful of Americans of Filipino ancestry have made their marks on major Division I and other college programs in the first decades of the twenty-first century. Early in the 2010s, Isaiah Umipig emerged as a fine guard for the Titans of California State University, Fullerton. After the 2010–2011

Korean American Emil Kim played big time hoops for the University of California, Irvine, in the early 2000s. Courtesy UC Irvine Athletic Media Relations.

season, Umipig was named the conference "Sixth Player of the Year." Umipig subsequently transferred to Seattle University, where he continued to excel. Maverick Ahanmansi, a Southern Californian possessing Filipino and Nigerian ancestry, got court time for the University of Minnesota Gophers. Around the same time, part–Filipino American Steve Holt played regularly and well for the highly respected St. Mary's Gaels basketball program. Holt came to Moraga with a reputation as a fine high school point guard, but because the Gaels already had experienced point guards on hand, he switched to shooting guard, with considerable success. Playing for USF, Michael Williams had been considered one of the brightest offensive performers in the conference. However, after the 2011–2012 season, he transferred to California State University, Fullerton. He did well for his new team during the 2013–2014 season. Steven Norwood played effectively for George Mason University in Virginia. Meanwhile, Ohio State was one of the NCAA's top-ranked teams, thanks in part to the gritty play of Aaron Craft, part-Filipino from his father's side. At Tulsa University, Jordan Clarkson stood out, averaging 16.5 points per game his second year.

Part-Filipino Jordan Clarkson excelled as a guard for both the University of Tulsa and the University of Missouri before he became a high draft choice of the NBA in 2014. Courtesy University of Missouri Department of Athletics.

A website devoted to Filipino athletes remarked of Clarkson, "His game is composed of both inside and out, he has an almost automatic jumper and a streaky three-pointer shooter. He has above average slashing skills where he can use his athleticism to outmaneuver his defender." Clarkson subsequently transferred to the University of Missouri, where he put together a fine 2013–2014 season, winding up as a second-round NBA draft choice. And at LIU, Jason Brickman has shown himself to be a clever point guard, leading the nation in assists during the 2013–2014 season.[66]

Asian American men performed beyond Division I basketball. During the early 2000s, Imran Sufi, brother of Kamran, starred for Jamestown College, a NAIA school in North Dakota. Hawaiian Casey Kushiyama captained Linfield College's hoops team during the 2004–2005 season. Joe Chin was a five-foot-five guard for New York City's Baruch College during the 2009–2010 season. At California State University in Monterey, Kyle Wong was a five-foot-eleven guard in 2011. Around the same time, *hapa* Ryan Matsuoka ranked as the University of California, Santa Cruz, top scorer, averaging 17.7 per game. Darren Lew, averaging 9.5, was the second-highest scorer. Raised in Whittier, David

Jason Brickman is another part–Filipino who led the nation in assists during the 2013–2014 season while a point guard for Long Island University. Courtesy Mike McLaughlin/LIU Brooklyn Athletics.

Hayashi did not have to go far for college. He became a guard for Whittier College in Southern California. Brandon Lin was a starting point guard for Chapman during the 2011–2012 season, while Taylor Hamasaki was on the team as well. At the brand new University of California, Merced, campus, Ben Nguyen played varsity hoops. And Bay Area–raised Ryan Tana became a starting guard for New York University.[67]

Title IX propelled women into highly competitive intercollegiate sports. For women of Asian ancestry with the desire and talent to play basketball at a fairly high level, this meant even greater opportunities than for Asian American men, who were often still perceived as too small to compete at a Division I level. Thus, during the latter decades of the twentieth century, perhaps a surprising number of Asian American women showed up on elite and nonelite college rosters.

Teiko Nishi was a UCLA Bruin from 1986 to 1988. Late in 1987, she was the subject of a piece in the *Los Angeles Times*. Journalist Irene Garcia called Nishi an "oriental" who stood out in high school and continued to excel in Westwood. But what made her rare, according to Garcia, was that "[s]he's the only Asian playing women's Division I basketball in Southern California." Nishi reportedly told Garcia, "When we played at a tournament in Hawaii ... the people couldn't believe we had an Asian player. When I was checking into the game, the guys at the table said, 'No way! You're Oriental!' They were so happy to see a Japanese playing basketball, especially for a big school like UCLA."[68]

After her excellent high school career in Oregon, Lindsey Yamasaki moved to Stanford in the late 1990s. At Stanford, she put together a nice four-year career. A daughter of a Japanese American father and a European American mother, Lindsay Yamasaki admitted to the media, "I never really thought about being Asian American until I came [to Stanford.] There are so many Asian Americans at Stanford."[69]

Asian Week columnist Emil Guillermo witnessed what he perceived as a disturbing incident after one Stanford game in 1998. Guillermo wrote that Yamasaki was greeted by Stanford fans with "yo-yo talk" after her play keyed the Cardinal to a victory. Guillermo explained, "This is when people who speak perfect English say the words 'yo-yo' at an increasingly fast pace to infinity in order to mimic Japanese…. It was loud. It was clear. I was stunned."[70]

Still, Yamasaki, who played varsity volleyball for a powerful Stanford squad, achieved a great deal as a Cardinal hoopster, especially once she gave up volleyball and concentrated on hoops. In 2001, she was named to the U.S. basketball team that competed in the World University Games. In January 2001, Yamasaki scored 27 points against Arizona State, 23 of which were achieved in what *Sports Illustrated* called a "scintillating first half." Indeed, Yamasaki tallied 18 of the Cardinal's first 19 points. Honors heading her way included being named the Pac-10's top first-year player in 1999 and to the all-Pac-10 team in 2002. She also made honorable mention for the Associated Press's All-American squad. Along the way, she set a record for most single-game three-pointers made when she netted nine—at the time it was a Pac-10 record, and still stands as a Stanford record. An opposing coach said of Yamasaki, "She does everything well—shoot, rebound, put the ball on the floor, and she's tough to keep off the boards."[71]

As the twenty-first century dawned, Natalie Nakase emerged as a spark plug point guard at UCLA. Barely five feet, Nakase got a scholarship offer from University of California, Irvine, but not from her dream school—UCLA. Still, the Bruins' coach, Kathy Oliver, convinced her to try to latch on to a UCLA roster spot as a walk-on. Nakase remembered that upon her arrival at Westwood, "everyone doubted me, even coaches…. Even on campus, people thought I was on the gymnastics team. Stuff like that I use as motivation to work even harder and I've been pretty much proving everyone wrong since." After Nakase not only made the team but eventually became the regular point guard, she stood tall as an inspiration to another Japanese American, Jamie Hagiya, who wound up starring for the rival USC Trojans. Hagiya maintained,

"One of the things that really helped me out when I was playing high school basketball was that when I saw Natalie ... play. When I saw her, I thought, 'Okay, that's something I can do.'" Kathy Oliver acknowledged the point guard was an inspiration to young girls who might think they were too short and too Asian to play hoops. "She give them that that dream, that the dream can be a reality," Oliver said, adding, "She's amazing, an amazing woman in my mind. She was a little spitfire on the court…. It wasn't about her size, it was about the size of her heart."[72]

Corrie Mizusawa surfaced as an adroit point guard for St. Mary's of Moraga and then the University of Oregon in the early 2000s. While at St. Mary's, she told the *Asian Week*, "I think I'm more noticeable because I don't look like everybody else on the floor…. To

be one of the only female Asian American basketball players in the nation is something I take seriously. It's an honor to know that I am good enough to play at the Division I level." Indeed, Mizusawa was named the West Coast Conference's freshman of the year for the 2000–2001 season. The high point of Mizusawa's St. Mary's career could well have been her effort against the University of Tennessee, a legendary women's basketball program. On national television, Mizusawa scored 13 points and dished out an impressive 11 assists. The transfer to Oregon did not appreciably affect her basketball skills. She led the Pac-10 conference in assists in both of her seasons as a Duck.[73]

In the late 1990s and early 2000s, Natalie Nakase was a dynamic point guard for UCLA. She subsequently made history by being the first female head coach of a Japanese professional team and then the first female assistant coach for an NBA summer league team. Courtesy Associated Students UCLA.

Jamie Hagiya shined as a guard for USC, from which she graduated in 2007. She tied the great Lisa Leslie in eighth place for games played by a Trojan woman. She was fourth in assists among all USC women's players, leading her team in her freshman, sophomore, and senior years. As a junior, she led the Pac-10 in assist/turnover ratio. Moreover, the Pac-10 named her twice to the all-academic team as a honorable mention. One writer noted that Hagiya received plenty of family and community support while competing at USC. Her mother and grandparents regularly attended home games. At the same time, many youthful competitors from local Asian American leagues were drawn to Hagiya's games on a regular basis.[74]

Emily Tay was so good at Harvard that a Columbia University journalist claimed she "saved" his Friday night when Harvard met Columbia in a women's basketball matchup. Aaron Stewart enthused,

> Officially a shooting guard with a 5-foot-8-inch athletic frame, Tay has a point guard's handle, a showtime crossover, a soft interior jumper, and three-point range. She wreaks havoc on defense, and more than anything has almost transcendent vision and a fundamentally sound passing repertoire to boot. She leads her team in scoring at over 13 points per game and leads the league in assists, with over five per game.[75]

Stewart remained riveted on Tay's game—a game he compared to that of the great University of Connecticut star, Diana Taurasi. That is, "Tay exhibited a rare kind of calmness and wherewithal throughout, like she was waiting for the game to come to her, all the while crossing up defenders and making daggerlike passes." Furthermore, after Tay made a sensational pass, one of Stewart's friends announced, "I've gotta Facebook her."[76]

Often likened to fellow Harvard student Jeremy Lin, Tay became a threetime Ivy League player of the week her senior year when she took upon herself more of the scoring load during the 2008–2009 season. The five-foot-eight guard could dish, shoot, and play defense. Co-captain Niki Finelli remarked of Tay, "She's just phenomenal…. It's just a privilege to be a teammate of hers." A Burmese American, Tay not only co-captained the Harvard squad her senior year but was a unanimous all–Ivy League choice after making the all–Ivy League team her sophomore and junior years. Subsequently, Tay was the subject of a documentary, "No Look Pass," which concentrated on her life not only as an exceptional scholar and athlete but also as the lesbian daughter of Burmese immigrants.[77]

Around the same time, Alyssa Shoji developed into a superb guard for Santa Clara University. An expert three-point shooter, Shoji was chosen as one of the eight participants in the State Farm Women's 3-Point Contest at Tulane University. The event, which Shoji did not win, was televised on ESPN as part of the network's coverage of the women's NCAA championships.[78]

Lower-division college basketball has been enlivened by Asian American women since 2000. Monica Tokoro was a prolific scorer at Los Angeles State in the early 2000s. At the Division II level, Anh Dao-Nguyen starred at the University of New Haven. A strong scorer and ball handler, she averaged 11.5 points per game her first year and made the Northeast 10's all-rookie team for the 2010–2011 season. Catie Kimura and Bea Chang played for Division III Haverford College in Pennsylvania. Filipino American Cassie Klockgether competed for New York, Stony Brook. Hawaiian Kepua Lee carved out an illustrious career at Menlo College in the Bay Area. In 2008, Shisty Kumar was hailed as the best three-point shooter in the history of women's hoops at California State University, Stanislaus. From 2007 to 2011, Tika Koshiyama-Diaz was one of the finest ever to play women's ball at Sacramento State. The point guard ranked second in assists in Hornets' history. In 2012 Miranda Seto started at guard for University of California, San Diego. Michelle Teng starred at Seattle Pacific. She was twice the team's "Most Inspirational," while receiving recognition for her academics. And Cyndi Matsuoka's career was so outstanding at Vassar in recent years that the Women's Basketball National Hall of Fame displayed her jersey among those of other stellar players.[79]

While Jeremy Lin excited Harvard hoops fans on the men's side, scintillating Emily Tay was doing the same on the women's side. Courtesy David Silverman and Harvard Athletics.

Asian American coaches, while still relatively rare, have popped up heading or assisting some basketball programs over the last generation or so. For example, Jeff Hironaka has accomplished a great deal in college coaching in the Pacific Northwest. Born and raised in Idaho, Hironaka attended Eastern Oregon in the early 1980s. While he lettered three years on Eastern Oregon's basketball team, he spent a great deal of time on the bench. Hironaka recalled, "I was a scrub college player.... So I always got to sit on the bench and just watch. I got interested in it. When you're sitting on the bench and watching you think, 'Hey, I kind of want to do this."[80]

Hironaka's love and knowledge of basketball propelled him into coaching, initially in high school in the Pacific Northwest. In the late 1980s, he served as an assistant coach at Idaho State and then did small college head coaching in Southern California at The Master's College. In 1991, Hironaka became an assistant coach at Seattle Pacific University. By the end of the decade, he was head coach of the school's male five. His teams won 134 games and lost 67; he was named conference coach of the year twice. Under Hironaka, Seattle Pacific had seven winning seasons and gained entry into five NCAA Division II tournaments. The 2005–2006 five won 26 games and reached the final four of the NCAA tournament. It also won a conference title, which it regained the next year.[81]

Hironaka eventually became assistant coach at Washington State. While an assistant, he voiced an ambition to become a Division I head coach. Hironaka lamented,

> I mean, Rex Walters, he's a *hapa* at the University of San Francisco and that's really it. Other than Bill Fujikawa [*sic*] at Arizona State back in the 50s, other than him, there's nobody. Dave Yanai was very successful at Cal State L.A [*sic*]. and I was fortunate enough to be fairly successful at SPU. But as an Asian male, you're not much of a commodity because there aren't any Asian players that are high caliber talent. So you don't bring a lot to the table that way. If you look at the coaches in the NCAA, you've got a lot of African American players, so you need African American coaches or assistants because you need someone on the staff who can identify with the players you're recruiting.[82]

After a few years at Pullman, Hironaka was let go as an assistant and reassigned an administrative role with the Cougars' basketball program. Apparently, "basketball smarts" was not an issue, but Hironaka's lack of enthusiasm as a recruiter drew fire. Hironaka, most recently, has taken a post as associate head coach of men's basketball at Portland State University.[83]

Rex Walters, after leaving the NBA, took up college coaching. His first head coaching job was at Florida Atlantic. Then, he returned to the Bay Area to assume the reins of the USF basketball program. The once-respected USF basketball program had fallen on hard times. However, under Walters the Dons have not necessarily become a national powerhouse, but they have regained a substantial amount of lost respectability.[84]

Other Asian American coaches have earned a presence, albeit perhaps too small, in men's college basketball. Dave Yanai coached winners at California State University, Dominguez Hills (CSUDH) for many years. Indeed, Yanai spent 19 seasons as CSUDH. In 1979, the Toros got into the NAIA elite eight. After CSUDH joined the NCAA, Yanai's teams continued to do well, advancing to NCAA tournaments in 1981, 1987, and 1989. In terms of individual honors, he was NAIA district coach of the year in 1979 and West Region NCAA coach of the year in 1987. In 1987 and 1988, his conference named him coach of the year. Around the same time, Daniel Chu served as an assistant coach at the University of Miami before taking over as head coach at the University of the South. More recently, Danny Yoshikawa was a very successful community college coach at West Valley in Saratoga, California, in the early 2000s before he took a position as Rex Walters' assistant at USF and then moved on to University of California, Santa Barbara, as an assistant. Raymond's brother, Kurt Townsend, has been a long-time assistant coach, mostly for the nationally respected University of Kansas program. Vinay Patel held the title of associate head coach of men's college basketball at West Texas A&M. Previously, Patel had been an assistant for both men's and women's hoops at the school.[85]

Elite women's college basketball on the mainland has been more willing to avail itself of the skills, passion, and knowledge of Asian Americans than its male counterpart. For several years, Aki Hill, a Japanese national who migrated to the United States, coached basketball at Oregon State during the late twentieth century. In 1979, *Portland Oregonian* sportswriter Bart Wright observed that she had been mentored in the United States by the likes of John Wooden and Pete Newell. After attending their coaching clinics, she coached in Japan, but she returned to the United States as assistant coach at Foothill Community College in Los Altos, California, and then Santa Clara University. With letters of recommendations from highly respected coaches such as Wooden and Newell, she wound up at Corvallis, Oregon. Stu Inman, a former coach turned NBA executive, noted her attendance at West Coast basketball clinics and admittedly wondered, "What can this little Japanese gal know about basketball and what does she want to do with it?"[86]

A truly respected figure in intercollegiate women's basketball, Colleen Matsuhara coached for several women's programs in the United States. In the mid- and late 1970s, Matsuhara assisted at California State University, Fullerton, for another pioneer of women's hoops—Billie Moore. Describing Matsuhara as a "Sacramento State University graduate and player," *Sacramento Bee* reporter Kent Johnson said Matsuhara had considerable success in guiding Fullerton's junior varsity to a winning record. When Moore transferred her extensive coaching abilities northward to UCLA, she took Matsuhara along with her to Westwood. Later, Matsuhara served as an assistant at Long Beach State, Notre Dame, and Texas. In the early 1980s, however, she was head coach of Nebraska University's women's team. Meanwhile, Matsuhara had also coached a community team in Sacramento called the Majestics.[87]

In the 1990s, Matsuhara headed to the University of California, Irvine, coaching the Anteaters to their first NCAA berth and receiving the honor as Big West Women's Coach of the Year. Her arrival on the Orange County campus was noted by the *Los Angeles Times'* journalist Gabe Hernandez, who informed readers that the five-foot-two-inch coach seemed to blend in with the student body. Matsuhara observed, "I noticed right away that there were a lot more Asian students around, which was something I hadn't experienced in the past.... You can't help but notice that there aren't a lot of others like you around."[88]

After departing from Irvine in the late 1990s, Matsuhara involved herself in a variety of coaching stints. The Los Angeles Sparks of the NBA employed her as an assistant. Then, Matsuhara moved on to USC to perform the same kind of work. USC's head coach at the time, Chris Gobrecht, extolled Matsuhara as "certainly ... one of the pioneers of women's basketball on the West Coast." Meanwhile, she was head coach of a traveling women's team called Love and Basketball. As of this writing, Matsuhara coaches the West Los Angeles Community College women's five. Meanwhile, Matsuhara served as technical advisor to the relatively popular movie, *Love and Basketball.*[89]

Michelle Sasaki Jacoby coached St. Mary's of Moraga in the early 2000s. After her playing career at University of the Pacific ended, Sasaki was an assistant at Washington State and Gonzaga, earning a reputation as a good recruiter. In 2001, she led the Gaels into the NCAA, where they stubbornly refused the expected humiliation at the hands of the powerful and eventually victorious University of Tennessee five.[90]

Asian Americans have coached for smaller college programs or have served as assistants. Marcia Murota coached several years at Los Angeles State, while Joyce Wong headed up the women's program at Rochester University. Jennifer Omana was an assistant coach at Haverford in the late 1990s. A former Long Beach State player, Tamara Inouye served as an assistant coach at Santa Clara University in the 2010s. Previously, she had done some coaching in Australia. Jamie Wong became a very successful head coach at San Francisco City College. Her five, for example, copped the California's community championship. Monica Quan served on the California State University, Fullerton, staff before her tragic murder early in 2013. Casey Kashiyama has been an assistant coach and head coach of women's basketball at Linfield and more recently, an assistant at Whitman. During the last few years, Hofstra hired Faisal Khan as an assistant coach. Khan had previous coached at various educational institutions and at one time served as student manager of the University of Maryland's men's team. Lindsey Yamasaki became the first women's basketball coach at San Francisco's Academy of Art University. At the newest University of California campus in Merced, Kevin Pham has been head coach of the women's team. Before getting the job, Pham was an assistant women's coach at Cosummes River College in Sacramento. And before that, he was a student assistant at Cal.[91]

Professionals

Between Wat Misaka and Jeremy Lin, a few elite professional hoopsters of Asian descent have competed in the United States. For example, in the late 1970s and early 1980s, Raymond Townsend had a taste of NBA basketball. Raymond Townsend was drafted by and played for the Oakland-based Golden State Warriors in the late 1970s. Townsend came off the bench during the 1978–1979 and 1979–1980 seasons. After the Warriors cut him, Townsend joined the Indiana Pacers during the 1981–1982 season. He subsequently went on to perform professionally in Europe before pursuing a career in education and youth coaching.[92]

Hapa hoopsters appeared in the NBA in the 1980s, 1990s, and 2000s. Corey Gaines was a *hapa* of African American and Japanese ancestry who was also drafted by the New Jersey Nets in 1989. He appeared over the next five seasons with not only the Nets but the Philadelphia 76ers, Denver Nuggets, and New York Knicks. Rex Walters was drafted in the first round by the New Jersey Nets in 1993. A decent three-point shooter, Walters competed several years as a bench player for the Nets, Toronto Raptors, Philadelphia 76ers, and Miami Heat.[93]

As for Jeremy Lin, he went undrafted by the NBA after his stint at Harvard. Unfazed, Lin took the opportunity to play in the NBA summer league. He made the most of that summer by impressing NBA scouts with his potential. Subsequently, the Golden State Warriors signed him for the 2010–2011 season. Korean American journalist Timothy Yoo recognized Lin as "a cultural pioneer" and, as a Harvard graduate, "a messiah to Asian parents." As the native-born Californian entered his first NBA season, Yoo added,

> For a cultural pioneer, Jeremy is surprisingly—almost maddeningly—unaffected. He tends to speak in platitudes, but with a genuineness that is believable. For instance, when he states with an aw-shucks earnestness that his paramount objectives are to "live a Godly life and to have fun playing basketball," it comes across as a legitimate recitation of his priorities, and not some throwaway PR line.[94]

Many critics considered the Warriors move as a publicity stunt aimed at attracting support from the Bay Area's large Asian Pacific American population. This charge seemed to have some legs in that Lin rarely played, and when he did, he did not do well, although few suggested that he lacked the will to succeed. To ostensibly give him more time on the court, the Warriors periodically dispatched Lin to the NBA Developmental League, where he put up nice numbers for the Warrior's D–league team. When they called him back up, Lin was supposedly set at the guard position with talented Monta Ellis and Stephen Curry, but the Warriors were not about to give him much playing time. However, his work in the D–league seemed to give him some confidence and his performance improved.

The next year the NBA faced a labor lockout, during which time Lin was expected by some to play professionally in Asia. Nevertheless, he wanted to stick it out with the NBA. After the lockout ended, the Warriors revealed they had other ideas about Lin's future. They still had Ellis and Curry handy, while drafting a gifted rookie guard from Washington State, Klay Thompson. Although both the team owner and coach Mark Jackson claimed they liked Lin, the Harvard grad was cut. Consequently, the Houston Rockets tried Lin out, but they, too, were deep in backcourt talent and let him go.

If nothing else, Lin was persistent. He could have taken his Harvard degree and moved on with his life. Instead, Lin accepted an offer from the New York Knicks, but it seemed as though he was facing a situation similar to that of the Warriors. That is, while shadowed by accusations that his signing was nothing but a gimmick, he would make the official roster but play little and get sent down to the D–league whenever it was convenient. However, in January 2012, an injury-riddled Knicks team turned to Lin to give them energy, and he did. For weeks Lin, playing in the hub of the American sports world, turned the NBA upside down with his surprisingly superb play.

Lin thrived in coach Mike D'Antoni's open-court, fast-breaking style of offense. However, injured, highly paid stars Carmelo Anthony and Amar'e Stoudemire excelled in a slower, half-court offense, and when they returned their needs clashed with D'Antoni's, as well as Lin's career path. The Knicks' management decided that someone had to go and that was D'Antoni, who was replaced by Mike Brown, a coach committed to a half-court offense in order to complement what he hoped would eventually be a stifling defense. Perhaps because of Brown's stress on defense, the Knicks managed to get into the playoffs, but Lin, while still doing decently, was showing signs of inexperience— committing too many turnovers and defensive lapses. To make matters worse, Lin got hurt before the Knicks moved into the playoffs and never returned to the team's lineup. Some observers inside and outside of the Knicks organization speculated that Lin could have played but did not want to take a chance of injuring himself more seriously, because he was going on the free agent market after the end of the season.

Given how well Lin performed and how much positive publicity he brought to the Knicks, it was assumed that the New York franchise would sign him for the 2012–2013 season. Nevertheless, he was not necessarily Mike Brown's type of point guard and was not necessarily close to key players like Anthony. Moreover, Lin and his agent were asking for a lot of money. Consequently, the Knicks passed on Lin, who wound up returning to the Houston Rockets.

Lin, in his first two seasons with the Rockets, displayed the capacity to be a good professional basketball player, but inconsistency still marked his performances and perhaps proved he was not quite worth all the money the Houston franchise paid him. More experience, greater focus on defense, a consistent outside shot, and the development of an ability to move left with the ball as dynamically as he moves to the right would have probably helped Lin's progress. Traded to the Los Angeles Lakers so that the Rockets would have money to sign free agents, Lin has shown, if nothing else, dedication to making himself a better NBA player.

Despite the relative success of Asian American women in NCAA basketball, less than a handful have played professionally in the United States—especially at an elite level. Leilani Mitchell has probably been the most successful elite professional of Asian descent. A daughter of an Australian woman of mixed Asian ancestry, Mitchell won the most improved WNBA player of the year in 2010 while performing for the New York Liberty.[95]

Lindsay Yamasaki and Natalie Nakase got a few sips of professional basketball in the United States. When her Stanford career ended, Lindsay Yamasaki, dogged by injuries, performed sparingly in the WNBA for the Miami Sol, New York Liberty, and the San Antonio Silver Spurs. Yamasaki also played for the San Jose Spiders of the National Women's Basketball League, which was something of a minor league to the WNBA in the early 2000s. Natalie Nakase, the former UCLA standout, also suited up for the Spiders. Nakase, after graduating from UCLA, had played for the Love and Basketball traveling team. Upon joining the Spiders, she surprised even her coach, Tracy Carpenter, who admitted that Nakase was smaller than she thought. Still, Nakase showed to Carpenter "great leadership, ball-handling, and superb on-ball defense.... [S]he plays with an incredible passion. She's shown real control and the players look up to her.... She's well respected."[96]

In recent years, former USC star Jamie Hagiya has tried to land a roster spot on a WNBA team, mainly the Los Angeles Sparks. In the process, she seemed very cognizant of what her efforts meant. Hagiya told a reporter late in August 2011, "Seeing someone from our community on the WNBA stage would be huge, that's why this is not only about me.... If I don't make it, maybe this will set the stage for someone else from our community to get there, and that would be great." Hagiya did not make the Sparks; perhaps her five-foot-four-inch frame worked against her. In any event, Jeremy Lin's emergence gave her hope. Journalist Jamilah King quoted her as saying, "I could be the next Jeremy Lin." Hagiya was not totally serious, according to King, but she still felt inspired by Lin, explaining, "This is something the Asian American community has been waiting for, for someone to break through and be given a chance." Meanwhile, Hagiya has put on basketball clinics for Los Angeles youth—clinics sponsored by the Sparks.[97]

Taking up professional hoops outside of the United States could be less rewarding emotionally and less lucrative, but, in any event, it could be more enjoyable and remunerative than working in some office or factory. Raymond Townsend played in Europe after his all-too-brief NBA career ended. After departing from the NBA, Corey Gaines took his skills abroad to Europe and Israel. Former California State Dominguez player, Dean Maki, played for the Tokyo Apaches. Kamran Sufi made some stops overseas in his professional playing career. *Hapa* Greg Stevenson became a top scorer in the Korean Basketball League. Playing as Moon Tae-Young, he led in scoring in 2010. Previously the University of Richmond standout was drafted by the LG Sakers as an "ethnic-Korean." According to journalist Timothy Yoo, Moon was learning Korean in the off-season, as well as seeking Korean citizenship. Part-Korean Tony Rutland played professionally in both Korea and the United States. The former Wake Forest hoopster declared, "I'm proud to have the Korean heritage in me. Knowing that others are proud is great. I know that in the past being half Korean was so bad. I'm not saying it's 100% better but hopefully it will get there." Another hoopster of Korean descent, Emil Kim, suited up for the Rizing Fukuoka franchise in the Japanese BJ League.[98]

Derrick Low has been paid for his skills in many parts of the globe. During one season, he played in Haifa, Israel, for the Maccabi five. Low came off the bench, averaging 5.5 points per game during the regular season, but nearly eight in the EuroChallenge competition. His shooting was accurate, hitting on more than 50 percent of his shots, below and beyond the three-point arc. When the Haifa five played the New Jersey Nets of the NBA in an exhibition game, Low scored 14 points, knocking down four of five three-pointers. Hawaiian sportswriter Cindy Luis wrote, "Low's passport stamps include half of Europe. He's played in France, Ukraine, Latvia, Germany, Russia, Bulgaria and Lithuania. His dream is still the NBA."[99]

Without Low's collegiate pedigree, Houston-raised Timir Patel has bounced around China and Romania, playing for pay. The son of Indian immigrants, Patel told journalist Karan Madhok that he felt he was representing a diasporic Indian community whenever he played basketball. "I am just trying to be an example for all young Indian basketball players that have a dream of playing in college and professionally. I know there is not many people that will put India and basketball in the same sentence but know if one person opens the door and lays the foundation then many more can follow."[100]

Beginning in the 1980s, Filipino Americans migrated across the Pacific to professional hoop leagues in the Philippines. Half-Filipino former Pepperdine star Ricardo Brown was a third-round NBA draft choice but did not make it in American basketball's most elite professional league. In 1983, he joined the Philippines Basketball Association (PBA). Some locals doubted he was legitimately Filipino in ancestry, while others fretted that he would be the first of too many Americans to play professionally in the Philippines. Moreover, Brown's talents did not fulfill everybody's high expectations. The short, muscular guard, nevertheless, averaged over 23 points per game during his career, the highest ever in the PBA. He won the league's MVP and was named to several all-star teams before he quit in 1990. Brown subsequently returned to the United States, where he took up an admirable career as an educator.[101]

In the 1990s, Paul Asi Taulava, Eric Menk, and Sonny Alvarado were identified as "Fil-Am" professionals. Several of these players were only partly Filipino. Paul Asi Taulava, in 1999, was called the "most dominant newcomer in this year's all Filipino cup." The six-foot-ten Taulava was born in Tonga to a Filipino mother and a half-Tongan, half-Ilocano father. Subsequently, his family moved to the United States. He told the press, "I was born poor. There were times when I had to skip meals in my early years in the United States where I grew up." Called the "blond-haired man mountain with a heart of gold," Taulava played first for the Blu Detergent of the Philippines Basketball League and then switched over to the older PBA, for which he played for Mobiline. Other Fil-Ams starting to perform professionally in the Philippines in the 1990s were Jeff Cariaso, Vince Hizon, and Dwight and Elmer Lago. Cariaso was named rookie of the year in 1995, while Hizon, a handsome three-point specialist, became something of a "heart throb."[102]

Rafe Bartholomew is an American writer who spent a few years in the Philippines in the first decade of the 2000s. He not only observed Filipino professional basketball closely, but he even played professionally a bit in the PBA. The Fil-Ams coming into the PBA in the 1990s, Bartholomew declared, seem to have an advantage over their Filipino competition. "These American-born Filipinos learned basketball on high school and traveling teams with bigger, stronger, more diverse competition than existed in the Philippines." In the process, they "developed guarding and ball handling skills while bigger than the average Filipino."[103]

Jeff Cariaso, Nic Belasco, Mike Cortez, and Alvin Castro were Fil-Ams who shined in the PBA in the early 2000s. Bartholomew insisted that the

Fil-Ams "brought a new style to Philippine basketball." They drove the lanes with more fury. Furthermore, "The American-raised players had a swagger that was more hip-hop and more NBA than the way Philippine-bred athletes carried themselves."[104]

Indeed, Filipino Americans seemingly enhanced the professional game in the Philippines. Point guard Mike Cortez transported to the Philippines a Southern California street basketball attitude. His surliness alienated locals, but few doubted his work ethic or the ball handling skills many considered the best in the PBA. Bartholomew wrote that "he didn't just try to beat his man to the rim, he wanted to demoralize the defender." Nic Belasco showed that a taller hoopster of Filipino descent could run the court. Jeff Cariaso, according to Bartholomew, emerged as a tenacious defender. Bartholomew asserted that he "brought technique and intensity to perimeter defense that hardly existed in the PBA before him."[105]

The appearance of Filipino Americans in Filipino professional basketball has not always been celebrated in the Philippines. Many Filipino nationals doubted that Fil-Ams were actually Filipino in descent. The term *Fil-Sham* arose to taint some of the players caught up in controversy. Forward Sonny Alvarado claimed he possessed Filipino ancestry in the 1990s, but he was actually a Latino. And Taulava could not prove he was sufficiently Filipino to doubters; he was deported in 2000.[106]

Bartholomew observed key cultural differences between Filipinos and Filipino American hoopsters. He averred, "The locals, no doubt, considered themselves just as manly as their Fil-Am teammates, but their notion of machismo didn't preclude a clutching of a teammate's inner thigh." Thus, relationships between Filipino and Filipino American professionals were usually amiable but not warm. Furthermore, one Filipino lamented to Bartholomew, "Some Fil-Ams are not even interested to learn the language. They just want to take Filipinos' money and bring it to the States." Many Filipino fans are raucous and unconventional by U.S. standards. Thus, according to Bartholomew, Fil-Ams have usually been civil to them but, unlike the local hoopsters, lacked the "common touch."[107]

Jeff Cariaso, Bartholomew testified, materialized as something of a bridge between Fil-Am hoopsters and local players, coaches, and fans. It was not always easy for the San Franciscan. His Filipino wife conceded that when she first saw him on television, he seemed "so *mayabang*"—so "stuck up," which apparently was how several American-born players appeared to local fans. However, while he could only speak English upon his arrival in the Philippines, Cariaso sought to acculturate as much as possible. Accordingly, Bartholomew maintained that he became "the key to team chemistry" on the Alaska team. Filipino nationals on the squad "felt at ease with Jeff's fluent Tagalog," while Fil-Ams appreciated him "as one of their own." Further, among Filipino hoops fans Cariaso was widely considered an "honorary local."[108]

In the meantime, American women seeking remuneration for their basketball skills were able to find outlets in foreign countries years before the WNBA surfaced. And since the WNBA has been only a summertime enterprise, elite American female hoopsters have been able to find fall and winter opportunities in Europe, the Middle East, and Asia. Lindsay Yamasaki, for example, played a season in Turkey. After leaving USC, Jamie Hagiya competed professionally in Greece. During the 2007–2008 season, she was named the best playmaker in the Greek league while playing for Iraklis in Thessaloniki. She enjoyed a banner year with Iraklis and then moved on to Megas for the 2008–2009 season. And Emily Tay has taken her talents to Europe, where she has suited up for teams such as Vienheim and Sandhausen in Germany.[109]

Coaches, Executives and Scouts

There has been only one NBA coach of Asian ancestry—part-Filipino Erik Spoelstra. Team president and legendary coach Pat Riley handed him the reins of the Miami Heat as the first decade of the twenty-first century ended. Before that Spoelstra had been a player-coach in Germany and then served the Heat in a variety of capacities, including that of an assistant coach for Riley.

The biracial Spoelstra told a *Pacific Citizen* reporter when he first got the Heat job that he experienced his "Asian roots" when he was younger: "I grew up looking different than most kids…. People were always wondering what I was." He added, "I would say the Asian influences were in food and cuisine … and commitment to family and extended family. My mom cooks a lot of fish and rice, and my uncle makes awesome lumpia."[110]

Coaching the Heat might have been harder for Spoelstra than coaching less talented teams. It was bad enough he succeeded a well-regarded veteran coach; Spoelstra's job became more volatile when the Heat signed superstar LeBron James and powerful big man Chris Bosh to go with Dwayne Wade, a marvelous backcourt veteran for the Miami franchise. Many fans in South Beach expected an NBA championship in the 2010–2011 season and blamed the relatively youthful Spoelstra when the Heat fell short of expectations. Perhaps because he replaced a coaching legend in Riley and perhaps because his "superstars" evidenced occasional disdain for him as a coach, Spoelstra continued to be criticized up to the end of the 2011–2012 season, when the Heat actually became the NBA champs. The next season the Heat repeated.

Nevertheless, while condemnations of Spoelstra at this time seemed muted, the nature of the NBA dictates that they will escalate whenever the Heat inevitably falls from its championship ways, which it did during the 2013–2014 finals to the San Antonio Spurs.

As of this writing, Kamran Sufi has joined the NBA as an advanced scout for the Detroit Pistons. Previously, he had played professionally overseas and minor league hoops in the United States. He has also worked in the Chinese Basketball Association and as an assistant coach in the NBA's Developmental League.[111]

A few Asian Americans have made into the front offices of NBA teams. One, Rich Cho, served as a general manager for the Portland Trail Blazers before he was fired after ten months. More recently, Michael Jordan hired Cho for the seemingly thankless job of general manager of the presently hapless Charlotte Hornets. A Burmese native, Cho arrived in the United States with his family in 1968. He began his NBA career in the early 1990s, when he served as an intern with the Seattle Supersonics while in law school. With the Supersonics and the Oklahoma City Thunder after the franchise left Washington, Cho served in a variety of capacities before becoming the first Asian American general manager in the NBA. Meanwhile, Mumbai-born Vivek Ranadive has been the Golden State Warriors' vice-chair and at present is the majority owner of the Sacramento Kings.[112]

In big league women's basketball, a few people of Asian ancestry stand out. Corey Gaines coached the WNBA Phoenix Mercury effectively in recent years and was subsequently named general manager of the franchise. After retiring from his peripatetic professional playing career, Gaines coached a while for the American Basketball Association, a minor league operation, as well as serving as a personal trainer for candidates for the NBA draft. Gaines, moreover, played a role in the Mercury's attempt at raising money for the victims of the 2011 earthquake and tsunami in Japan. *Arizona Republic* writer Odeen Domingo wrote, "It's an effort that Gaines, whose mother is Japanese, takes to heart." Mentioning that Gaines had played professionally in Japan, Domingo reported the former Loyola star as saying, "It means a lot to me. I've been connected with Japan since 1997. That was the first time I went to Japan to play … I stayed at a Japanese house with a host family [in Tokyo]. I didn't speak Japanese. They didn't speak English. And I was young. But I kept going to Japan ever since." Domingo added that while most of Gaines' mother's family had moved to Hawai'i, he still had many friends who called Japan their home.[113]

Demonstrating concerns beyond the basketball court, Gaines wrote an article in 2012 for the *Huffington Post*. Celebrating Black History Month, Gaines' piece told of his experiences growing up in a home in which both parents were police officers. He informed readers, "My dad is black and my mom is Japanese, so there is a lot of culture and history in my family, which gives us a lot to celebrate." He conceded that "Black History Month was not something celebrated while I was growing up." Nevertheless, Gaines added, "The month is dedicated to remembering and honoring African American achievements. Growing up in a bi-racial home, I had a unique look at the impact minorities have had on our culture."[114]

Unfortunately for Gaines, he met the fate of many professional coaches, however successful. The Phoenix Mercury fired him amidst a disappointing downturn in fortunes during the 2012–2013 season. The Mercury had expected to do well, not only because the magnificent Diana Taurasi was the team, but the franchise had just drafted from Baylor University six-foot-seven Brittney Griner, who was expected to become a dominating force in the WNBA.

The WNBA has also utilized the skills of a couple of women of Asian ancestry. The Seattle Reign of the WNBA employed part-Filipino Karen Bryant as general manager. Meanwhile, after years of college coaching in the late twentieth century, Colleen Matsuhara was an assistant for the Los Angeles Sparks of the WNBA in the late 1990s. And the Sparks honored her several years later at an "Inspiring Women's Night."[115]

Natalie Nakase, finally, should be noted as the first female foreigner to coach women's professional basketball in Japan after coaching in Germany. Upon arriving in Japan, Nakase served as an assistant to former NBA coach Bob Hill, who was in charge of the Tokyo Apache. When the Apache folded, she found a job as an assistant for the Tokyo Broncos. The head coach of the Broncos was fired and Nakase took over. Subsequently, Nakase told the press she would like to coach in the NBA, and Bob Hill claimed he would not bet against the former UCLA standout. Nakase, nevertheless, wound up losing her job in Tokyo only to find a noncoaching position with the Los Angeles Clippers in the NBA. Subsequently, however, she made history by assuming the duties of an assistant coach for the Clippers' summer league team in 2014.[116]

As of this writing, Jeremy Lin is the only non-*hapa* American hoopster of Asian descent playing in either the NBA or the WNBA. Significantly, there seems to be no one of similar racial and ethnic background on the horizon to join him in the ranks of the NBA. Meanwhile, given the relative success of Asian American women in the NCAA, one would think that their presence in the WNBA would have become more pronounced.

Still, we should honor pioneers such as Buck Lai Sr., Art Kim, and Wat Misaka, as well as the efforts of Raymond Townsend, Rex Walters, and Lindsay Yamasaki, even if they did not become professional stars. We should also recognize the coaching achievements of Eric Spoelstra and Corey Gaines. After all, even if Spoelstra never gains widespread recognition as a coaching genius, how many NBA coaches of Asian ancestry have won two NBA championships as of 2014? Indeed, how many NBA coaches have won two NBA championships?

In the meantime, Asian American hoopsters have shined in college basketball as well as taken up regular spots on the bench. This has been true of women mostly, but men have also found some fulfillment and notoriety in college hoops. Moreover, college coaches of Asian descent have put together respectable careers.

Still, while we can celebrate the apparently growing inclusiveness of elite American basketball, perhaps we should keep the celebration muffled for a while. We focus too much on the failures and successes of Asian Americans in elite college or professional basketball. The marvelous competitors who comprise NBA rosters and Division I NCAA rosters should certainly inspire admiration for their very rare and entertaining skills. Yet a democratic culture inspires admiration and joy not just in the rare but in the ordinary. Accordingly, we should bear in mind the stereotype-busting efforts of Asian American hoopsters of both sexes who set picks and box out on numerous community, high school, and small college courts.

Epilogue

The Lessons of "Linsanity" and Other Musings

While some embraced Jeremy Lin's ascendancy to NBA fame as a "feel good" story about a young man overcoming the doubts of coaches, fellow players, and fans, others were not ready to jump on the bandwagon. Fox commentator Jason Whitlock tweeted a racist joke in response to Lin's notching 38 points against the Lakers. Whitlock subsequently apologized. ESPN proved even more provocative. Its mobile website disclosed a headline, "Chink in the Armor" after Lin had a less-than-stellar game. Further, commentators on both ESPN television and radio voiced a similar phrase in reference to Lin. ESPN did fire the headline writer and at least one of the commentators was disciplined.[1]

Writing for the *Huffington Post*, historian Scott Kurashige understandably worried about the media and the public response to Lin's performance in early 2012. It was great, he said, that culturally diverse people have enjoyed Lin's play, "but the road to hell is paved with good intentions and right now they are combined with bad analogies being put forward by writers who've caught wind of Linsanity but don't realize how dangerous a little bit of partial knowledge can be. So please follow these simple steps to ensure that Linsanity doesn't jump the shark before its time."[2]

First, Kurashige emphatically cautioned against turning "Linsanity" into a "Black-Asian rivalry thing." He admitted evidence of "folks hating on Jeremy—people of all races including Asians." But, he countered, there was more evidence of stories of "how Linsanity has cut across social boundaries." When African American boxing standout Floyd Mayweather complained that Lin was nothing but a "yellow version" of the "great white hype," African Americans, including but not just Knicks superfan Spike Lee, "rushed to get Jeremy's back."[3]

Second, Kurashige feared that Lin's story would be used to justify neo-conservative propaganda about "bootstrap success." Kurashige insisted, "Look, we were all unbelievably impressed and moved to tears when Jeremy lit up the Lakers for 38 points and upstaged Kobe Bryant. But it didn't happen because Lin believes in 'hard work' and Kobe is a 'lazy' person who gets by on 'natural' ability."[4]

Finally, Kurashige warned readers away from accepting Lin "as a validation of the 'Tiger Mother' theory of parenting." To Kurashige it was distressing that someone could read in the *Washington Post* that Lin represented a "stereotype that should be celebrated." Kurashige declared that "it's not a compliment to insinuate that Asian Americans exhibit a dedication to education that you presume is lacking in other ethnic groups you wrongly believe are skating through on affirmative action."[5]

A critical sportswriter and historian, David Zirin observed in the *Nation* that Lin had become "the dream-carrier for masses of Asian Americans." But the dreams Lin represented were not necessarily that of "basketball greatness but dreams of being acknowledged as a living, breathing part of this country." To Zirin, Lin's well-publicized performance in early 2012 provoked bigotry, but also "a national discussion about media depictions of Asian Americans, the daily racism they faced and their history."[6]

Zirin hoped that the racism incited by the media attention to Lin early in 2012 would ultimately persuade sportswriters from thinking that Lin signified a postracial phenomenon in contemporary America. He reminded readers that the "[t]he kind of casual bigotry Lin has faced—the Twitter jokes, the Yellow Mamba signs, the mock Chinese talk, the catcalls from people attending the games—is something Asian-Americans have experienced across the country."[7]

Zirin cited two Asian American writers to sustain his argument. William Wong insisted, "There's never been a Jeremy Lin in our collective community history." After all the racism Asian Americans have faced, "we finally have our first sports superstar." Jeff Chang claimed that Lin's incredible string of superb games produced a moment in time when people could discuss more openly "how Asian Americans are racialized." Chang explained, "In two weeks, the discourse on Asian-Americans in general and Asian-American men in particular has moved up from the college campus level to the highest levels of the media. Issues that we've been talking about for years are now on the minds of the entire world. That has blown me away."[8]

Activist Helen Gym's voice was heard through Zirin's piece. A member of Asian Americans United, Gym said that the previously mentioned tweet by Jason Whitlock aroused "an overwhelming rejection of long-held stereotype." She added, "I couldn't keep up with my Twitter feed anymore, and I couldn't put it down. I think I fell asleep with my phone in my hand, and as soon as I woke up I was checking in and talking with everyone I knew."[9]

Gym expressed support for Lin's play and his off-court behavior. But more than that, she told Zirin,

> I am just as proud of a new generation of Asian-Americans that has not only rallied around Lin but is articulating a distinct Asian-American experience and identity and shifting the discussion toward a more multiracial understanding of this country. And although there have been shocking instances of racial prejudice and ignorance, I've been far more encouraged about a multiracial outpouring of support and consciousness building that is just inspiring.[10]

Across the continent from New York City, Sacramento High School coach Robert Fong declared that "basketball shaped me, made me who I am today." Interviewed after Lin's rise to hoops prominence, Fong admitted that the then Knick "is a great feel-good story, and the fact that he's Asian American makes it special for me." Fong, however, did not think Lin fame would cause a "spike" in Asian American basketball participation, mainly because Asian Americans had been playing basketball for years. Asian Americans, Fong conceded, would still find it hard to break into high school varsity basketball where "size—not desire—often reduces numbers." Nevertheless, Lin's story resonated with Asian Americans. Fong declared, "We all face adversity, and Lin speaks volumes in how he's dealt with it—not recruited, cut in the NBA—and he's done it on the biggest stage.... It doesn't have to be just [in] sports that you overcome adversity. It can be anything."[11]

Coach Fong told a tale about the possibilities and limitations of not only basketball but of constructing a democratic culture in the United States—a democratic culture in which sport has become an essential ingredient. "Culture is ordinary," Raymond Williams once wrote. By that the great cultural historian and analyst meant that "culture" was not something that just people in the rarified world of elite art and literature do, but lower-, middle-, and working-class people do as well—that we all seek and express meaning. A democratic society should encourage a culture that allows ordinary people to express themselves, including, among many other things, "representing" their communities through sports.[12]

Through basketball the Mei Wahs and Mangoes could express the significance of community and cultural citizenship to Chinese and Filipino Americans, respectively. The athletes comprising these teams did not possess NBA height, quickness, or leaping ability. They were certainly not privileged with wealth, as they were generally ordinary young women and men from lower-middle or working-class backgrounds. Perhaps it is regrettable that Chinese American women and Filipino American men felt the need to form ethnic teams. Why, we might ask, did community lines ever have to be drawn in ways mirroring hierarchical racial and ethnic divisions? However, race and ethnicity helped to construct community borders in the American past and many would say continue to do so in the American present. And the experiences of the Mei Wahs and the Mangoes speak to the need of ordinary people to address the existence of stratified racial and ethnic divisions in ways that may seem trivial, because, after all, we are only talking about basketball. Yet community basketball was and remains very meaningful to participants and supporters desirous of connecting with people they have deemed ethnically similar while not surrendering their right to cultural citizenship—their right to take part in American civic culture.

As culture is transportable, ordinary Asian Americans have conveyed their love of basketball across stratified racial and ethnic distinctions and have played the game under the cover of cosmopolitan canopies. They dared try out for high school basketball teams. They packed themselves into a car and carried their passions and skills to "Middle America," as did the Hong Wah Kues. Some might also recognize that racial and ethnic borders were not the only frontiers they had to traverse. Young Asian American women and men had to dribble and defend their way through class, gender, and sexual conventions seeking to control access to court time.

The more naturally gifted, persistent, and fortunate might find their way on to college, even elite college fives. The fact that some Asian Americans have been able to play for universities and colleges from New England to Hawai'i suggests the democratic potential of basketball. The fact that the numbers still seem so few suggests the restraints as well. If nothing else, Jeremy Lin has shown how mistaken, if mistaken is really the word that fits, Division I coaches were in overlooking his stellar performance for Palo Alto High School. Stanford, across the way from Palo Alto High, has had decent point guards in recent years, but none as good as Lin.

Much the same, but even more so, could be said of elite professional basketball in the United States. To be sure, I do not wish to overemphasize the NBA or Division I NCAA when I have already made such a big deal over a democratic sport culture fostering the participation of those of us who could only replicate Lin's spin move in our dreams. However, a democratic sport culture should also nurture those with the talent and desire to take their game to a high level. A worthwhile question is whether parents, coaches, teammates, and others involved in providing the organizational muscle for the sport of basketball in the United States have done all they could to cultivate the basketball skills of young Asian American men and women, without losing sight that there are more important things in life than playing basketball.

In the late 1990s, *Asian Week* journalist Brian Liou declared that "to get to NBA land far, far away, we'll need more than a wand and a pair of shoes to click us there. We'll need to filter out all our parents' open laughter as we divulge our hoop dreams. We need to convince our parents that the NBA can be a reality. We need our parents' faith." To Liou, it was "unfortunate" that Asian American parents had diverted the basketball ambitions of their children because of their insistence upon education as a higher priority than driving the paint.[13]

Liou argued that "Asian American parents have been sending the wrong message to their kids." They should "push ... them to reach for the [basketball] stars" rather than using their "ultra-conservative and suppressive principles" to channel their children toward a complete devotion to classroom success. Liou complained, "In their half-hearted attempts to uphold the values of fairness and equal opportunity, Asian American parents have created a double-edged hypocrisy that limits their kids from full access to what's most beneficial for themselves."[14]

Liou even accused Asian American parents of racism or at least racial stereotyping. These parents might very well compliment African Americans for their "innate" talents in the game. At the same time, Liou complained, "Within our parents' eyes, we simply don't belong. Essentially, Asian American parents just prefer the security from a computer-fixing son than a hopeless, ball-hogging jock."[15]

Liou approvingly quoted Rex Walters when the then-veteran NBA player and future NCAA coach said that Asian American young people could balance education and basketball. However, according to Walters, "If Asian American parents don't risk anything, the rewards aren't going to be anything either.... And if parents keep protecting kids from being hurt, the kids will never know what it's like to put [themselves] out there." Walters added that he believed Asian Americans had constructed a "predetermined excuse" not to succeed in basketball—"I'm Japanese and I'm not going to grow, I'm not going to do this and I'm never going to [be] big enough and fast enough and I think that's all bullshit."[16]

Both Walters and Liou insisted that Asian American hoopsters should stop playing with one another exclusively. Able and taller Asian Americans hurt their hoops careers by competing against shorter and less talented opposition. "With a little courage," Liou urged, "talented Asian Americans can develop their abilities against a more NBA-reflective surrounding."[17]

Nearly a decade later, Michael Wong perhaps unwittingly bought into Walters' and Liou's argument while defending Asian American community leagues. Sensitive to charges that such leagues are racist because they ostensibly discriminate against non–Asian Americans, Wong, a former president of the

Buddhist Church of San Francisco's youth athletics program, claimed that Asian American community leagues were not racist. At that time, the Buddhist Church of San Francisco was staging an 80-game tournament in the city; Wong told journalist Vanessa Hua, "As a group we don't have the size and strength of other basketball players, so we create our own little world of basketball.... We're not trying to lock people out because we're better. We're protecting our weaker status."[18]

Maybe, though, we can temper our frustrations at the inability of Asian Americans to break into the ranks of elite basketball, or elite basketball's failure at inclusiveness. Maybe we can recognize that basketball, and culture in general, contains a hodgepodge of possibilities, not the least of which is the possibility that it has quite undemocratically reflected and reinforced the estrangement of Asian Americans.

We should honor the legacy of Asian American community basketball rather than condemn it or be defensive about it. We should cherish the memories of Asian American hoopsters who no doubt braved at least the occasional insult to play with and against other races, from the playgrounds to professional hoops. Nevertheless, race has rendered Asian Americans strangers on the court in the past and continues to do so, as the ambivalent public response to Jeremy Lin more than suggests.

We cannot know how many Asian Americans were cut from teams, denied college scholarships, or kept on the bench because of the way they have been identified by race and ethnicity. We do know, for example, that Wat Misaka's Utah coach, while perhaps less bigoted than many of his contemporaries, was unwilling to give him the court time he deserved. We do know that Division I college programs somehow did not think that Lin deserved a college scholarship. And we do know that Asian American hoopsters were penned in and stereotyped by Orientalist press accounts.

Aside from the biased actions of individual coaches, teammates, opponents, and journalists, Asian American basketball has been shaped by racial nativism's impact on American immigration laws. Unlike European immigrants who could not escape nativism but generally escaped immigration restriction, Asians faced severe immigration laws for nearly a century—from the Page Law of 1875, which managed to discourage the movement of Chinese women into the United States, to the liberal Immigration Act of 1965. Thus, Asian ethnic groups were quite small compared to other ethnic groups. In 1930, there were 275,665 Asian immigrants in the United States, while nearly 12 million European immigrants claimed America as their home. Is it really then so surprising that aside from Hank Luisetti, Italian American basketball could call upon the services of many talented hoopsters in the 1930s, 1940s, and 1950s? Is it really so surprising that the Ted Ohashis and Al Mars were relatively few and far between? And is it really so surprising that in Hawai'i, where Asian Americans comprised a substantial portion of the population, Asian Americans played a comparatively prominent role in high school, college, and independent hoops?[19]

However, while acknowledging that race and ethnicity shadowed Asian American hoopsters, we should keep in mind that they often have had to jump other barriers to get on the court. Basketball crossed class barriers in Asian American communities, but census data suggest that those young men and women most likely to surface as community, high school, and college hoopsters in the mid-twentieth century came from lower-middle and working-class backgrounds. That is, their often immigrant-headed families might have had sufficient, albeit limited, funds to allow their children time to play basketball rather than spend their off-school hours working or helping out at home with their younger siblings. Asian American females, furthermore, played basketball before 1965. Even so, community teams were usually male. And while Asian American boys could represent their high schools in varsity and nonvarsity hoops 60 years ago, their sisters were largely confined to the shadows of GAA sports, which, to be fair, may have been very enjoyable and probably better than nothing.

Democracy, as thinkers as varied as John Dewey and Amartya Sen have reminded us, would seem to thrive best in a society that values heterogeneity. Democracy needs cultural diversity so that healthy and hopefully civil policy discussions can occur. Cultural citizenship would, therefore, appear invaluable to a democracy, since it allows varied social groups to retain a sense of distinctiveness while remaining engaged in the vital affairs of a society. Democracy would likewise nurture cosmopolitan canopies as social spaces capable of stimulating civil civic engagement.[20]

Yet Asian Americans remain strangers in the United States. Through basketball, however, Asian Americans have been able to assert their cultural citizenship. Through fierce defending and adroit dribbling on asphalt and shining hardwood, they have fashioned enduring connections to their ethnic communities but also connections to a broader national community—a democratic cosmopolitan canopy imagined and sometimes realized as America.

Chapter Notes

Preface

1. Elaine Kim, "Preface," in *Charlie Chan Is Dead: An Anthology of Contemporary Asian American Fiction*, ed. Jessica Hagedorn (New York: Penguin Books, 1993).

2. Shelley Sang-Hee Lee, *A New History of Asian America* (New York: Routledge, 2013); "The Rise of Asian Americans," Pew Research Center, http://www.pewsocialtrends.org/2012/06/19/the-rise-of-asian-americans, accessed 18 August 2014.

3. David B. Welky, "Viking Girls, Mermaids, and Little Brown Men: U.S. Journalism and the 1932 Olympics," *Journal of Sport History* 24 (Spring 1997): 24–50.

Introduction

1. Robert Dahl, *On Democracy* (New Haven: Yale University Press, 1998); Benjamin Barber, *Strong Democracy: Participatory Politics for a New World* (Berkeley: University of California Press, 2004).

2. Amartya Sen, *The Idea of Justice* (Cambridge: Harvard University Press, 2011).

3. Larry R. Gerlach, "Not Quite Ready for Prime Time: Baseball History, 1983–1993," *Journal of Sport History* 21 (Summer 1994): 103–137.

4. Henry Louis Gates, *Loose Cannons: Notes on the Culture Wars* (New York: Oxford University Press, 1992), 175.

5. Renato V. Rosaldo and William V. Flores, "Ideology, Conflict and Evolving Latino Communities: Cultural Citizenship in San Jose, California," in *Latino Cultural Citizenship: Claiming Identity, Space, and Rights*, ed. William V. Flores and Rina Benmayor (Boston: Beacon Press, 1997), 57.

6. Benedict Anderson, *Imagined Communities: Reflections on the Origins and Spread of Nationalism* (London: Verso, 1983).

7. Raymond Williams, *Keywords: A Vocabulary of Culture and Society* (New York: Oxford University Press, 1983), 76.

8. Robert Bellah et al. *Habits of the Heart: Individualism and Commitment in American Life* (Berkeley: University of California Press, 1985).

9. Ibid., 333.

10. Elijah Anderson, *The Cosmopolitan Canopy: Race and Civility in Everyday Life* (New York: W.W. Norton, 2011), xiv.

11. Pierre Bourdieu, *Distinction: A Social Critique of the Judgment of Taste* (London: Routledge, 1986); Richard White, *The Middle Ground: Indians, Empires and Republics in the Great Lakes Region, 1650–1815* (London: Cambridge University Press, 1991); Mary Louise Pratt, *Imperial Eyes: Travel Writing and Transculturation* (London: Routledge, 1992).

12. Ronald Takaki, *Strangers from a Different Shore: A History of Asian Americans* (Boston: Little, Brown, 1998). Among the many other fine works of Asian American history I have consulted are Takaki, *A Different Mirror: A History of Multicultural America* (Boston: Back Bay Books, 2005); Helen Zia, *Asian American Dreams: The Emergence of an American People* (New York: Farrar, Straus & Giroux, 2001); Sucheng Chan, *Asian Americans: An Interpretive History* (Boston: Twayne, 1991); Sang-Hee Lee, *A New History* (see preface, n. 2); Gary Okihiro, *Margins and Mainstreams: Asians in American History and Culture* (Seattle: University of Washington Press, 1994); Okihiro, *Island World: A History of Hawai'i and the United States* (Berkeley: University of California Press, 2008); Evelyn Nakano Glenn, *Issei, Nisei, Warbride: Three Generations of Japanese American Women in Domestic Service* (Philadelphia: Temple University Press, 1986); and Valerie J. Matsumoto, *Farming the Home Place: A Japanese Community in California, 1919–1942* (Ithaca: Cornell University Press, 1993).

13. Sara Vowell, *Unfamiliar Fishes* (New York: Riverhead Books, 2011), 1.

14. Allson Varzally, *Making a Non-White America: Californians Coloring Outside Ethnic Lines, 1925–1955* (Berkeley: University of California Press, 2008); Shelley Sang-Hee Lee, *Claiming the Oriental Gateway: Prewar Seattle and Japanese*

America (Philadelphia: Temple University Press, 2011).

15. Bill Ong Hing, *Making and Remaking Asian America Through Immigration Policy, 1850–1990* (Stanford: Stanford University Press, 1994).

16. Michael Omi and Howard Winant, *Racial Formation in the United States: From the 1960s to the 1990s* (London: Routledge, 1994).

17. Amy Chua, *Battle Hymn of the Tiger Mother* (New York: Penguin Books, 2011).

18. Edward Said, *Orientalism* (New York: Vintage, 1979), 54; John Kuo Tchen, *New York Before Chinatown: Orientalism and the Shaping of American Culture, 1776–1882* (Baltimore: Johns Hopkins University Press, 2001).

19. Yunte Huang, *Charlie Chan: The Untold Story of the Honorable Detective and His Rendezvous with American History* (New York: W.W. Norton, 2011).

Chapter 1

1. Some of the works I have consulted for the early history of basketball include James B. Naismith, *Basketball: Its Origins and Development* (Lincoln: University of Nebraska Press, 1996); Pamela Grundy and Susan Shackelford, *Shattering the Glass: The Remarkable History of Women's Basketball* (Chapel Hill: University of North Carolina Press, 2007); Robert Ikard, *Just for Fun: The Story of AAU Women's Basketball* (Little Rock: University of Arkansas Press, 2008); Joan S. Hult and Marianna Trekell (eds.), *A Century of Women's Basketball* (Reston, VA: American Alliance for Health, Physical Education, Recreation, and Dance, 1991); Kathleen S. Yep, *Outside the Paint: When Basketball Ruled at the Chinese Playground* (Philadelphia: Temple University Press, 2009); and Linda S. Peavy and Ursula Smith, *Full-Court Quest: The Girls from Fort Shaw Indian School, Basketball Champions of the World* (Norman: University of Oklahoma Press, 2008).

2. Peter Levine, *Ellis Island to Ebbets Field: Sport and the American Jewish Experience* (New York: Oxford University Press, 1992), 27–28.

3. Ibid., 27.

4. Ibid.

5. Ibid., 29.

6. *San Francisco Examiner*, 28 September 1900; *Oakland Tribune*, 6 March 1905; *San Jose Mercury*, 28 January 1917.

7. Peavy and Smith, *Full-Court Quest.*

8. Susan K. Cahn, *Coming on Strong: Gender and Sexuality in Twentieth-Century Women's Sports* (Cambridge: Harvard University Press, 1998).

9. *Rockford Star*, 17 November 1905.

10. *Portland Oregonian*, 19 June 1916.

11. *Mind and Body* (University of California), December 1916; *San Francisco Evening News*, 15 March 1918.

12. *Oakland Tribune*, 29 June 1919.

13. *San Jose Mercury*, 30 March 1922; *Los Angeles Times*, 28 March 1922; *Daily Palo Alto*, 9 April 1923.

14. *New York Times*, 15 March 1923; *Janesville (WI) Daily Courier*, 11 November 1921.

15. *Chinese Digest*, 24 January 1936, 6 November 1937; *Seattle Times*, 14 April 1938; Stanford University Yearbook, 1937, http://www.ancestry.com, accessed 1 August 2013.

16. *Colorado Springs Gazette*, 18 March 1918.

17. *Maui News*, 10 October 1919, 8 December 1922, 9 December 1922.

18. Loui Leong Hop, "History of Chinese Sports in Hawaii," in *The Chinese of Hawaii*, ed. C. Lun, L. F. Kwock, D. C. Chang, and M. H. Li (Honolulu: Overseas Penman Club, 1929), 29; Loui Leong Hop, "Chinese Contributions to Sports," in *A History of Recreation in Hawaii*, Honolulu Recreation Commission (Honolulu: T.H., 1936), 104; *Honolulu Star-Bulletin*, 3 January 1927, 12 January 1927.

19. *Honolulu Star-Bulletin*, 17 January 1927; *Honolulu Advertiser*, 3 March 1935; T. C. Goo, "Wonderful Athletes When They Want to Be," in *The Chinese in Hawaii: A Historical Sketch*, ed. Robert Lee (Honolulu: Advertiser Publishing Co., 1961), 70.

20. *Honolulu Star-Bulletin*, 1 January 1927, 8 January 1927; Hop, "History of Chinese Sports," 29.

21. Hop, "History of Chinese Sports," 29.

22. *Chinese Digest*, May 1938; Yep, *Outside the Paint*, 21–24.

23. Yep, *Outside the Paint*, 26, 33.

24. Ibid., 27–30.

25. Yep, *Outside the Paint*, 32–33; William V. Flores and Rina Benmayor (eds.), *Latino Cultural Citizenship: Claiming Identity, Space, and Rights* (Boston: Beacon Press, 1997).

26. *San Francisco Chronicle*, 18 January 1928, 6 January 1930, 8 January 1930, 8 March 1935, 9 March 1935.

27. Ibid., 4 January 1931, 9 January 1931, 1 March 1932, 14 March 1941; *Chinese Digest*, 13 November 1936, January 1937; Alex Edelstein, "145s and Jayvees," San Francisco State Yearbook, 1939, http://www.classmaates.com, accessed 7 January 2012.

28. *Chinese Digest*, 15 November 1935.

29. Ibid., 3 January 1936.

30. Ibid., 15 November 1935, 22 November 1935, 27 December 1935, 17 January 1936.

31. *Chinese Digest*, 22 November 1935, 10 January 1936; U.S. Census Bureau, Manuscript Census Schedules, City and County of San Francisco, 1930.

32. *Chinese Digest*, May 1938.

33. Ibid., 3 January 1936, 24 January 1936.

34. *San Francisco Chronicle*, 20 March 1934; Judy Yung, *Unbound Voices: A Documented History of Chinese Women in San Francisco* (Berkeley: University of California Press, 1999), 351.

35. Florence Chinn, correspondence with the author, 3 July 1997; Susan Zieff, "From Badminton to the Bolero: Physical Recreation in San

Francisco's Chinatown, 1895–1950," *Journal of Sport History* (Spring 2000): 13.

36. *Chinese Digest*, January 1938; Yep, *Outside the Paint*, 63–65, 76; Katherine Lawrence, *Laurence Yep* (New York: The Rosen Publishing Company, 2003), 13; Polk's Crocker-Langley San Francisco City Directory, 1935, http://www.ancestry.com, accessed 25 April 2013; U.S. Census Bureau, Manuscript Census Schedules, City and County of San Francisco, 1940.

37. Yep, *Outside the Paint*, 64–66, 71, 75, 78.

38. Ibid., 65–66.

39. Ibid., 72–73.

40. *Chinese Digest*, 8 May 1936, April 1938, May 1938, September 1938.

41. Ibid., 5 June 1936.

42. *Chinese Digest*, 17 April 1936, May 1937, May 1938, October 1938; U.S. Census Bureau, Manuscript Schedules, City and County of San Francisco, 1930.

43. *Chinese Digest*, May and June 1938; *California Chinese Press*, 20 December 1940, 28 February 1941; *San Francisco Chronicle*, 14 March 1941.

44. *Oakland Tribune*, 2 March 1920, 4 May 1920, 11 September 1927, 21 January 1932, 14 February 1932, 10 February 1934, 5 May 1940; *Chinese Digest*, 31 January 1936, May 1937, April 1938; L. Eve Armentrout Ma, Jeong Hui Ma, and Forrest Gok, *The Chinese of Oakland: Unsung Builders* (Oakland: Chinese History Research Committee, 1982), 54–55.

45. *California Chinese Press*, 13 December 1940.

46. *California Chinese Press*, 28 March 1941; *Chinese Digest*, 6 December 1935, 27 December 1935, 3 January 1936, 17 January 1936, 24 January 1936; *San Jose Mercury*, 4 February 1936, 14 February 1936, 2 November 1937; U.S. Census Bureau, Manuscript Census Schedules, City of San Jose and County of Santa Clara, 1920, 1940.

47. *Chinese Digest*, January 1937.

48. *Sacramento Bee*, 1 February 1923, 5 January 1929, 11 January 1938; *Chinese Digest*, 30 October 1936, 27 November 1936, January 1937, February 1937, April 1937, March 1938, January 1939; *Bakersfield Californian*, 6 January 1940; U.S. Census Bureau, Manuscript Census Schedules, City and County of Sacramento, 1940.

49. *Chinese Digest*, February 1937.

50. Ibid., 24 April 1936; Lynn Fauley Emery and Margaret Toohey-Costa, "Hoops and Skirts: Women's Basketball on the West," in *A Century of Women's Basketball*, ed. Joan S. Hult and Marianna Trekell (Reston, VA: American Alliance for Health, Physical Education, Recreation, and Dance, 1991), 152.

51. *Chinese Digest*, 30 December 1935, 24 January 1936, January 1937; *San Diego Union*, 16 November 1936.

52. *Chinese Digest*, 24 April 1936; *Los Angeles Times*, 27 March 1937; *California Chinese Press*, 7 February 1941, 14 March 1941, 18 April 1941;

Lucille Cheng et al. *Linking Our Lives: Chinese American Women in Los Angeles* (Los Angeles: Chinese American Society of Southern California, 1984), 109.

53. *Chinese Digest*, May 1938.

54. *Chinese Digest*, January 1937; *San Diego Evening Tribune*, 21 November 1933, 2 December 1938; *San Diego Union*, 7 February 1936, 28 February 1936, 16 November 1936, 17 February 1938, 21 April 1938.

55. *Portland Oregonian*, 28 November 1922, 30 October 1932, 12 November 1933, 29 December 1933; *Chinese Digest*, 16 December 1935; *Seattle Times*, 2 December 1925, 1 December 1926, 12 January 1936, 17 January 1937, 21 January 1938; *Seattle Post-Intelligencer*, 3 January 1941, 4 January 1941.

56. *Chinese Digest*, 17 April 1936; Lee, *Claiming*, 164–166 (see intro., n. 14).

57. *Chinese Digest*, 17 April 1936.

58. Lee, *Claiming*, 164–166.

59. *Seattle Times*, 28 February 1940; *Seattle Post-Intelligencer*, 14 January 1941; *Walla Walla Union*, 21 December 1947.

60. *Seattle Times*, 30 November 1930; U.S. Census Bureau, Manuscript Census Schedules, City of Seattle and County of King, 1930.

61. *Chinese Digest*, 31 January 1936.

62. *Seattle Times*, 19 October 1934; U.S. Census Bureau, Manuscript Census Schedules, City of Seattle and County of King, 1930.

63. *Seattle Times*, 20 March 1940.

64. *Portland Oregonian*, 24 December 1933, 31 January 1935, 8 February 1935, 24 February 1935, 20 March 1935, 11 December 1935.

65. *Seattle Times*, 27 December 1934.

66. *Portland Oregonian*, 6 February 1933, 23 December 1934.

67. *Chinese Digest*, 29 November 1935, 24 January 1936, 7 February 1936, January 1937.

68. Ibid., 27 November 1936, February 1937.

69. Ibid., 24 January 1936, January 1937.

70. *Arizona Republic*, 15 February 1940, 16 February 1940.

71. *Brooklyn Daily Standard Union*, 19 December 1915; *New York Herald*, n.d., 1918; *New York Tribune*, 27 October 1918; *Philadelphia Public Ledger*, 5 February 1921, 17 February 1921; *Miami Herald*, 17 November 1922; *Schenectady Gazette*, 25 December 1934; *Chinese Digest*, 4 April 1936; *Augusta Chronicle*, 8 January 1939; *San Antonio Express*, 14 January 1940.

72. *Buffalo Evening News*, 29 January 1926.

73. *Chinese Digest*, 29 November 1935; U.S. Census Bureau, Manuscript Census Schedules, City and County of Baltimore, 1930, 1940.

74. *Providence News*, 4 June 1928; *Boston Herald*, 4 March 1928, 24 March 1928, 8 April 1929; Dorothy Lindsay, "Women in Sports," 5 January 1930, 21 February 1935, 4 March 1930, 11 March 1930, 21 February 1935; U.S. Census Bureau,

Manuscript Census Schedules, City of Boston, County of Suffolk, 1930.

75. *New Orleans Times-Picayune*, 22 April 1928.

76. *Bellingham Herald*, 13 March 1910; *San Francisco Chronicle*, 23 January 1916; *Oakland Tribune*, 29 August 1917.

77. *Garden Island*, 26 July 1921; *Maui News*, 9 December 1921.

78. John Christgau, *The Origins of the Jump Shot: Eight Men Who Shook the World of Basketball* (Lincoln: University of Nebraska Press, 1999), 38–39.

79. Harry H. L. Kitano, *Japanese Americans: The Evolution of a Subculture* (New York: Prentice Hall, 1969), 89.

80. *San Francisco Chronicle*, 19 January 1930, 12 February 1930, 18 March 1934, 10 February 1936, 15 March 1936; *Berkeley Gazette*, 16 March 1933; *San Francisco Examiner*, 10 January 1934.

81. *Oakland Tribune*, 7 February 1934; *Berkeley Gazette*, 5 January 1940; *Buddhist Churches of America* (Chicago: Norbart Inc., 1974), 271.

82. *San Jose Mercury*, 14 January 1925, 7 March 1964; San Jose Zebra Youth Foundation, http://sjzebra.org/web/public/site/pages/about.html, accessed 29 April 2013.

83. *San Jose Mercury*, 17 January 1934, 18 January 1934, 25 December 1936, 14 January 1937, 2 November 1937; *Pacific Citizen*, 24 March 1944.

84. *Buddhist Churches*, 219; *Bakersfield Californian*, 6 January 1940; Samuel Regalado, "Sport and Community in California's Japanese American 'Yamato County,' 1930–1945," *Journal of Sport History* 19 (Summer 1992), 134; http://www.nikkeiwest.com/index.php/obituary-notice/202-obituaries-oct-10, accessed 30 November 2013; Yoshi Grace Hattori, http://www.legacy.com/obituaries/montereyherald/obituary-print.aspx?pid=142512798, accessed 30 November 2013.

85. *San Jose Mercury*, 14 January 1937.

86. *Sacramento Bee*, 17 January 1938.

87. *Lodi News-Sentinel*, 26 February 1940.

88. *Los Angeles Times*, 21 January 1937, 26 January 1939, 12 April 1939; Emery and Toohey-Costa, "Hoops and Skirts," 152; Nisei Athletic Union Basketball League, http://ncnau.org/history/index.html, accessed 9 July 2013.

89. *San Diego Evening Tribune*, 24 February 1932.

90. *Riverside Daily Press*, 11 January 1935; *San Diego Union*, 25 February 1927.

91. Nisei Athletic Union Basketball League, http://ncnau.org/history/index.html, accessed 9 July 2013.

92. *Seattle Times*, 16 February 1924, 21 February 1925, 2 December 1925, 1 December 1926, 12 January 1928, 27 October 1932, 4 January 1933, 6 February 1939; *Portland Oregonian*, 18 December 1932.

93. King County Snapshots, "Basketball team, Auburn, 1939–1940," http://content.lib.washington.edu/cdm4/item_viewer.php?CISOROOT=/imlswrvm&CISOPTR=148&CISOBOX=1&REC=1, accessed 24 January 2014.

94. *Portland Oregonian*, 19 December 1931, 12 January 1932, 13 January 1933, 15 January 1933, 26 January 1941.

95. *Salt Lake Tribune*, 13 March 1939.

96. *Honolulu Advertiser*, 3 March 1935, 14 March 1935; *Seattle Times*, 7 January 1926; *Chinese Digest*, May 1938; Center for Oral History, Social Science Research Institute, *Lana'i Ranch: The People of Ko'ele and Keomuku* (Honolulu: University of Hawai'i at Manoa, 1989), 834–835; Marie Booty, "Korean Contributions," in *A History of Recreation in Hawaii*, Honolulu Recreation Commission (Honolulu: T.H., 1936), 133.

97. Peter Jamero, *Vanishing Filipino Americans: The Bridge Generation* (Lanham, MD: University Press of America, 2011), 21.

98. *Salinas Index-Journal*, 26 February 1942; *Fresno Bee Republican*, 5 March 1942; Bill Staples Jr., *Kenichi Zenimura: Japanese American Baseball Pioneer* (Jefferson, NC: McFarland, 2011).

99. Franklin S. Odo, *No Sword to Bury: Japanese Americans in Hawai'i During World War II* (Philadelphia: Temple University Press, 2003), 208.

100. *San Francisco Chronicle*, 5 March 1942.

101. *Pacific Citizen*, 8 October 1942.

102. *New York Times*, 31 December 1942.

103. *Pacific Citizen*, 25 March 1944.

104. Ibid.

105. Ibid.

106. Ibid., 17 November 1942, 14 December 1942.

107. *Santa Anita Pacemaker*, 2 June 1942, 24 April 1942, 29 July 1942; *Tanforan Totalizer*, 25 July 1942, 8 August 1942.

108. *Heart Mountain Sentinel*, 9 January 1943; Samuel O. Regalado, "Incarcerated Sport: Nisei Women's Softball and Athletics During Japanese Internment," *Journal of Sport History* 27 (Fall 2000), 437.

109. *Heart Mountain Sentinel*, 17 April 1943, 3 May 1943, 31 December 1943, 8 January 1944; Japanese Americans Relocated During World War II, http://www.ancestry.com, accessed 21 December 2013.

110. *Heart Mountain Sentinel*, 30 January 1943, 6 February 1943, 13 February 1943, 20 February 1943, 6 March 1943, 3 April 1943, 10 April 1943; *Pacific Citizen*, 8 January 1944, 9 February 1944.

111. *Heart Mountain Sentinel*, 19 February 1944, 26 February 1944.

112. *Heart Mountain Sentinel*, 20 February 1943, 24 April 1943, 29 January 1944, 8 April 1944; Mikey Hirano Culbrass, "His Speed Was the Stuff of Legend," http://www.rafu.com/2011/11/his-speed-was-the-stuff-of-legend, accessed 2 November 2013; Japanese Americans Relocated During World War II, http://www.ancestry.com, accessed 21 December 2013.

113. *Heart Mountain Sentinel*, 8 April 1944; U.S. Census Bureau, Manuscript Census Schedules, City of San Jose and County of Santa Clara, 1940.

114. *Rohwer Outpost*, 16 January 1943, 20 January 1943.

115. Ibid., 16 February 1945, 2 March 1945.

116. *Pacific Citizen*, 21 January 1943, 28 January 1943.

117. Ibid., 4 February 1943, 18 February 1943, 25 February 1943, 18 March 1943, 15 January 1944; *Ogden Standard-Examiner*, 24 February 1943.

118. *Pacific Citizen*, 4 February 1943, 15 January 1944; *Heart Mountain Sentinel*, 8 January 1944; *Rohwer Outpost*, 19 January 1944, 23 February 1945; *Rocky Shimpo*, 17 January 1945, 2 February 1945, 23 February 1945.

119. *Rohwer Outpost*, 26 January 1944; *Pacific Citizen*, 25 March 1944; *Rocky Shimpo*, 5 February 1945; Bob Okizaki, "Chicagoans Organize Basketball League," *Rocky Shimpo*, 7 February 1945.

120. *Salinas Index-Journal*, 1–2 January 1942, 4–5 January 1945.

121. *San Francisco Chronicle*, 7 January 1942, 9 March 1942, 22 November 1942.

122. Ellen D. Wu, *Color of Success: Asian Americans and the Origins of the Model Minority* (Princeton: Princeton University Press, 2013), 55.

123. *Monitor*, 27 January 1945, 10 February 1945, 10 March 1945, 17 March 1945; *San Francisco Chronicle*, 14 February 1945; *San Francisco Examiner*, 5 April 1945.

124. *Korean Independence*, 17 May 1945.

Chapter 2

1. Regimental Report, 442nd Regiment, United States Army, November 1945, 26 January 1946, 20 May 1946, 20 April 1947.

2. John Ito, "Nisei Basketball Team Tours Northern Italy," *Pacific Citizen*, 4 May 1946.

3. Ibid.

4. John Ito, "Nisei Basketball Team Plays Series in Northern Italy," *Pacific Citizen*, 11 May 1946.

5. Ibid.

6. World War II Army Enlistment Records, 1938–1946, http://www. ancestry.com, accessed 25 April 2013; 442nd photos, http://www.javadc.org/java/docs/1946–02–14_Leghorn%20Basketball%20for%20442nd%20RCT.pdf, accessed 18 April 2013.

7. *Pacific Citizen*, 22 September 1945.

8. Ibid., 27 March 1948, 1 January 1954.

9. Ibid., 18 September 1948.

10. *Honolulu Star-Bulletin*, 5 November 1948.

11. *Honolulu Star-Bulletin*, 6 November 1948; *Hawaii Herald*, 23 January 1951.

12. *Hawaii Herald*, 18 February 1950, 3 March 1950; *Pacific Citizen*, 11 March 1950.

13. *Hawaii Herald*, 8 March 1950, 11 March 1950.

14. *Pacific Citizen*, 15 January 1949, 18 March 1955; *San Francisco Evening News*, 11 March 1950.

15. *Pacific Citizen*, 20 February 1950, 13 January 1951, 3 March 1951; *Seattle Times*, 22 December 1948.

16. *Pacific Citizen*, 25 November 1950.

17. *Hawaii Herald*, 7 February 1951; *Honolulu Advertiser*, 13 February 1954.

18. *San Jose News*, 14 January 1946, 16 January 1946; *San Jose Mercury*, 23 March 1947, 2 December 1949, 7 December 1949, 14 December 1949, 25 December 1949, 6 February 1950, 3 March 1950, 15 March 1950, 4 February 1955, 3 July 1960; San Jose City Directory, 1956, http://www.ancestry.com, accessed 12 December 2013.

19. *San Jose Mercury*, 8 January 1948, 11 January 1948, 15 January 1948, 18 January 1948; *Fresno Bee Republican*, 16 January 1948, 4 February 1948; Nisei Athletic Union Basketball League, http://ncnau.org/history/index.html, accessed 9 July 2013; Colleen Matsuhara, correspondence with the author, 21 July 2014.

20. *Riverside Daily Press*, 18 January 1949; Nisei Athletic Union Basketball League, http://ncnau.org/history/index.html, accessed 9 July 2013.

21. *Pacific Citizen*, 20 March 1948; *Seattle Times*, 18 April 1956; Pio DeCano II, "Integrity Guides Life of Legendary Coach," *Northwest Asian Weekly*, 12 June 2004.

22. *Pacific Citizen*, 16 February 1946.

23. *Pacific Citizen*, 7 February 1948, 25 November 1950, 13 January 1951, 23 January 1953; *Provo Daily Herald*, 25 March 1956.

24. Alec Yoshio McDonald, "Voices of Chicago: Sports, Community, and History: Reflections on Recording the Japanese American Experience in Chicago," http://www.discovernikkei.org/en/journal/2006/9/12/voices-of-chicago, accessed 21 February 2014; Wu, *Color of Success*, 40 (see chap. 1, n. 122).

25. McDonald, "Voices."

26. *Pacific Citizen*, 31 October 1952.

27. Ibid., 29 November 1947, 7 January 1950, 31 March 1951, 1 March 1952, 29 March 1952, 10 April 1953; *San Jose Mercury*, 3 December 1949; http://www.cjahs.org/cjahs/index.php?option=com_content&view=article&id=57:-interacttive-gallery&catid=39:history&Itemid=76, accessed 30 November 2013.

28. *Pacific Citizen*, 18 November 1948, 1 January 1954; *San Jose Mercury*, 18 January 1948.

29. *Pacific Citizen*, 13 December 1947, 18 November 1948, 23 February 1952; *Utah Nippo*, 16 January 1950.

30. *San Jose Mercury*, 23 March 1947.

31. *Pacific Citizen*, 20 March 1948.

32. Ibid., 2 April 1949.

33. Ibid., 1 March 1952.

34. Ibid., 31 March 1951; *Lodi News-Sentinel*, 27 December 1957.

35. *Seattle Times*, 23 March 1948.

36. *Pacific Citizen*, 2 March 1946, 4 March 1950.

37. Ibid., 3 February 1951.

38. *Chicago Tribune*, 28 November 1948; *Pacific Citizen*, 1 April 1953.

39. *Utah Nippo*, 29 March 1950; *Pacific Stars and Stripes*, 31 March 1953.

40. *Idaho Falls Register*, 29 March 1956.

41. *Deseret News*, 28 March 1957.

42. *Seattle Times*, 28 March 1958.

43. Ibid., 27 March 1959; *Hayward Daily Review*, 30 March 1959.

44. *Nichi Bei Times*, 13 June 1993.

45. *Pacific Citizen*, 1 April 1955; Nisei Athletic Union Basketball League, http://ncnau.org/history/index.html, accessed 9 July 2013.

46. *Pacific Citizen*, 1 April 1955.

47. *Honolulu Star-Bulletin*, 12 May 1951.

48. *San Francisco Examiner*, 5 December 1945.

49. Ibid., 18 February 1946, 23 February 1946; *San Francisco Chronicle*, 23 February 1946.

50. *San Francisco Chronicle*, 24 February 1946; *San Francisco Examiner*, 24 February 1946.

51. *San Francisco Examiner*, 23 February 1947, 24 February 1947, 1 March 1947, 4 March 1947.

52. Ibid., 5 March 1947; *San Francisco Chronicle*, 18 February 1948; *Oakland Tribune*, 2 March 1948.

53. *San Francisco Examiner*, 22 January 1950, 3 March 1950, 5 March 1950, 29 November 1950.

54. Ibid., 2 March 1947; Yep, *Outside the Paint*, 82; U.S. Census Bureau, Manuscript Census Schedules, City and County of San Francisco, 1940; Dwight Chapin, "Willie 'Woo Woo' Wong," *San Francisco Chronicle*, 8 September 2005.

55. *San Francisco Examiner*, 22 January 1950; *Chinese Press*, 7 January 1949; 10 November 1950; Chapin, "Willie 'Woo Woo' Wong."

56. *Syracuse Herald-Journal*, 9 April 1948.

57. *Monitor*, 6 February 1948, 13 February 1948, 12 March 1948, 6 January 1950.

58. Ibid., 22 December 1945, 14 December 1946, 23 November 1947, 7 December 1947, 9 January 1949; *Chinese Press*, 14 January 1949, 23 December 1949; U.S. Census Bureau, Manuscript Census Schedules, City and County of San Francisco, 1940.

59. Yep, *Outside the Paint*, 102; http://www.asianweekly.com, 5–11 January 2001.

60. *Troy Times*, 17 June 1948.

61. *San Francisco Chronicle*, 23 December 1947; *San Francisco Examiner*, 9 January 1948, 10 January 1948, 21 January 1948.

62. *San Francisco Examiner*, 5 January 1950, 7 January 1950, 19 January 1950; *San Francisco Chronicle*, 19 February 1952, 21 February 1952; *Pacific Citizen*, 1 March 1952.

63. *San Francisco Examiner*, 9 January 1949, 10 January 1949, 16 March 1950; *Chinese Press*, 7 January 1949; *San Francisco Chronicle*, 10 January 1949.

64. Yep, *Outside the Paint*, 32; *Chinese Press*, 2 June 1950.

65. *San Francisco Examiner*, 2 March 1953, 4 March 1953, 1 March 1955; *New York Times*, 19 November 1956.

66. Wu, *Color of Success*, 126.

67. Ibid., 136.

68. Ibid., 137.

69. Ibid.

70. Ibid., 299; http://www.stmaryschoolsf.org/about/history, accessed 24 January 2014.

71. *Oakland Tribune*, 5 February 1946; *Chinese Press*, 19 May 1950; *Sacramento Bee*, 21 March 1946; *Fresno Bee Republican*, 3 January 1946, 13 January 1949; *Pacific Citizen*, 13 December 1947; *Los Angeles Times*, 12 January 1964; Cheng, *Linking*, 109 (see chap. 1, n. 52).

72. *Portland Oregonian*, 30 November 1948; *Seattle Times*, 18 April 1956; Robert Heilman, "Dragon's Fierceness Skin Deep," *Seattle Times*, 4 August 1960.

73. *Brooklyn Eagle*, 11 September 1952, 31 December 1952, 26 June 1953; *Boston Herald*, 27 December 1959; *Washington Post*, 7 April 1962.

74. *Honolulu Star-Bulletin*, 15 September 1948, 9 October 1948, 2 November 1948, 4 November 1948; *Honolulu Record*, 11 November 1948, 23 December 1948, 27 January 1949.

75. DeCano, "Integrity Guides Life"; *San Francisco Chronicle*, 16 February 1949; *Philippine News*, 10–16 January 1974; Filipino American National Historical Society, Manilatown Heritage Foundation, Pin@y Educational Partnership, *Filipinos in San Francisco*, (Charleston, SC: Arcadia Publishing, 2011), 87; Juanita Tamayo Lott, *Common Destiny: Filipino American Generations* (Lanham, MD: Rowman and Littlefield, 2006), 44; Jamero, *Bridge Generation*, 22, 65–66.

76. U.S. Census Bureau, Manuscript Census Schedules, City and County of San Francisco, 1930, 1940.

77. *Philippines Star Press*, 23 January 1946, 9 April 1948, 12 December 1948; *Philippines Mail*, 1 April 1948; *San Jose Mercury*, 2 March 1950, 4 March 1950; *San Diego Union*, 29 November 1960; http://www.peterjamero.net/Pages/Photos.aspx, accessed 4 October 2013; Jamero, *Bridge Generation*, 23–24.

78. Jamero, *Bridge Generation*, 24–25.

79. *San Francisco Examiner*, 21 January 1949, 25 January 1949.

80. Jamero, *Bridge Generation*, 50, 56, 69, 74, 81–82, 87–88, 94, 98.

81. *Seattle Post-Intelligencer*, 31 December 1948; *Seattle Times*, 25 January 1961; Jamero, *Bridge Generation*, 24.

82. *Korean Independence*, 30 October 1946; *Honolulu Star-Bulletin*, 1 April 1950.

83. *San Francisco Chronicle*, 16 March 1948; *Pacific Citizen*, 20 March 1948.

84. *Seattle Post-Intelligencer*, 15 December 1947, 23 December 1947, 25 December 1947.

85. Jim O'Leary, "Guard Rates as Top Set Shot," *Greensboro Record*, 2 January 1950.

86. *Walla Walla Union Bulletin*, 21 December 1947.

87. *Seattle Times,* 27 December 1947.

88. *Pacific Citizen,* 18 September 1948; *Seattle Post-Intelligencer,* 29 December 1947.

89. Alex Shults, "Oriental Antagonism Vanish in this Basketball Tourney," *Seattle Times,* 21 December 1948.

90. Ibid.

91. Ibid.

92. Ibid., 11 December 1948; *Seattle Post-Intelligencer,* 22 December 1948, 24 December 1948.

93. *Walla Walla Union-Bulletin,* 24 December 1948; *Seattle Times,* 25 December 1948; *San Francisco Examiner,* 27 December 1948.

94. *Chinese Press,* 18 November 1949; *Seattle Times,* 20 December 1949; *San Francisco Examiner,* 4 December 1949.

95. *San Jose Mercury,* 12 December 1949, 20 December 1949, 21 December 1949, 22 December 1949.

96. *Seattle Times,* 23 December 1949, 25 December 1949.

97. *San Francisco Examiner,* 26 December 1949; *San Jose Mercury,* 26 December 1949.

Chapter 3

1. *Pacific Commercial Advertiser,* 13 April 1912, 16 December 1916; *Hawaiian Star,* 13 April 1912; *Honolulu Star-Bulletin,* 21 December 1916, 17 January 1927.

2. *Pacific Commercial Advertiser,* 2 February 1912, 18 March 1913, 16 November 1915, 28 November 1915, 5 October 1916, 17 October 1916.

3. Ibid., 4 March 1919; *Maui News,* 10 October 1916, 15 August 1919.

4. *Maui News,* 10 August 1920, 18 February 1921, 25 February 1921, 9 December 1922; *Garden Island,* 27 August 1920, 24 January 2 1922, 31 January 1922; E. L. Damrogger, "Basketball on Maui," *Honolulu Star-Bulletin,* 3 January 1927; *Honolulu Star-Bulletin,* 11 January 1927.

5. *Honolulu Star-Bulletin,* 6 January 1927, 12 January 1927, 15 January 1927, 19 January 1927.

6. Loui Leong Hop, "Two Contests of Bankers' League Program for the Opening Night," *Honolulu Star-Bulletin,* 1 January 1927, 15 January 1927; *Honolulu Advertiser,* 2 March 1933.

7. *Honolulu Advertiser,* 2 March 1933, 2 March 1935, 3 March 1935, 22 March 1935; *Honolulu Star-Bulletin,* 2 December 1934, 3 December 1934, 3 March 1936, 11 March 1936; U.S. Census Bureau, Manuscript Census Schedules, City and County of Honolulu, 1940.

8. *Honolulu Advertiser,* 20 April 1940.

9. Mrs. E. P. Reppert, "Agriculture Big Business in Hawaii," *Dallas Morning News,* 10 August 1941; Takaki, *Strangers,* chapter 4 (see intro., n. 12); Ronald T. Takaki, *Pau Hana: Plantation Life and Labor in Hawai'i, 1835–1920* (Honolulu: University of Hawai'i Press, 1983).

10. *Honolulu Advertiser,* 12 March 1944, 14 March 1944.

11. U.S. Census Bureau, Manuscript Census Schedules, District 27, Hilo, 1930; Leila Wai, "Goo Truly Had Magic Touch," honoluluadvertiser.com, 30 July 2004; Bob Hogue, "Ah Chew Goo, Hoops Magician," midweekauwai.com, 28 March 2007.

12. Wai, "Goo Truly Had Magic Touch"; Hogue, "Ah Chew Goo."

13. Bob Hogue, "Hawaii's Connections to Jeremy Lin," midweekauai.com, 8 March 2012; Dave Reardon, "UH Basketball's First AC Shares Gift With Others," http://www.starbulletin.com, 9 September 2001.

14. Robert Edgren, " Duke Kahanamoku Rules as Guardian of the Island," *Moorhead Daily News,* 13 April 1940.

15. *Oakland Tribune,* 11 April 1941; *Salt Lake Tribune,* 24 April 1941; Reardon, "UH Basketball"; Wai, "Goo Truly Had Magic Touch."

16. Wai, "Goo Truly Had Magic Touch"; Mark Kriegel, *Pistol: The Life of Pete Maravich* (New York: Free Press, 2008), 64.

17. Joel S. Franks, *Hawaiian Sports in the Twentieth Century* (Lewiston, ME: Edwin Mellen Press, 2002); Joel S. Franks, *The Barnstorming Hawaiian Travelers: A Multiethnic Baseball Team Tours the Mainland, 1912–1916* (Jefferson, NC: McFarland, 2012).

18. *Oakland Tribune,* 9 January 1923; *San Francisco Chronicle,* 11 January 1923, 13 January 1923.

19. *San Francisco Chronicle,* 14 January 1923, 19 January 1923; *Oakland Tribune,* 16 January 1923; *San Diego Union,* 23 January 1923.

20. *Sacramento Bee,* 24 January 1923, 2 February 1923; *San Francisco Chronicle,* 3 February 1923; *Woodland Daily Democrat,* 25 January 1923.

21. *Fresno Bee Republican,* 6 February 1923.

22. *Portland Oregonian,* 8 February 1923.

23. U.S. Census Bureau, Manuscript Census Schedules, City of Chicago and County of Cook County, 1930; U.S. Census Bureau, Manuscript Census Schedules, City and County of Honolulu, 1930.

24. Honolulu, Hawaii, Passenger and Crew Lists, 1900–1959, http://www.ancestry.com, accessed 18 January 2013.

25. *Portland Oregonian,* 5 December 1936; *Prensa,* 4 January 1937.

26. *Chinese Digest,* January 1937.

27. *Dallas Morning News,* 5 December 1937; *Abilene Reporter News,* 7 December 1937, 12 December 1937, 14 December 1937.

28. *New York Post,* 6 January 1937; *Albuquerque News,* 5 December 1937.

29. *San Jose News,* 14 December 1932; *Riverside Daily Press,* 9 December 1932; *Berkeley Daily Gazette,* 30 November 1935; *Chinese Digest,* 24 January 1936; *Sacramento Bee,* 12 January 1938, 26 January 1938; *Fresno Bee Republican,* 9 January

1942; California Voter Registrations, http://www.ancestry.com, accessed 5 April 2014.

30. *Boston Journal*, 9 February 1909; *Brooklyn Standard Union*, 28 November 1923.

31. *Rockford Morning Star*, 17 October 1941; Yung, *Unbound Voices*, 492 (see chap. 1, n. 32); *Sporting News*, 5 November 1947.

32. *Heart Mountain Sentinel*, 5 February 1944.

33. *San Jose Mercury*, 30 April 1905, 7 January 1933, 13 January 1933; *Oakland Tribune*, 20 November 1927; *Berkeley Gazette*, 16 March 1933; *Sacramento Bee*, 22 January 1938; *San Mateo Times and Daily News Leader*, 23 February 1944.

34. *Helena Independent*, 8 January 1930; *Ogden Standard-Examiner*, 17 February 1939; Josh Ferrin and Tres Ferrin, *Blitz Kids: The Cinderella Story of the 1944 University of Utah National Championship Basketball Team* (Layton, UT: Gibb Smith, 2012), 27–28.

35. *Hawaiian Gazette*, 21 March 1899; *Pacific Commercial Advertiser*, 16 March 1903; *Honolulu Evening Bulletin*, 7 November 1905; *Garden Island*, 14 March 1922; *Honolulu Star-Bulletin*, 20 January 1927.

36. *Pacific Commercial Advertiser*, 19 January 1915; *Honolulu Star-Bulletin*, 27 January 1917, 3 February 1917, 30 October 1917, 16 November 1917; *Garden Island*, 14 June 1921, 28 March 1922; *Maui News*, 22 March 1922; Leilehua High School Yearbook 1941, http://www.ancestry.com, accessed 3 July 2013.

37. *Honolulu Star-Bulletin*, 17 December 1917, 15 January 1927, 18 January 1927, 2 February 1927.

38. McKinley High School Yearbook 1931, http://www.ancestry.com, accessed 2 January 2012; McKinley High School Yearbook 1936, http://www.ancestry.com, accessed 9 February 2013.

39. Punahou High School Yearbook 1930, http://www.ancestry.com, accessed 13 July 2012.

40. *Honolulu Star-Bulletin*, 2 February 1927.

41. Franks, *Hawaiian Sports*; Hilo High School Yearbook 1941, http://www.ancestry.com, accessed 9 February 2013.

42. *Pacific Citizen*, 28 January 1950.

43. *San Francisco Evening Post*, 26 October 1912; *Tanforan Totalizer*, 20 June 1942; *San Francisco Chronicle*, 11 January 1919, 18 January 1919, 10 January 1931, 22 January 1934, 16 February 1935, 11 March 1936, 15 March 1936; *San Mateo Times*, 6 December 1930; *Oakland Tribune*, 21 January 1931, 18 January 1932.

44. Bob Stevens, "Indians Challenge Eagles," *San Francisco Chronicle*, 18 January 1941; Bob Stevens, "Commerce Prep Cagers Maul Lincoln," 13 February 1941, 1 March 1941; Bob Stevens, "Eagles Score in Cage Riot," 7 March 1941; Bob Stevens, "Mission Smears Commerce Preps," 31 January 1942; Bob Stevens, "Men of Commerce Deserve Praise," 3 March 1942; Bob Stevens, "Sacred Heart Whips Commerce in Extra Period," 4 March 1942; *San Francisco Examiner*, 21 February

1941; Galileo High School Yearbook 1944, http://www.classmates.com, accessed 21 March 2012.

45. *San Jose Mercury*, 10 January 1930, 6 February 1930, 8 February 1930, 2 February 1935, 16 January 1937; *San Jose News*, 17 December 1932; Palo Alto High School Yearbook, 1933, http://www.ancestry.com, accessed 1 August 2013; San Mateo High School Yearbook, 1933, http://www.classmates.com, accessed 20 December 2012; San Jose High School Yearbook, 1933, http://www.classmates.com, accessed 26 March 2014.

46. Stockton High School Yearbook, 1930, http://www.classmates.com, accessed 19 September 2012; Ron Kroichick, "Theodore 'Ted' Ohashi—Cal Basketball Player, YMCA Coach," *San Francisco Chronicle*, 9 November 2006.

47. *Oakland Tribune*, 29 January 1930; *Sacramento Bee*, 15 June 1935, 13 January 1938, 14 January 1938, 18 January 1938; *Fresno Bee Republican*, 10 January 1942; Stockton High School Yearbook, 1933, http://www.classmates.com, accessed 19 September 2012; Grass Valley High School Yearbook, 1934, http://www.ancestry.com, accessed 8 July 2009; Livingston High School Yearbook, 1941, http://www.ancestry.com, accessed 5 April 2013; Fresno High School Yearbook, 1938, http://www.ancestry.com, accessed 28 December 2013; High School Basketball Team, Dinuba, Calif., 1919, Tulare County Library, calisphere, University of California, http://content.cdlib.org/ark:/13030/c8tm78dh/?layout=metadata&brand=calisphere, accessed 9 June 2014.

48. *Los Angeles Times*, 9 January 1935, 18 January 1936, 16 January 1937, 23 January 1937; Lincoln High School Yearbook, 1930, http://www.ancestry.com, accessed 5 April 2014; Belmont High School Yearbook, 1938, http://www.classmates.com, accessed 5 May 2012.

49. *Los Angeles Times*, 16 January 1940, 24 January 1940, 27 January 1940, 16 January 1942; Hollywood High School Yearbook, 1940, http://www.classmates.com, accessed 20 February 2012; Helms Foundation Press Release, 16 February 1940.

50. *Riverside Daily Press*, 6 January 1932; Charles Byrne, "Sweetwater Beats La Jolla in CIF Thriller," *San Diego Union*, 26 February 1934; Garden Grove High School Yearbook, 1935, http://www.ancestry.com, 26 November 2012.

51. Bob Jacobsen, "A Man for All Seasons," http://www.asu.edu/alumnivision, accessed 19 October 2012; Phoenix High School Yearbook, 1933, http://www.ancestry.com, accessed 27 May 2006.

52. *Chinese Digest*, 31 January 1936; *Seattle Post-Intelligencer*, 11 January 1941, 15 January 1941, 18 January 1941, 25 January 1941; *Seattle Times*, 9 March 1941; Garfield High School Yearbook, 1941, http://www.ancestry.com, accessed 22 March 2013.

53. Lee, *Claiming*, 165–166 (see intro., n. 14); *Seattle Post-Intelligencer*, 5 January 1941; *Seattle Times*, 4 February 1942.

54. *Seattle Times*, 3 March 1922, 9 March 1941, 13 March 1941, 4 February 1942, 22 February 1942; *Ogden Standard-Examiner*, 13 January 1940; Matt Wyse, "Orange Streaks Lands Three on All-Division," 16 March 1941; *Seattle Post Intelligencer*, 15 January 1941, 18 January 1941, 29 January 1941; *Portland Oregonian*, 13 January 1918, 2 February 1941; *Pacific Citizen*, 22 February 1944, 4 February 1955; Queen Anne High School Yearbook, 1941, http://www.ancestry.com, 1 June 2013.

55. *Philadelphia Public Ledger*, 11 January 1915; *Rockford Republic*, 21 January 1924; *New York Times*, 22 February 1928; *Augusta Chronicle*, 3 January 1936; *Cleveland Plain Dealer*, 20 December 1939.

56. Ralph Wheeler, "Freshman Johnny Paredes Makes Sports History at Cambridge Latin," *Boston Herald*, 2 February 1943, 19 January 1944.

57. *San Francisco Chronicle*, 4 March 1913, 25 January 1919.

58. *San Francisco Chronicle*, 22 January 1938; Bob Stevens, "Sacred Heart Whips Commerce in Extra Period," *San Francisco Chronicle*, 4 March 1942; Bob Stevens, "1942 Prep Basketball Quintets are Named," *San Francisco Chronicle*, 16 March 1942; *San Francisco Chronicle*, 2 March 1944, 10 February 1945; Bob Stevens, "Lincoln Prep Quintet Rally Over Commerce," *San Francisco Chronicle*, 17 February 1945; Commerce High School Yearbook, http://www.worldvitalrecords.com, accessed 26 October 2012; Commerce High School Yearbook, 1925, http://www.ancestry.com, accessed 21 December 2008; Commerce High School Yearbook, 1941, http://www.ancestry.com, accessed 21 May 2013.

59. *San Francisco Chronicle*, 3 March 1934; Bob Stevens, "Galileo Basketballers Defeat Balboa, 46 to 23," *San Francisco Chronicle*, 16 January 1937; *San Francisco Chronicle*, 13 February 1942; Bob Stevens, "Men of Commerce," *San Francisco Chronicle*, 3 March 1942; Galileo High School Yearbook, 1933, http://www.classmates.com, accessed 18 July 2012; Galileo High School Yearbook, 1944, http://www.ancestry.com, accessed 21 March 2013; Galileo High School Yearbook, 1945, http://www.ancestry.com, accessed 21 March 2012.

60. Bob Stevens, "Inexperience Hits Parrot Hoops Men Where It Hurts," *San Francisco Chronicle*, 3 January 1938; Bob Stevens, "Eagle Score in Cage Riot," *San Francisco Chronicle*, 7 March 1941; Bob Stevens, "Chuck Lerable Leads All-City Basketball Five," *San Francisco Chronicle*, 11 March 1941; George Washington High School Yearbook, 1943, http://www.ancestry.com, accessed 19 April 2014.

61. *San Francisco Chronicle*, 21 September 1937; Bob Stevens, "Balboa Cagers Defeat Irish," *San Francisco Chronicle*, 15 January 1938 ; Bob Stevens, "Egg Foo Lum," *San Francisco Chronicle*, 17 January 1938; Bob Stevens, "Barbi Leads Mission to 36–23 Cage Victory," *San Francisco Chronicle*, 20 January 1938; *San Francisco Chronicle, 2 February 1938.

62. Bob Marcus, "Prep Quintets Take to the Boards in Kezar," *San Francisco Chronicle*, 15 January 1945; Bob Marcus, "Guerin's Twenty-One Points Give St. Ignatius Win," *San Francisco Chronicle*, 26 January 1945; Bob Stevens, "Ten Prep Hoop Teams Deadlocked for Title," *San Francisco Chronicle*, 5 February 1945; Bob Marcus, "Title Final Results in Irish Loss to Galileo," *San Francisco Chronicle*, 26 February 1945.

63. *San Francisco Evening News*, 10 December 1918; *Oakland Tribune*, 21 March 1926, 11 February 1931; Ed Wilkes, "Bearcats Top P.A.L. as Race Nears Finish," *San Mateo Times*, 4 February 1933; Douglas Guy, "Trys for Third Win Against Stronger S," *San Francisco Chronicle*, 23 January 1942; Berkeley High School Yearbook, 1933, http://www.ancestry.com, accessed 20 December 2012.

64. *San Jose Mercury*, 6 January 1933, 23 January 1937, 4 March 1942.

65. *San Jose Mercury*, 20 January 1934; Les Herman, "Loss of Star by Graduation Impairs Records of Local Preps," *San Jose Mercury*, 4 February 1935; San Jose High School Yearbook, 1931, http://www.classmates.com, accessed 2 December 2011; San Jose High School Yearbook, 1933, http://www.classmates.com, accessed 26 March 2014; San Jose High School Yearbook, 1935, http://www.classmates.com, accessed 13 February 2012; San Jose High School Yearbook, 1939, http://www.classmates.com, accessed 2 December 2011; San Jose High School Yearbook, 1940, http://www.ancestry.com, accessed 31 October 2013; San Jose High School Yearbook, 1942, http://www.ancestry.com, accessed 31 October 2013.

66. *San Jose Mercury*, 6 January 1925, 16 January 1933, 21 January 1933, 13 January 1937, 16 January 1937, 22 January 1937, 28 January 1937, 5 November 1937; Campbell High School Yearbook, 1940, http://www.ancestry.com, 18 June 2013.

67. *Salinas Index-Journal*, 16 March 1942; Salinas High School Yearbook, 1941, http://www.ancestry.com, accessed 6 December 2013; Salinas High School Yearbook, 1942, http://www.ancestry.com, accessed 6 December 2013; Salinas High School Yearbook, 1945, http://www.ancestry.com, accessed 6 December 2013.

68. *Sacramento Bee*, 15 January 1929, 8 June 1935, 8 January 1938, 14 January 1938, 15 January 1938, 18 January 1938; *Fresno Bee Republican*, 10 January 1942, 4 March 1942; Stockton High School Yearbook, 1929, http://www.ancestry.com, accessed 1 June 2013; Livingston High School Yearbook, 1932, http://www.ancestry.com, accessed 18 November 2013; Livingston High School Yearbook, 1934, http://www.ancestry.com, accessed 18 November 2013; Livingston High School Yearbook, 1941, http://www.ancestry.com, accessed 5 April 2013; Fresno High School Yearbook, 1938, http://www.ancestry.com, accessed 28 December 2013; Fresno High School

Yearbook, 1941, http://www.classmates.com, accessed 15 July 2012.

69. *Los Angeles Times*, 2 February 1923, 5 January 1935, 9 January 1935, 12 January 1935; Gardena High School Yearbook, 1929, http://www. ancestry.com, accessed 28 December 2013; Polytechnic High School Yearbook, 1930, http:// www.ancestry.com, accessed 3 July 2013; Lincoln High School Yearbook, 1930, http://www.ancestry. com, accessed 5 April 2014; Belmont High School Yearbook, 1938, http://www.classmates.com, accessed 5 May 2012; Hollywood High School Yearbook, 1938, http://www.ancestry.com, accessed 18 July 2013; Hollywood High School Yearbook, 1939, http://www.ancestry.com, accessed 18 July 2013; Hollywood High School Yearbook, 1940, http://www.classmaates.com, accessed 20 February 2012; San Pedro High School Yearbook, 1941, http://www.classmates.com, accessed 18 June 2012.

70. Broadway High School Yearbook, 1924, http://www.ancestry.com, accessed 22 March 2013; Broadway High School Yearbook, 1928, http://www.ancestry.com, accessed 22 March 2013; Broadway High School Yearbook, 1934, http://www.classmates.com, accessed 6 July 2013; Broadway High School Yearbook, 1937, http:// www.classmates.com, accessed 6 July 2013; Garfield High School Yearbook, 1933, http:// www.ancestry.com, accessed June 2013; Garfield High School Yearbook, 1938, http://www.ancestry. com, accessed 22 March 2013; Astoria High School Yearbook, 1941, http://www.ancestry.com, accessed 27 April 2013.

71. Gardena High School Yearbook, 1929, http://www.ancestry.com, accessed 28 December 2013; Livingston High School Yearbook, 1932, http://www.ancestry.com, accessed 18 November 2013; Galileo High School Yearbook, 1932, http:// www.classmates.com, accessed 25 April 2013; Galileo High School Yearbook, 1934, http://www. classmates.com, accessed 18 July 2012; Fresno High School Yearbook, 1934, http://www.ancestry. com, accessed 13 December 2013; Fresno High School Yearbook, 1941, http://www.ancestry. com, accessed 25 July 2012; Chico High School Yearbook, 1935, http://www.ancestry.com, accessed December 20, 2012; San Jose High School Yearbook, 1935, http://www.ancestry.com, accessed 13 February 2012; San Jose High School Yearbook, 1939, http://www.ancestry.com, accessed 2 December 2011; San Jose High School Yearbook, 1942, http://www.ancestry.com, accessed 31 October 2013; McClatchy High School Yearbook, 1939, http://www.ancestry.com, accessed 18 November 2013; Campbell High School Yearbook, 1940, http://www.ancestry. com, accessed 18 June 2013.

72. *Chinese Digest*, 16 December 1936, January 1937, May 1938; Broadway High School Yearbook, 1937, http://www.ancestry.com, accessed 6 July 2013; Garfield High School Yearbook, 1938, http://www.ancestry.com, accessed 22 March 2013; Queen Anne High School Yearbook, 1941, http://www.ancestry.com, accessed 1 June 2013.

Chapter 4

1. *Honolulu Star-Bulletin*, 14 September 1948, 22 January 1951; *Hawaii Herald*, 8 March 1950; *Pacific Stars and Stripes*, 11 February 1951.

2. *Honolulu Star-Bulletin*, 17 March 1947, 15 September 1948, 4 November 1948, 1 January 1949.

3. *Hawaii Herald*, 4 January 1951; *Honolulu Advertiser*, 13 February 1954.

4. *Pacific Citizen*, 27 January 1951; *Hawaii Herald*, 1 February 1951; *San Francisco Chronicle*, 17 February 1952; *Portland Oregonian*, 19 October 1952; *Lewiston Morning Tribune*, 30 November 1952; *St. Helena Chronicle*, 2 December 1952; *Honolulu Star-Bulletin*, 3 January 1953; *Stars and Stripes*, 10 March 1953; Andrew Mitsukado, "Broncos Trip Universals," *Honolulu Advertiser*, 13 February 1954.

5. *Honolulu Star-Bulletin*, 6 January 1953, 10 January 1953.

6. *Honolulu Star-Bulletin*, 14 November 1949, 29 November 1949, 30 January 1951.

7. *Dixon Evening Telegraph*, 26 February 1947; *Ogden Standard-Examiner*, 27 February 1947.

8. Air Passenger Manifest, Pan American Airways, Inc., 30 March 1947, http://www.ancestry. com, accessed 29 December 2012.

9. *Los Angeles Times*, 30 January 1947; *Ogden Standard-Examiner*, 23 February 1947, 26 February 1947; *Pacific Citizen*, 16 August 1947.

10. *Ogden Standard-Examiner*, 23 February 1947, 26 February 1947.

11. *Los Angeles Times*, 3 February 1947, 4 February 1947; *Syracuse Herald Journal*, 4 February 1947; *Dixon Evening Telegram*, 28 February 1947; *Ogden Standard-Examiner*, 7 March 1947; *Portland Oregonian*, 17 February 1949.

12. *Kingston Daily Freeman*, 20 January 1948; *Benton Harbor News-Palladium*, 10 March 1948.

13. *Ogden Standard-Examiner*, 27 January 1952, 28 January 1952; *Pampa Daily News*, 22 February 1953; U.S. Census Bureau, Manuscript Schedules, City and County of Honolulu, 1930 and 1940.

14. *Stars and Stripes*, 10 March 1953; *Provo Daily Herald*, 25 March 1956.

15. *Day*, 14 June 1954; *Bennington Evening Banner*, 27 August 1955; *Amsterdam Evening Bulletin*, 7 November 1955; *New Mexican*, 11 March 1957; *Salina Journal*, 19 March 1957.

16. Adolph H. Grundman, *The Golden Age of Amateur Basketball: The AAU Tournament, 1921–1968* (Lincoln: University of Nebraska Press, 2004).

17. *Humboldt Standard*, 4 January 1952, 8 January 1952.

18. Ray Haywood, "Engineers Host Denver Bank Tonight," *Oakland Tribune*, 10 January 1952,

14 March 1952; Ray Haywood, "Engineers Meet Ford Five in AAU Tourney Tonight," *Oakland Tribune*, 17 March 1952; *San Francisco Chronicle*, 22 February 1952.

19. *San Jose Mercury*, 23 March 1947, 21 December 1949, 14 January 1951, 5 January 1952, 9 January 1952; *Valley News*, 14 February 1947; *Fresno Bee*, 15 January 1948; *Long Beach Independent*, 6 January 1955; *Pasadena Star-News*,12 December 1956.

20. *Seattle Times*, 21 February 1946, 26 February 1948; Lee, *Claiming*, 175.

21. Lee, *Claiming*, 175; *Seattle Times*, 20 February 1953.

22. *Pacific Citizen*, 20 March 1948, 15 October 1949, 21 January 1950, 29 March 1952, 5 April 1952; *Boston Herald*, 11 January 1953.

23. *Pacific Citizen*, 1 October 1949, 10 April 1953; *Fresno Bee*, 16 December 1951; Jamero, *Bridge Generation*, 89.

24. *Lodi News-Sentinel*, 5 February 1955, 20 December 1955; *Pasadena Star-News*, 14 December 1957; *San Jose Mercury*, 10 January 1960; *Sacramento Bee*, 25 January 1954.

25. *Aberdeen Daily News*, 10 April 1952, 28 May 1953; *Springfield Union*, 19 February 1946.

26. *San Francisco Examiner*, 18 December 1948.

27. *San Francisco Examiner*, 22 December 1948, 23 December 1948, 26 December 1948, 28 December 1948, 7 January 1949.

28. *San Francisco Examiner*, 8 December 1949, 16 December 1949, 21 December 1949, 23 December 1949.

29. *Honolulu Star-Bulletin*, 2 November 1948, 7 January 1953; *Honolulu Advertiser*, 13 February 1954.

30. McKinley High School Yearbook, 1956, http://www.classmates.com, accessed 31 May 2012.

31. *Honolulu Star-Bulletin*, 9 January 1953, 11 January 1953; http://www.hawaiiprepworld.com/author/jcampany, accessed 15 April 2013.

32. *Honolulu Star-Bulletin*, 2 December 1949, 6 April 1950, 9 January 1953; http://www.k12.hi.us/~jnako/afookchinen.htm, accessed 10 July 2013; Dan Cisco, *Hawai'i Sports, Facts, and Statistics* (Honolulu: University of Hawai'i Press, 1999), 47; U.S. Census Bureau, Manuscript Census Schedules, City of Hilo, Island of Hawai'i, 1940; Kauai High School Yearbook, 1958, http://www.ancestry.com, accessed 30 September 2013.

33. *Honolulu Star-Bulletin*, 8 May 1956; *Hayward Daily Review*, 29 December 1966; Stacy Kaneshiro, "Walter Wong, St. Louis Coach," 10 August 2002, http://www.the.honoluluadvertiser.com; U.S. Census Bureau, Manuscript Census Schedules, City and County of Honolulu, 1940; Robert Lee, *The Chinese in Hawaii: A Historical Sketch*, (Honolulu: Honolulu Advertiser Publishing Company, 1961); St. Louis Preparatory School Yearbook, 1959, http://www.ancestry.com, accessed 19 February 2014; Roosevelt High School

Yearbook, 1962, http://www.ancestry.com, accessed 29 August 2013.

34. *San Francisco Examiner*, 5 March 1947, 10 March 1947; Don Selby, "Chin Racks Up Record 21 Points," 9 January 1948; *San Francisco Examiner*, 24 January 1948, 21 January 1949, 10 December 1949, 6 January 1950; Bob Marcus, "Bears' Triandos Hits 22 Points," *San Francisco Chronicle*, 23 January 1947; Commerce High School Yearbook, 1947, http://www.classmates.com, accessed 17 June 2011.

35. *San Francisco Call-Bulletin*, 26 January 1949; *San Francisco Examiner*, 7 December 1949; Don Selby, "Calsa Hurt Again," *San Francisco Examiner*, 14 January 1950; Don Selby, "Moh, Postel Led Lincoln to Victory," *San Francisco Examiner*, 17 January 1950; *San Francisco Chronicle*, 17 January 1950; Commerce High School Yearbook, 1949, http://www.ancestry.com, accessed 24 February 2014.

36. *San Francisco Chronicle*, 19 January 1962; George Washington High School Yearbook, 1954, http://www.ancestry.com, accessed 26 November 2012; Lowell High School Yearbook, 1958, http://www.classmaates, accessed 11 July 2013; George Washington High School Yearbook, 1959, http://www.ancestry.com, accessed 7 May 2014; Lowell High School Yearbook, 1961, http://www.ancestry.com, accessed 11 July 2013; Lowell High School Yearbook, 1963, http://www.classmates.com, accessed 11 September 2013.

37. *Oakland Tribune*, 9 January 1946, 23 January 1960; *San Jose News*, 19 January 1946; *San Jose Mercury*, 1 February 1946, 16 January 1965; *San Francisco Chronicle*, 7 January 1950, 21 January 1950, 17 February 1951, 16 February 1952, 22 February 1952, 21 February 1953; Don Selby, "San Jose Makes Bid for Title," *San Francisco Examiner*, 20 February 1947; *San Francisco Examiner*, 14 January 1950; *Fremont Argus*, 2 December 1964; *Monitor*, 19 March 1948; Oakland Technical High School Yearbook, 1966, http://www.ancestry.com, accessed 23 May 2013; Mel Orphilla, correspondence with the author, 20 June 2013.

38. *San Jose Mercury*, 2 February 1946, 14 January 1948, 3 December 1949, 17 December 1949, 6 January 1950, 1 February 1950, 6 January 1960, 9 January 1960, 20 February 1960, 1 December 1960, 16 January 1965, 3 February 1965; *Pacific Citizen*, 11 February 1950; *San Francisco Examiner*, 6 March 1955; Bob Mattson, "Carlmont Quintet Wins," *San Mateo Times*, 19 December 1956; Andrew Hill Yearbook, 1963, http://www.classmates.com, accessed 26 March 2010; Campbell High School Yearbook, 1961, http://www.classmates.com, accessed 8 September 2010; Mountain View High School Yearbook, 1963, http://www.classmates.com, accessed 24 October 2009.

39. *San Jose Mercury*, 6 January 1960, 9 January 1960, 13 January 1960, 16 January 1960, 19 January 1960, 16 February 1960.

40. *San Jose News*, 2 February 1946, 11 February 1946; *Pacific Citizen*, 11 February 1950; *San Jose Mercury*, 17 January 1948; Salinas High School Yearbook, 1947, http://www.classmates.com, accessed 16 January 2012; Watsonville High School Yearbook, 1949, http://www.ancestry.com, accessed 27 April 2013.

41. *Fresno Bee Republican*, 25 January 1946; *Modesto Bee and Herald*, 23 February 1946, 11 December 1960; *Pacific Citizen*, 11 February 1950, 13 January 1951, 2 February 1952; *Sacramento Bee*, 30 March 1950, 21 January 1958, 25 January 1958; *Lodi News-Sentinel*, 29 December 1961; Livingston High School Yearbook, 1951, http://www.classmates.com, accessed 17 January 2014; Sacramento High School Yearbook, 1952, http://www.ancestry.com, accessed 8 July 2013; Sacramento High School Yearbook, 1958, http://www.ancestry.com, accessed 16 July 2013.

42. *Pacific Citizen*, 28 January 1950, 20 February 1950, 25 November 1950, 13 January 1951.

43. *Pacific Citizen*, 28 January 1950, 13 January 1951, 27 January 1951.

44. *Pacific Citizen*, 11 February 1950; *Los Angeles Times*, 4 February 1950, 25 January 1956, 7 December 1961, 11 January 1964; *Valley News*, 22 November 1956; *Pasadena Star-News*, 19 January 1957; Helms Athletic Foundation, Press Release, 12 March 1952, http://www.la84.org/sports-library-digital-collection/, accessed 20 July 2012; Helms Athletic Foundation, Press Release, 5 February 1954, http://www.la84.org/sports-library-digital-collection/, accessed 10 July 2012; Helms Athletic Foundation, Press Release, 24 March 1955, http://www.la84.org/sports-library-digital-collection/, accessed 3 September 2012; Roosevelt High School Yearbook, 1954, http://www.classmates.com, accessed 24 August 2013.

45. *Seattle Times*, 14 February 1948; Bob Schwartzman, "Fiddler Building Strong Offensive Quintet," 22 December 1948; *Seattle Times*, 12 February 1949; Garfield High School Yearbook, 1949, http://www.ancestry.com, accessed 15 June 2013.

46. Bob Sutton, "Garfield Basketball Star Earning Way Through School," *Seattle Times*, 20 February 1949.

47. *Pacific Citizen*, 28 January 1950, 11 February 1950, 11 March 1950; Bob Sutton, "Garfield Faces Defense of Title With Only Two Lettermen," *Seattle Times*, 1 January 1950; *Seattle Post-Intelligencer*, 4 March 1955, 6 March 1955; Garfield High School Yearbook, 1946, http://www.classmates.com, accessed 6 July 2013; Garfield High School Yearbook, 1955, http://www.classmates.com, accessed 23 July 2013.

48. *Pacific Citizen*, 28 January 1950; *Lowell Sun*, 28 January 1953; Carbon High School Yearbook, 1965, http://www.ancestry.com, accessed 5 April 2013.

49. *San Francisco Examiner*, 28 February 1947, 4 January 1949, 5 January 1950, 14 January 1950;
Don Selby, "Mohr, Postel Led Lincoln to Victory," *San Francisco Examiner*, 17 January 1950; *San Francisco Examiner*, 23 February 1951; Tom Barclay, "Commerce Coach Has His Way," *San Francisco Call-Bulletin*, 22 January 1949; *San Francisco Call-Bulletin*, 31 January 1949; Commerce High School Yearbook, 1947, http://www.classmates.com, accessed 17 June 2011.

50. *San Francisco Examiner*, 23 February 1953, 4 March 1953; *San Francisco Chronicle*, 8 March 1953; Galileo High School Yearbook, 1957, http://www.classmates.com, accessed 11 July 2013; Galileo High School Yearbook, 1960, http://www.classmates.com, accessed 30 May 2011; Galileo High School Yearbook, 1963, http://www.classmates.com, accessed 11 September 2013.

51. Lowell High School Yearbook, 1958, http://www.ancestry.com, accessed 11 July 2013; Lowell High School Yearbook, 1960, http://www.ancestry.com, accessed 11 July 2013.

52. *San Francisco Examiner*, 18 January 1950, 20 February 1951; *San Francisco Chronicle*, 4 March 1951, 16 January 1962; George Washington High School Yearbook, 1954, http://www.classmates.com, accessed 24 August 2012; George Washington High School Yearbook, 1955, http://www.classmates.com, accessed 9 October 2012; George Washington High School Yearbook, 1959, http://www.ancestry.com, accessed 7 May 2014; http://www.stmaryschoolsf.org/about/history/, accessed 24 January 2014.

53. *Oakland Tribune*, 8 January 1946; *San Mateo Times*, 16 February 1952, 21 January 1953; *San Jose Mercury*, 5 February 1955.

54. *San Jose Mercury*, 2 February 1946, 7 October 1949, 22 October 1954, 5 February 1955, 2 March 1962; *San Jose News*, 9 October 1946, 23 October 1946, 20 September 1947, 9 December 1950, 5 February 1955, 2 March 1962; San Jose High School Yearbook, 1946, http://www.ancestry.com, accessed 3 July 2013; San Jose High School Yearbook, 1951, http://www.classmates.com, accessed 26 March 2014; James Lick High School Yearbook, 1954, http://www.ancestry.com, 16 July 2013; James Lick High School Yearbook, 1964, http://www.classmates.com, accessed 21 May 2011; Mountain View High School Yearbook, 1966, http://www.classmates.com, accessed 24 January 2013.

55. *San Jose News*, 11 February 1946; *San Jose Mercury*, 7 January 1950, 5 February 1955; Watsonville High School Yearbook, 1954, http://www.ancestry.com, accessed 5 April 2013.

56. *Fresno Bee Republican*, 14 January 1948; *Pacific Citizen*, 3 February 1950; *Sacramento Bee*, 20 March 1950, 18 January 1958; *Lodi News-Sentinel*, 7 March 1957, 10 December 1961; *Modesto Bee*, 11 December 1960; Sacramento High School Yearbook, 1952, http://www.ancestry.com, accessed 8 July 2013; Sacramento High School Yearbook, 1958, http://www.ancestry.com, accessed 16 July 2013.

57. *Long Beach Independent*, 18 December 1954; Calipatria High School Yearbook, 1950, http://www.classmates.com, accessed 31 May 2012; Polytechnic High School (Los Angeles) Yearbook, 1951, http://www.classmates.com, 7 July 2012; Roosevelt High School Yearbook, 1954, http://www.classmates.com, accessed 24 August 2013; Lincoln High School Yearbook, 1955, http://www.classmates.com, accessed 7 July 2012; Garfield High School (Los Angeles) Yearbook, 1962, http://www.ancestry.com, accessed 23 July 2013; Polytechnic High School (Long Beach) Yearbook, 1964, http://www.classmates.com, accessed 11 May 2011.

58. Bob Ries, "Gene Sue is City's First Chinese Hopeful," *Canton Repository*, 31 March 1946; Wapato High School Yearbook, 1951, http://www.ancestry.com, accessed 29 August 2013; Garfield High School (Seattle) Yearbook, 1955, http://www.ancestry.com, 23 July 2013.

59. *Seattle Times*, 20 July 1959; Berkeley High School Yearbook, 1947, http://www.classmates.com, accessed 8 September 2012; Commerce High School Yearbook, 1947, http://www.classmates.com, accessed 24 June 2011; Watsonville High School Yearbook, 1949, http://www.ancestry.com, accessed 19 February 2014; San Jose High School Yearbook, 1951, http://www.classmates.com, accessed 26 March 2014; Monterey High School Yearbook, 1953, http://www.classmates.com, accessed 24 January 2013; George Washington High School Yearbook, 1954, http://www.classmates.com, accessed 9 October 2012.

60. *Monitor*, 22 February 1947, 8 March 1947, 15 March 1947, 12 April 1947, 5 March 1948, 19 March 1948, 17 March 1950, 16 March 1951; Star of the Sea Academy Yearbook, 1953, http://www.classmates.com, accessed 30 May 2011; Star of the Sea Academy Yearbook, 1955, http://www.classmates.com, accessed 17 November 2011.

61. James Lick High School Yearbook, 1954, http://www.ancestry.com, accessed 16 July 2013; http://www.placersports, 25 October 2012; Brian Bainum, "Legendary Prep Coach Ed Chavez Feeling the Love During His Recovery From Stroke," 21 April 2008, http://www.marinij.com/sports/ci_9005534, accessed 21 April 2008.

Chapter 5

1. *Garden Island*, 28 March 1922; *Honolulu Star-Bulletin*, 17 January 1927; University of Hawai'i Yearbook, 1928, http://www.ancestry.com, accessed 4 October 2013.

2. *Honolulu Advertiser*, 3 March 1935, 14 March 1935; *Honolulu Star-Bulletin*, 11 March 1936; University of Hawai'i Yearbook, 1932, http://www.worldvitalrecords.com, accessed 30 January 2012.

3. University of Hawai'i Yearbook, 1944, http://www.world vitalrecords.com, accessed 27 April 2012.

4. *New York Times*, 18 February 1947; *Honolulu Star-Bulletin*, 3 November 1948, 7 January 1949, 1 December 1949, 21 January 1950; Air Passenger Manifest, Pan American Airways, SF to Honolulu, http://search.ancestry.com/iexec?htx=View&r=an&dbid=1502&iid=40299_169764-00326&fn=Bert+Chan&ln=WA&st=r&ssrc=&pid=14215022, accessed 29 December 2012.

5. *Portland Oregonian*, 26 February 1948; *New York Times*, 1 January 1950; University of Hawai'i Yearbook, 1949, http://www.worldvitalrecords.com, accessed 3 March 2012.

6. *Pacific Citizen*, 27 March 1951.

7. University of Hawai'i Yearbook, 1951, http://www.ancestry.com, accessed 29 December 2013; University of Hawai'i Yearbook, 1953, http://www.ancestry.com, accessed 29 December 2013.

8. *Honolulu Star-Bulletin*, 9 January 1953.

9. *Pacific Citizen*, 23 February 1952; *Honolulu Advertiser*, 13 February 1954; Jack Geyer, "Trojans Down Hawaiians in Overtime," *Los Angeles Times*, 6 December 1952.

10. *San Francisco Chronicle*, 10 December 1953; *San Francisco Examiner*, 18 December 1953, 19 December 1953, 20 December 1953, 22 December 1953, 23 December 1953.

11. *Los Angeles Times*, 10 December 1953; *San Francisco Chronicle*, 18 December 1953, 20 December 1953.

12. *Los Angeles Times*, 13 December 1954.

13. *Los Angeles Times*, 12 December 1956; *Twin Falls News*, 5 December 1956.

14. *Seattle Times*, 7 December 1958; University of Hawai'i Yearbook, 1959, http://www.worldvitalrecords.com, accessed 27 April 2012.

15. *Pasadena Star-News*, 12 December 1958, 18 December 1958.

16. University of Hawai'i Yearbook, 1951, http://www.ancestry.com, accessed 31 December 2013; University of Hawai'i Yearbook, 1953, http://www.ancestry.com, accessed 31 December 2013; University of Hawai'i Yearbook, 1959, http://www.ancestry.com, accessed 7 February 2014.

17. University of Hawai'i Yearbook, 1949, http://www.worldvitalrecords.com, accessed 3 March 2012.

18. University of Hawai'i Yearbook, 1953, http://www.worldvitalrecords.com, accessed 27 April 2012.

19. *Daily Palo Alto*, 1 January 1923; *San Francisco Chronicle*, 13 January 1923; *Washington Post*, 5 February 1924; *Gastonia Daily Gazette*, 12 November 1926; Greg Robinson, "Gridiron Pioneer: Art Matsu, a Multi-racial Nikkei, Broke Ground, *Nichi Bei Times*, 5 April 2007; William and Mary University Yearbook, 1925, http://www.ancestry.com, accessed 29 August 2013.

20. *Berkeley Gazette*, 29 December 1932; *San Francisco Chronicle*, 20 December 1932.

21. *Oakland Tribune*, 22 January 1931; Art Potter, "Bruin Series Will Decide Standings," *Oakland Tribune*, 2 February 1931; *San Jose News*, 26 January 1931; http://bigcsociety.org/tedohashi/tedohashi.htm, accessed 19 January 2013.

22. Milt Phinney, "Fast Breaking Game May Settle Question of East, West Basketball Supremacy," *Oakland Tribune*, 28 December 1931; *Oakland Tribune*, 17 January 1932, 18 February 1932, 26 February 1932; *San Jose Mercury*, 6 January 1932; Stanford University Yearbook, 1932, http://www.worldvitalrecords.com, accessed 1 June 2012.

23. *Oakland Tribune*, 8 January 1933; Milt Phinney, "Ohashi Ready for Open With UCLA," *Oakland Tribune*, 11 January 1933; *Oakland Tribune*, January 13, 1933; Milt Phinney, "Bears Win From Bruins Again," *Oakland Tribune*, 15 January 1933; Milt Phinney, "Bears Slight Edge Over Stanford," *Oakland Tribune*, 21 January 1933; *Oakland Tribune*, 7 February 1933.

24. http://bigcsociety.org/tedohashi/tedohashi.htm., accessed 19 January 2013.

25. Art Cohn, "Bob Chalmers Stars for U.C.," *Oakland Tribune*, 26 January 1937; Roger Philips, "Stockton Hall of Famer Dies at 95," *Stockton Record*, 8 November 2006.

26. *Pacific Citizen*, 21 October 1951; http://bigcsociety.org/tedohashi/tedohashi.htm, accessed 19 January 2013.

27. *San Diego Evening Tribune*, 20 January 1930; *Chinese Digest*, 27 December 1935; *Los Angeles Times*, 21 January 1940, 4 January 1941; *Portland Oregonian*, 26 January 1941; University of Idaho Yearbook, 1934, http://www.ancestry.com, accessed 15 April 2014; University of Redlands Yearbook, 1940, http://www.worldvitalrecords.com, accessed 27 April 2013.

28. *San Jose Mercury*, 22 January 1937.

29. *Brooklyn Eagle*, 5 January 1943.

30. *Seattle Times*, 4 February 1942, 5 February 1942, 10 February 1942, 6 March 1942; *Spokane Daily-Chronicle*, 23 February 1942; *Spokane Spokesmen-Review*, 25 February 1942, 1 January 1943; Whitman College Archives, clippings, accessed 25 June 2014.

31. *Seattle Times*, 15 October 1943; Bruce Hamby, "Washington Given Edge as Northern Teams Get Set," *Portland Oregonian*, 26 December 1943.

32. *Seattle Times*, 31 December 1943, 20 February 1944; George Varnell, "Mar Added to Husky Basket Roster," *Seattle Times*, 5 December 1944; *Bend Bulletin*, 25 January 1944, 12 February 1944; *Lewiston Morning Tribune*, 23 February 1944; Seattle City Directory, 1956, http://www.ancestry.com, accessed 9 March 2013; University of Washington Yearbook 1944, http://content.lib.washington.edu/cdm4/document.php?CISOROOT=%2Fuwdocs&CISOPTR=32424&REC=2&CISOBOX=Al+Mar, accessed 7 April 2014.

33. *Portland Oregonian*, 22 January 1945; U.S. Census Bureau, Manuscript Census Schedules, City of Astoria and County of Clatsop, 1930 and 1940.

34. Bruce Hamby, "Washington Given Edge"; *Portland Oregonian*, 9 January 1944, 22 January 1945; George Varnell, "Huskies Drill to Stop O.S.C. Scoring Stars, *Seattle Times*, 2 February 1944; *Seattle Times*, 13 February 1944, 20 February 1944, 10 March 1944.

35. University of Washington Yearbook 1944, http://content.lib.washington.edu/cdm4/document.php?CISOROOT=%2Fuwdocs&CISOPTR=32424&REC=2&CISOBOX=Al+Mar, accessed 7 April 2014.

36. *Eugene Register-Guard*, 4 January 1948; *Seattle Times*, 14 February 1949; Keith Hansen, "Portland Five Avenges Loss," *Portland Oregonian*, 25 January 1948; *Portland Oregonian*, 16 January 1949, 5 February 1948, February 6, 1949; Bill Hulen, "Portland Led by Happy Lee," *Portland Oregonian*, 12 December 1949; *Portland Oregonian*, 11 February 1950; University of Portland Yearbook, 1948, http://www.ancestry.com, accessed 13 March 2013.

37. *Pacific Citizen*, 15 November 1947; *Ogden Standard-Examiner*, 27 April 1954; *Salt Lake Tribune*, 7 October 1973; U.S. Census Bureau, Manuscript Census Schedules, City of Ogden, County of Weber, 1930.

38. Ferrin and Ferrin, *Blitz Kids*, 76, 96, 129 (see chap. 3, n. 34).

39. *Helena Independent*, 22 March 1944.

40. *Washington Post*, 27 March 1944, 28 March 1944; Ferrin and Ferrin, *Blitz Kids*, 139–140.

41. *Kansas City Star*, 27 March 1944.

42. Ibid.

43. *Pacific Stars and Stripes*, 1 April 1944.

44. Wilbur Wood, "Indians Made Favorite Over Utah Tonight," *New York Sun*, 30 March 1944; Ferrin and Ferrin, *Blitz Kids*, 157–160.

45. *Pacific Citizen*, 8 April 1944, 15 April 1944; *Ogden Standard-Examiner*, 1 April 1944.

46. *Pacific Citizen*, 15 November 1947.

47. *New York Times*, 20 March 1947.

48. Louis Effrat, "Wildcats Toppled by the Utes," *New York Times*, 25 March 1947; *San Jose Mercury*, 24 March 1947; *Oxnard Press*, 25 March 1947; *Ogden Standard-Examiner*, 25 March 1947; *Pacific Citizen*, 28 June 1947.

49. *New York Evening Record*, 24 March 1947.

50. Ibid.

51. *Hayward Daily*, 1 April 1947.

52. *Ogden Standard-Examiner*, 2 April 1947, 29 April 1947; *Pacific Citizen*, 26 April 1947.

53. *Pacific Citizen*, 19 April 1947.

54. DeCano, "Integrity guides life of Legendary Coach" (see chap. 2, n. 21).

55. Ferrin and Ferrin, *Blitz Kids*, 109–114; Irving Marsh, "The Taller the Player, the More Money for Irish," *Sporting News*, 3 March 1948.

56. Ferrin and Ferrin, *Blitz Kids*, 78, 81.

57. *Los Angeles Times,* 24 January 1940, 24 January 1942; *Heart Mountain Sentinel,* 22 January 1944; *Pacific Citizen,* 12 February 1944, 1 October 1949, 14 January 1950; *San Jose Mercury,* 23 March 1947, 18 December 1949; Gary Y. Okihiro, *Storied Lives: Japanese American Students and World War II* (Seattle: University of Washington Press, 1999), 92, 94, 95, 97.

58. Bill Clegg, "Utes Await Springfield," *Salt Lake Tribune,* 17 December 1947; *Salt Lake Tribune,* 19 December 1947; *San Francisco Chronicle,* 24 December 1947; *Portsmouth Herald,* 7 January 1949; Springfield College Yearbook, 1947, http://www.ancestry.com, accessed 29 August 2013; Springfield College Yearbook, 1948, http://www.ancestry.com, 29 August 2013.

59. Jim O'Leary, "Guard Rates as Top Set Shot Player," *Greensboro Record,* 2 January 1950; *San Francisco Chronicle,* 23 February 1949; *Oakland Tribune,* 23 February 1949; *Moberly Monitor Index,* 3 March 1949; Yep, *Outside the Paint,* 82.

60. University of San Francisco vs. Fordham University, Football Program, Kezar Stadium, San Francisco, 20 November 1949; *Monitor,* 2 December 1949; *San Francisco Examiner,* 9 December 1949; *Chinese Press,* 26 December 1949.

61. *Trenton Evening Times,* 29 January 1960.

62. *San Francisco Examiner,* 9 December 1949, 14 December 1949.

63. *San Francisco Examiner,* 22 December 1949; *New York Times,* 22 December 1949, 23 December 1949; *Dixon Evening Telegram,* 6 January 1950.

64. O'Leary, "Guard Rates."

65. Bob Brachman, "Dons Cool Broncos," *San Francisco Examiner,* 11 January 1950; Santa Clara University Yearbook, 1950, http://www.worldvitalrecords.com, accessed 1 June 2012; Yep, *Outside the Paint,* 86–87.

66. Yep, *Outside the Paint,* 88, 93; Dwight Chapin, "Willie 'Woo Woo' Wong," *San Francisco Chronicle,* 8 September 2005.

67. Yep, *Outside the Paint,* 94–95.

68. Chapin, "Willie 'Woo Woo' Wong."

69. *San Francisco Examiner,* 16 January 1949, 21 January 1949; *San Jose Mercury,* 6 December 1949, 14 January 1941; Santa Clara University Yearbook, 1950, http://www.ancestry.com, accessed 3 July 2013.

70. *San Jose Mercury,* 3 January 1951; *Pacific Citizen,* 13 November 1953; *Sacramento Bee,* 18 January 1954; Sacramento State College Yearbook, 1954, http://www.ancestry.com, accessed 27 April 2013; http://www.sierracollege.edu/about-us/foundation/alumni/spotlight/george-goto.php, accessed 3 October 2013.

71. *Pacific Citizen,* 13 November 1953; *Sacramento Bee,* 18 January 1954; *Los Angeles Times,* 27 January 1954; Bill Dunbar, "Trojans Challenge Bears Lead," *Oakland Tribune,* 5 February 1954, 8 January 1955; *Idaho Falls Register,* 23 December

1954; *San Diego Union,* 29 December 1954; *Long Beach Independent,* 30 December 1954; *Portland Oregonian,* 5 February 1956; U.S. Census Bureau, Manuscript Census Schedules, City and County of Los Angeles, 1940.

72. *Pacific Citizen,* 2 February 1952.

73. *Seattle Times,* 28 November 1950, 8 December 1950, 5 January 1951, 20 April 1951.

74. *Seattle Times,* 8 December 1951; John Lindwed, "Seattle U Wins Ninth Straight Hoops Game," *Seattle Times,* 6 February 1952; Rev. Erle Powell, "Prayer Creates Unity," *Seattle Times,* 6 March 1955; Jack Hewing, "Seattle's Standout Cage Team Really a United Nations' Outfit," *Moberly Monitor-Index,* 6 March 1952.

75. *San Francisco Chronicle,* 30 November 1947; *San Francisco Examiner,* 9 January 1949, 11 December 1949, 9 March 1950; *Pacific Citizen,* 27 January 1951; *Canton Repository,* 24 January 1953; *Cleveland Plain Dealer,* 10 December 1954; *Valley News,* 11 November 1956; *San Diego Union,* 27 January 1957; *Los Angeles Times,* 23 January 1954, 2 March 1958, 12 January 1964; *Sacramento Bee,* 16 January 1958; Westmont College Yearbook, 1952, http://www.ancestry.com, accessed 29 August 2013; http://issuu.com/hornetsports/docs/1314_mbb_book_c850a1856d02c7, accessed 7 April 2014.

76. *Pacific Citizen,* 30 September 1950, 1 March 1952; *Humboldt Standard-Examiner,* 16 January 1952, 31 January 1953; Don Terbush, "Lumberjacks Win Opener in Hoop Title Play," *Humboldt Standard-Examiner,* 28 February 1953; *Humboldt Standard-Examiner,* 18 March 1953; *Walla Walla Union-Bulletin,* 14 January 1953; *Nevada State Journal,* 25 March 1953; *Portland Oregonian,* 17 December 1953, 8 February 1954, 13 February 1954; *Reno Evening Gazette,* 22 January 1954.

77. *San Jose Mercury,* 19 January 1933, 10 February 1935, 2 February 1936, 8 February 1936; *Los Angeles Times,* 31 January 1935; *Chinese Digest,* 15 November 1935; *Heart Mountain Sentinel,* 16 January 1943, 6 February 1943; *Portland Oregonian,* 13 January 1948, 6 February 1948; *Riverside Daily Press,* 25 February 1949; *Sacramento Bee,* 16 January 1958; Stanford University Yearbook, 1922, http://www.worldvitalrecords.com, accessed 1 June 2012; Stanford University Yearbook, 1925, http://www.worldvitalrecords.com, accessed 1 June 2012; Stanford University Yearbook, 1940, http://www.mocavo.com, accessed 7 April 2014; University of California Yearbook, 1933, http://www.worldvitalrecords.com, accessed 7 May 2012; University of California Yearbook, 1950, http://www.worldvitalrecords.com, accessed 1 June 2012; University of California, Los Angeles, Yearbook, 1941, http://www.ancestry.com, accessed 9 July 2013.

78. *San Jose Mercury,* 10 January 1936, 12 January 1936, 25 January 1936, 2 February 1936; August G. Kettmann, "Santa Clara Trims S.J. State Five," *San Jose Mercury,* 13 February 1936.

79. *Riverside Daily Press*, 1 December 1922; *San Francisco Examiner*, 17 February 1941, 14 January 1950, 10 March 1950, 20 March 1950, 22 March 1950; *Pacific Citizen*, 15 November 1947, 10 April 1953; *Modesto Bee and Herald* News, 24 January 1949; U.S. Census Bureau, Manuscript Census Schedules, City of Anaheim and County of Orange, 1940; Fullerton High School Yearbook, 1938, http://www.ancestry.com, accessed 2 July 2014; Fullerton Junior College Yearbook, 1940, http://www.ancestry.com, accessed 2 July 2014.

80. *San Francisco Examiner*, 6 January 1949, 20 January 1949.

81. *San Francisco Examiner*, 8 January 1950; *Pacific Citizen*, 14 January 1950, 25 February 1950; U.S. Census Bureau, Manuscript Census Schedules, County of Placer, 1930.

82. *Pacific Citizen*, 13 January 1951, 27 January 1951.

83. *Pacific Citizen*, 1 March 1952; *San Francisco Chronicle*, 18 February 1953; *Oakland Tribune*, 7 January 1955, 8 January 1955; *San Jose Mercury*, 4 February 1955; *Los Angeles Times*, 10 March 1955, 21 January 1956, 22 January 1956; *Springfield Union*, 30 March 1955.

84. *Sacramento Bee*, 21 January 1954, 25 January 1954, 30 January 1954; http://wserver.scc.losrios.edu/~physed/forms/mensbasketball/performancelist.pdf, accessed 5 July 2013.

85. Bob Jacobsen, "A Man For All Seasons."

86. *Arizona Republic*, 26 January 1940, 16 February 1940, 12 April 1940; *Pacific Citizen*, 15 January 1949; http://www.asulonline.edu, accessed 16 November 2002.

87. *Arizona Daily Sun*, 29 June 1949; http://www.asuonline.edu., accessed 16 November 2002.

88. *Pacific Citizen*, 14 January 1950.

89. *New York Times*, 29 December 1951; *Troy Record*, 8 February 1952.

90. *Pacific Citizen*, 18 March 1955; *Abilene Reporter News*, 2 February 1956; 22 February 1957; *New York Times*, 22 February 1957; *Oakland Tribune*, 24 April 1967.

91. Bob Jacobsen, "A Man for All Seasons."

92. *Sporting News*, 5 November 1947; *Berkshire Eagle*, 8 October 1956; Keoni Everington, "Remembering Buck Lai, APA Baseball Pioneer," *Asian Week*, http://www.asianweek.com, 23–28 November 2002; Mary Lai, conversation with the author, 7 March 2008.

93. Randy Roberts and James Olson, *Winning is the Only Thing: Sports in America Since 1945* (Baltimore: Johns Hopkins University Press, 1989), 74–75; Milton Gross, "Basketball Busiest Bee," *Sport*, March 1951, 40.

94. Roberts and Olson, *Winning*, 77.

95. *New York Times*, 16 January 1951; Ace Bushell, "Will LIU Crack Cat Streak," *Brooklyn Eagle*, 23 August 1950; Mary Lai, conversation with the author, 7 March 2008.

96. *Brooklyn Eagle*, 22 February 1951; *Gloversville*

and Johnson Morning-Herald, 9 February 1952; *Springfield Union*, 6 December 1955.

97. *Traverse City Record Eagle*, 6 December 1955; Harold Burr, "Hitler Spoilsport in Buck Lai Jr.'s Life," *Brooklyn Eagle*, 7 January 1955; *Springfield Union*, 6 December 1955.

98. Howard Tucker, "Lai Wants No Neon Lights in L.I.U. Basketball," *New York Times*, 11 December 1956.

99. William J. Briody, "First L.I.U. Quintet Since '51 Lacks Height," *New York Times*, 10 December 1957; *Portland Oregonian*, 27 March 1957.

100. *Marietta Journal*, 20 January 1960.

101. William T. "Buck" Lai, *Winning Basketball: Individual Play and Team Strategy*, (Englewood Cliffs, NJ: Prentice Hall, 1955), 6, 210, 211.

102. John Chevalier, "Springfield Beats Long Island In Homecoming Basketball Game," *Springfield Union*, 19 February 1961; Michael Strauss, "LIU Plots to Confuse Foes," *New York Times*, 5 December 1959; *New York Times*, 7 March 1961.

103. Gordon S. White, "LIU's Wandering Five Awaits Home," *New York Times*, 2 June 1963; *Bridgeport Post*, 8 March 1966; http://www.liu.edu, 19 August 2001.

104. *Oakland Tribune*, September 12, 1950; *San Francisco Examiner*, December 6, 1950; *Portland Oregonian*, September 24, 1950.

105. *Syracuse Herald*, 16 December 1921; *New York Evening World*, 14 December 1921; Murry R. Nelson, *The Originals: The New York Celtics Invent Modern Basketball* (Bowling Green, OH: Bowling Green University Popular Press, 1999); Robert Peterson, *Cages to Jump Shots: Pro Basketball's Early Years* (Lincoln: University of Nebraska Press, 1990).

106. *New York Evening World*, 15 December 1921; *Bridgeport Telegram*, 20 December 1921; Franks, *Hawaiian Travelers*.

107. *Philadelphia Inquirer*, 3 January 1922, 6 January 1922, 13 January 1922.

108. *St. Alban's Weekly* Messenger, March 13, 1924.

109. Yep, *Beyond the Paint*, 38; U.S. Census Bureau, Manuscript Census Schedules, City and County of San Francisco, 1930.

110. Al Young, "Hoop Dreams," *A Magazine*, February–March 1998; Yep, *Beyond the Paint*, 38–39.

111. *California Chinese Press*, 20 December 1940; Darra Akko Tom, "Great Chinese Warriors Play for Fun and Money," *San Jose Mercury*, 9 September 1996; Young, "Hoop Dreams"; Yep, *Beyond the Paint*, 38, 41.

112. Tom, "Chinese Warriors"; Yep, *Beyond the Paint*, 43.

113. Yep, *Beyond the Paint*, 46–47.

114. Ibid., 52

115. Tom, "Chinese Warriors"; Young, "Hoop Dreams"; Yep, *Beyond the Paint*, 46.

116. Yep, *Beyond the Paint*, 41.

117. Yep, *Beyond the Paint*, 40; Young "Hoop Dreams."

118. *Seattle Times*, 10 January 1940; Young, "Hoop Dreams."

119. Yep, *Beyond the Paint*, 57.

120. Ibid., 58, 59.

121. Young, "Hoop Dreams"; Quoted in Yep, *Beyond the Paint*, 46; *California Chinese Press*, 28 March 1941.

122. *Southtown Economist*, 15 November 1939; Yep, *Beyond the Paint*, 39, 40.

123. *Appleton Post-Crescent*, 29 November 1939; *Ironwood Daily Globe*, 1 December 1939, 8,December 8 1939; *Wakefield News*, 10 December 1954.

124. *Helena Independent*, 20 December 1939, 24 December 1939.

125. Ibid., 24 December 1939, 29 December 1939.

126. *Butte Standard*, 23 February 1940.

127. *Ogden Standard-Examiner*, 17 November 1940; *Twin Fall Evening Times*, 7 December 1940.

128. *Cook County Herald*, 14 January 1941; *Wisconsin Rapids Daily Tribune*, 17 January 1941, 22 January 1941.

129. *Washington Post*, 13 February 1941; *Circleville Herald* 13 February 1941,14 February 1941.

130. *San Francisco Examiner*, 5 February 1947.

131. *San Francisco Chronicle*, 18 February 1945; *Chicago Defender*, 21 April 1945, 28 April 1945.

132. *San Francisco Chronicle*, 18 February 1946, 24 February 1946; *San Jose News*, 18 February 1946; *San Jose Mercury*, 19 February 1946, 25 March 1947; *Oakland Tribune*, 24 February 1946.

133. *Pacific Citizen*, 28 June 1947; *Ogden Standard-Examiner*, 18 January 1953.

134. *Honolulu Advertiser*, 25 July 1947.

135. *Pacific Citizen*, 26 July 1947, 25 October 1947.

136. *Pacific Citizen*, 15 November 1947; *Salt Lake Tribune*, 6 November 1947; *New York Times*, 11 November 1947; *Brooklyn Eagle*, 13 November 1947.

137. *Pacific Citizen*, 15 November 1947, 29 November 1947.

138. Samuel R. Cacas, "The Professional Pioneer Wat Misaka Reflects on Being First," *Asian Week*, 17 December 1994; Louinn Lota, "Misaka is NBA's Forgotten Minority," *Los Angeles Times*, 7 May 2000.

139. *Transcending: The Wat Misaka Story*, directors Bruce Alan Johnson and Christine Toy Johnson, 2010; George Vecsey, "Pioneering Knick Returns to Garden," *New York Times*,10 August 2009, http://www.nytimes.com/2009/08/11/sports/basketball/11vecsey.html?_r=0, accessed 3 June 2012.

140. Cacas, "The Professional Pioneer"; *Pacific Citizen*, 21 January 1950; *Transcending: The Wat Misaka Story*.

141. *New York Times*, 17 June 1959; *Milwaukee Sentinel*, 8 July 1959; *Chicago Defender*, 3 December 1959.

142. Mike Sugarman, "Decades Before Lin, SF Man Paved Way For Asian-Americans in NBA," *CBS SF Bay Area*, 1 March 2012, http://san francisco.cbslocal.com/2012/03/01/decades-before-lin-sf-man-paved-way-for-asian-americans-in-nba, accessed 3 May 2014.

143. Franks, *Hawaiian Travelers*, chapter 7.

144. *Gettysburg Times*, 1 February 1932 ; *Frederick News*, 2 February 1932.

145. *Frederick News*, 6 February 1932; *Rochester Democrat and Chronicle*, 12 March 1932; *Trenton Evening Times*, 4 November 1932; *Gettysburg Times*, 16 December 1933; *Washington Post*, 28 January 1934; *Yonkers Herald*, 16 March 1934.

146. Franks, *Hawaiian Travelers*, chapter 7; *Trenton Evening Times*, 20 January 1939.

147. *Ogden Standard-Examiner*, 23 December 1958; *St. Joseph Herald Press*, 8 November 1960.

148. Murray R. Nelson, *Abe Saperstein and the American Basketball League, 1960–1963: The Upstarts Who Shot for Three and Lost to the NBA* (Jefferson, NC: McFarland, 2013), 3.

149. Frank Finch, "Chiefs' Owner Predicts ABL Success," *Los Angeles Times*, 12 December 1961; *Long Beach Independent*, 9 January 1972.

150. *Long Beach Independent*, 5 February 1969; "Anaheim Amigos," http://www.remembertheaba.com/anaheim-amigos.html, accessed 7 November 2008.

Chapter 6

1. Daniel Buffington and Tod Fraley, "Racetalk and Sport: The Color Consciousness of Contemporary Discourse on Basketball," *Sociological Inquiry* 81 (August 2011): 336.

2. *Pacific Citizen*, 4 December 1948.

3. Jamilah King, "The Asian American Basketball Leagues That Created Linsanity," http://www.colorlines.com, 21 February 2012.

4. Ibid.

5. Ibid.

6. Ibid.

7. Colin Moynihan, "A Passion for Basketball Made Even Stronger by Lin's Emergence," *New York Times*, 26 February 2012.

8. Ibid.

9. Ibid.

10. Sean Gregory, "Linsanity," *Time*, 27 February 2012, http://www.time.com/time/magazine/article/0,9171,2106983,00.html#ixzz2KQNEMNK.

11. Pasadena Bruins, http://www.pasadenabruins.org/about.php, accessed 15 March 2013.

12. http://www.asianweek.com, 5 January 2011; San Jose CYS Basketball Invitational Tournament Program, 2003; http://www.berkeleysangha.org/yc/index.html, accessed 7 May 2000.

13. Bob Manalo, "Asian Basketball League Keeps Kids Off Streets," *Asian Week*, 18 August 2010.

14. http://www.aabl-norfolk.com/aabl/, accessed 14 July 2008; http://www.austinasian bball.webs.com/, accessed 24 September 2013.

15. http://www.aabl-norfolk.com/aabl/, accessed 14 July 2008.

16. Ibid.

17. Monica Rhor, "Filipinos and Basketball: Setting a Cultural Pick," http://www.facaa.us/~facaa/html/features.html, accessed 8 December 2012.

18. Ibid.

19. Ibid.

20. http://events.hmoodle.com/event/all-hmong-j4-basketball-tournament/, accessed 4 October 2013; MaxPreps, Hmong Academy Basketball Record Book, http://www.maxpreps.com/local/team/records/default.aspx?gendersport=boys,basketball&schoolid=091d4624-4ce4-4171-a2e7-2e705bd2316b, accessed 14 October 2013; http://www.hmongfoundation.com/page/show/757122-hmong%20basketball%20league%20of%20colorado, accessed 4 October 2013.

21. Stanley Thangaraj, "Ballin' Indo-Pak Style: Pleasures, Desires, and ExpressivePractices of 'South Asian American' Masculinity," *International Review for the Sociology of Sport* 45, No. 3 (2010); Stanley Thangaraj, "'Liting it up': Popular Culture, Indo-Pak Basketball, and South Asian American Institutions," *Cosmopolitan Civil Societies: An Interdisciplinary Journal* 2, No.2 (2010); South Asian Sports, http://www.southasianbasketball.com/live/index.php, accessed 14 September 2013.

22. Tony Chai, "Dallas to Host 2nd Annual Korean-American Basketball Tournament of North America," mijudaily.com, accessed 2 April 2013.

23. Ibid.

24. *East/West*, 10 September 1969.

25. Sam Le, "Hoop Dreams," Asian American Journalists Association, http://www.aaja.org, 9 August 2002.

26. Rachel Graves, "Asian Community Goes Wow For Yao," http://www.HoustonChronicle.com, accessed 19 July 2003.

27. Raymond Wong, letter to editor, *Asian Week*, 30 January 2004.

28. Amy Huang, "Chinese WNBA Players Debut in Seattle," nwasianweekly.com, 9 July 2005.

29. http://www.youtube.com/watch?v=bLCebxCFK40ploaded PacificRimVideoPress on Nov 29, 2009; http://www.asianweek.com/2009/10/29/faae-to-partner-with-warriors-to-host-filipino-heritage-night-on-nov-6/, accessed 13 February 2013; http://hoopistani.blogspot.com/2011/03/golden-state-warriors-to-celebrate.html, accessed 3 August 2013.

30. Sean Gregory, "Can Jeremy Lin's Appeal in China Really Help Houston's Bottom Line," 19 July 2012, http://keepingscore.blogs.time.com, accessed 7 February 2014; http://www.khou.com/sports/Houstons-Asian-community-going-Linsane-over-newest-Rocket—163103766.html, accessed 13 February 2013.

31. John Horton et al., *The Politics of Diversity: Immigration, Resistance, and Change in Monterey Park, California* (Philadelphia: Temple University Press, 1995), 44.

32. Ibid., 46

33. West San Jose National Junior Basketball Yearbook, 1999–2000.

34. http://www.nj.com/sports/jjournal/index.ssf?/base/sports-4/123252276338390.xml&coll=3, accessed 2 August 2013.

35. Grace Tzeng, "Filipina Female Basketball Players With Fast Feet," 20 November 2007, http://www.asianweek.com.

36. http://superstarbasketball.org/2011_spring/stats.html, accessed 4 October 2013.

37. *Oakland Tribune*, 29 December 1966; Stacy Kaneshiro, "Walter Wong, St. Louis Coach," 10 August 2002, http://www.honoluluadvertiser.com; Stanley Lee, "Twin Towers Lifted Saints to a Dynasty," 29 July 2007, http://honoluluadvertiser.com; St. Louis Preparatory School Yearbook, 1969, http://www.classmates.com, accessed 9 October 2012.

38. http://archives.starbulletin.com, 3 March 2003.

39. David Kiefer, "The Changing Face of Basketball," *San Jose Mercury*, 17 January 2007.

40. Ibid.

41. *San Jose Mercury*, 4 February 1988; Keith Peters, "Paly Boys Advance in CCS Basketball," *Palo Alto Weekly*, 26 February 2006; SFGate.com, 16 December 2008.

42. Joe Davidson, "Long Before Lin, Asian Americans Thrived on Local Courts," *Sacramento Bee*, 29 February 2012, http://sacbee.com.

43. Paul McLeod, "A Community of Basketball Going Strong," *Los Angeles Times*, 3 May 2001.

44. Ibid.

45. *East/West*, 20 July 1983; *Augusta Chronicle*, 25 May 1979, 1 December 1979, 1 March 1994.

46. *Anchorage Daily News*, 17 July 1999; *Dallas Morning News*, 17 December 1996; *Providence Journal*, 8 March 2000; *Rochester Democrat and Chronicle*, 4 December 2002; http://www.bradley braves.com/ViewArticle.dbml?DB_OEM_ID=3400&ATCLID=123048, accessed 25 May 2013; http://www.lohud.com/article/20130131/SPORTS02/301310090/Boys-basketball-notebook-took-two-North-Salem-s-Umar-Singh-Joey-Tunas-outduel-one-Somers-John-Decker-?nclick_check=1, accessed 25 March 2013.

47. *Registrar Star*, 23 February 1999; *Sports Illustrated*, 2 March 1998.

48. http://www.maxpreps.com/news/TP2_8AXCC0-JBuL7FGDN8g/new-york-city-has-jeremy-lin,-ossining-girls-basketball-has-saniya-chong.htm, accessed 30 November 2013.

49. *Hayward Daily Review*, 10 March 1969, 11 December 1971; *Pacific Citizen*, 30 March 1973; *Hokubei Mainichi*, 14 December 1977; *Seattle Times*, 30 September 1998; *Registrar Star*, 23 February 1999; *San Jose Mercury*, 29 March 2000, 4 March 2004, 3 June 2009; Hooptown Basketball, http://www.hooptown-bball.com, accessed 1 December 2012; James Lick High School Yearbook, 1954, http://www.ancestry.com, accessed 16 July 2013.

50. Cindy Lewis, "Itoman is Big Trouble for Her Opponents," www.starbulletin.com, January 30, 1997, accessed 21 January 2000; www.starbulletin.com, 3 September 1999.

51. http://waynejoseph.wordpress.com/2009/02/24/living-legend-jimmy-yagi/, accessed 27 September 2012; Steve Sinclair, "Hawaii-Hilo Coach Ecstatic," *Omaha World Herald*, 2 December 1976.

52. http://uhathletics.hawaii.edu/WBasket/honors.html, accessed 12 October 2012; http://hawaiiathletics.com/coaches.aspx?rc=161, accessed 12 October 2012; http://hawaiiathletics.com/coaches.aspx?rc=162, accessed 12 October 2012; http://www.hawaiiathletics.com/news/2009/5/28/WBB_0528091816.aspx, accessed 12 October 2012.

53. Joseph Craig, "Southern California Native Thrives as Assistant Basketball Coach," *Pacific Citizen*, 24 January 2011; http://goseawarriors.com/coaches.aspx?path=&rc=117, accessed 3 August 2013.

54. Mal Florence, "Wooden's Legend Keeps Heat on UCLA's Barton," *Sporting News*, 3 April 1976; Mark Purdy, "Townsend Has Golden Touch," *Los Angeles Times*, 7 February 1978.

55. *Seattle Times*, 5 December 1978; *Omaha World Herald*, 28 December 1978; *Spokane Daily-Chronicle*, 3 February 1978.

56. Nick Peters, "Plenty of Points to Go Around," *Sporting News*, 22 February 1988; *Gettysburg Times*, 12 January 1990; *Valley Independent*, 9 March 1990, 26 March 1993; *Elyria Chronicle*, 22 December 1991; *Zanesville Times Recorder*, 20 December 1993.

57. Lydia Lin, "The Heat Is On for NBA's 1st APA Head Coach," *Pacific Citizen*, 6 May 2008; http://www.branchwest.com/imran_sufi.htm, accessed 24 May 2014; Crush Sign Sufi, http://articles.dailypilot.com/2004-10-18/news/export7727_1_sufi-utah-state-olympic-title, accessed 24 May 2014; http://statsheet.com/mcb/players/player/saint-marys/kamran-sufi accessed 24 May 2014; http://www.halfkorean.com/?page_id=4972, accessed 7 February 2014.

58. Hogue, "Ah Chew Goo" (see chap. 3, n. 11); Harold Nedd, "Big Business of College Hoops Await Derrick Low," *Pacific Business News*, 19 March 2004; *Asian Week*, 11 February 2005.

59. Bryan Chu, "Asian Americans Remain Rare in Men's College Basketball," http://www.sfgate. com/cgi-bin/article.cgi?f=/c/a/2008/12/15/SPD213J9RD.DTL, 16 December 2008.

60. Ibid.

61. Ibid.

62. http://www.bradleybraves.com/ViewArticle.dbml?DB_OEM_ID=3400&ATCLID=123048, accessed 25 May 2013; http://goriverhawks.com/roster.aspx?rp_id=357, accessed 25 May 2013; http://www.minerathletics.com/roster.aspx?rp_id=1571, accessed 10 June 2013; http://www.gotiffindragons.com/roster/11/27/2901.php, accessed 10 June 2013; http://www.csmorediggers.com/sports/mbkb/2013-14/boxscores/20131108_9rxq.xml, accessed 13 November 2013.

63. David Gao, "Emil Kim: Walking Onwards," http://www.newuniversity.org/2011/01/sports/emil-kim-walking-onwards/, accessed 17 July 2013.

64. Ibid.

65. Ibid.

66. http://www.fullertontitans.com/sports/m-baskbl/mtt/umipig_isiah00.html, accessed 21 June 2012; http://www.goseattleu.com/ViewArticle.dbml?SPSID=89900&SPID=10773&DB_LANG=C&DB_OEM_ID=18200&ATCLID=205719146&Q_SEASON=2013, accessed 28 February 2014; http://www.asianjournal.com/galing-pinoy/59-galing-pinoy/7386-pinoys-in-ncaa-basketball.html?start=1, accessed 27 September 2012; http://www.cbssports.com/collegebasketball/players/playerpage/1715800/michael-williams, accessed 7 April 2014; http://gomason.cstv.com/sports/m-baskbl/mtt/norwood_gabe00.html, accessed 23 October 2012; http://www.insidehoops.com/forum/showthread.php?t=53103, accessed 23 October 2012; http://www.hooptown-bball.com/, accessed 1 December2012; http://www.happypunter.com/sports/kelly-williams/, accessed 5 July 2013; http://sportspinas.blogspot.com/2012/09/top-filipino-americans-ncaa-division-1.html, accessed 5 July 2013; http://www.cbssports.com/collegebasketball/players/playerpage/1780900/jordan-clarkson, accessed 18 July 2013; http://espn.go.com/mens-college-basketball/player/_/id/51323/jordan-clarkson, accessed 7 April 2014; Kim Darcy, "Jason Brickman Earns 1,000[th] Assist," http://espn.go.com/new-york/mens-college-basketball/story/_/id/10538434/liu-brooklyn-brickman-reaches-1000-assists-final-game, accessed 26 May 2014.

67. http://www.branchwest.com/imran_sufi.htm, accessed 24 May 2014; http://athletics.baruch.cuny.edu/roster.aspx?rp_id=632, accessed 25 May 2013; http://www.reed.edu/sports_center/sports_clubs/basketball.html, accessed 31 May 2012; http://www.wcpoets.com/sports/mbkb/2009-10/bios/David_Hayashi, accessed 31 May 2012; http://www.otterathletics.com/roster.aspx?rp_id=1325, accessed 25 May 2013; http://www.chapmanathletics.com/sports/mbkb/2011-12/bios/lin_brandon_27xz, accessed 6

June 2013; http://www.chapmanathletics.com/sports/mbkb/2012–13/bios/hamasaki_taylor_1ojl, accessed 6 June 2013; http://www.gonyu athletics.com/roster.aspx?rp_id=5416&path=mbball, accessed 15 June 2013; http://www.whitman.edu/whitman-athletics/womens-basketball/assistant-coach-casey-kushiyama, accessed 12 July 2013; http://www.d3independents.org/statistics/mensbasketball1011/ucsc.htm, accessed 12 July 2013; http://www.ucmerced bobcats.com/roster/11/1/385.php, accessed 28 February 2014.

68. Irene Garcia, "Only 5–8 but Bruin Cager is a Real Standout," *Los Angeles Times*, 31 December 1987.

69. Emil Guillermo, "Two Modern Takes on Racism," *Asian Week*, 3 December 1998.

70. Ibid.

71. Bob Rodman, "Yamasaki Thrives as One Sport Athlete, *Eugene Register-Guard*, 7 February 2001; http://www.gostanford.com, accessed 15 August 2001; http://sportsillustrated.cnn.com/basketball/college/women/recaps/2002/01/26/sca_aar/m 1/26/2001; *Aberdeen Daily News*, 13 March 2002.

72. Dylan Hernandez, "Natalie Nakase Continues to Dream Big, Beat Odds," http://articles.latimes.com/2012/feb/17/sports/la-sp-0218-natalie-nakase-20120218; Bryan Chu, "Natalie Nakase Becomes First Asian American Female in Pro Basketball League," http://iousports.org/blog-news/natalie-nakase-becomes-first-asian-american-female-pro-basketball-league, accessed 29 August 2012; Mikey Hirano Culross, "Time to Let Spark Fly," http://rafu.com/news/2011/08/time-to-let-a-spark-fly, accessed 23 July 2012.

73. Eten Leiser, "Immediate Gael Impact," *Asian Week*, 4 May 2001–10 May 2001; Yukiya Jerry Waki, "St. Mary's Put Up Valiant Effort Against Lady Vols," http://www.nichibeitimes.com, 20 March 2001.

74. http://www.hagiya.com, accessed 23 July 2013; Mikey Hirano Culross, "Time."

75. Aaron Stewart, "How Emily Tay Saved My Friday Night," *Columbia Spectator*, 8 February 2007.

76. Ibid.

77. http://www.thecrimson.com/article/2009/3/10/athlete-of-the-week-emily-tay, accessed 21 June 2012; http://www.gocrimson.com/sports/wbkb/2006–07/bios/Tay_Emily, accessed 21 June 2012; http://viss.wordpress.com/2012/03/04/documentary-on-a-burmese-american-harvard-basketball-player, accessed 21 June 2012.

78. http://www.santaclarabroncos.com/sports/w-baskbl/mtt/shoji_alyssa00.html, accessed February 12, 2010; http://www.santa clarabroncos.com/sports/w-baskbl/2011–12/releases/201203300yx74x, accessed 12 February 2010.

79. Kelley Jones, "Women's Basketball: Stanis-laus Routs in Finale," *Modesto Bee*, 1 March 2008; Chris Hunn "Women's Basketball," *Milford-Orange Bulletin*, 10 November 2011; http://www.csula athletics.com/custompages/mediaguides/0809_WBB.pdf, accessed 7 September 2013; http://www.haverford.edu., accessed 10 September 2005; http://www.goseawolves.org/sports/w-baskbl/mtt/klockgether_cassie00.html; Leila Wai, "Menlo Milestone for Basketball Star Lee," http://the.honoluluadvertiser.com/article/2007/Jan/10/sp/FP701100379.html, accessed 25 July 2013; http://www.hornetsports.com/assets/sports/wbball/2012–13%20WBB%20Media%20Guide%204%20Record%20Book.pdf, accessed 29 March 2013; http://www.pe.pomona.edu/sports, accessed 26 March 2010; Culross, "Time"; http://www.goslugs.com/sports/wbkb/2011–12/bios/joo_erin_5lkl, accessed 2 April 2013; http://www.hooptown-bball.com/, accessed 1 December 2012; http://www.ucsdtritons.com/ViewArticle.dbml?SPSID=29897&SPID=2338&DB_LANG=C&DB_OEM_ID=5800&ATCLID=205733282&Q_SEASON=2012; accessed 10 June 2013; http://www.spufalcons.com/roster.aspx?rp_id=1279&path=, accessed 29 June2013; http://alums.vassar.edu/news/2013–2014/131101-cydni-matsuoka.html, 28 February 2014.

80. Jordan Ikeda, "The Consistent Coach," *Rafu Shimpo,* 15 November 2009; http://goviks.com/news/2013/6/5/MBB_0605131512.aspx, accessed 25 July 2013; Ryan Foley, "Falcon Basketball Pre-Season Heats Up," *Falcon,* 20 November 2002, http://www.falcononline.com.

81. Ikeda, "Consistent."

82. Ibid.

83. http://goviks.com/news/2013/6/5/MBB_0605131512.aspx, 25 accessed July 2013; http://www.cougcenter.com/2013/6/3/4392174/wsu-basketball-jeff-hironaka-ken-bone-washington-state, accessed 25 July 2013.

84. http://www.usfdons.com/coaches.aspx?rc=11&path=mbball, accessed 9 October 2013.

85. http://www.gobuffsgo.com/coaches.aspx?rc=427, accessed 29 June 2013; http://ucsbgauchos.com/sports/m-baskbl/mtt/yoshikawa_danny00.html, accessed 25 July 2013; http://www2.kusports.com/mens_basketball/roster/2012_13/, accessed 26 July 2013; http://www.usfdons.com/staff.aspx?staff=87, accessed 26 July 2013; http://www.linkedin.com/pub/daniel-chu/9/823/668, accessed 23 August 2013.

86. *Portland Oregonian*, 22 November 1979.

87. Kent Johnson, "Women's Basketball," *Sacramento Bee*, 13 January 1977; University of California Los Angeles Yearbook, 1979, http://www.ancestry.com, accessed 13 March 2013; *Omaha World Telegram*, 12 January 1983; http://www.wnba.com, accessed 4 October 1999; Greg Hernandez, "Coach Helping UCI Program Rebound," *Los Angeles Times*, 2 May 1992; Colleen Matsuhara, correspondence with the author, 19 July 2014.

88. http://ucirvine.prestosports.com/sports/ w-baskbl/history/index, accessed 9 October 2013; Greg Hernandez, "Coach Helping."

89. Aarne Heikkala, "USC to Hire New Women's Coach," *Daily Trojan*, 17 May 2000; Arizona Women's Basketball, press release, 1 November 2000, accessed 9 February 2013; http://www. wlac.edu/athletics/basketball_womens/roster/ 11roster.html#contact, accessed 17 June 2012.

90. http://www. smcgaels.com, accessed 28 October 2000; Yukiya Jerry Waki, "St. Mary's."

91. *Indiana Gazette*, 22 July 1999; Gwen Knapp, "Yamasaki Fakes Out Asian Jock Stereotypes," SFGate.com, 30 January 2000; http:// www.angelfire.com/stars4/lindsey_yamasaki/ article013000.html, accessed 26 July 2013; *Filipinas*, May 1998; http://www.santaclarabroncos. com/sports/w-baskbl/mtt/inoue_tamara00. html, accessed 12 February 2010; James Fang, "Where Are the Asian American Athletes," 19 May 2006, http://www.asianweek.com; http://www. fullertontitans.com/sports/w-baskbl/mtt/quan_ monica00, accessed 23 July 2013; http://laist. com/2013/02/04/woman_shot_dead_in_irvine_ was_basketball_coach.php, accessed 26 July 2013; http://artuathletics.com/coaches.aspx?path= wbball&rc=253, accessed 26 July 2013; http:// www.hooptown-bball.com/, accessed 1 December 2012; http://www.ucmercedbobcats.com/ article/54.php, accessed 6 June 2013; http:// www.gohofstra.com/ViewArticle.dbml?DB_ OEM_ID=22200&ATCLID=205461480, accessed June 10, 2013; http://www.whitman.edu/whitman-athletics/womens-basketball/assistant-coach-casey-kushiyama, 12 accessed July 2013.

92. http://prosydelacruz.com/provencal/my-filipino-heritage-huge-filipino-nba-player-raymond-townsend-graces-fil-am-gala/, accessed 3 May 2011.

93. Cacas, "The Professional Pioneer" (see chap. 5, n. 138); *Annapolis Capital*, 23 January 1997.

94. Timothy Yoo, "Jeremy Lin's Long Awaited Shot," KoreAm.com, accessed 5 October 2010.

95. http://half-asians.com/leilani-mitchell, accessed 8 September 2010.

96. http://www.goldsea.com, accessed 29 June 2005; Chu, "Natalie Nakase."

97. Culross, "Time" ; King, "Leagues that Created Linsanity."

98. http://prosydelacruz.com/provencal/my-filipino-heritage-huge-filipino-nba-player-raymond-townsend-graces-fil-am-gala/, accessed 3 May 2011; http://amirbogen.blogspot.com/ 2005/11/where-they-are-today-corey-gaines. html, accessed 7 June 2012; Hernandez, "Nakase"; Yoo, "Jeremy Lin's Long-Awaited Shot"; http:// zotcubed.wordpress.com/2011/11/23/where-are-they-now-qa-with-anteater-alum-emil-kim/, accessed 17 July 2013; http://www.halfkorean. com/?page_id=4972, accessed 7 February 2014; http://www.nba.com/pistons/news/detroit-

pistons-finalize-coaching-staff, accessed 24 May 2014.

99. Cindy Luis, "Low Getting Assists While Waiting to Play," *Honolulu Star-Bulletin*, 12 July 2011; Hogue, "Hawaii's Connections" (see chap. 3, n. 13).

100. http://hoopistani.blogspot.com/2011/ 03/timir-patel-q-i-want-be-example-for.html, accessed 3 August 2013.

101. Rafe Barholomew, *Pacific Rims:Beermen Ballin' in Flip-Flops and the Philippines' Unlikely Love Affair with Basketball* (New York: New American Library, 2010), 202–203.

102. *Manila Times*, 13 May 1999; *Philippine Daily Inquirer*, 9 April 1999; Bartholomew, *Pacific Rims*, 205.

103. Bartholomew, *Pacific Rims*, 205.

104. Ibid.

105. Ibid., 234–235.

106. Ibid., 217, 221–223.

107. Ibid., 200–201, 213, 214–215.

108. Ibid., 236.

109. http://www.stanfordfbc.org/FBCFiles/ alumni_alphabetical.htm, accessed 10 December 2012; http://www.hagiya.com, accessed 23 July 2013; http://basketball.eurobasket.com/player/ Emily_Tay/Germany/TG_1889_Sandhausen/ 94467?Women=1#Player Stats, accessed 27 May 2014.

110. Lin, "The Heat Is On."

111. http://www.nba.com/pistons/news/ detroit-pistons-finalize-coaching-staff, accessed 24 May 2014.

112. http://www.hoopsvibe.com/nba-news-and-rumors/articles/167207-blazers-again-look-foolish-firing-gm-richie-cho-after-10-months, accessed 27 March 2013; http://www.nba.com/ bobcats/bio_rich_cho.html, accessed 25 April 2013; http://hoopistani.blogspot.com/2011/03/ golden-state-warriors-to-celebrate.html, accessed 3 August 2013.

113. Odeen Domingo, "Phoenix Mercury's Corey Gaines Proves to be Player's Coach," *Arizona Republic*, 23 May 2011; http://amirbogen. blogspot.com/2005/11/where-they-are-today-corey-gaines.html, accessed 27 February 2013.

114. Corey Gaines, "Inspire Yourself," http:// www.huffingtonpost.com/corey-gaines/wnba-black-history-month_b_1264102.html, accessed 27 February 2013.

115. *Seattle Times*, 30 September 1998; Alexander J. Ige, "Coach Matsuhara Is an Inspiration to Young Women,"*Culver City News*, 29 July 2012; http://www.usctrojans.com/sports/w-baskbl/mtt/ matsuhara_colleen00.html, accessed 23 June 2000.

116. Hernandez, "Nakase."

Epilogue

1. David Zirin, "Jeremy Lin: Taking the Weight," *Nation*, 19 March 2012.

2. Scott Kurashige, "Dear America, Please Don't Ruin Jeremy Lin's Story," *Huffington Post*, 21 February 2012, http://www.huffingtonpost.com/scott-kurashige/jeremy-lin_b_1286428.html.

3. Ibid.

4. Ibid.

5. Ibid.

6. Zirin, "Taking the Weight."

7. Ibid.

8. Ibid.

9. Ibid.

10. Ibid.

11. Davidson, "Long Before Lin."

12. Raymond Williams, *Resources of Hope* (London: Verso, 1989).

13. Brian Liou, "Tall Order," *Asian Week*, 29 November 1999.

14. Ibid.

15. Ibid.

16. Ibid.

17. Ibid.

18. Vanessa Hua, "Asian American Basketball Leagues Boost Game Skills and Ethnic Pride," SFGATE,10 April 2006, http://www.sfgate.gate.com.

19. http://www.census.gov/population/www/documentation/twps0029/tab02.html, accessed 18 April 2014.

20. Robert Westbrook, *John Dewey and American Democracy* (Ithaca: University Press, 1989); Sen, *The Idea of Justice* (see intro., n. 2).

References

Archives and Special Collections

California State University, Sacramento, Special Collections and University Archives
Fullerton Community College Library
Japanese American National Museum
Radcliffe Institute, Harvard University
San Jose State University Special Collections
Santa Clara University Special Collections
University of Portland Archives
University of San Francisco Special Collections
University of Southern California Special Collections
Whitman University Special Collections

Books and Articles

Anderson, Benedict. *Imagined Communities: Reflections on the Origins and Spread of Nationalism.* London: Verso, 1983.

Anderson, Elijah. *The Cosmopolitan Canopy: Race and Civility in Everyday Life.* New York: W.W. Norton, 2011.

Barber, Benjamin. *Strong Democracy: Participatory Politics for a New World.* Berkeley: University of California Press, 2004.

Bartholomew, Rafe. *Pacific Rims: Beermen Ballin' in Flip-Flops and the Philippines' Unlikely Love Affair with Basketball.* New York: New American Library, 2010.

Bellah, Robert, Richard Madsen, William Sullivan, Ann Swidler, and Steven Tipton. *Habits of the Heart: Individualism and Commitment in American Life.* Berkeley: University of California Press, 1985.

Booty, Marie. "Korean Contributions." In *A History of Recreation in Hawaii,* Honolulu Recreation Commission. Honolulu: T.H., 1936.

Bourdieu, Pierre. *Distinction: A Social Critique of the Judgment of Taste.* London: Routledge, 1986.

Buddhist Churches of America. Chicago: Norbart, Inc., 1974.

Buffington, Daniel, and Tod Fraley. "Racetalk and Sport: The Color Consciousness of Contemporary Discourse on Basketball," *Sociological Inquiry* 81 (August 2011): 333–352.

Cahn, Susan K. *Coming on Strong: Gender and Sexuality in Twentieth-Century Women's Sports.* Cambridge: Harvard University Press, 1998.

Center for Oral History, Social Science Research Institute. *Lana'i Ranch: The People of Ko'ele and Keomuku.* Honolulu: University of Hawai'i at Manoa, 1989.

Chan, Sucheng. *Asian Americans: An Interpretive History.* Boston: Twayne, 1991.

Cheng, Lucie, University of California, Los Angeles, Asian American Studies Center, and Chinese

Historical Society of Southern California. *Linking Our Lives: Chinese American Women in Los Angeles*. Los Angeles: The Society, 1984.

Christagu, John. *The Origins of the Jump Shot: Eight Men Who Shook the World of Basketball*. Lincoln: University of Nebraska Press, 1999.

Chua, Amy. *Battle Hymn of the Tiger Mother*. New York: Penguin Books, 2011.

Cisco, Dan. *Hawai'i Sports, Facts, and Statistics*. Honolulu: University of Hawai'i Press, 1999.

Dahl, Robert. *On Democracy*. New Haven: Yale University Press, 1998.

Filipino American National Historical Society, Manilatown Heritage Foundation, Pin@y Educational Partnership. *Filipinos in San Francisco*. Charleston, SC: Arcadia Publishing, 2011.

Ferrin, Josh, and Tres Ferrin. *Blitz Kids: The Cinderella Story of the 1944 University of Utah National Championship Basketball Team*. Layton, UT: Gibb Smith, 2012.

Franks, Joel S. *The Barnstorming Hawaiian Travelers: A Multiethnic Baseball Team Tours the Mainland, 1912–1916*. Jefferson, NC: McFarland, 2012.

_____. *Hawaiian Sports in the Twentieth Century*. Lewiston, ME: Edwin Mellen Press, 2002.

Gates, Henry Louis. *Loose Cannons: Notes on the Culture Wars*. New York: Oxford University Press, 1992.

Gerlach, Larry R. "Not Quite Ready for Prime Time: Baseball History, 1983–1993." *Journal of Sport History* 21 (Summer 1994): 103–137.

Glenn, Evelyn Nakano. *Issei, Nisei, Warbride: Three Generations of Japanese American Women in Domestic Service*. Philadelphia: Temple University Press, 1986.

Gook, T. C. "Wonderful Athletes When They Want to Be." In *The Chinese in Hawaii: A Historical Sketch*. Edited by Robert Lee. Honolulu: Advertiser Publishing Co., 1961.

Grundman, Adolph H. *The Golden Age of Amateur Basketball: The AAU Tournament, 1921–1968*. Lincoln: University of Nebraska Press, 2004.

Grundy, Pamela, and Susan Shackelford. *Shattering the Glass: The Remarkable History of Women's Basketball*. Chapel Hill: University of North Carolina Press, 2007.

Hing, Bill Ong. *Making and Remaking Asian America Through Immigration Policy, 1850–1990*. Stanford: Stanford University Press, 1994.

Hop, Loui Leong. "Chinese Contributions to Sports." *A History of Recreation in Hawaii*, Honolulu Recreation Commission. Honolulu: T.H., 1936.

_____. "History of Chinese Sports in Hawaii." In *The Chinese of Hawaii*. Edited by Chock Lun, L. F. Kwock, Dormant C. Chang, and Min Hin Li. Honolulu: Overseas Penman Club, 1929.

Horton, John. *The Politics of Diversity: Immigration, Resistance, and Change in Monterey Park, California*. Philadelphia: Temple University Press, 1995.

Huang, Yunte. *Charlie Chan: The Untold Story of the Honorable Detective and His Rendezvous with American History*. New York: W.W. Norton, 2011.

Hult, Joan S., and Marianna Trekell, eds. *A Century of Women's Basketball*. Reston, VA: American Alliance for Health, Physical Education, Recreation, and Dance, 1991.

Ikard, Robert. *Just for Fun: The Story of AAU Women's Basketball*. Little Rock: University of Arkansas Press, 2008.

Jamero, Peter. *Vanishing Filipino Americans: The Bridge Generation*. Lanham, MD: University Press of America, 2011.

Kim, Elaine. "Preface." In *Charlie Chan is Dead: An Anthology of Contemporary Asian American Fiction*. Edited by Jessica Hagedorn. New York: Penguin Books, 1993.

Kitano, Harry H. L. *Japanese Americans: The Evolution of a Subculture*. New York: Prentice Hall, 1969.

Kriegel, Mark. *Pistol: The Life of Pete Maravich*. New York: Free Press, 2008.

Lai, William T. "Buck." *Winning Basketball: Individual Play and Team Strategy*. Englewood Cliffs, NJ: Prentice Hall, 1955.

Lawrence, Katherine. *Laurence Yep*. New York: The Rosen Publishing Company, 2003.

Lee, Robert. *The Chinese in Hawaii: A Historical Sketch*. Honolulu: Honolulu Advertiser Publishing Company, 1961.

Lee, Shelly Sang-Hee. *Claiming the Oriental Gateway: Prewar Seattle and Japanese America*. Philadelphia: Temple University Press, 2011.

_____. *A New History of Asian America*. New York: Routledge, 2014.

Levine, Peter. *Ellis Island to Ebbets Field: Sport and the American Jewish Experience*. New York: Oxford University Press, 1992.

Lott, Juanita Tamayo. *Common Destiny: Filipino American Generations*. Lanham, MD: Rowman and Littlefield, 2006.

Ma, L. Eve Armentrout, Jeong Hui Ma, and Forrest Gok. *The Chinese of Oakland: Unsung Builders*. Oakland, CA: Oakland Chinese History Research Committee, 1982.

Matsumoto, Valerie J. *Farming the Home Place: A Japanese Community in California, 1919–1942*. Ithaca: Cornell University Press, 1993.

Naismith, James B. *Basketball: Its Origins and Development*. Lincoln: University of Nebraska Press, 1996.

Nelson, Murry R. *Abe Saperstein and the American Basketball League, 1960–1963: The Upstarts Who Shot for Three and Lost to the NBA*. Jefferson, NC: McFarland, 2013.

_____. *The Originals: The New York Celtics Invent Modern Basketball*. Bowling Green, OH: Bowling Green University Popular Press, 1999.

Odo, Franklin S. *No Sword to Bury: Japanese Americans in Hawai'i During World War II*. Philadelphia: Temple University Press, 2003.

Okihiro, Gary. *Island World: A History of Hawai'i and the United States*. Berkeley: University of California Press, 2008.

_____. *Margins and Mainstreams: Asians in American History and Culture*. Seattle: University of Washington Press, 1994.

_____. *Storied Lives: Japanese American Students and World War II*. Seattle: University of Washington Press, 1999.

Omi, Michael, and Howard Winant. *Racial Formation in the United States: From the 1960s to the 1990s*. London: Routledge, 1994.

Peavy, Linda S., and Ursula Smith. *Full-Court Quest: The Girls from Fort Shaw Indian School, Basketball Champions of the World*. Norman: University of Oklahoma Press, 2008.

Peterson, Robert. *Cages to Jump Shots: Pro Basketball's Early Years*. Lincoln: University of Nebraska Press, 1990.

Pratt, Mary Louise. *Imperial Eyes: Travel Writing and Transculturation*. London: Routledge, 1992.

Regalado, Samuel. "Sport and Community in California's Japanese American 'Yamato County' 1930–1945." *Journal of Sport History* 19 (Summer 1992): 130–143.

_____. "Incarcerated Sport: Nisei Women's Softball and Athletics During the Japanese American Internment Period." *Journal of Sport History* 27 (Fall 2000): 431–444.

Roberts, Randy, and James Olson. *Winning Is the Only Thing: Sports in America Since 1945*. Baltimore: Johns Hopkins University Press, 1989.

Rosaldo, Renato V., and William V. Flores. "Ideology, Conflict, and Evolving Latino Communities: Cultural Citizenship in San Jose, California," *Latino Cultural Citizenship: Claiming Identify, Space, and Rights*. Edited by William V. Flores and Rina Benmayor. Boston: Beacon Press, 1997.

Said, Edward. *Orientalism*. New York: Vintage, 1979.

Sen, Amartya. *The Idea of Justice*. Cambridge: Harvard University Press, 2011.

Staples, Bill. *Kenichi Zenimura: Japanese American Baseball Pioneer*. Jefferson, NC: McFarland, 2011.

Takaki, Ronald. *A Different Mirror: A History of Multicultural America*. Boston: Back Bay Books, 2005.

_____. *Pau Hana: Plantation Life and Labor in Hawai'i, 1835–1920*. Honolulu: University of Hawai'i Press, 1983.

_____. *Strangers from a Different Shore: A History of Asian Americans*. Boston: Little Brown, 1998.

Tchen, John Kuo. *New York Before Chinatown: Orientalism and the Shaping of American Culture, 1776–1882*. Baltimore: Johns Hopkins University Press, 2001.

Thangaraj, Stanley. "Ballin' Indo-Pak Style: Pleasures, Desires, and Expressive Practices of 'South Asian American' Masculinity." *International Review for the Sociology of Sport* 45, No. 3 (2010): 372–389.

_____. "'Liting it up': Popular Culture, Indo-Pak Basketball, and South Asian American Institutions." *Cosmopolitan Civil Societies: An Interdisciplinary Journal* 2, No. 2 (2010): 71–91.

Varzally, Allison. *Making a Non-White America: Californians Coloring Outside Ethnic Lines, 1925–1955.* Berkeley: University of California Press, 2008.

Vowell, Sara. *Unfamiliar Fishes.* New York: Riverhead Books, 2011.

Welky, David B. "Viking Girls, Mermaids, and Little Brown Men: U.S. Journalism and the 1932 Olympics." *Journal of Sport History* 24 (Spring 1997): 24–49.

Westbrook, Robert. *John Dewey and American Democracy.* Ithaca: University Press, 1989.

White, Richard. *The Middle Ground: Indians, Empires and Republics in the Great Lakes Region, 1650–1815.* London: Cambridge University Press, 1991.

Williams, Raymond. *Keywords: A Vocabulary of Culture and Society.* New York: Oxford University Press, 1983.

_____. *Resources of Hope.* London: Verso, 1989.

Wu, Ellen D. *Color of Success: Asian Americans and the Origins of the Model Minority.* Princeton: Princeton University Press, 2013.

Yep, Kathleen S. *Outside the Paint: When Basketball Ruled at the Chinese Playground.* Philadelphia: Temple University Press, 2009.

Yung, Judy. *Unbound Voices: A Documented History of Chinese Women in San Francisco.* Berkeley: University of California Press, 1999.

Zia, Helen. *Asian American Dreams: The Emergence of an American People.* New York: Farrar, Straus & Giroux, 2001.

Zieff, Susan. "From Badminton to the Bolero: Physical Recreation in San Francisco's Chinatown, 1895–1950. *Journal of Sport History* 27 (Spring 2000): 1–29.

Government Documents

United States Census Bureau. Manuscript Census Schedules. City and County of Baltimore, 1930, 1940.

_____. Manuscript Census Schedules. City and County of Honolulu, 1940.

_____. Manuscript Census Schedules. City and County of Los Angeles, 1940.

_____. Manuscript Census Schedules. City and County of Sacramento, 1940.

_____. Manuscript Census Schedules. City and County of San Francisco, 1930, 1940.

_____. Manuscript Census Schedules. City of Anaheim and County of Orange, 1940.

_____. Manuscript Census Schedules. City of Astoria and County of Clatsop, 1930, 1940.

_____. Manuscript Census Schedules. City of Boston, County of Suffolk, 1930.

_____. Manuscript Census Schedules. City of Chicago and County of Cook, 1930.

_____. Manuscript Census Schedules. City of Hilo, Island of Hawai'i, 1940.

_____. Manuscript Census Schedules. City of Ogden, County of Weber, 1940.

_____. Manuscript Census Schedules. City of San Jose and County of Santa Clara, 1920, 1940.

_____. Manuscript Census Schedules. City of Seattle and County of King, 1930.

_____. Manuscript Census Schedules. County of Placer, 1930.

_____. Manuscript Census Schedules. District 27, Hilo, 1930.

Internet Sources

http://www.aabl-norfolk.com/aabl/, accessed 14 July 2008.

Air Passenger Manifest, Pan American Airways, Inc. 30 March 1947. http://www.ancestry.com, accessed 29 December 2012.

http://alums.vassar.edu/news/2013–2014/131101-cydni-matsuoka.html, 28 February 2014.

http://amirbogen.blogspot.com/2005/11/where-they-are-today-corey-gaines.html, accessed 7 June 2012.

http://www.angelfire.com/stars4/lindsey_yamasaki/article013000.html, accessed 26 July 2013.

http://artuathletics.com/coaches.aspx?path=wbball&rc=253, accessed 26 July 2013.

http://athletics.baruch.cuny.edu/roster.aspx?rp_id=632, accessed 25 May 2013.

http://www.austinasianbball.webs.com/, accessed 24 September 2013.

Bainum, Brian. "Legendary Prep Coach Ed Chavez Feeling the Love During His Recovery From Stroke," http://www.marinij.com/sports/ci_9005534, accessed 21 April 2008.

http://basketball.eurobasket.com/player/Emily_Tay/Germany/TG_1889_Sandhausen/94467?Women=1#Player Stats, accessed 27 May 2014.

http://www.berkeleysangha.org/yc/index.html, accessed 7 May 2000.

http://bigcsociety.org/tedohashi/tedohashi.htm, accessed 19 January 2013.

http://www.bradleybraves.com/ViewArticle.dbml?DB_OEM_ID=3400&ATCLID=123048, accessed 25 May 2013.

http://www.branchwest.com/imran_sufi.htm, accessed 24 May 2014.

http://www.cbssports.com/collegebasketball/players/playerpage/1715800/michael-williams, accessed 7 April 2014.

http://www.cbssports.com/collegebasketball/players/playerpage/1780900/jordan-clarkson, accessed 18 July 2013.

http://www.census.gov/population/www/documentation/twps0029/tab02.html, accessed 18 April 2014.

Chai, Tony. "Dallas to Host 2nd Annual Korean-American Basketball Tournament of North America." http://mijudaily.com, accessed 2 April 2013.

http://www.chapmanathletics.com/sports/mbkb, accessed 6 June 2013.

Chu, Bryan. "Natalie Nakase Becomes First Asian American Female in Pro Basketball." http://iousports.org/blog-news/natalie-nakase-becomes-first-asian-american-female-in-pro-basketball-league, accessed 29 August 2012.

Chu, Bryan. "Asian Americans Remain Rare in Men's College Basketball." http://www.sfgate.com/cgi-bin/article.cgi?f=/c/a/2008/12/15/SPD213J9RD.DTL, 16 December 2008.

http://www.cjahs.org/cjahs/index.php?option=com_content&view=article&id=57:-interacttive-gallery&catid=39:history&Itemid=76, accessed 30 November 2013.

http://content.cdlib.org/ark:/13030/c8tm78dh/?layout=metadata&brand=calisphere, accessed 9 June 2014.

http://content.lib.washington.edu/cdm4/item_viewer.php?CISOROOT=/imlswrvm&CISOPTR=148&CISOBOX=1&REC=1, accessed 24 January 2014.

http://www.cougcenter.com/2013/6/3/4392174/wsu-basketball-jeff-hironaka-ken-bone-washington-state, accessed 25 July 2013.

http://www.csmorediggers.com/sports/mbkb/2013–14/boxscores/20131108_9rxq.xml, accessed 13 November 2013.

http://www.csulaathletics.com/custompages/mediaguides/0809_WBB.pdf, accessed 7 September 2013.

Culbrass, Mikey Hirano. "His Speed Was the Stuff of Legend." http://www.rafu.com/2011/11/his-speed-was-the-stuff-of-legend/, accessed 2 November 2013.

http://www.d3independents.org/statistics/mensbasketball1011/ucsc.htm, accessed 12 July 2013.

Darcy, Kim. "Jason Brickman Earns 1,000th Assist." http://espn.go.com/new-york/mens-college-basketball/story/_/id/10538434/liu-brooklyn-brickman-reaches-1000-assists-final-game, accessed 26 May 2014.

http://espn.go.com/mens-college-basketball/player/_/id/51323/jordan-clarkson, accessed 7 April 2014.

http://events.hmoodle.com/event/all-hmong-j4-basketball-tournament/, accessed 4 October 2013.

"First and Only Filipino American NBA Basketball Player Raymond Townsend." PacificRimVideo-Press, 29 November 2009. http://www.youtube.com/watch?v=bLCebxCFK40ploaded, accessed 3 March 2014.

Foley, Ryan. "Falcon Basketball Pre-Season Heats Up." *Falcon*, 20 November 2002. http://www.thefalcononline.com/2002/11/falcon-basketball-pre-season-heats-up.

http://www.fullertontitans.com/sports/m-baskbl/mtt/umipig_isiah00.html, accessed 21 June 2012.

Gaines, Corey. "Inspire Yourself." http://www.huffingtonpost.com/corey-gaines/wnba-black-history-month_b_1264102.html, accessed 27 February 2013.

Gao, David. "Emil Kim: Walking Onwards." http://www.newuniversity.org/2011/01/sports/emil-kim-walking-onwards/, accessed 17 July 2013.

http://www.gobuffsgo.com/coaches.aspx?rc=427, accessed 29 June 2013.

http://www.gocrimson.com/sports/wbkb/2006–07/bios/Tay_Emily, accessed 21 June 2012.

http://www.gohofstra.com/ViewArticle.dbml?DB_OEM_ID=22200&ATCLID=205461480, accessed 10 June 2013.

http://gomason.cstv.com/sports/m-baskbl/mtt/norwood_gabe00.html, accessed 23 October 2012.

http://www.gonyuathletics.com/roster.aspx?rp_id=5416&path=mbball, accessed 15 June 2013.

http://goriverhawks.com/roster.aspx?rp_id=357, accessed 25 May 2013.

http://goseawarriors.com/coaches.aspx?path=&rc=117, accessed 3 August 2013.

http://www.goseattleu.com/ViewArticle.dbml?SPSID=89900&SPID=10773&DB_LANG=C&DB_OEM_ID=18200&ATCLID=205719146&Q_SEASON=2013, accessed 28 February 2014.

http://www.goseawolves.org/sports/w-baskbl/mtt/klockgether_cassie00.html, accessed 12 February 2014.

http://www.gostanford.com, accessed 15 August 2001.

http://www.gotiffindragons.com/roster/11/27/2901.php, accessed 10 June 2013.

Gregory, Sean. "Can Jeremy Lin's Appeal in China Really Help Houston's Bottom Line." 19 July 2012. http://keepingscore.blogs.time.com, accessed 7 February 2014.

http://www.hagiya.com, accessed 23 July 2013.

http://half-asians.com/leilani-mitchell, accessed 8 September 2010.

http://www.halfkorean.com/?page_id=4972, accessed 7 February 2014.

http://www.haverford.edu., accessed 10 September 2005.

http://hawaiiathletics.com/coaches., accessed 12 October 2012.

http://www.hawaiiathletics.com/news/2009/5/28/WBB_0528091816.aspx, accessed 12 October 2012.

http://www.hawaiiprepworld.com/author/jcampany/, accessed 15 April 2013.

http://www.hmongfoundation.com/page/show/757122-hmong%20basketball%20league%20of%20colorado, accessed 4 October 2013.

Hogue, Bob. "Ah Chew Goo, Hoops Magician." midweekauwai.com, 28 March 2007.

_____. "Hawaii's Connections to Jeremy Lin," midweekauai.com, 8 March 2012.

Honolulu, Hawaii, Passenger and Crew Lists, 1900–1959. http://www.ancestry.com, accessed 18 January 2013.

http://hoopistani.blogspot.com, accessed 3 August 2013.

http://www.hoopsvibe.com/nba-news-and-rumors/articles/167207-blazers-again-look-foolish-firing-gm-richie-cho-after-10-months, accessed 27 March 2013.

http://www.hooptown-bball.com/, accessed 1 December 2012.

http://www.hornetsports.com/assets/sports/wbball/2012–13, accessed 29 March 2013.

Hua, Vanessa. "Asian American Basketball Leagues Boost Game Skills and Ethnic Pride." *SFGate*, 10 April 2006. http://www.sfgate.com.

http://www.insidehoops.com/forum/showthread.php?t=53103, accessed 23 October 2012.

http://issuu.com/hornetsports/docs/1314_mbb_book_c850a1856d02c7, accessed 7 April 2014.

Jacobsen, Bob. "A Man for All Seasons." http://www.asu.edu/alumnivision, accessed 19 October 2012

Japanese Americans Relocated During World War II. http://www. ancestry.com, accessed 21 December 2013.

http://www.javadc.org/java/docs/1946–02-14_Leghorn%20Basketball%20for%20442nd%20RCT.pdf, accessed 18 April 2013.

http://www.k12.hi.us/~jnako/afookchinen.htm, accessed 10 July 2013

http://www.khou.com/sports/Houstons-Asian-community-going-Linsane-over-newest-Rocket—163103766.html, accessed 13 February 2013.

King, Jamilah. "The Asian American Basketball Leagues that Created Linsanity." www.colorlines.com, 21 February 2012.

Knapp, Gwen. "Yamasaki Fakes Out Asian Jock Stereotypes," *SFGate*, 30 January 2000. http://www.sfgate.com.

Kurashige, Scott. "Dear America, Please Don't Ruin Jeremy Lin's Story." *Huffington Post*, 21 February 2012. http://www.huffingtonpost.com/scott-kurashige/jeremy-lin_b_1286428.html.

http://www2.kusports.com/mens_basketball/roster/2012_13/, accessed 26 July 2013.

http://laist.com/2013/02/04/woman_shot_dead_in_irvine_was_basketball_coach.php, accessed 26 July 2013.

Le, Sam. "Hoop Dreams." http://www.aaja.org 9 August 2002.

http://www.legacy.com/obituaries/montereyherald/obituary-print.aspx?pid=142512798, accessed 30 November 2013.

http://www.linkedin.com/pub/daniel-chu/9/823/668, accessed 23 August 2013.

http://www.maxpreps.com/local/team/records/default.aspx?gendersport=boys,basketball&schoolid=091d4624–4ce4–4171-a2e7–2e705bd2316b, accessed 14 October 2013.

http://www.maxpreps.com/news/TP2_8AXCC0-JBuL7FGDN8g/new-york-city-has-jeremy-lin,-ossining-girls-basketball-has-saniya-chong.htm, accessed 30 November 2013.

McDonald, Alec Yoshio. "Voices of Chicago: Sports, Community, and History: Reflections on Recording the Japanese American Experience in Chicago." http://www.discovernikkei.org/en/journal/2006/9/12/voices-of-chicago, accessed 21 February 2014.

http://www.minerathletics.com/roster.aspx?rp_id=1571, accessed 10 June 2013.

http://www.nba.com/bobcats/bio_rich_cho.html, accessed 25 April 2013.

http://www.nba.com /pistons/news/detroit-pistons-finalize-coaching-staff, accessed 24 May 2014.

http://ncnau.org/history/index.html, accessed 9 July 2013.

http://www.nikkeiwest.com/index.php/obituary-notice/202-obituaries-oct-10, accessed 30 November 2013.

http://www.nj.com/sports/jjournal/index.ssf?/base/sports-4/123252276338390.xml&coll=3, accessed 2 August 2013.

http://www.otterathletics.com/roster.aspx?rp_id=1325, accessed 25 May 2013.

http://www.pasadenabruins.org/about.php, accessed 15 March 2013.

http://www.pe.pomona.edu/sports, accessed 26 March 2010.

http://www.peterjamero.net/Pages/Photos.aspx, accessed 4 October 2013.

http://www.placersports.com, accessed 25 October 2012.

http://prosydelacruz.com/provencal/my-filipino-heritage-huge-filipino-nba-player-raymond-townsend-graces-fil-am-gala/, accessed 3 May 2011.

http://www.reed.edu/sports_center/sports_clubs/basketball.html, accessed 31 May 2012.

http://www.remembertheaba.com/anaheim-amigos.html, accessed 7 November 2008.

Rhor, Monica. "Filipinos and Basketball: Setting a Cultural Pick." http://www.facaa.us/~facaa/html/features.html, accessed 8 December 2012.

http://www.santaclarabroncos.com/sports/w-baskbl/, accessed 12 February 2010.

http://wserver.scc.losrios.edu/~physed/forms/mensbasketball/performancelist.pdf, accessed 5 July 2013.

http://www.sierracollege.edu/about-us/foundation/alumni/spotlight/george-goto.php, accessed 3 October 2013.

http://sjzebra.org/web/public/site/pages/about.html, accessed 29 April 2013.

http://www.smcgaels.com, accessed 28 October 2000.

http://www.southasianbasketball.com/live/index.php, accessed 14 September 2013.

http://sportspinas.blogspot.com/2012/09/top-filipino-americans-ncaa-division-1.html, accessed 5 July 2013.

http://www.spufalcons.com, accessed 29 June 2013.

http://www.stanfordfbc.org/FBCFiles/alumni_alphabetical.htm, accessed 10 December 2012.

http://statsheet.com/mcb/players/player/saint-marys/kamran-sufi, accessed 24 May 2014.

http://www.stmaryschoolsf.org/about/history/, accessed 24 January 2014.

Sugarman, Mike. "Decades Before Lin, SF Man Paved Way For Asian-Americans In NBA." http://sanfrancisco.cbslocal.com/2012/03/01/decades-before-lin-sf-man-paved-way-for-asian-americans-in-nba, accessed 3 May 2014.

http://superstarbasketball.org/2011_spring/stats.html, accessed 4 October 2013.

http://ucirvine.prestosports.com/sports/w-baskbl/history/index, accessed 9 October 2013.

http://www.ucmercedbobcats.com/roster/11/1/385.php, accessed 28 February 2014.

http://ucsbgauchos.com/sports/m-baskbl/mtt/yoshikawa_danny00.html, accessed 25 July 2013

http://uhathletics.hawaii.edu/WBasket/honors.html, accessed 12 October 2012.

http://www.usctrojans.com/sports/w-baskbl/mtt/matsuhara_colleen00.html, accessed 23 June 2000.

http://www.usfdons.com/coaches.aspx?rc=11&path=mbball, accessed 9 October 2013.

http://viss.wordpress.com/2012/03/04/documentary-on-a-burmese-american-harvard-basketball-player/, accessed 21 June 2012.

http://waynejoseph.wordpress.com/2009/02/24/living-legend-jimmy-yagi/, accessed 27 September 2012.

http://www.wcpoets.com/sports/mbkb/2009–10/bios/David_Hayashi, accessed 31 May 2012.

http://www.whitman.edu/whitman-athletics/womens-basketball/assistant-coach-casey-kushiyama, accessed 12 July 2013.

http://www.wlac.edu/athletics/basketball_womens/roster/11roster.html#contact, accessed 17 June 2012.

http://www.wnba.com, accessed 4 October 1999.

World War II Army Enlistment Records, 1938–1946. http://www.ancestry.com, accessed 25 April 2013.

Yoo, Timothy. "Jeremy Lin's Long Awaited Shot." KoreAm.com, accessed 5 October 2010.

http://zotcubed.wordpress.com/2011/11/23/where-are-they-now-qa-with-anteater-alum-emil-kim/, accessed 17 July 2013.

Interviews

Florence Chinn, mail correspondence with the author, 3 July 1997.

Mary Lai, telephone conversation with the author, 7 March 2008.

Colleen Matsuhara, e-mail correspondence with the author, 19 July 2014, 21 July 2014.

Mel Orphilla, e-mail correspondence with the author, 20 June 2013.

Movies

Transcending: The Wat Misaka Story. Directed by Bruce Alan Johnson and Christine Toy Johnson, 2010.

Reports, Programs, and Press Releases

Arizona Women's Basketball, Press Release. 1 November 2000.

California Voter Registrations. http://www.ancestry.com, accessed 5 April 2014.

Helms Athletic Foundation, Press Release. 16 February 1940. http://www.la84.org/sports-library-digital-collection/, accessed 20 July 2012.

_____. 12 March 1952. http://www.la84.org/sports-library-digital-collection/, accessed 20 July 2012.

_____. 5 February 1954. http://www.la84.org/sports-library-digital-collection/, accessed 10 July 2012.

_____. 24 March 1955. http://www.la84.org/sports-library-digital-collection/, accessed 3 September 2012.

Polk's Crocker-Langley San Francisco City Directory, 1935. http://www.ancestry.com, accessed 25 April 2013.

Regimental Report, 442nd Regiment. November 1945, 26 January 1946, 20 May 1946, 20 April 1947.

San Jose City Directory, 1956. http://www.ancestry.com, accessed 12 December 2013.

San Jose CYS Basketball Invitational Tournament Program, 2003.

Seattle City Directory, 1956. http://www.ancestry.com, accessed 9 March 2013.

University of San Francisco vs. Fordham University Football Program. Kezar Stadium. San Francisco. 20 November 1949.

Yearbooks

Andrew Hill Yearbook. 1963. http://www.classmates.com, accessed 26 March 2010.

Astoria High School Yearbook. 1941. http://www.ancestry.com, accessed 27 April 2013.

Belmont High School Yearbook. 1938. http://www.classmates.com, accessed 5 May 2012.

Berkeley High School Yearbook. 1933. http://www.ancestry. com, accessed 20 December 2012.

_____. 1947. http://www.classmates.com, accessed 8 September 2012.

Broadway High School Yearbook. 1924. http://www.ancestry. com, accessed 22 March 2013.

_____. 1928. http://www.ancestry. com, accessed 22 March 2013.

_____. 1934. http://www.classmates.com, accessed 6 July 2013.

_____. 1937. http://www.classmates.com, accessed 6 July 2013.

Calipatria High School Yearbook. 1950. http://www.classmates.com, accessed 31 May 2012.

Campbell High School Yearbook. 1940. http://www. ancestry.com, 18 June 2013.

_____. 1961. http://www.classmates.com, accessed 8 September 2010.

Carbon High School Yearbook. 1965. http://www.ancestry.com, accessed 5 April 2013.

Chico High School Yearbook. 1935. http://www.ancestry.com, accessed 20 December 2012.

Commerce High School Yearbook. 1916. http://www.worldvital records.com, accessed 26 October 2012.

_____. 1925. http://www.ancestry.com, accessed 21 December 2008.

_____. 1941. http://www.ancestry.com, accessed 23 May 2013.

_____. 1947. http://www.classmates.com, accessed 17 June 2011.

_____. 1949. http://www.ancestry.com, accessed 24 February 2014.

Fresno High School Yearbook. 1938. http://www.ancestry.com, accessed 28 December 2013.

_____. 1941. http://www.classmates.com, accessed 15 July 2012.

Fullerton High School Yearbook. 1938. http://www.ancestry.com, accessed 2 July 2014.

Fullerton Junior College Yearbook. 1940. http://www. ancestry.com, accessed 2 July 2014.

Galileo High School Yearbook. 1932. http://www.classmates.com, accessed 25 April 2013.

_____. 1933. http://www.classmates.com, accessed 18 July 2012.

_____. 1934, http://www.classmates.com, accessed 18 July 2012.

_____. 1944. http://www.classmates.com, accessed 21 March 2012.

_____. 1945. http://www.ancestry.com, accessed 21 March 2012.

_____. 1957. http://www.classmates.com, accessed 11 July 2013.

_____. 1960. http://www.classmates.com, accessed 30 May 2011.

_____. 1963. http://www.classmates.com, accessed 11 September 2013.

Gardena High School Yearbook. 1929. http://www.ancestry.com, accessed 28 December 2013.

Garden Grove High School Yearbook. 1935. http://www.ancestry.com, accessed 26 November 2012.

Garfield High School (Los Angeles) Yearbook. 1962. http://www.ancestry.com, accessed 23 July 2013.

Garfield High School (Seattle) Yearbook. 1933. http://www.ancestry.com, accessed 15 June 2013.

_____. 1938. http://www.ancestry.com, accessed 22 March 2013.

_____. 1941. http://www.ancestry.com, accessed 22 March 2013.

_____. 1946. http://www.classmates.com, accessed 6 July 2013.

_____. 1949. http://www.ancestry.com, accessed 15 June 2013.

_____. 1955. http://www.classmates.com, 23 accessed July 2013.

George Washington High School Yearbook. 1943. http://www.ancestry.com, accessed 7 May 2014.

_____. 1949. http://www.ancestry.com, accessed 19 April 2014.

_____. 1954. http://www.classmates.com, accessed 24 August 2012.

_____. 1955. http://www.classmates.com, accessed 9 October 2012.

_____. 1959. http://www.ancestry.com, accessed 7 May 2014.

Grass Valley High School Yearbook. 1934. http://www. ancestry.com, accessed 8 July 2009.

Hilo High School Yearbook. 1941. http://www.ancestry.com, accessed 9 February 2013.

Hollywood High School Yearbook. 1938. http://www.ancestry.com, accessed 18 July 2013.

_____. 1939. http://www.ancestry.com, accessed 18 July 2013

_____. 1940. http://www.classmates.com, accessed 20 February 2012.

James Lick High School Yearbook. 1954. http://www.ancestry.com, 16 July 2013.

Kauai High School Yearbook. 1958. http://www.ancestry.com, accessed 30 September 2013.

Leilehua High School Yearbook. 1941. http://www.ancestry.com, accessed 3 July 2013.

Lincoln High School Yearbook. 1930. http://www.ancestry.com, accessed 5 April 2014.

_____. 1955. http://www.classmates.com, accessed 7 July 2012.

Livingston High School Yearbook. 1932. http://www.ancestry.com, accessed 18 November 2013.

_____. 1934. http://www.ancestry.com, accessed 18 November 2013.

_____. 1941. http://www.ancestry.com, accessed 5 April 2013.

_____. 1951. http://www.classmates.com, accessed 17 January 2014.

Lowell High School Yearbook. 1958. http://www.ancestry.com, accessed 11 July 2013.

_____. 1960. http://www.ancestry.com, accessed 11 July 2013.

_____. 1961. http://www.ancestry.com, accessed 11 July 2013.

_____. 1963. http://www.classmates.com, accessed 11 September, 2013.

McClatchy High School Yearbook. 1939. http://www.ancestry.com, accessed 18 November 2013.

McKinley High School Yearbook. 1931. http://www.ancestry.com, accessed 2 January 2012.

_____. 1936. http://www. ancestry.com, accessed 9 February 2013.

_____. 1956. http://www.classmates.com, accessed 31 May 2012.

Monterey High School Yearbook. 1953. http://www.classmates.com, accessed 24 January 2013.

Mountain View High School Yearbook. 1963. http://www.classmates.com, accessed 24 October 2009.

_____. 1966. http://www.classmates.com, accessed 24 January 2013.

Oakland Technical High School Yearbook. 1966. http://www.ancestry.com, accessed May 23, 2013.

Palo Alto High School Yearbook. 1933. http://www.ancestry.com, 1 August 2013.

Phoenix High School Yearbook. 1933. http://www.ancestry.com, accessed 27 May 2006.

Polytechnic High School (Long Beach) Yearbook. 1964. http://www.classmates.com, accessed 11 May 2011.

Polytechnic High School (Los Angeles) Yearbook. 1930. http://www.ancestry.com, accessed 3 July 2013.

_____. 1951. http://www.classmates.com, accessed 7 July 2012.

Punahou High School Yearbook. 1930. http://www.ancestry.com, accessed 13 July 2012.

Queen Anne High School Yearbook. 1941. http://www.ancestry.com, accessed 1 June 2013.

Roosevelt High School (Honolulu) Yearbook. 1962. http://www.ancestry.com, accessed 29 August 2013.

Roosevelt High School (Los Angeles) Yearbook. 1954. http://www.classmates.com, accessed 24 August 2013.

Sacramento High School Yearbook. 1952. http://www.ancestry.com, accessed 8 July 2013.

_____. 1958. http://www.ancestry.com, accessed 16 July 2013.

Sacramento State College Yearbook. 1954. http://www.ancestry.com, accessed 27 April 2013.

St. Louis Preparatory School Yearbook. 1959. http://www.ancestry.com, accessed 19 February 2014.

_____. 1969. http://www.classmates.com, accessed 9 October 2012.

Salinas High School Yearbook. 1941. http://www.ancestry.com, accessed 6 December 2013.

_____. 1942. http://www.ancestry.com, accessed 6 December 2013.

_____. 1945. http://www.ancestry.com, accessed 6 December 2013.

_____. 1947. http://www.classmates.com, accessed 16 January 2012.

San Francisco State Yearbook. 1939. http://www.classmaates.com, accessed 7 January 2012.

San Jose High School Yearbook. 1931. http://www.classmates.com, accessed 2 December 2011.
_____. 1933. http://www.classmates.com, accessed 26 March 2014.
_____. 1935. http://www.classmates.com, accessed February 13, 2012.
_____. 1939. http://www.classmates.com, accessed 2 December 2011.
_____. 1940. http://www.ancestry.com, accessed 31 October 2013.
_____. 1942. http://www.ancestry.com, accessed 31 October 2013.
_____. 1946. http://www.ancestry.com, accessed 3 July 2013.
_____. 1951. http://www.classmates.com, accessed 26 March 2014.
San Mateo High School Yearbook. 1933. http://www.classmates. com, accessed 20 December 2012.
San Pedro High School Yearbook. 1941. http://www.classmates.com, 18 accessed June 2012.
Santa Clara University Yearbook. 1950. http://www.worldvitalrecords.com, accessed 1 June 2012.
Springfield College Yearbook. 1947. http://www.ancestry.com, accessed 29 August 2013.
_____. 1948. http://www.ancestry.com, 29 August 2013.
Stanford University Yearbook. 1922. http://www.worldvitalrecords.com, accessed 1 June 2012.
_____. 1925. http://www.worldvitalrecords.com, accessed 1 June 2012
_____. 1932. http://www.worldvitalrecords.com, accessed 1 June 2012.
_____. 1937. http://www.ancestry.com, accessed 1 August 2013.
_____. 1940. http://www.mocavo.com, accessed 7 April 2014.
Star of the Sea Academy Yearbook. 1953. http://www.classmates.com, accessed 30 May 2011.
———. 1955. http://www.classmates.com, accessed 17 November 2011.
Stockton High School Yearbook. 1929. http://www.ancestry.com, accessed 1 June 2013.
_____. 1930. http://www.classmates.com, accessed 19 September 2012.
_____. 1933. http://www.classmates.com, accessed 19 September 2012.
University of California Yearbook. 1933. http://www.worldvitalrecords.com, accessed 7 May 2012.
_____. 1950. http://www.worldvitalrecords.com, accessed 1 June 2012.
University of California, Los Angeles, Yearbook. 1941. http://www.ancestry.com, accessed 9 July 2013.
_____. 1979. http://www.ancestry.com, accessed 13 March 2013.
University of Hawai'i Yearbook. 1932. http://www.worldvitalrecords.com, accessed 30 January 2012.
_____. 1944. http://www.worldvitalrecords.com, accessed 27 April 2012.
_____. 1949. http://www.worldvitalrecords.com, accessed 3 March 2012.
_____. 1951. http://www.ancestry.com, accessed 29 December 2013.
_____. 1953. http://www.ancestry.com, accessed 29 December 2013.
_____. 1959. http://www.worldvitalrecords.com, accessed 27 April 2012.
University of Idaho Yearbook. 1934. http://www.ancestry.com, accessed 15 April 2014.
University of Portland Yearbook. 1948. http://www.ancestry.com, accessed 13 March 2013.
University of Redlands Yearbook. 1940. http://www.worldvitalrecords.com, accessed 27 April 2013.
Wapato High School Yearbook. 1951. http://www.ancestry.com, accessed 29 August 2013.
Watsonville High School Yearbook. 1949. http://www.ancestry.com, accessed 27 April 2013.
_____. 1954. http://www.ancestry.com, accessed 5 April 2013.
Westmont College Yearbook, 1952. http://www.ancestry.com, accessed 29 August 2013.
West San Jose National Junior Basketball Yearbook. 1999–2000.
William and Mary University Yearbook. 1925. http://www.ancestry.com, accessed 29 August 2013.

Index

Page numbers in **_bold italics_** indicate pages with illustrations

265

6-21-16